WRIGHTSLAW

No Child Left Behind

Peter W. D. Wright

Pamela Darr Wright

Suzanne Whitney Heath

Harbor House Law Press, Inc.
Hartfield, Virginia 23071

Wrightslaw: No Child Left Behind
By Peter W. D. Wright, Pamela Darr Wright and Suzanne Whitney Heath

Library of Congress Cataloging-in-Publication Data

Wright, Peter W. D., Pamela Darr Wright and Suzanne Whitney Heath
Wrightslaw: No Child Left Behind /1ˢᵗ. ed.
p. cm.
Includes bibliographical references and index.
ISBN-13: 978-1-892320-12-4; ISBN: 1-892320-12-6
1. Education – law – United States. I. Title
2. Education– parent participation – United States.
Library of Congress Catalog Card Number: 2003109590

10 9 8 7 6 5 4

Printing History
Harbor House Law Press, Inc. issues new printings and new editions to keep our books current. New printings include technical corrections and minor changes. New editions include major revisions of text and/or changes.
First Edition: February 2004   Fourth Printing: March 2007

Disclaimer
The purpose of this book is to educate and inform. While every effort has been made to make this book as accurate as possible, there may be mistakes, both typographical and in content. The authors and Harbor House Law Press, Inc. shall have neither liability nor responsibility to any person or entity with respect to any loss or damage caused, or alleged to be caused, directly or indirectly, by the information contained in this book. If you do not wish to be bound by the above, you may return this book to the publisher for a full refund. Every effort has been made to ensure that no copyrighted material has been used without permission. The authors regret any oversights that may have occurred and are happy to rectify them in future printings of this book.

When You Use a Self-Help Law Book
Law is always changing. The information contained in this book is general information and may or may not reflect current legal developments. This book is designed to provide general information in regard to the subject matter covered. It is sold with the understanding that the publisher and author are not engaged in rendering legal or other professional services. For legal advice about a specific set of facts, you should consult with an attorney.

Bulk Purchases
Harbor House Law Press books are available at quantity discounts for bulk purchases, academic sales or textbook adoptions. For information, contact Harbor House Law Press, P. O. Box 480, Hartfield VA 23071. Please provide the title of the book, ISBN number, quantity, how the book will be used, and date needed.
Toll Free Phone Orders: (877) LAW IDEA or (877) 529-4332. Toll Free Fax Orders: (800) 863-5348.
Internet Orders: http://www.harborhouselaw.com

WHAT PEOPLE ARE SAYING ABOUT . . .

WRIGHTSLAW: NO CHILD LEFT BEHIND

"Easy to read, incredibly informative – a 'must read' for all parents in America." — Dr, Elaine Holden, The Reading Foundation

"Incredible and right on the money! Gives me ammunition to help more parents and kids . . . inspires me and makes me feel like slaying windmills again. Another win for the kids!" — Fran Dobrowolski, advocate

"Makes a complex law easily understandable . . . another outstanding *Wrightslaw* book" — Cynthia Gardner, Esq.

"Does an amazing job of making this law understandable and accessible to lay folk, like me." — Sandra Rief, master teacher and author of ***How to Reach and Teach ADD/ADHD Children***

"This book is great!" — Diane Smith, Esq., National Protection and Advocacy Systems

"Excellent work . . . straightforward and easy-to-read." — Bill Matthew, Director, Student Support Services

"Folks can make headway for their kids with this book in their amory." — Robert Crabtree, Esq.

"Fascinating material . . ." — Dr. Janet Lerner, author and editor

"No Child Left Behind will make schools accountable for educating all kids – this is an American law!" — William Byrne, Esq.

"You did a Herculean job of analyzing the No Child Left Behind Act . . . that will pay dividends for parents and advocates." — Torin Togut, Esq.

ACKNOWLEDGEMENTS

We wish to acknowledge and thank these people who selflessly gave their time and provided comments, insight, recommendations and advice for *Wrightslaw: No Child Left Behind*.

William F. Byrne, Esq., attorney in West Virginia

Robert Crabtree, Esq., attorney in Massachusetts

Cynthia Gardner, Esq., attorney with Tennessee Protection & Advocacy, Inc.

Ruth Heitin, Ed.D., educational consultant in Virginia

Elaine Holden, Ph.D., educational consultant, The Reading Foundation, New Hampshire

Pat Howey, special education consultant and advocate in Indiana

Lauri Isham, advocate in Massachusetts

Margaret J. Kay, Ed.D., psychologist in Pennsylvania

Shirley Leak, parent advocate in California

Janet W. Lerner, Ph.D., learning disabilities specialist and author in Illinois

Bill Matthew, Ph.D., psychologist and special education director in California

Rob Mead, Esq., attorney and law professor, University of Kansas

Cathy Pratt, Ph.D., Indiana Institute on Disability and Community

Sandra F. Rief, master teacher and author in California

Lori Sheri, advocate in New Jersey

Diane Smith, Esq., attorney, National Association of Protection and Advocacy Systems

John Willis, Ed.D., evaluator from New Hampshire

We offer special thanks to **Fran Dobrowolski**, an advocate from New Hampshire, and **Torin Togut**, an attorney from Georgia. Fran and Torin spent hours going through the manuscript and made dozens of excellent suggestions that we incorporated into *Wrightslaw: No Child Left Behind*.

We thank **Mayapriya Long** who designed the wonderful cover for *Wrightslaw: No Child Left Behind*.

Finally, we thank our creative, resourceful staff, **Debra Pratt** and **Traci Wright**, who make Wrightslaw and warm and wonderful place.

DEDICATION

We dedicate this book to advocates for children.

When you are wrestling with a gorilla, you don't stop when you are tired; you stop when the gorilla is tired. —Robert Strauss

CONTENTS

Contents

Contents

INTRODUCTION

The No Child Left Behind Act is a large, complex statute. What does the law say about reading? What are the essential components of a reading program? What is scientifically based reading research?

What does the law say about annual proficiency tests? Who must be tested? In what subjects? Whose scores must be reported? What does the law say about accommodations? Who is exempt from annual proficiency tests?

What does the law say about accountability? School and school district report cards? What does the law say about schools in need of improvement? What are the sanctions for schools that do not improve? What does the law say about public school choice? Supplemental educational services and tutoring?

What are the requirements for highly qualified teachers? When do these requirements go into effect? How do the highly qualified teacher requirements affect special education teachers? English language teachers?

What are the educational requirements for paraprofessionals? Do all paraprofessionals have to meet these requirements? When do these requirements go into effect? How does the law limit the duties paraprofessionals may perform?

What does the law say about parental involvement? Parents' right to know the qualifications of their child's teachers? The parent's right to observe their child's classroom? Parental access to instructional material?

Wrightslaw: No Child Left Behind will help you find answers to your questions in the No Child Left Behind statute, regulations, and publications from the U. S. Department of Education.

WHO SHOULD READ THIS BOOK?

If you are the parent of a child who attends school, you represent your child's interests. To effectively advocate for your child, you need to learn about your rights and responsibilities under the No Child Left Behind Act and how this law affects your child's education. You need to know what your child is entitled to.

If you work as a teacher, principal, pupil personnel specialist, or administrator, No Child Left Behind will have a profound impact on you and your job. You may have received inaccurate information and conflicting advice about this law. You need to know what the law actually says. If you are knowledgeable about the law, you will be able to meet the challenges of The No Child Left Behind Act.

If you are a teacher or principal, you may be interested to learn about mentoring, bonus pay, scholarships and fellowships for advanced certification, and other financial incentives. You will want to take advantage of training opportunities. You may be interested in the new teacher liability protections.

Introduction

If you are a school board member, you need to know your responsibilities. If you are a superintendent, you need to collect data, assess curriculums, monitor progress, and determine staff qualifications for specific roles.

If you are a tutor or school administrator in the private sector, you may want to provide services as a supplemental educational service provider. If you are an entrepreneur, you may wish to apply for grant money that is available for innovative programs and cooperative ventures with school districts and states.

If you are an employee of a state department of education, you may be responsible for monitoring compliance in your state, collecting data, aligning state assessments with academic standards, writing assessments, or other activities to improve compliance or achievement. If you are a state legislator, you need to know the law that accompanies the federal money that your state applied for and received.

If you are an attorney or advocate who represents children with disabilities, you need to have the statutes, regulations, and guidance publications. In *Wrightslaw: No Child Left Behind*, your primary legal references are in one place.

If you are a taxpayer, you may be interested in accountability in federal programs.

WHO IS COVERED BY NCLB?

Accountability follows the money in No Child Left Behind. All states applied for and received NCLB funds. In return, states agreed to implement annual academic assessments of student proficiency to measure their progress in accomplishing the purpose for which the money was intended. "The purpose of this title is to ensure that all children have a fair, equal, and significant opportunity to obtain a high-quality education and reach, at a minimum, proficiency on challenging State academic achievement standards and state academic assessments." (20 U. S. C. § 6301 Statement of Purpose) States will issue annual report cards to report on their progress toward reaching this goal.

Ninety percent of school districts applied to their states for a portion of the funds available under Title I of No Child Left Behind. Sixty percent of schools received Title I funds from their school districts. School districts must provide detailed annual report cards about the progress of their schools toward meeting the goals for which they accepted these funds.

The federal definitions of reading, scientific research, diagnostic reading assessment, essential components of reading instruction and other definitions apply nationally. If you are defining reading in a legal context, you will find the definition of reading in the No Child Left Behind Act. If you are evaluating a reading program, the program must include the essential components of reading instruction specified in No Child Left Behind.

The federal minimum standards for teacher quality, reading instruction, research based instructional programs, and professional development in No Child Left Behind are now the standards nationally.

Ten percent of school districts in the country did not apply for Title I funds under NCLB. These school districts do not face federal penalties if they do not have highly qualified teachers in the classroom or do not meet other quality standards of NCLB. However, if they do not meet these standards, they are operating below the nationally recognized minimum standards. This may have implications in special education disputes regarding the provision of an appropriate education.

HOW THIS BOOK IS ORGANIZED

Wrightslaw: No Child Left Behind is divided into four sections. **Section One** is **Learning About the Law**. Chapter 1 is **A Short History of No Child Left Behind**. In this chapter, you learn how the law has evolved since it was enacted as the Elementary and Secondary Education Act of 1965. Chapter 2 is **Law, Regulations and Caselaw**. Chapter 3, **An Overview No Child Left Behind by Title** provides the high points of the law by Title. Chapter 4 is **Frequently Asked Questions about No Child Left Behind**.

Section Two is **How No Child Left Behind Will Affect You**. Chapter 5 is **No Child Left Behind for Parents**. In this chapter, you learn about annual proficiency testing, accountability and adequate yearly progress (AYP), school and school district report cards, public school choice, supplemental educational services, reading, highly qualified teachers, parental involvement and empowerment, and parents' right to know the qualifications of their child's teachers. This chapter also includes information for parents of children with special educational needs.

Chapter 6 is **No Child Left Behind for Teachers, Principals and Paraprofessionals**. In this chapter, you learn how NCLB affects teachers who teach different grade levels and subjects. You learn about the new highly qualified teacher requirements, parent involvement requirements, parent's right to know the teacher's qualifications. You learn about adequate yearly progress, annual proficiency testing, and training and professional development, teacher retention and recruitment, and teacher liability protection.

Chapter 7 is **No Child Left Behind for Attorneys and Advocates**. In this chapter, you learn about reading, reading instruction, reading research, and assessments. You also learn about highly qualified teachers, accountability and adequate yearly progress (AYP), requirements for English language learners and immigrant children, report cards and notices to parents, transfers, privacy and instructional materials. This chapter includes *Questions for the Attorney and Advocate.*

Chapter 8 is **No Child Left Behind for School Leaders and Academics**. In this chapter, you learn about accountability and assessments, parent options, new requirements for teachers and paraprofessionals, research-based instruction, and the need to "know the rules" about data collection and analysis.

Section Three is **Advocacy Strategies**. In Chapter 9, **How to Obtain Information and Request Action**, you learn how to write letters, how to use the Freedom of Information Act and Open Government laws to obtain information, and strategies for writing good letters. Chapter 10 is **How to Report a Problem or File a Complaint**. In this chapter, you learn how to write persuasive complaint letters and about letter writing pitfalls. In Chapter 11, **Sample Letters**, you will find fifteen sample letters about No Child Left Behind issues that you can tailor to your circumstances.

Section Four is the **No Child Left Behind Statute with Commentary**. Chapter 12 is **Table of Statutes of the No Child Left Behind Act**. Chapter 13 is the full text of **Title I of the No Child Left Behind Act** with overviews, commentary, and cross-references.

You will find two **Appendices** at the end of the book. Appendix A is the **Glossary of No Child Left Behind Acronyms, Abbreviations and Terms**. Appendix B includes the **List of Publications and Resources** on the *Wrightslaw NCLB CD-ROM*. The book also includes a comprehensive index.

The *Wrightslaw NCLB CD-ROM* includes the full text of Titles I through X of the No Child Left Behind Act with overviews, commentary, cross-references, and resources, the No Child Left Behind regulations published by the U. S. Department of Education, and the No Child Left Behind Act (Public Law 107-110).

The *Wrightslaw NCLB CD-ROM* also includes the *No Child Left Behind Deskbook, A Parent's Guide to No Child Left Behind, A Toolkit for Teachers*, and dozens of Fact Sheets and Guidance publications on key topics from the U. S. Department of Education.

Icons

This book includes icons that alert you to Overviews and Comments, Resource publications, Cross-references, and Internet resources.

➔ Overview or Comment

📖 Resource publication

🗁 Cross-reference

🖰 Internet resource

STRATEGIES: HOW TO USE THIS BOOK

First, read the chapters that precede the No Child Left Behind statute. Some chapters will approach the law from your perspective, some from the viewpoints of others. When you see the law from several angles, you will have a clearer picture of the law. Next, read a few Guidance publications on the *Wrightslaw NCLB CD-ROM*. Select publications on subjects that interest you.

Guidance publications are official U. S. Department of Education publications that are one step short of being regulations. If you are looking for clarification about an issue, you are likely to find relevant information quickly in the Guidance publications or the *No Child Left Behind Desktop Reference*. When you read these publications, you will begin to understand the scope and depth of this law.

The No Child Left Behind Act specifies that the U.S. Department of Education would write regulations for the Act. The U. S. Department of Education published regulations on December 2, 2002 and December 9. 2003. The U. S. Department of Education has published Guidance publications for clarification and will issue formal regulations on other issues in the future. Guidance publications issued after this book is published will be available on the Wrightslaw NCLB website at www.wrightslaw.com/nclb/index.htm

After you read Guidance publications that interest you, review the *NCLB Desktop Reference,* the **Table of Statutes of the NCLB Act** (Chapter 11), and the **Glossary of Abbreviations, Acronyms and Terms** (Appendix A). When you have an idea about how the law is structured and what it covers, begin reading sections of the statute.

📖 Guidance publications, the *No Child Left Behind Desktop Reference*, and the NCLB regulations are on the *Wrightslaw NCLB CD-ROM*.

In this book, the statutes are set in Minion font. We used **bold type** to emphasize important words and phrases in the statute. Commentary in Helvetica font preceded by a large arrow like this ➔ is **not** part of the statute. Look at the example below.

➔ **OVERVIEW:** The Statement of Purpose is the **most important statute** in No Child Left Behind because it describes the overall purpose of the law: "that all children will have a fair, equal, and significant opportunity to receive a high-quality education" and reach "at a minimum, proficiency on challenging State academic achievement standards and state academic assessments."

CONTACT US

What did you like about *Wrightslaw: No Child Left Behind*? How can we improve the book so it meets your needs? Send your ideas, thoughts and comments to: Harbor House Law Press, Inc., P. O. Box 480, Hartfield, VA 23071. (877) 529-4332 or (877) LAW IDEA or by email to ideas@harborhouselaw.com

1 | A SHORT HISTORY OF THE NO CHILD LEFT BEHIND ACT

In this chapter, you learn that the No Child Left Behind Act is the reauthorization of the Elementary and Secondary Education Act of 1965. You will learn about several comprehensive studies and reports about educational quality have been published, including *A Nation at Risk,* the *Nation's Report Card* and *Our Schools and Our Future: Are We Still at Risk?*

In the years since Congress enacted the Elementary and Secondary Education Act in 1965, the federal government has spent more than $321 billion to help educate disadvantaged children. Forty years later, only 32 percent of fourth-graders can read skillfully at grade level. Many of the 68 percent who cannot read well are minority children and those who live in poverty.[1]

In 2001, Congress added benchmarks, measurements and sanctions to the Elementary and Secondary Education Act and called it The No Child Left Behind Act. The President signed this bill into law on January 8, 2002.

ELEMENTARY AND SECONDARY EDUCATION ACT (1965)

The Elementary and Secondary Education Act of 1965 (ESEA) provided a comprehensive plan to address the inequality of educational opportunity for economically underprivileged children.

On April 11, 1965, when President Lyndon B. Johnson signed the Elementary and Secondary Education Act of 1965 into law, he said:

> *"No law I have signed or will ever sign means more to the future of America."*

The Elementary and Secondary Education Act of 1965 included Title I programs of federal aid to disadvantaged children who live in poor urban and rural areas. The ESEA was the statutory basis on which early special education legislation was drafted. Because education is primarily a state and local responsibility, ESEA funds are intended to supplement state and local education expenditures.

Since 1965, Congress has amended the law several times. Each time Congress reauthorized the law, political leaders spoke to the potential impact of the law.

> *"Today, and for generations to come, America will benefit from this law which expresses our national commitment to quality education for all children."* – President Gerald Ford

> *"We have together taken an historic step in the evolution of the Federal role in education."*
> – President Jimmy Carter

---

[1] *Why No Child Left Behind is Important to America* from the U. S. Department of Education.
http://www.ed.gov/nclb/overview/importance/edlite-index.html

Chapter 1

"It is not an overstatement to say that this is the most important reauthorization in this legislation's history."
– Senator Edward Kennedy (1994)

A Nation at Risk (1983)

By the mid 1970s, the quality of public school education had declined. In response, the President appointed the National Commission on Excellence in Education. In 1983, the Commission published *A Nation at Risk*, a hard-hitting report about educational quality that ignited a firestorm of controversy.

> *Our nation is at risk . . . the educational foundations of our society are presently being eroded by a rising tide of mediocrity that threatens our very future as a Nation and a people . . . If an unfriendly foreign power had attempted to impose on America the mediocre educational performance that exists today, we might well have viewed it as an act of war.*[2]

The Commission reported that:

- 23 million adults were functionally illiterate on the simplest tests of reading and writing.
- 13 percent of 17-year olds were functionally illiterate.
- 40 percent of minority children were functionally illiterate.
- Only 30 percent of high school students could solve multi-step mathematics problems.
- Only 20 percent of high school students could write a persuasive essay.
- On the Scholastic Aptitude Tests, verbal scores dropped more than 50 points and math scores dropped 40 points between 1963 and 1982.

The Commission examined high school courses in four areas: content, expectations, time, and teaching. They reported:

- Grades have risen as academic achievement has declined.
- Secondary school education has been homogenized, diluted, and diffused to the point that it has no central purpose . . . We have a cafeteria-style curriculum in which appetizers and desserts can be easily mistaken for the main course.
- Time spent learning how to cook and drive counts as much toward a high school diploma as time spent studying mathematics, English, chemistry, U. S. history, and biology.
- 25 percent of credits earned by high school students are from physical and health education courses, work experience outside the school, remedial English and mathematics, and personal development courses like training for adult life and marriage.
- Some schools provide as little as 17 hours of academic instruction a week; an average school provides about 22 hours. In other industrialized countries, high school students spend 8 hours a day at school, 220 days a year.
- Expenditures for books and instructional materials have dropped by 50 percent during the last 17 years.

Based on these concerns, the Commission made the following recommendations:

- Strengthen high school graduation requirements for all students.
- Adopt higher, measurable standards of academic performance.
- Increase time devoted to learning.
- Raise standards for teachers.

---

[2] *A Nation at Risk: The Imperative for Educational Reform.* http://www.ed.gov/pubs/NatAtRisk/risk.html

THE NATION'S REPORT CARD

The National Assessment of Educational Progress (NAEP) publishes *The Nation's Report Card*, the only nationally representative and continuing assessment of what American students know and can do in various subject areas. Since 1969, the NAEP has conducted assessments in reading, mathematics, science, writing, United States history, civics, geography, and the arts.[3]

Fifteen years after *A Nation at Risk* was published, the United States Department of Education reported that:

- 10 million high school students cannot read at the basic level.
- More than 25 million students do not know basic U.S. history.
- More than 20 million high school students cannot do basic math.

According to the United States Department of Education:

- Per pupil spending increased by 75 percent.
- The number of students per teacher fell 25 percent.
- The number of teachers with advanced degrees more than doubled.
- Student student achievement remained flat.[4]

IMPROVING AMERICA'S SCHOOLS ACT OF 1994

In 1994, Congress amended the Elementary and Secondary Education Act as The Improving America's Schools Act. States were required to develop or adopt challenging content, proficiency standards, and assessments. Schools that received Title I funds must make adequate yearly progress (AYP) toward ensuring that students who receive Title I services meet these standards. Schools that did not make adequate progress must develop corrective action plans.

NO CHILD LEFT BEHIND ACT OF 2001

In 2001, Congress amended the Elementary and Secondary Education Act (ESEA) as the No Child Left Behind Act. The centerpiece of the No Child Left Behind Act is the requirement that public schools bring all students to proficiency in reading and math by the 2013-2014 school year. The law includes sanctions for schools that fail to make acceptable progress.

Each school's progress will be measured with reading and math proficiency tests of all students. The school will report on students by subgroup (i.e., ethnicity, disability, English language learners, and low-income). To meet the No Child Left Behind standard, all subgroups must make sufficient academic progress to ensure that all students are proficient by 2014. If the school does not educate any subgroup, the school will fail to meet this standard.

OUR SCHOOLS AND OUR FUTURE: ARE WE STILL AT RISK? (2003)

The Hoover Institute of Stanford University commissioned the Koret Task Force on K-12 Education to examine changes in education after *A Nation at Risk* was published. The Task Force published its findings in *Our Schools and Our Future: Are We Still at Risk?*

---

[3] An overview of The Nation's Report Card is at http://nces.ed.gov/nationsreportcard/about/
[4] Speech by the Secretary of Education (April 14, 2003)

Chapter 1

The Task Force found that fewer teachers specialized in their subject areas, the school day and school year were even shorter, and students did no more homework than students did in 1982. The Task Force found:

> Since the National Commission published **A Nation at Risk**, nearly two generations of students have passed through U. S. schools. Real per pupil spending has risen by 50 percent. Twenty years of entering first graders–about 80 million children–have walked into schools where they have scant chance of learning much more than the youngsters in 1983.[5]

The Task Force reported.

- Education outcomes have not improved since 1970.
- Achievement gaps have not narrowed. Problems that affect disadvantaged children have not been addressed.
- Higher-quality teachers are key to improving schools. The appropriate gauge of teacher quality is classroom effectiveness.
- Standards-based reforms have not achieved their potential.
- Choice based reforms have not been given a fair test.
- Elementary and middle schools need to be reformed.
- Americans need timely, accurate information about student performance.

The Task Force recommended reforms in three areas: accountability, choice, and transparency.

Accountability

Children, teachers, schools and school districts need to know what they must produce, how progress will be measured, and what will happen if they do not attain the desired results. Every school and education provider should subscribe to rigorous academic standards, assessments of student and school performance, and a system of incentives and interventions that is tied to results.

The components of accountability are: clear goals, accurate measures, and consequences.

Clear Goals

Every state needs to adopt challenging academic standards and curricular guidelines, subject by subject, and grade by grade. These standards should not be limited to basic skills but should include history, science, geography, civics, and literature. Every state also needs to develop coherent "proficiency" levels to be attained by all children in these subjects that encompass essential knowledge and necessary skills.

Accurate Measures

Every state needs to use tests and assessments that accurately measure the performance of children, schools, and school systems in relation to its standards. These assessments should form the basis for evaluating each school. Incentives should be linked to how much schools contribute to student learning.

Consequences

Every state needs to develop an accountability system in which the consequences fall on responsible adults. Success should be rewarded. Failing schools should be closed, reconstituted, or taken over. All students should have the right to leave poor schools for better schools.

---

[5] *Are We Still At Risk* by the Koret Task Force on K-12 Education. http://www.educationnext.org/20032/10.html

School Choice

Parents, not bureaucrats, should make decisions about the education of their children. Parents should be free to abandon low-performing schools for stronger ones. The consumers of educational services should be free to select providers that teach their children effectively. The Task Force made specific recommendations about charter schools, vouchers, full funding for high-risk students, and incentives for quality teachers.

Transparency

Information systems need to provide full transparency in public education. Individuals who seek information about a school or school district should be able to get this information easily. The information should be provided in formats that make it easy to compare one school, system, or state with others.

The Task Force concluded:

> *The tide of mediocrity remains high . . . In the years since **A Nation at Risk**, the incremental changes that passed for reform have not improved schools' performance or students' achievement. Fundamental changes are needed in the incentive structures and power relationships of schooling.*

In Summation

In this chapter, you learned about the background of the No Child Left Behind Act and factors that led Congress to include stronger accountability measures when they reauthorized the law. In the next chapter, *Law, Regulations and Caselaw*, you learn about statutes, regulations, caselaw, and legal research strategies.

References

National Commission on Excellence in Education. *A Nation at Risk: The Imperative for Educational Reform*, 1983.
URL: http://www.ed.gov/pubs/NatAtRisk/index.html

Thomas, M. Donald and Billy R. Reagan. *A Nation at Risk Revisited*, Education News (2003)
URL: http://www.educationnews.org/a-nation-at-risk-revisited.htm

Peterson, Paul E. ed. *Our Schools and Our Future: Are We Still at Risk?* The Hoover Institution Press, 2003.
URL: http://www.educationnext.org/20032/10.html

Coeyman, Marjorie. "Twenty years after A Nation at Risk." *Christian Science Monitor* (April 23, 2003)
URL: http://www.csmonitor.com/2003/0422/p13s02-lepr.html

For Your Notes

2 | LAW, REGULATIONS AND CASELAW

Congress enacted the No Child Left Behind Act during the first session of the 107th Congress. The President signed the statute into law on January 8, 2002. When Congress passes a bill and the President signs it, the statute becomes law immediately, unless it specifically states otherwise.

The authorization of any new law typically brings about a spate of interpretations and even more questions. Certainly, the No Child Left Behind Act will raise its fair share of questions. Self-styled experts may spread wrong interpretations, misinformation and deliberate dis-information. Do not rely on the opinions of others or advice you may find in articles or at training programs.

To find answers to your questions about The No Child Left Behind Act, you may want to do your own legal research. The intention of this book is to bridge the gap between the law itself and one's understanding of the legal language within it, in an accurate, objective manner and through direct reference to the law itself.

In this book, you will read the law. In the beginning, this is more difficult than having the law explained to you. As you read, the law will begin to fit together in your mind. When you learn how the law is organized, you can find sections or regulations that are relevant to your questions.

STATUTES

Statutes are laws passed by federal, state and local legislatures. A statute is called an "Act." The original federal education statute was "The Elementary and Secondary Education Act of 1965" (ESEA). When Congress amended the statute in 2001, they gave the law a new name, "The No Child Left Behind Act of 2001." The No Child Left Behind Act is Public Law 107-110 and is often cited as Pub. L. 107-110.

> 🗁 The full text of Public Law 107-110 is available on the *Wrightslaw NCLB CD-ROM*.

Congress first publishes laws in the *Statutes at Large* and then organizes laws by subject in the *United States Code (U.S.C)*. Thus, the No Child Left Behind Act is printed in both the *Statutes at Large* and in the *United States Code*. The numbering system used to categorize it in the *Statutes at Large* is different from the system used in the *United States Code*.

The *United States Code* has fifty subject classifications called Titles. For example, Title 20 is about education, Title 26 is the Internal Revenue Code, and Title 42 is about public health and welfare. In each title, laws are indexed and assigned section numbers. The No Child Left Behind Act of 2001 is cited as 20 U.S.C. § 6301 *et.seq*.

References to law are called legal citations. Legal citations are standardized formats that explain where you will find a particular statute, regulation, or case.

Chapter 2

→ **LEGAL CITATIONS**: When you see a legal citation such as 20 U. S. C. § 6301 *et. seq.*, the term *"et. seq."* means "at Section 6301 and continuing thereafter." The "§" (symbol of two superimposed S's) is legal shorthand for the section. (To insert a § into a Microsoft Word document, click on Insert, Symbol, Normal Text, and click on the §.)

Statutes published in the *Statutes at Large* have sections (section 1, 2, 3, 4, etc.) and may have subsections ((a), (b), (c), (d), etc.). The first section in the No Child Left Behind Act is "Section 1001 Statement of Purpose" as published in the *Statutes at Large*.

The Statement of Purpose of NCLB is in Section 1001 of the Act. When the Act was published in the *United States Code*, the Statement of Purpose was placed in Section 6301 of Title 20. The legal citation for the Statement of Purpose is 20 U.S.C. § 6301. You may refer to Statement of Purpose as "20 U. S. C. § 6301" or "Section 1001 of the NCLB Act."

→ *Wrightslaw: No Child Left Behind* uses the format of the United States Code. A cross-reference to the No Child Left Behind Act is at the end of each section. For example, Statement of Purpose is at 20 U. S. C. § 6301 of the statute. The cross-reference to Statutes at Large in parentheses at the end of this code section is Section 1001 of the NCLB Act.

Findings & Purposes

The first four code sections of Title I set the stage for the No Child Left Behind Act.

20 U. S. C. § 6301. Statement of Purpose
20 U. S. C. § 6302. Authorization of Appropriations
20 U. S. C. § 6303. School Improvement
20 U. S. C. § 6304. State Administration

The Statement of Purpose is the most important section in No Child Left Behind because it describes the overall purpose of the law: "that **all children** will have a fair, equal, and significant opportunity to **receive a high-quality education and reach, at a minimum, proficiency** on challenging State academic achievement standards and state academic assessments." (emphasis added)

20 U. S. C. § 6301, Statement of Purpose, lists twelve steps to accomplish these purposes. The law seeks to close the gap between low- and high-achieving students by holding states, local school districts, and schools accountable for improving the academic achievement of all students. The law requires schools to meet the educational needs of poor children, children with disabilities, children with limited English proficiency, minority and migratory children, and other neglected groups of children, and to publicly report their progress in educating these children every year.

If you are confused about a section in No Child Left Behind, re-read this Statement of Purpose to see how a particular section fits into the overall purpose of No Child Left Behind.

U. S. C. § 6336(a) includes Congressional Findings about economically disadvantaged students, poverty rates, the percentage of poor children in schools, and the need for adequate funding to educate disadvantaged children. If more than 2 percent of students live below the poverty level, the school district qualifies for funds under NCLB. When this book went to press, the U. S. Department of Education reported that ninety percent of school districts and fifty-nine percent of schools receive Title I funds.

→ **TITLE I SCHOOL DISTRICTS**: A List of Title I School Districts is on the U. S. Department of Education (USDOE) website at http://www.ed.gov/offices/OUS/TitleILEAs/FY02allocations/index.html

→ **BROKEN LINKS**: From time to time, the U.S. Department of Education moves files on their websites. If a file is not at the given address, use www.google.com/unclesam for a specialized "Uncle Sam" government-focused search engine.

Other Federal Statutes

In addition to No Child Left Behind, other important federal acts and statutes that affect educational issues are:

- The Individuals with Disabilities Education Act of 1997, begins at 20 U. S. C. § 1400 *et. seq.*
- Section 504 of the Rehabilitation Act of 1973, begins at 29 U. S. C. §794
- The Family Educational and Rights and Privacy Act, begins at 20 U. S. C. § 1232, *et. seq.*

📁 The full text of the Individuals with Disabilities Education Act, Section 504 of the Rehabilitation Act, and the Family Educational and Privacy Rights Act, with analysis and commentary, are in *Wrightslaw: Special Education Law* (ISBN: 1-892320-03-7) published by Harbor House Law Press, Inc. and available at the www.wrightslaw.com website.

States must ensure that their statutes and regulations are consistent with the United States Code (U. S. C.) and the Code of Federal Regulations (C. F. R.). While state statutes and regulations may provide more rights than federal laws, they cannot provide fewer rights than guaranteed by federal law.

REGULATIONS

Regulations clarify and explain statutes. A regulation has the same force of law as a statute and must be consistent with the statute that it interprets and or implements.

Before the federal government can publish federal regulations in the Code of Federal Regulations (C. F. R.), the agency must publish proposed regulations in the Federal Register (F. R.) to solicit comments about the proposed regulations from citizens.

✍ **USDOE**: NCLB legislation, regulations, and guidance are available from the U. S. Department of Education URL: http://www.ed.gov/offices/OESE/asst.html

The U. S. Department of Education developed and published the No Child Left Behind regulations. These regulations went into effect on January 2, 2003. The regulations are in Volume 34, Part 200 of the Code of Federal Regulations. The legal citation for the NCLB regulations is 34 C. F. R. § 200.

📁 **NCLB REGULATIONS**: The NCLB Regulations are on the *Wrightslaw NCLB CD-ROM*.

JUDICIAL INTERPRETATIONS OR CASELAW

Evolving Caselaw

Caselaw is always changing and evolving. NCLB will evolve and be defined and re-defined by caselaw. When a state court issues a decision, the decision may be appealed to a higher state court. For example, a Virginia trial judge's interpretation of a statute is governed by earlier rulings from the highest state court in Virginia. The highest state court is usually the state Supreme Court.

Federal judges are bound by rulings of their Circuit Court of Appeals. Since Virginia, Maryland, North Carolina, South Carolina, and West Virginia are in the Fourth Circuit, a U. S. District Court judge in any of those states must follow rulings from the United States Court of Appeals for the Fourth Circuit. The judge is not required to follow legal rulings from other circuits although these opinions may be cited as persuasive authority.

All state and federal courts must follow rulings by the U. S. Supreme Court. If the U. S. Supreme Court issues a ruling with which Congress disagrees, Congress may enact a new law to overrule the decision of the Supreme Court.

Chapter 2

Judicial Interpretations

Compelling facts may cause a judge to want to rule in one direction, even if the ruling is contrary to current caselaw. The decision-maker who faces this situation often finds and uses unique facts in the case to create an exception to general caselaw. These "exceptions to the rule" decisions cause the body of law to change and grow.

How a court interprets a law or regulation may be dictated by a single word (e.g., "may " instead of "shall"). When Congress wants to pass a bill but cannot agree on the wording of a statute, they often use vague compromise wording. Confusing words or phrases often lead to litigation. For example, in special education law, the term "appropriate education" has been litigated for more than twenty-five years.

Over time, a "majority rule " evolves when courts agree on the same interpretation. A "minority rule" may also develop. If a majority rule does not develop, the issue becomes more confusing. Sometimes, U. S. Courts of Appeal in different circuits issue conflicting rulings. This leads to a "split among circuits." When there is a split among circuits, the U. S. Supreme Court may agree to hear the case to clarify the issue and resolve the conflict among the circuits.

Legislative Intent

Judges look at legislative intent when analyzing the meaning of a statute. When you read decisions by the United States Supreme Court, you will see that the Justices often discuss legislative history and legislative intent in their decisions. Legislative intent can be based on Committee Reports, transcripts of debate in the Congressional Record and other sources. These can be found at http://thomas.loc.gov.

The No Child Left Behind Act is a reauthorization of Public Law 89-10, The Elementary and Secondary Education Act of 1965 (ESEA) that was signed into law by President Lyndon Johnson on April 11, 1965. The law is a comprehensive plan to redress and address the unequal educational opportunities for economically underprivileged children.

Legal Interpretations

Law is subject to different interpretations. Different attorneys and judges will interpret a statute differently, depending on their perspectives. If you read an article about education law, the interpretations and conclusions are likely to represent the author's opinions. If you read the statute and regulations for yourself, you will form your own interpretations and conclusions about the law and impact it is likely to have on you.

LEGAL RESEARCH

When you do research on a legal issue, you should study three types of law:

- Statutes
- Regulations
- Judicial decisions or caselaw

If you have questions about a legal issue, read the statute about your issue. Next, read the regulation that discusses or clarifies your issue. Expect to read the statute and regulation several times.

Find out if there are any cases about your legal issue. At present, there are very few reported cases regarding No Child Left Behind. Critical cases will be published on the Wrightslaw.com website.

NCLB CASELAW: As cases are decided, they will be added to the NCLB section of Wrightslaw at http://www.wrightslaw.com/nclb/index.htm

If you find cases about your issue, read the earlier decisions first, then tackle the recent decisions. If you know a case was appealed, read the decision that was appealed and reversed (or appealed and affirmed). When you read earlier decisions, you will learn how law in this area is evolving.

➜ **LEGAL SITES:** In addition to Wrightslaw.com, Findlaw.com and Versuslaw.com are good sources of legal information. Many cases are only available in print and must be located at a court or academic law library.

For every position taken by one court that a legal issue is clear black letter law, it is likely that another court has taken the opposite position, claiming their ruling is black letter law. In law, black is white, white is black, truth is shades of gray.

This is the nature of law.

IN SUMMATION

In this chapter, you learned about statutes, regulations and caselaw. You learned about legal research, legislative intent and judicial interpretations. The next chapter is an *Overview of the No Child Left Behind Act by Title*.

FOR YOUR NOTES

3 | An Overview of the NCLB Act

This chapter provides overview of the No Child Left Behind Act by Title. The Act is a massive statute, nearly 700 pages in length. Important information is not always be located where you expect to find it. For example, requirements about highly qualified teachers are in Title I, but the definition of "highly qualified teacher" is in Title IX.

The *Wrightslaw NCLB CD-ROM* that accompanies this book has the full text of Titles I through X with overviews and commentary, NCLB regulations, fact sheets, guidance publications from the U. S. Department of Education, and other NCLB resources.

The **Statement of Purpose** is the first and most important section in the No Child Left Behind Act:

> The purpose of this title is to ensure that all children have a fair, equal, and significant opportunity to obtain a high-quality education and reach, at a minimum, proficiency on challenging State academic achievement standards and state academic assessments. (20 U. S. C. § 6301)

The No Child Left Behind Act provides funding and grants, mandates accountability and results for grant recipients, and authorizes funds to supplement state and local education funding.

CLOSING THE GAP

Nationally, there is a significant gap between the achievement test scores of children from low-income families, racial minorities, children with disabilities, English language learners, and the test scores of other children. No Child Left Behind seeks to close the achievement gap by holding states, local school districts, and schools accountable for improving the academic achievement of all children.

No Child Left Behind requires schools to teach all children to proficiency in reading, math and science by 2014. The key requirements of the law—annual proficiency tests in grades 3-8, highly qualified teachers in every classroom, research-based instruction, increased parental rights, public school choice, and state, district and school report cards—are strategies to accomplish this goal.

Schools and school districts are required to meet the educational needs of all children, including poor children, children with disabilities, English language learners, minority and migratory children, and other neglected groups of children, and to publicly report their progress in educating children every year. (20 U. S. C. § 6301)

Children will have access to effective, scientifically based instruction and challenging academic content. Children are to receive an enriched, accelerated educational program that includes additional services that increase quality instructional time. (20 U. S. C. § 6301)

No Child Left Behind covers all states, school districts, and schools that accept federal Title I grants. Title I grants provide funding for remedial education programs for poor and disadvantaged children in public schools, and in some private programs. States shall give priority to school districts that serve the lowest-achieving schools that demonstrate the greatest need and strongest commitment to improve. (20 U. S. C. § 6303)

NCLB applies differently to schools that receive Title I funds than to schools that do not. You need to remember this concept and determine if a school or school district receives Title I funds. In some instances, the impact is different if a school district receives Title I funds but a particular school in that district does not receive Title I funds. The lack of Title I funds for a school or school district does not eliminate many No Child Left Behind requirements. One way or another, this law covers all public schools in all states.

NAVIGATING AROUND NCLB

The No Child Left Behind Act includes ten Titles. These Titles include parts, subparts, and chapters.

The print version of *Wrightslaw: No Child Left Behind* includes the full text of Title I with overviews, commentary and references. The *Wrightslaw No Child Left Behind CD-ROM* includes:

- Full text of **The No Child Left Behind Act, Titles I-X,** with overviews and commentary
- **No Child Left Behind Act of 2001** (Public Law 107-110)
- **No Child Left Behind regulations** (34 C.F.R. Part 200)
- *No Child Left Behind Deskbook* published by The U. S. Department of Education
- *Parent's Guide to NCLB* published by The U. S. Department of Education
- *NCLB: A Toolkit for Teachers* published by The U. S. Department of Education
- *Guidance Publications* from the U. S. Department of Education
- *NCLB Fact Sheets* from the U. S. Department of Education

🗁 **NCLB CD-ROM**: Appendix B includes a complete list of publications on the *Wrightslaw NCLB CD-ROM*.

TITLE I - IMPROVING THE ACADEMIC ACHIEVEMENT OF THE DISADVANTAGED

No Child Left Behind authorizes grants to states and school districts (local educational agencies or LEAs). In return for these funds, states and school districts agree to provide certain reports, programs, and results. Title I schools and programs are schools and programs that receive funds through grants authorized by Title I of the No Child Left Behind Act.

In general, states distribute funds to school districts. School districts distribute funds to Title I schools. A "Title I school" is a school that receives any portion of its funds from a Title I grant. All states accept Title I funds. About 90 percent of school districts and 60 percent of schools receive these funds. Title I funds go to both **schoolwide programs** and **targeted assistance programs**.

Schoolwide Programs

Schoolwide programs is a specialized term in the statute that describes a Title I program. A "schoolwide program" upgrades the entire educational program of a school with 40 percent or more of the children from low-income families. (20 U. S. C. § 6314)

Targeted Assistance Programs

Targeted assistance programs is a specialized term. It describes a Title I program that provides services to children identified as failing, or at risk of failing, to meet the State's challenging student academic achievement standards. (20 U. S. C. § 6315)

Title I has nine parts:

Part A: Improving Basic Programs Operated by Local Educational Agencies
Part B: Student Reading Skills Improvement Grants
Part C: Education of Migratory Children
Part D: Prevention and Intervention Programs for Children and Youth who are Neglected, Delinquent, or At-Risk
Part E: National Assessment of Title I
Part F: Comprehensive School Reform
Part G: Advanced Placement Programs
Part H: School Dropout Prevention
Part I: General Provisions

PART A - IMPROVING BASIC PROGRAMS OPERATED BY LOCAL EDUCATIONAL AGENCIES

Part A includes:

- state and local educational agency plans
- schoolwide programs and targeted assistance schools
- academic assessments and school improvement plans
- school recognition programs
- parental involvement
- new qualifications for teachers and paraprofessionals
- rules about children enrolled in private schools
- fiscal and coordination requirements

Adequate Yearly Progress (AYP)

Each state must define the **adequate yearly progress (AYP)** that school districts and schools must make to ensure that all students are proficient in reading, math, and science by 2014. Adequate yearly progress is a concept that applies to schools and school districts, not to individual children. School districts and schools must report their overall progress and their progress in educating specific groups of children who are often left behind, including:

- low-income students
- students with disabilities
- English language learners (limited English proficiency students)
- students from racial/ethnic groups

States are required to set annual yearly progress targets and annual measurable objectives for student progress and ensure that school districts test at least 95 percent of students. This data is used to determine if school districts and schools make adequate yearly progress. (20 U. S. C. § 6311) Data must also be reported for other groups including homeless children, migratory children, and children who dropout.

Accountability for Student Performance

No Child Left Behind requires states to implement accountability systems to ensure that all schools make adequate yearly progress and report their progress to the public.

If a Title I school district or school fails to make adequate yearly progress for **two consecutive years**, the state must identify the district or school as "in need of improvement." Students in the school may choose to attend a non-failing school in the school district. The school district may not use lack of capacity to deny students the option to transfer.

If a Title I school fails to make adequate yearly progress for **three consecutive years**, the school must also provide supplemental educational services (SES) to the children from low-income families who remain. Supplemental educational services include tutoring, after-school programs, and summer school, all at no cost to the parents. Parents may choose a tutor, or other service provider, from a list of providers approved by the state. The state will ensure that all providers on this list have a history of success.

If a Title I school fails to make adequate yearly progress for **four consecutive years**, the district may replace school staff, hire outside experts, implement a new curriculum, and/or reorganize the management structure.

If a Title I school fails to make adequate yearly progress for **five consecutive years,** the district shall either replace the staff, contract with a private firm to run the school, or reopen the school as a charter school. If these options are not successful, the state will take over management of the school. (20 U. S. C. § 6311)

Annual Academic Assessments

Beginning in 2005, schools that receive Title I funds must test all children in grades 3-8 in math and reading every year. Academic assessment or proficiency test scores will be used to determine if schools and school districts are making adequate yearly progress (AYP). Science assessments are required in 2007.

State academic standards must describe two levels of high proficiency (proficient and advanced) and a third level of achievement (basic) to describe progress by lower-achieving children toward the proficient and advanced levels. (20 U. S. C. § 6316)

All students in grades 3 through 8 will participate in the annual proficiency testing of reading and math, and less frequently in science, including students with disabilities and English language learners. Schools must provide reasonable adaptations and accommodations for students with disabilities. (20 U. S. C. § 6316(b))

School districts must test English language learners (students with limited English proficiency) every year to measure their oral language, reading, and writing skills in English. (20 U. S. C. § 6311)

To ensure that all states adopt high academic standards, states must participate in assessments of reading and math skills for fourth and eighth graders by the National Assessment of Educational Progress (NAEP).

State and School District Report Cards

Each state must publish an annual report card that includes specific information about the professional qualifications of teachers, graduation rates, overall academic achievement, and academic achievement of these subgroups:

* children from low-income families
* children with disabilities
* children with limited English proficiency
* racial and ethnic minorities

Title I school districts must report school test scores in the school district report card. The school district report card must include scores for each school as a whole and scores for those specific groups of children. The school district report card will tell parents and the public if the school and school district have been successful in teaching all groups of children. People can compare the report card from one school with report cards from other schools in the school district and state. Some states and school districts publish the report cards on the Internet. (20 U. S. C. § 6311)(h)

Public School Choice

If a Title I school fails to meet its adequate yearly progress (AYP) goals for **two consecutive years**, all children in that school may attend a non-failing school in the school district. If all schools in a district fail, children may attend a non-failing school in another school district. When a child transfers to a better school, the child may remain there until he or she completes the highest grade in that school. The sending school district is responsible for providing transportation to the receiving school until the sending school meets its Adequate Yearly Progress goal for 2 consecutive years. (20 U. S. C. § 6316(b))

If a Title I school fails to meet its adequate yearly progress (AYP) goals, the school must spend at least 10 percent of its Title I funds on professional development for teachers and principals.

Supplemental Educational Services

If a Title I school fails to meet its adequate yearly progress (AYP) goals for **three consecutive years**, the school must provide supplemental educational services to the students from low-income families who remain in the school. Supplemental educational services include tutoring, remediation, after-school programs, and summer school at no cost to parents.

Parents may choose a tutor or other service provider from a list of state-approved providers. The school district must promptly notify parents of eligible children of their option to transfer to a better-performing school or receive supplemental educational services at the district's expense. (20 U. S. C. § 6316(b))

Parent Empowerment and Parent's Right-to-Know

If a school does not receive Title I funds but is in a school district that does, the public is to be advised if the school is improving at the required rate and what subgroups the school is teaching successfully. If the child attends a school that receives Title I funds, parents have more options.

At the beginning of each school year, schools that receive Title I funds must notify all parents of their right to request information about the education, training and qualifications of their child's teachers and paraprofessionals. Schools must also notify parents if a teacher who is not "highly qualified" teaches the child for four consecutive weeks. (20 U. S. C. § 6311)

In the statute, the term "Right-to-Know" is hyphenated. If you are using a "search" or "find" feature to find this term, use hyphens. The authority for "Right-to-Know" is located in 20 U. S. C. § 63311(h)(6).

Title I schools must meet with parents to develop a parental involvement policy and distribute the policy to parents and the community. Parents of children who attend Title I schools shall have access to school staff, opportunities to participate in the child's class and to observe classroom activities. (20 U. S. C. § 6318)

The school must notify parents of English language learners of the child's level of English proficiency. Further, the school must define how the level was assessed, the child's academic achievement levels, the methods being used to teach the child, how the language program will help the child learn English, and when the child is expected to complete the program.

Highly Qualified Teachers

No Child Left Behind includes new educational requirements for teachers. New teachers and teachers who work in Title I programs at the beginning of the 2002-2003 school year must be "highly qualified."

At a minimum, a highly qualified teacher must have an undergraduate degree and be certified or licensed by the state. Elementary school teachers must demonstrate knowledge of teaching math and reading. Middle school and high school teachers must have a major in the subjects they teach or demonstrate knowledge of the subject.

Teachers who worked for school districts before 2002 must meet the highly qualified requirements by the 2005-2006 school year. (20 U. S. C. § 6319)

Higher Qualifications for Paraprofessionals

New paraprofessionals who work in Title I programs must complete two years of college or pass a rigorous skills test. Currently employed paraprofessionals must meet these requirements by 2006. Paraprofessionals may not provide instruction, except under the direct supervision of a teacher. (20 U. S. C. § 6319)

PART B - STUDENT READING SKILLS IMPROVEMENT GRANTS

Part B includes four subparts:

Subpart 1: Reading First
Subpart 2: Early Reading First
Subpart 3: William Goodling Even Start Family Literacy Programs
Subpart 4: Improving Literacy Through School Libraries

Effective Research-Based Reading Instruction

The purpose of Reading First is to ensure that every child can read at or above grade level by the end of third grade.

Reading First provides funds for screening, diagnostic, and classroom-based instructional reading assessments. Schools must use Reading First funds for research-based reading programs for children in Kindergarten through third grade. School districts and schools are required to use Title I funds for instructional programs, materials and assessments based on scientific research. Teacher training programs and school improvement plans must have proven records of effectiveness. Schools with high percentages of non-proficient readers, low-performing schools, and high-poverty schools are eligible for Reading First grants.

Because teachers must learn to screen, identify, and overcome children's reading problems, Reading First provides funds for training so teachers have the knowledge and skills to teach children to read. Teachers must make classroom decisions informed by scientifically based reading research. (20 U. S. C. § 6319)

Reading and the Essential Components of Reading Programs

No Child Left Behind defines **reading** as "A complex system of deriving meaning from print that requires all of the following:

- The skills and knowledge to understand how phonemes or speech sounds are connected to print
- The ability to decode unfamiliar words
- The ability to read fluently
- Sufficient information and vocabulary to foster reading comprehension
- The development of appropriate active strategies to construct meaning from print
- The development and maintenance of the motivation to read." (20 U. S. C. § 6368(5))

No Child Left Behind defines the **essential components of reading instruction** as explicit, systematic instruction in phonemic awareness, phonics, fluency, vocabulary, and reading comprehension. (20 U. S. C. § 6368(3))

Scientifically Based Reading Research

No Child Left Behind defines **scientifically based reading research** as research that:

- Applies rigorous, systematic, and objective procedures to obtain valid knowledge about reading development, reading instruction, and reading problems
- Includes research that uses systematic, empirical methods that use observation or experiment
- Uses rigorous data analysis that justifies the conclusions drawn
- Relies on measurements or methods that provide valid data across evaluators and across multiple measurements and observations
- Is accepted by a peer-reviewed journal or approved by a panel of independent experts through a rigorous, objective, scientific review (20 U. S. C. § 6368(6))

Early Reading First: Early Identification & Early Intervention

Early Reading First focuses on early identification and early intervention of reading problems. Early Reading First programs are required to:

- Use instructional materials based on sound research about language acquisition, reading, and spoken vocabulary
- Identify and help children who have trouble with spoken language and early reading skills.

NCLB lists these age-appropriate preschool language skills:

- recognizes letters of the alphabet
- knows letter sounds, sounds blends, uses increasingly complex vocabulary
- knows that written language is composed of phonemes and letters that make up syllables, words, and sentences
- has spoken language, vocabulary, and oral comprehension
- knows the purposes and conventions of print (20 U. S. C. § 6371)

Even Start Family Literacy Programs

The purpose of **Even Start Family Literacy Programs** is to break the cycle of poverty and illiteracy by ensuring that children and adults learn to read. Parents and children are eligible for testing, counseling, related services, and support services in Even Start Programs. (20 U. S. C. § 6381)

Even Start provides funds for intensive, high-quality family literacy programs that include these components:

- adult education
- childhood education
- parenting education
- interactive literacy activities

Funds must be used for scientifically based reading programs, including:

- family literacy programs
- reading readiness programs for preschool children
- summer reading programs to prevent children from losing skills in the summer (20 U. S. C. § 6381d)

Chapter 3

Improving Literacy Through School Libraries

The purpose of **Improving Literacy Through School Libraries** is to improve literacy skills and academic achievement by providing access to well-equipped school libraries staffed by certified school library specialists.

Improving Literacy provides funds for:

- books and media
- Internet linkages and networks
- access to school libraries before and after school, on weekends, and during the summer (20 U. S. C. § 6383)

PART C - EDUCATION OF MIGRATORY CHILDREN

The purposes of Part C are to improve educational outcomes for migratory children by:

- providing high-quality educational programs
- reducing educational disruptions associated with repeated moves
- preventing schools from penalizing migratory children
- requiring schools to provide educational programs and services to address the special educational needs of migratory children
- developing educational programs and services that help migratory children overcome cultural and language barriers, social isolation, and health problems
- preparing migratory children for postsecondary education and employment (20 U. S. C. § 6391)

Each state must report the performance of migratory students in the State Report Card. School districts and schools must provide parents of migratory students with academic achievement information. Schools must provide migratory children with opportunities to meet state academic and achievement standards.

Educational programs for migratory children may include:

- advocacy and outreach for migrant children and their families
- professional development for teachers and other pupil personnel
- family literacy programs (20 U. S. C. § 6394)

NCLB established a national information system to electronically exchange health and educational information about migratory students at no cost to school districts, including:

- immunization and health records
- academic history and credits
- results of State assessments
- eligibility under the Individuals with Disabilities Education Act (20 U. S. C. § 6398)

Schools are required to meet with parents of migratory children to develop written parent involvement policies and school-parent compacts. These documents will describe how the school will work with parents and students to improve academic achievement.

PART D - PREVENTION AND INTERVENTION PROGRAMS FOR NEGLECTED, DELINQUENT OR AT-RISK CHILDREN

Part D focuses on the needs of **at-risk children** in institutions or community day programs for neglected or delinquent youth. The purposes of Part D are to:

- improve educational services for neglected or delinquent children and youth in institutions
- provide transition services so neglected or delinquent children can attend school or secure employment
- prevent at-risk youth from dropping out of school
- provide a support system to dropouts and youth who return from correctional facilities so they can continue their education (20 U. S. C. § 6421)

The state is required to work with parents to improve educational achievement of at-risk children and youth. Each state must ensure that teachers and other personnel are trained to work with children with disabilities and other students with special needs. (20 U. S. C. § 6434)

School districts may use Title I funds for transition programs to help at-risk children and youth remain in school. Title I funds may be used for dropout prevention programs for delinquent children, gang members, pregnant and young parents, migratory children, immigrant children, and children who have been retained. The school may also use Title I funds for mentoring and peer mediation programs. (20 U. S. C. § 6454)

The state may eliminate funding if a school district does not show measurable progress in reducing dropout rates. (20 U. S. C. § 6456)

PART E - THE NATIONAL ASSESSMENT OF TITLE I

Part E authorizes the National Assessment of Title I, and includes information about state standards, state assessment systems, and accountability. Part E authorizes an independent review panel to advise the U. S. Department of Education about the effectiveness of the National Assessment of Title I and the National Longitudinal Study. (20 U. S. C. § 6491)

PART F - COMPREHENSIVE SCHOOL REFORM

Part F provides financial incentives to school districts that develop school reform strategies for basic academics and parental involvement. School districts can use Part F funds for school reform. (20 U. S. C. § 6511)

PART G - ADVANCED PLACEMENT PROGRAMS

Because 600,000 students who take advanced placement courses every year do not take advanced placement exams, Part G provides funds to:

- increase participation in advanced placement courses
- improve access to highly trained teachers
- increase the number of students who take advanced placement exams. (20 U. S. C. § 6532)

PART H - SCHOOL DROPOUT PREVENTION

The School Dropout Prevention Act provides Title I funds for effective school dropout prevention and reentry programs. Funds may be used for various programs, including:

- providing teacher training and professional development
- purchasing curricular materials
- providing remedial education
- reducing pupil-teacher ratios
- meeting state academic achievement standards
- providing counseling and mentoring
- developing school reform models (20 U. S. C. § 6561a)

The School Dropout Prevention Act establishes a national recognition program to recognize and financially reward schools that develop effective programs that reduce dropout rates. (20 U. S. C. § 6555)

PART I - GENERAL PROVISIONS

Part I authorizes the U. S. Department of Education to issue No Child Left Behind regulations. The No Child Left Behind regulations went into effect on January 2, 2003. The regulations are in Volume 34, Part 200 of the Code of Federal Regulations. (20 U. S. C. § 6571)

States must create committees of practitioners to review proposed regulations and ensure that state rules, regulations, and policies conform to the purposes of the No Child Left Behind statute. (20 U. S. C. § 6573)

TITLE II - PREPARING, TRAINING, AND RECRUITING HIGH QUALITY TEACHERS AND PRINCIPALS

Title II of the No Child Left Behind Act authorizes funds for teacher recruitment, hiring, and retention. States and school districts may offer scholarships, signing bonuses, differential pay, and other financial incentives. Teachers in high-need academic subjects and in high-poverty schools and districts are eligible for bonus pay. No Child Left Behind provides additional funds to encourage teachers to get advanced certification or credentials.

Title II has four Parts:

Part A - Teacher and Principal Training and Recruiting Fund
Part B - Mathematics and Science Partnerships
Part C - Innovation for Teacher Quality
Part D - Enhancing Education Through Technology

PART A - TEACHER AND PRINCIPAL TRAINING AND RECRUITING FUND

Each state may apply for teacher and principal training and recruitment grants. State applications must describe how activities will improve student academic achievement, how funds will improve the quality of teachers and principals, and how the state will hold local school districts accountable. States may use funds to:

- reform teacher and principal certification
- establish alternate routes to teaching
- reform tenure systems
- establish teacher advancement programs
- develop multiple career paths for teachers
- fund programs to encourage men to become elementary school teachers (20 U. S. C. § 6613)

School districts may receive grants for teacher recruitment. To receive funds, districts must agree to target schools with the lowest number of highly qualified teachers, largest class sizes, and/or schools identified for improvement. Financial incentives are available for new principals and for principals who mentor new principals. Grants are available for public and private entities that provide teacher training and professional development. (20 U. S. C. § 6623)

PART B - MATHEMATICS AND SCIENCE PARTNERSHIPS

The purposes of Part B are:

- to improve mathematics and science teaching
- to bring mathematics and science teachers together with scientists, mathematicians, and engineers
- to increase the knowledge and teaching skills of mathematics and science teachers (20 U. S. C. § 6661)

To recruit mathematics, engineering, and science majors into teaching, NCLB authorizes performance incentives, stipends and scholarships. NCLB also authorizes grants for math and science distance learning programs. (20 U. S. C. § 6662) ,

PART C - INNOVATION FOR TEACHER QUALITY

Part C includes programs to recruit and retain teachers and improve teacher quality.

Troops-to-Teachers authorizes bonuses and stipends to members of the Armed Forces who become highly qualified teachers. Individuals must agree to teach in high-need schools for at least three years to receive financial incentives. (20 U. S. C. § 6673)

Transition to Teacher seeks to recruit mid-career professionals to work as teachers in high-need schools. This program provides alternate routes to teacher certification by using the individual's experiences, expertise, and academic qualifications. Participants who agree to teach in high-need schools are eligible for scholarships, stipends, bonuses, and other financial incentives. (20 U. S. C. § 6683)

The **National Writing Project** supports and promotes effective practices and research to improve the quality of student writing and learning. (20 U. S. C. § 6701)

The purposes of the **Education for Democracy Act** are:

- to improve the quality of civics and government education
- to educate students about the Constitution and the Bill of Rights
- to foster civic competence and responsibility (20 U. S. C. § 6712)

Congress enacted the **Teacher Liability Protection** statute to help schools maintain order and control in the classroom and school. This statute protects teachers, principals, and other school personnel from liability if they act within the scope of their employment and do not violate Federal, State, and local laws. (20 U. S. C. § 6732)

PART D - ENHANCING EDUCATION THROUGH TECHNOLOGY

The purposes of Part D are:

- to use technology to improve academic achievement
- to increase access to technology
- to ensure that every student is technologically literate by the end of eighth grade (20 U. S. C. § 6752)

States and school districts may use technology grants for various projects, including:

- to create electronic networks and distance learning
- to promote parent and family involvement in education
- to facilitate communication between students, parents, teachers, and administrators (20 U. S. C. § 6766)

The U. S. Department of Education is required to conduct an independent, long-term study of educational technology that uses scientifically based research methods and control groups. An independent panel will review the findings of the study and advise the Secretary about its implications. (20 U. S. C. § 6771)

Grants and cooperative agreements with public telecommunications entities are available to produce and distribute educational and instructional video programs for preschool and elementary school children and their parents. (20 U. S. C. § 6775)

Schools must develop and implement policies to block visual depictions of obscene and pornographic materials. (20 U. S. C. § 6777)

TITLE III - LANGUAGE INSTRUCTION FOR LIMITED ENGLISH PROFICIENT AND IMMIGRANT STUDENTS

Title III includes three Parts:

Part A - English-Language Acquisition, Language Enhancement, and Academic Achievement Act
Part B - Improving Language Instructional Programs
Part C - General Provisions

PART A - ENGLISH LANGUAGE ACQUISITION, LANGUAGE ENHANCEMENT, AND ACADEMIC ACHIEVEMENT ACT

The purposes of Part A are:

- to ensure that English language learners and immigrant children become proficient in the English language and in core academic subjects
- to help states and school districts develop high-quality language instruction programs that prepare these children to enter all-English classes (20 U. S. C. § 6812)

NCLB requires states and local school districts to establish standards and objectives for increasing English proficiency in four areas: speaking, listening, reading, and writing. School districts must use research-based language instruction curricula for English language learners that are effective with this population. (20 U. S. C. § 6823)

Schools must assess English language learners to measure the child's progress toward English proficiency and the child's comprehension, speaking, listening, reading, and writing skills in English. If the child has been in the United States for three or more years, the school must test the child in English every year. (20 U. S. C. § 6826)

NCLB funds are available for professional development programs that teach principals and teachers to use research-based curricula, tests, and strategies that increase English proficiency. Colleges and universities can receive grants for professional development programs that improve classroom instruction for English language learners. Professional development must be sufficiently intense to have a lasting impact on a teacher's classroom performance; one-day and short-term workshops and conferences do not qualify. (20 U. S. C. § 6825)

Recipients of Title III funds are required to provide information about the percentage of children who are making progress toward English proficiency, the percentage who achieved English proficiency, and the percentage that made the transition to general education classes. (20 U. S. C. § 6842)

PART B - IMPROVING LANGUAGE INSTRUCTION EDUCATIONAL PROGRAMS

The purpose of Part B is to ensure that English language learners master English and the same standards of academic achievement that other children are required to master. (20 U. S. C. § 6892)

Part B funds may be used to recruit and train educators. Grants are available for professional development, curricula, and resources to improve educational services and results for English language learners. NCLB authorizes undergraduate, graduate, doctoral, and post-doctoral fellowships and scholarships to recruit and train language teachers. (20 U. S. C. § 6951)

NCLB authorizes emergency financial assistance for school districts that experience large, unexpected increases in their immigrant populations. School districts may use Emergency Immigrant Education funds for family literacy and parent outreach, staff training, student tutorials, mentoring, career or academic counseling, and basic instructional services. (20 U. S. C. § 6951)

NCLB authorizes funds to pay staff to participate in professional development programs. (20 U. S. C. § 6981)

The school must notify parents of English language learners about:

- the child's progress in the language program
- the child's academic skill levels
- how the child's progress is being measured
- when the child will complete the program and enter a general education program
- how the language program is meeting the child's educational needs
- how the language program is helping the child learn English and meet standards for promotion and graduation
- exit requirements for the language program (20 U. S. C. § 7012)

Parents have the right to remove their child from a language program at any time. (20 U. S. C. § 7012)

If the school fails to make progress on their annual measurable achievement objectives, the school must advise all parents of this failure within 30 days. The school must provide this notice to parents in an understandable, uniform format and in a language the parent can understand, to the extent practicable. (20 U. S. C. § 7012)

TITLE IV - 21ST CENTURY SCHOOLS

The purposes of Title IV are:

- to create safe, orderly schools
- to protect students and teachers
- to encourage discipline and personal responsibility
- to combat drugs.

Title IV includes three parts:

Part A – Safe and Drug-Free Schools and Communities
Part B – 21st Century Community Learning Centers
Part C – Environmental Tobacco Smoke

PART A – SAFE AND DRUG-FREE SCHOOLS AND COMMUNITIES

The purposes of Part A are:

- to support programs that prevent violence
- to prevent the illegal use of alcohol, tobacco, and drugs
- to involve parents and communities
- to support student academic achievement (20 U. S. C. § 7102)

Funds are available for school drug and violence prevention programs with priority to programs that prevent violence and drug use for at-risk populations. (20 U. S. C. § 7112)

Grants must include performance indicators, including reductions in risk factors, increases in protective factors, and how progress will be reported to the public. Program effectiveness will be evaluated and this information will be used to refine, improve, and strengthen programs. (20 U. S. C. § 7113)

Schools must have a comprehensive plan to keep the school safe, including school discipline policies, security procedures, prevention activities, a crisis management plan, and a student code of conduct. (20 U. S. C. § 7114)

Programs must include objective data about violence and illegal drug use, consequences, performance measures. They must also be based on research that shows the program will reduce violence and illegal drug use. (20 U. S. C. § 7115)

Funds are available for educational programs that prevent hate crimes and improve the conflict or dispute resolution skills of students, teachers, and administrators. (20 U. S. C. § 7133)

PART B - 21ST CENTURY COMMUNITY LEARNING CENTERS

The purpose of Part B is to provide opportunities for communities to establish or expand community learning centers. 21st Century Community Learning Centers offer before- and after-school programs, summer programs, and family literacy programs and services, including:

- academic enrichment
- tutorials
- remediation
- counseling
- recreation
- technology education (20 U. S. C. § 7171)

PART C - ENVIRONMENTAL TOBACCO SMOKE

Schools, agencies, clinics, and service providers must prohibit smoking within any indoor facility used for educational or library services to children. (20 U. S. C. § 7183)

TITLE V - PROMOTING INFORMED PARENTAL CHOICE AND INNOVATIVE PROGRAMS

The purposes of Title V are to:

- support educational reform
- fund school improvement programs based on scientifically based research
- meet the educational needs of at-risk students, and
- improve school, student and teacher performance (20 U. S. C. § 7201)

Title V provides funds to school districts for innovative programs in various areas, including:

- educational reform
- programs to meet the needs of at-risk and high-need students
- public charter schools and magnet schools
- counseling, character education, and mental health programs
- gifted and talented programs
- foreign language and arts programs
- smaller learning communities
- physical education programs (20 U. S. C. § 7215)

The purposes of Part B, Public Charter Schools, are to:

- provide charter schools with funding
- evaluate the effects of charter schools
- increase the number of high-quality charter schools
- encourage states to provide financial support to charter schools (20 U. S. C. § 7221)

Part C authorizes financial assistance for magnet schools. (20 U. S. C. § 7231)

Part D authorizes funding for dozens of programs, including counseling, character education, mental health, gifted and talented, reading, small learning communities, the arts, foreign languages, physical education, and economics. (20 U. S. C. § 7243)

TITLE VI - FLEXIBILITY AND ACCOUNTABILITY

The purposes of Title VI are to:

- give states and school districts flexibility in using federal funds
- encourage local solutions for local problems
- help administrators improve student progress.

Title VI includes three Parts.

Part A – Improving Academic Achievement
Part B – Rural Education Initiative
Part C – General Provisions

PART A - IMPROVING ACADEMIC ACHIEVEMENT

Part A describes:

- state academic assessments
- statewide reporting systems
- state assessment systems
- information about student and school achievement (20 U. S. C. § 7301)

PART B - RURAL EDUCATION INITIATIVE

Part B focuses on the unique needs of small rural school districts, especially districts with a large proportion of low-income students. Title VI funds can be used for:

- teacher recruitment and retention
- professional development
- educational technology
- parent involvement activities (20 U. S. C. § 7341a)

PART C - GENERAL PROVISIONS

Part C describes the roles of the federal government and the National Assessment of Educational Progress (NAEP). The federal government will not:

- control the instructional content, standards, or curriculum of a state, district or school
- require states or school districts to equalize spending per pupil (20 U. S. C. § 7371)

The National Assessment of Educational Progress (NAEP) will:

- conduct assessments in reading and math every two years
- provide information about academic progress by race, ethnicity, socioeconomic status, gender, disability, and English proficiency (20 U. S. C. § 9010)

TITLE VII - INDIAN, NATIVE HAWAIIAN AND ALASKA NATIVE EDUCATION

PART A - INDIAN EDUCATION

The purposes of Part A about Indian Education are to:

- support Indian tribes, organizations, colleges and universities
- meet the unique educational, cultural and academic needs of American Indian and Alaska Native students
- help these students meet challenging state academic achievement standards (20 U. S. C. § 7402)

Title VII funds are available for various programs, including:

- programs to improve the education of Indian children
- remedial instruction, early childhood education, health and nutrition programs
- dropout prevention programs

- research into effective educational programs for Indian children and adults
- in-service training for teachers of Indian children
- fellowships and stipends for Indian students who attend college
- centers for gifted and talented Indian students (20 U. S. C. § 7425)

PART B - NATIVE HAWAIIAN EDUCATION

The purposes of Part B about Native Hawaiian Education are to:

- develop innovative educational programs for Native Hawaiians
- provide resources for Native Hawaiian education
- encourage Native Hawaiians to plan and manage education programs (20 U. S. C. § 7513)

Funds are available for an array of programs and services, including:

- reading and literacy activities in the Hawaiian or English language
- programs to meet the special needs of Native Hawaiian students with disabilities
- programs to meet the special needs of Native Hawaiian students who are gifted and talented
- professional development activities for educators
- community-based learning centers for Native Hawaiian families
- scholarships for undergraduate or graduate study
- family literacy services (20 U. S. C. § 7515)

PART C - ALASKA NATIVE EDUCATION

The purposes of Part C about Alaska Native Education are to:

- recognize the unique educational needs of Alaska Natives
- authorize supplemental educational programs
- supplement current programs
- provide flexibility about how funds will be spent (20 U. S. C. § 7543)

Part C funds are available for an array of programs and services, including:

- curricula and educational programs
- innovative educational methods and strategies
- professional development
- home instruction programs for preschool children
- family literacy programs
- math and science enrichment
- remedial programs
- parenting education
- dropout prevention (20 U. S. C. § 7444)

TITLE VIII - IMPACT AID PROGRAM

The purpose of Title VIII is to replace revenue that is lost because parents live and/or work on federal property. Title VIII authorizes several forms of impact aid, including:

- support payments to districts with federally connected children
- supplemental assistance for children with disabilities
- construction funds
- facilities maintenance

TITLE IX - GENERAL PROVISIONS

Title IX addresses diverse issues including:

- flexibility and consolidation of funds
- equitable services and benefits for private school children and teachers
- coordination of service delivery systems
- privacy of assessment results
- school prayer
- access by military recruiters
- unsafe school choice

Part A includes several key legal definitions of terms from "average daily attendance" to "technology." (20 U. S. C. § 7801)

Public school officials must consult with private school officials to ensure that **private school children and teachers** receive special educational services and benefits under these programs. Services and benefits for private school students and teachers must be equitable to services and benefits for public school children. (20 U. S. C. § 7881)

No Child Left Behind does not apply to children who attend **private schools** or **home schools.** The law does not permit, allow, encourage, or authorize any Federal control over any aspect of any private, religious, or home school, nor require any State educational agency or local educational agency to mandate, direct, or control the curriculum of a private or home school. (20 U. S. C. § 7886)

School districts that receive NCLB funds must certify, in writing, that they do not have any policy that prevents **school prayer** in public schools. (20 U. S. C. § 7904)

School districts that receive funds must provide **military recruiters** with access to student names, addresses, and telephone listings, with some limitations. (20 U. S. C. § 7908)

The **Unsafe School Choice option** requires states to implement a policy that allows children who attend persistently dangerous schools and children who are victims of violent criminal offense to transfer to another school that is safe. (20 U. S. C. § 7912)

TITLE X - REPEALS, REDESIGNATIONS, AND AMENDMENTS TO OTHER STATUTES

Title X does not follow the format of the first nine titles (codified in the United States Code beginning at 20 U. S. C. § 6301 in Title I to 20 U. S. C. § 7941 in Title IX). Part A is about repeals. Part B is re-designations. Title X also includes amendments to other statutes and technical corrections.

PART C - HOMELESS EDUCATION ASSISTANCE _____

Part C is the McKinney-Vento Homeless Education Assistance Act of 2001. The Act begins with a Statement of Congressional Policy: ". . . that each child of a homeless individual and each homeless youth has access to the same free, appropriate public education, including a public preschool education, as provided to other children and youth." (42 U. S. C. § 11431)

States that have compulsory residency requirements that may act as a barrier to homeless children must review and revise these laws, regulations, policies, and practices to ensure that homeless children receive the same free, appropriate public education that other children receive. (42 U. S. C. § 11431)

States must establish an Office of Coordinator of Homeless Children and Youth to gather valid, reliable information on problems and innovative practices. States and school districts must provide assurances that they have policies and practices to ensure that homeless children and youth are not segregated nor stigmatized, and that educational decisions are in the child's best interest. (42 U. S. C. § 11432)

School districts may receive grants for tutoring, supplemental education, enrichment, health and dental services, mentoring, summer programs, tutoring, parent training, school supplies, and emergency assistance. (42 U. S. C. § 11433)

PART D - NATIVE AMERICAN EDUCATION IMPROVEMENT ACT OF 2001 _____

Part D begins with a declaration of a policy: that the federal government has sole responsibility for operating and financing Bureau of Indian Affairs (BIA) schools established on or near Indian reservations and Indian trust lands and that BIA-funded schools "are of the highest quality" and meet "the unique educational and cultural needs of those children." (25 U. S. C. § 2000)

Students who attend these schools are to be provided with educational opportunities that ". . . equal or exceed those for all other students in the United States." (25 U. S. C. § 2001)

All schools, dormitories, and Indian education-related facilities shall be brought into compliance with applicable tribal, federal, state health and safety standards, Section 504 of the Rehabilitation Act, and the Americans with Disabilities Act. The Secretary of Interior must submit a detailed plan about how these facilities will be brought into compliance, including specific cost estimates and specific timelines to bring each school into compliance. (25 U. S. C. § 2005)

The United States has a policy "to facilitate Indian control of Indian affairs in all matters relating to education." (25 U. S. C. § 2005)

PART F – GENERAL EDUCATION PROVISIONS ACT _____

Part F includes the statute about **student privacy** and **parent access to information**.

This statute gives parents the right to inspect any instructional material used in their child's educational curriculum. Instructional material is defined as "instructional content that is provided to a student, regardless of its format, including printed or representational materials, audio-visual materials, and materials in electronic or digital formats (such as materials accessible through the Internet). The term does not include academic tests or academic assessments." (Section 1061)

IN SUMMATION

In this chapter, you learned how the No Child Left Behind Act is organized and where to find information on key topics. In the next chapter, you get answers to more than forty frequently asked questions about accountability, public school choice, research based instruction, reading, safe schools, teachers, and annual testing.

RESOURCES

You will find many excellent publications for parents in the *Wrightslaw: No Child Left Behind CD-ROM* and on the Internet. Here is a short list of recommended resources.

In the Wrightslaw No Child Left Behind CD-ROM

NCLB Fact Sheets. Fact sheets from the U. S. Department of Education about many No Child Left Behind topics, including reading, math, supplemental services, and public school choice.

No Child Left Behind: A Desktop Reference. This publication from the U. S. Department of Education outlines the No Child Left Behind program supported under the Elementary and Secondary Act of 1965 and other statues and describes how the Act's four guiding principles (accountability, flexibility and local control, parental choice, and what works) are brought to bear on these programs.

Report Cards: Non-Regulatory Guidance. Publication from the U. S. Department of Education answers questions about state and school district (local educational agency) report cards.

On the Internet

➔ **BROKEN LINKS:** Internet links change often and many links are quickly outdated. If you find an article or publication is no longer available, use a search engine to find the document. Type the title of the article into the search box.

A New Wave of Evidence: The Impact of School, Family and Community Connections on Student Achievement published by the Southwest Educational Development Laboratory.
URL: http://www.sedl.org/connections/resources/evidence.pdf

An Action Guide for Community and Parent Leaders - Using NCLB to Improve Student Achievement by Public Education Network. URL: http://www.publiceducation.org/pdf/NCLBBook.pdf

No State Left Behind: The Challenges and Opportunities of ESEA 2001 published by Education Commission of the States. URL: http://www.ecs.org/ecsmain.asp?page=/html/special/ESEA_main.htm

4 | FREQUENTLY ASKED QUESTIONS ABOUT NCLB

No Child Left Behind includes new responsibilities and requirements for states, school districts, and schools. The law also includes new rights and responsibilities for children who attend public schools that receive Title I funds and their parents. These frequently questions and answers are from the No Child Left Behind site at www.nclb.gov/
:

- Accountability
- Choice
- Doing What Works
- Reading
- Safe Schools
- Teachers
- Testing

ACCOUNTABILITY
1. How do I know how my child is doing?
2. When will the states have to follow this new law?
3. My child has special needs. How does this bill help my child?
4. What are the requirements of the No Child Left Behind Act for states and school districts to publish "report cards" on school performance?
5. How can I see these school report cards?
6. Will these tests measure the progress of the schools?
7. How will measuring "adequate yearly progress" help improve my school?
8. What if a school fails to improve?
9. Are there any rewards for schools or teachers that do well?

PUBLIC SCHOOL CHOICE
10. Do the public school choice options include only schools in the same district, or might they include schools in neighboring school districts?
11. Will transportation be offered to pupils exercising public school choice options?
12. Which pupils will be eligible for public school choice?
13. How do I know if my child is eligible for supplemental services?
14. How can I find out what kind of extra help is available from the school?
15. Who will provide supplemental services?
16. Can community-based organizations participate in programs funded under No Child Left Behind?
17. If my child is in a charter school, do testing and accountability apply?
18. Does No Child Left Behind provide for the facility financing of charter schools?

DOING WHAT WORKS

19. Does No Child Left Behind do anything to prevent education fads, bad ideas or untested curricula from being used in my child's classroom?
20. What is scientifically based research?
21. How does scientifically based research apply to other federal education programs?

READING

22. How are America's children doing in reading?
23. What's the key to helping children become successful readers?
24. Why is it so important for children to read better so early in school?
25. What is being done to help children learn to read well by the end of the third grade?
26. What is Reading First exactly, and what are its specific goals?
27. What's different about Reading First?
28. How will Reading First help classroom teachers?
29. What are the expectations of Reading First?
30. How will we know if Reading First is working?

CREATING SAFER SCHOOLS

31. I am concerned about my child's safety. How does this law help secure safer schools?
32. What is the "Unsafe School Choice Option" in the No Child Left Behind Act?
33. How will this law help teachers keep the classroom safe?

TEACHERS

34. How will this law help my child's teacher?
35. How can I help my child's teacher?

TESTING

36. What effect will testing have on my child?
37. Will the results of my child's test be private?
38. Some people say that testing will make teachers "teach to the test." Are those people right?
39. Will testing help teachers?
40. What about principals? Will testing help them?
41. Reading and math and eventually science will be tested. What about other subjects?
42. Who will pay for these tests?
43. What if I want to home school my child? Does the new law require tests at home?
44. What is the National Assessment of Educational Progress (NAEP), and what is its purpose?

ACCOUNTABILITY ─────────────────────────────────

1. How do I know how my child is doing?

No Child Left Behind gives parents new tools to help their children learn and to help improve America's schools. No Child Left Behind is designed to highlight success and shine a light on failure. It will give you objective data. Every state will test students in grades three through eight on what they know in math and reading. And by 2007, students will be tested in science, too. Many parents have children who are getting straight A's, but find out only later that their child is not prepared for college. That's why No Child Left Behind seeks to give parents objective data about how their children are doing.

2. When will the states have to follow this new law?

The new law took effect in the Fall of 2002. That's why it is critical that parents and educators are informed about the new reforms and improvements brought about by No Child Left Behind.

3. My child has special needs. How does this bill help my child?

No Child Left Behind gives districts new flexibility and freedom with Federal funds so children with disabilities can be better served. President Bush and the Department of Education will work with Congress to make sure reform starts with getting children help, focusing on results, and reducing the regulations that hinder outreach to these children.

4. What are the requirements of the No Child Left Behind Act for states and school districts to publish "report cards" on school performance?

Starting with the 2002-2003 school year, state test results will be reported to the public in order to hold schools accountable for improving the academic achievement of each one of their students. The following information will be on the report card:

- student academic achievement on statewide tests disaggregated by subgroup;
- a comparison of students at basic, proficient, and advanced levels of academic achievement (these levels are determined by your state);
- high school graduation rates (how many students drop out of school);
- the number and names of schools identified for improvement;
- the professional qualifications of teachers; and
- the percentages of students not tested

School districts must prepare annual reports for parents and the public on the academic achievement of all schools combined and of each individual school. The school district report cards will include the same information in the state report card. In the case of an individual school, the report card will include whether it has been identified for school improvement and how its students performed on the state test compared to the school district and state as a whole.

5. How can I see these school report cards?

In addition to student report cards, schools will report overall results for student learning. These campus report cards must be disseminated widely through public means, which could be posted on the Internet, distributed to the media, or distributed through public agencies.

6. Will these tests measure the progress of the schools?

Yes. No Child Left Behind received bipartisan support of both Democrats and Republicans because it demands results from every school for the benefit of every child. Every year, Americans will be able to find out whether their school is improving - or to put it another way: whether it is making adequate yearly progress.

7. How will measuring "adequate yearly progress" help improve my school?

Adequate Yearly Progress (AYP) is an individual state's measure of yearly progress toward achieving state academic standards. It sets the minimum level of improvement that states, school districts, and schools must achieve each year. No Child Left Behind raises the bar of expectations for all students - especially those ethnic groups and those disadvantaged students who are falling farther and farther behind and who are most in danger of being left behind.

It works like this: States start by defining adequate yearly progress - the measurements of academic improvement a school must achieve to ensure that, at the end of 12 years, every student graduating will have a mastery of the basics.

Each state chooses where to set the initial academic achievement bar based on the lowest-achieving demographic group or based on the lowest-achieving schools in the state, whichever is higher. Once the initial bar is established, the state is required to "raise the bar" gradually to reach 100 percent proficiency at the end of 12 years. The initial bar must be raised after two years and subsequent thresholds must be raised at least once every three years.

This guarantees every school will be striving to improve.

8. What if a school fails to improve?

Parents will get options for their children and districts will have ways to get children extra help. Schools that have not made state-defined adequate yearly progress for two consecutive school years will be identified as needing school improvement before the beginning of the next school year.

Immediately after a school is found to be in need of improvement, officials will receive help and technical assistance. These schools will develop a two-year plan to turn around the school. Every student in the school will be given the option to transfer to a better public school in the district.

If the school does not make adequate yearly progress for three consecutive years, the school remains in school improvement and the district must continue to offer public school choice to all students. The school must also provide supplemental educational services to disadvantaged children. Parents can chose the services their child needs from a list of approved providers.

If the school fails to make adequate yearly progress for four consecutive years, the district must implement certain corrective actions to improve the school, such as replacing certain staff or fully implementing a new curriculum, as well as continuing to offer public school choice and pay for supplemental services.

If a school fails to make adequate yearly progress for five consecutive years, it will be identified for restructuring. First, it would have to develop a plan and make the necessary arrangements to implement significant alternative governance actions, state takeover, the hiring of a private management contractor, converting to a charter school, or significant staff restructuring.

During this entire time of getting the school help, parents and children will get public school choice and supplemental services, so they won't be trapped in schools consistently identified as in need of improvement and risk being academically left behind.

9. Are there any rewards for schools or teachers that do well?

The law authorizes state academic achievement awards to schools that close achievement gaps between groups of students or exceed academic achievement goals. States may use Federal funds to financially reward teachers in schools that receive academic achievement awards. In addition, states may designate schools that make the greatest achievement gains as "Distinguished Schools."

PUBLIC SCHOOL CHOICE

10. Do the public school choice options include only schools in the same district, or might they include schools in neighboring school districts?

Options may include a neighboring school district. If a school is identified for school improvement, corrective action, or restructuring, your district must provide all students in the school the option to transfer to another public school that is not in need of improvement, no later than the first day of the school year following identification.

However, if all public schools served by the district are in school improvement, corrective action, or restructuring, the district must try to establish a cooperative agreement with other districts to provide students the option to transfer to another public school. In addition, nothing in the No Child Left Behind Act prohibits districts from establishing cooperative agreements, regardless of whether all schools in a particular district are in need of improvement. Public school choice must be provided unless state law prohibits it.

11. Will transportation be offered to pupils exercising public school choice options?

Yes. Districts must provide transportation required for a student to exercise public school choice under school improvement, corrective action, restructuring, or inter-district choice offered as part of corrective action for a school.

12. Which pupils will be eligible for public school choice?

All children attending schools identified for school improvement, corrective action, or restructuring are eligible to exercise public school choice, but districts must give priority to low-income students (as defined by the district) if it is not possible to serve all students.

13. How do I know if my child is eligible for supplemental services?

Eligible children are those from low-income families (as defined by the school district) who are attending a school in its second year of school improvement, in corrective action, or identified for restructuring.

14. How can I find out what kind of extra help is available from the school?

Your school must provide you with a list of the programs available in the area, so you have a full set of options to find whatever services your child needs to get caught up.

Schools that are required to provide supplemental services must:

- annually notify parents of the availability of those services, including the identity and qualifications of approved providers and a description of the services they provide;
- help parents select a provider, if such help is requested; and
- enter into an agreement with a provider for each student that includes goals and a timetable for improving the student's achievement, regular progress reports, a provision for termination if the provider fails to meet the goals, timetables, and payment terms.

15. Who will provide supplemental services?

Providers can be non-profit, including faith-based organizations, or for-profit entities with a "demonstrated record of effectiveness" in increasing student academic achievement. The provider must be capable of providing supplemental educational services consistent with the instructional program of the district and the state's academic standards.

In addition, providers must give parents and the school information on the progress of the children served, ensure that instruction is consistent with state and local standards, including state student academic achievement standards, and meet applicable health, safety, and civil rights laws.

16. Can community-based organizations participate in programs funded under No Child Left Behind?

Yes. Community-based organizations and other public entities and private organizations, including faith-based organizations that provide safety and drug abuse programs, can apply for Federal funds under the law.

17. If my child is in a charter school, do testing and accountability apply?

The accountability and testing provisions in No Child Left Behind must also be applied to charter schools in accordance with states' charter school laws. As public schools, charter schools are subject to the same accountability and testing requirements, but state authorized chartering agencies, as established by state law, are responsible for ensuring charter schools are meeting the requirements and being held accountable.

18. Does No Child Left Behind provide for the facility financing of charter schools?

Yes. No Child Left Behind includes two measures that provide for the facility financing of charter schools. The first measure provides facility-financing assistance to states and localities that support charter schools by allowing the Secretary of Education to award matching incentive grants to those states that provide charter schools with per-pupil expenditure funds.

The second measure extends the Charter School Facility Financing Demonstration Project for an additional two years. The Charter School Facility Financing Demonstration Project encourages the development of innovative approaches to credit enhancement and leverages private capital for charter schools to use for infrastructure needs.

DOING WHAT WORKS

19. There are a lot of education fads. Does No Child Left Behind do anything to prevent bad ideas or untested curricula from being used in my child's classroom?

The No Child Left Behind Act puts a special focus on doing what works. The new law stresses the importance of selecting instructional approaches that have a proven track record. For too many years, too many schools have experimented with lessons and materials that failed and have not proven effective.

20. What is scientifically based research?

To say that an instructional practice or program is research-based, we must have carefully obtained, reliable evidence that the program or practice works. For example, an evaluation might measure a group of children who are learning how to read using different methods, and then compare the results to see which method is most successful.

No Child Left Behind moves the testing of educational practices toward the medical model. Whenever the results of scientifically controlled studies (like clinical trials) are available, educators are expected to consider their results before making instructional decisions. Under the new law, federally funded education programs or practices must be based on evidence that validates their usefulness in achieving the stated outcome specified in law.

For instance, there are five essential components of reading instruction:

- phonemic awareness,
- phonics,
- oral reading fluency,
- vocabulary development, and
- comprehension strategies.

These have all been validated through years of peer-reviewed and replicated scientific research into the practice of reading instruction. These findings were reported in the Congressionally mandated National Reading Panel report in April 2000 and have now been written into the new law. If you are more interested in this subject, call 1-800-USA-LEARN and request "Putting Reading First" for parents and "Reading Tips for Parents."

21. How does scientifically based research apply to other federal education programs?

The Department of Education is striving to conduct and collect additional research using the same high scientific standards we use for reading and to apply results to math, science, and comprehensive school reform.

READING

22. How are America's children doing in reading?

Not well. Approximately 40 percent of students across the nation cannot read at a basic level. Almost 70 percent of low-income fourth grade students cannot read at a basic level. In other words, these children struggle with fundamental reading skills like understanding and summarizing a story. Almost half the students living in urban areas cannot read at a basic level. Average-performing students have made no progress over the past 10 years, and the lowest-performing readers have become less successful over this same time period.

23. What is the key to helping children become successful readers?

We know what works. Research has consistently identified the critical skills that young students need to become good readers. Teachers across different states and districts have demonstrated that sound, scientifically-based reading instruction can and does work with children. The critical missing piece lies in helping teachers benefit from the relevant research in every classroom. Real, nationwide progress can be made when we bring together proven methods and actually use them in America's classrooms to make sure that every child becomes a successful reader.

24. Why is it so important for children to read better so early in school?

Research shows that children who read well in the early grades are far more successful in later years. Putting it another way, reading is a gateway skill to all learning. Young, capable readers can take greater advantage of school opportunities and develop invaluable confidence in their own abilities. Reading success leads directly to success in other subjects such as social studies, math, and science. In the long term, students who cannot read well are much more likely to drop out of school and be limited to lower-paying jobs throughout their lifetimes. Reading is undeniably one of the foundations for success in society.

25. What is being done to help children learn to read well by the end of the third grade?

Improving the reading skills of children is a top national and state priority. The President, the First Lady, the Secretary of Education, governors, business leaders, elected officials, citizens, community organizations, parents, and teachers are deeply committed to doing whatever it takes to ensure that every child can read. In the past few years, science has provided tremendous insight into exactly how children learn to read, and related research has identified the most essential components of reading instruction.

26. What is Reading First exactly, and what are its specific goals?

Reading First is a bold new national initiative, squarely aimed at helping every child in every state become a successful reader. For this purpose, up to nearly $6 billion will be distributed among the 50 states, the District of Columbia, and Puerto Rico over the next several years. These funds are specifically dedicated to helping states and local school districts establish high-quality, comprehensive reading instruction for all children in kindergarten through third grade.

27. What is different about Reading First?

Reading First, unlike previous national reading programs, is a classroom-focused nationwide effort designed to help each and every student become a successful reader. Every state will be eligible to apply, and the most needy schools and districts will receive the funds and other support they will need to succeed. It differs from earlier initiatives by establishing clear, specific expectations for what can and should happen for every single student in a classroom. Reading First specifies that teachers' classroom instructional decisions must be informed by scientifically-based reading research.

Through Reading First funds, grants will be available for state and local programs in which students are systematically and explicitly taught five key early reading skills:

- Phonemic awareness: the ability to hear, identify, and play with individual sounds - or phonemes - in spoken words
- Phonics: the relationship between the letters of written language and the sounds of spoken language
- Fluency: the capacity to read text accurately and quickly
- Vocabulary: the words students must know to communicate effectively
- Comprehension: the ability to understand and gain meaning from what has been read

28. How will Reading First help classroom teachers?

Reading First appropriately concentrates attention on classroom learning. After all, during the average school day, students spend most of their time in classrooms. Classroom instructional time should reflect the most accurate and up-to-date knowledge about the science of teaching children how to read. For that reason, Reading First provides funds to states and local districts to help classroom teachers improve the reading instruction they deliver to all of their children.

States will ensure that primary grade teachers deliver reading instruction that is informed by scientifically-based reading research. For those teachers in schools and districts with the greatest need, Reading First funds may be used to organize additional professional development, purchase or develop high-quality instructional materials, or administer assessments or diagnostic tests. The common goal is to make sure that teachers have all the necessary tools to provide coherent, skills-based reading instruction for all children.

29. What are the expectations of Reading First?

Students are expected to become proficient readers by the end of third grade. Teachers are expected to deliver consistent and coherent skills-based reading instruction. District and state leaders are expected to provide educators with ongoing, high-quality support that makes a difference in the classroom. Reading First contributes to these high expectations by steadfastly supporting high-quality local and state reading initiatives with the funds needed to make real improvements.

30. How will we know if Reading First is working?

Reading First will be working when every child in our country becomes a successful and proficient reader, irrespective of economic circumstances or family background. Further, these efforts work when every child can read and understand a mathematics problem, social studies textbook, or science experiment because of a firm reading foundation established in the early elementary years through well-delivered, strong instruction. These efforts work when every child is ready for success and achievement in the later grades because every child mastered reading in the early grades.

CREATING SAFER SCHOOLS

31. I am concerned about my child's safety. How does this law help secure safer schools?

No child can learn in a climate of fear. The first job of government is to protect its citizens—whether the threat is terrorists abroad or criminals at home.

Under No Child Left Behind, the Administration is working with the states to better protect children, to define a "persistently dangerous school," and to provide families with an alternative when in danger of being trapped in an unsafe and threatening environment.

32. What is the "Unsafe School Choice Option" in the No Child Left Behind Act?

States receiving any funds under the Act must establish and implement a statewide policy requiring that a student be allowed to attend a safe public elementary or secondary school within the local education agency, including a public charter school, if he or she:

- attends a persistently dangerous public elementary and secondary school, as determined by the state in consultation with a representative sample of local educational agencies, or
- becomes a victim of a violent criminal offense, as determined by state law, while in or on the grounds of a public elementary or secondary school that the student attends.

States must certify in writing to the Secretary of Education that they are in compliance with this provision as a condition of receiving funds under No Child Left Behind.

33. How will this law help teachers keep the classroom safe?

No Child Left Behind ensures that teachers, principals, and other school professionals can undertake reasonable actions to maintain order and discipline in the classroom without fear of litigation.

TEACHERS

34. How will this law help my child's teacher?

Nothing is more important to a child's education at school than having a well-prepared teacher. That's why No Child Left Behind puts special emphasis on teaching. Right now, some children aren't getting teachers who have mastered what they are teaching:

- Just 41 percent of teachers of mathematics had math as an area of study in school. That's 30 percentage points lower than the international average.
- In English classes, one-fifth of all public school students in grades seven through twelve were taught by teachers who did not have at least a minor in English, literature, communications or journalism.
- In history and physical science, more than one out of every two children is being taught by a teacher who has never studied or practiced the subject in any concentrated way.

That's more than 4 million students in physics, chemistry, and history classes with teachers lacking the best preparation for teaching their subjects.

35. How can I help my child's teacher?

The best thing to do is get involved and make sure your school knows about all the new opportunities in the law including grants for retraining. Talk to your school board members and meet with your child's principal. Remind them that No Child Left Behind gives states and districts the flexibility to find innovative ways to improve teacher quality, including alternative certification, merit pay, and bonuses for people who teach in high-need subject areas like math and science.

You have a right to know how your child is doing. That starts with meeting with your child's teacher, working with your child on homework, and spending time reading and talking. But the most important thing is to understand how education is changing and to help your schools enter the new era of No Child Left Behind.

TESTING

36. What effect will testing have on my child?

For some parents, testing causes stress and anxiety. But in reality, children have always been assessed throughout the year to ensure they know the academic content taught in the classroom. Testing once a year using a standardized test gives an independent insight into the school's progress in order to ensure that your child isn't left behind or trapped in a failing school before it is too late to face the real tests in life. Handled by the school, testing becomes a normal, expected way of assessing whether curriculum has been taught.

37. Will the results of my child's test be private?

Absolutely. Only you and the school will get to see how your child is improving and progressing. Although states and districts will release report cards on their student test results, individual student scores will not be made public.

38. Some people say that testing will make teachers "teach to the test." Are those people right?

No Child Left Behind does not encourage teachers to cover the exact test questions. The state tests are expected to measure the state's academic standards. The material should be taught in the classroom. If teachers cover the subject matter required by the standards and teach it well, students should do well on the test. It's like taking a driver's test. The instructor covers all the important content the state wants you to know and much more.

Many of the nation's best schools and those improving the fastest don't just think testing is important. They think that without it, improving education would be impossible. Don McAdams, a member of the Houston Independent School District Board of Education, says: "School systems and schools exist to educate students. The core activity is teaching and learning. How can a school system or a school continuously improve if it does not measure growth in student achievement? As quality management teaches: What you value, you measure; what you measure, you get. It is almost inconceivable that a school system would not want to know the answer to the most fundamental of all questions: Are the children learning?"

39. Will testing help teachers?

Annual testing tells teachers the strengths and weaknesses of every child. With this knowledge, teachers can craft lessons to make sure each student meets or exceeds state standards. It also tells the teacher if he or she has been effective teaching particular content. If your child's teacher is spending weeks before the test cramming in material, that is a sign that the curriculum at your child's school may not be aligned with the academic standards being tested.

40. What about principals? Will testing help them?

Absolutely. Annual tests show principals exactly how much progress each teacher's students have made, so they can make good decisions about program selection, curriculum arrangement, and professional development. Along with other provisions in No Child Left Behind, they'll have the information and the freedom to get funding for exactly what teachers need to meet the needs of every child.

41. Reading and math and eventually science will be tested. What about other subjects?

No Child Left Behind doesn't require annual statewide testing of other subjects, but that doesn't mean your state won't test history, geography, or writing skills, for example. Many states recognize how important it is to measure whether the schools are getting results in every academic area and to make sure parents aren't disappointed with their child's education. Reading and math are key to the mastery of all other subjects and to a child's success in life. That's why No Child Left Behind focuses on those subjects.

42. Who will pay for these tests?

No Child Left Behind authorized $387 million for states to develop and administer the tests. Many states began this process years ago using state funds.

43. What if I want to home school my child? Does the new law require tests at home?

Nothing in the No Child Left Behind Act affects a home school or permits any Federal control over any aspect of a home school, whether that home school is treated as a home school or a private school under state law. Students who are home-schooled are not required to take any test referenced in the law.

44. What is the National Assessment of Educational Progress (NAEP), and what is its purpose?

NAEP tests are administered to a sample of students in each state from a variety of backgrounds to get an overall picture of a state's progress. Beginning with the 2002-2003 school year, the Department of Education will pay for your state to participate in the NAEP reading and math assessments for fourth and eighth grade students every two years. That way you'll know how your state is comparing with others.

In Summation

This chapter answered frequently asked questions about the No Child Left Behind Act.

In the next chapter, you learn about key provisions of the law that will be of interest to parents. These provisions include annual proficiency testing, school and school district report cards, public school choice and supplemental educational services, requirements about teaching children to read by the end of third grade, highly qualified teachers, the right to know the qualifications of teachers, and parent involvement policies.

FOR YOUR NOTES

5 | NCLB FOR PARENTS

In this chapter, you learn about key provisions in No Child Left Behind for parents and children. These provisions include annual proficiency testing, school and school district report cards, public school choice and supplemental educational services, teaching children to read by the end of third grade, highly qualified teacher requirements, parents' right to know the qualifications of teachers, and parent involvement and empowerment. The chapter includes additional information for parents of children with disabilities, English language learners, and children who attend dangerous schools.

When No Child Left Behind was enacted in 2002, millions of children graduated from high school without the basic skills they need to make it in the real world. According to the *2002 Nation's Report Card*:

- Only 36 percent of 12th graders were proficient in reading
- Only 18 percent of 12th graders were proficient in science
- Only 17 percent of 12th graders were proficient in math
- Only 11 percent of 12th graders were proficient in U. S. history

No Child Left Behind requires schools to teach all children to proficiency in reading, math and science by 2014. The key requirements of the law—annual testing of reading, math and science, a highly qualified teacher in every classroom, research-based instruction, increased parental rights, and state, school district and school report cards—are strategies to accomplish this goal.

Parents are natural advocates for their children. Who is responsible for your child's welfare? You are. Who represents your child's interests? You do. No Child Left Behind gives you the power to make educational decisions for your child.

Do not be afraid to use your power. Use it wisely. A good education is the most important gift you can give to your child.

HOW WILL NO CHILD LEFT BEHIND AFFECT PARENTS?

No Child Left Behind require schools to educate all children, including poor children, children with disabilities, migratory children and English language learners, minority children, and other neglected groups of children, and to publicly report their progress every year.

If your child attends a school that accepts Title I funds, you have more choices and options than parents of children who do not attend Title I schools. If your child attends a school that does not receive Title I funds, but is in a school district that does, you will receive information about whether your child's school is improving at the required rate. You will also be informed about what subgroups your school is teaching successfully.

✒ **TITLE I SCHOOLS:** To get information about Title I schools, go to The National Center for Education Statistics site at http://nces.ed.gov/ Enter your zip code, click public school, then click search. When the list of local schools appears, click your school, then click "more information." A box with information about your school will appear. This program will tell you if your school receives Title I funds.

ANNUAL PROFICIENCY TESTING

Testing is the normal way to assess academic progress. Beginning in 2005, schools must test all children in grades 3-8 every year in math and reading. By 2007, schools must test science. (20 U. S. C. § 6311)

➔ **LEGAL CITATIONS:** The legal citations in *Wrightslaw: No Child Left Behind* are in the format of the United States Code. For example, "Statement of Purpose" is at 20 U. S. C. § 6301 of the statute. To learn about legal citations, read Chapter 2.

Annual assessments or proficiency tests will give you information about the school's progress in teaching your child and other groups of children. This information will help you ensure that your child is not left behind or trapped in a failing school. Annual testing also provides useful information to your child's teachers. Teachers will know the strengths and weaknesses of their students. This information will help teachers develop lessons and ensure that all students meet or exceed state standards.

📁 **FAQs:** Learn about proficiency testing in Chapter 4, Frequently Asked Questions.

ADEQUATE YEARLY PROGRESS

Test scores are used to determine if schools are making Adequate Yearly Progress (AYP) toward the goal of proficiency for all children by 2014. Your state will set goals for schools and for specific subgroups within schools. Schools must report their overall progress, and their progress in educating subgroups of children, including:

- children with disabilities
- English language learners
- racial minorities
- children from low-income families

If your child's school or a subgroup of children in the school do not meet the AYP goals, the school will move into the "needs improvement" category. No Child Left Behind requires parents and school personnel to design an improvement plan for schools in the "needs improvement" category. (20 U. S. C. § 6311)

SCHOOL AND DISTRICT REPORT CARDS

The school must provide a report card to every parent whose child attends a Title I school. This report card will tell you if the school has been successful in teaching all groups of children. You can compare the report card from your child's school with report cards from other schools and school districts in your state.

Your school district must also publish a report card. If you cannot find your school or school district report cards, call or write your state department of education to request this information. (20 U. S. C. § 6311)

✒ **TIP:** Contact information for your state department of education is available at:

http://www.nochildleftbehind.gov/next/where/statecontacts.html and
http://www.yellowpagesforkids.com/help/seas.htm

If this required information is not available, you may want to contact the U.S. Department of Education to advise them of this.

ACCOUNTABILITY

Accountability follows money. Your state applied to the federal government for Title I funds. In return for these funds, your state agreed to test all children in grades 3-8 annually and to publicly report these test scores by school and school district.

School districts and schools apply to the state for a share of this money. In return for Title I funds, school districts and schools agree to follow specific rules to account for how the money is spent. Approximately ninety percent of school districts and 60 percent of schools receive Title I funds.

To help states and school districts improve and close the achievement gap, NCLB offers flexibility in combining federal grants. However, states and districts may use these funds only for research-based programs that have an established record of effectiveness.

PUBLIC SCHOOL CHOICE

If your child attends a Title I School that fails to meet its AYP goal for **two consecutive years**, your child may transfer to a non-failing school within the district. If all schools in your district fail to meet their AYP goals for two consecutive years, your child may attend a better-performing school in another school district. If your child transfers to a better-performing school, the child may remain there until he or she completes the highest grade in that school. (20 U. S. C. § 6316(b))

The sending school district will provide transportation to the receiving school until the sending school raises its AYP rate to an acceptable level. The district may limit the money it spends on transportation. If the district does not have enough money under a designated formula to pay transportation costs, the district may give preference to the lowest achieving children from low-income families. (20 U. S. C. § 6316(b))

📁 **FAQs:** Learn about public school choice in Chapter 4, "Frequently Asked Questions."

📖 **Public School Choice – Draft Non-Regulatory Guidance** from the U.S. Department of Education answers frequently asked questions about public school choice. This publication is available on the **Wrightslaw NCLB CD-ROM**.

SUPPLEMENTAL EDUCATIONAL SERVICES

If your child attends a Title I school that fails to meet its AYP goal for **three consecutive years**, the school must provide supplemental educational services to the students from low-income families who remain in the school. The school will notify parents of eligible children. Supplemental educational services include tutoring, after-school programs, and summer programs. Supplemental services must be free to parents.

Parents may choose a tutor or other supplemental service provider from a provider list provided by the state. The state must ensure that all providers on the list have a history of success. Again, the district may give preference to the lowest-achieving children from low-income families who request supplemental services. (20 U. S. C. § 6316)

Providers of supplemental services must give information about student progress to the parents and the school. Providers must ensure that instruction meets state and local standards, including state student academic achievement standards. Providers must also comply with health, safety, and civil rights laws.

📁 **FAQs:** Learn about supplemental educational services in Chapter 4, "Frequently Asked Questions."

📖 **A Parents' Guide to Supplemental Services** published by the U. S. Department of Education answers questions about obtaining supplemental educational services. This publication is available on the **Wrightslaw NCLB CD ROM**.

TRANSFERS FROM UNSAFE SCHOOLS _____

All children need a safe environment in which to learn. Under No Child Left Behind, no child is required to attend a persistently dangerous school. Your state must identify persistently dangerous schools every year and make this information available to the public.

If your child attends a persistently dangerous school, your school district must notify you of your right to transfer your child to a safe school in the district. Transfers should take place within **30 days.** If your child is the victim of a violent crime at a Title I school, you can transfer your child to a safe school in the district within **10 days** of the incident. (20 U. S. C. § 7912)

> 📖 *Unsafe School Choice Option – Draft Non-Regulatory Guidance* published by the U.S. Department of Education includes answers to frequently asked questions about school choice options for children who attend unsafe schools. This publication is available on the *Wrightslaw NCLB CD ROM.*

TEACHING CHILDREN TO READ _____

The U. S. Department of Education published these findings about reading in *The Nation's Report Card:*

- Only 32 percent of 4th graders are proficient readers
- Only 33 percent of 8th graders are proficient readers.
- Only 36 percent of 12th graders are proficient readers. [6]

Because two-thirds of students are not proficient readers when they graduate from high school, No Child Left Behind focuses on teaching young children to read. School districts and schools may only use Reading First grants for research-based reading programs that have a proven record of success.

Schools that receive Title I funds may use Reading First grants for classroom reading instruction in Kindergarten through third grade. Schools may also use NCLB funds to train K-3 teachers and K-12 special education teachers to use research-based instructional methods.

Legal Definition of Reading

No Child Left Behind includes the legal definition of **reading.**

"Reading is a complex system of deriving meaning from print that requires all of the following:

(A) The skills and knowledge to understand how phonemes, or speech sounds, are connected to print,
(B) The ability to decode unfamiliar words,
(C) The ability to read fluently,
(D) Sufficient background information and vocabulary to foster reading comprehension,
(E) The development of appropriate active strategies to construct meaning from print,
(F) The development and maintenance of a motivation to read." (20 U. S. C. § 6368(5))

_____

[6] National Assessment of Educational Progress (NAEP) 2002 Reading Assessments

Essential Components of Reading Instruction

The NCLB statute defines the **five essential components of reading instruction.**

"The term 'essential components of reading instruction' means explicit and systematic instruction in-

>   (A) phonemic awareness,
>   (B) phonics,
>   (C) vocabulary development,
>   (D) reading fluency, including oral reading skills, and
>   (E) reading comprehension strategies." (20 U. S. C. § 6368(3))

Diagnostic Reading Assessments

No Child Left Behind defines **diagnostic reading assessments**.

"The term 'diagnostic reading assessment' means an assessment that is-

>   (i) valid, reliable, and based on scientifically based reading research; and
>   (ii) used for the purpose of-
>   (I) identifying a child's specific areas of strengths and weaknesses so that the child has learned to read by the end of grade 3;
>   (II) determining any difficulties that a child may have in learning to read and the potential cause of such difficulties; and
>   (III) helping to determine possible reading intervention strategies and related special needs." (20 U. S. C. § 6368(7))

Scientifically Based Reading Research

The law also defines **scientifically based reading research**.

"The term 'scientifically based reading research' means research that-

(A) applies rigorous, systematic, and objective procedures to obtain valid knowledge relevant to reading development, reading instruction, and reading difficulties; and
(B) includes research that-
>   (i) employs systematic, empirical methods that draw on observation or experiment;
>   (ii) involves rigorous data analyses that are adequate to test the stated hypotheses and justify the general conclusions drawn;
>   (iii) relies on measurements or observational methods that provide valid data across evaluators and observers and across multiple measurements and observations; and
>   (iv) has been accepted by a peer-reviewed journal or approved by a panel of independent experts through a comparably rigorous, objective, and scientific review." (20 U. S. C. § 6368(6))

📁 **FAQs**: Learn about reading in Chapter 4, "Frequently Asked Questions."

📖 ***Guidance for the Reading First Program*** from the U.S. Department of Education answers questions about reading and reading programs. This publication is available on the ***Wrightslaw NCLB CD ROM***.

HIGHLY QUALIFIED TEACHERS _____

Teachers who have strong academic backgrounds boost the academic performance of their students. No Child Left Behind requires highly qualified teachers in every classroom by the end of the 2005-2006 school year.

Because all states accept Title I funds, the standards for highly qualified teachers apply to all public schools in all states.

All new teachers and all teachers who work in Title I programs must meet the highly qualified criteria:

- Certified by the state
- Pass the state teacher examination
- Have training in the subject area taught
- Hold a license to teach in the State (20 U. S. C. § 6319)

Elementary school teachers must demonstrate their knowledge of teaching math and reading. Middle and high school teachers must have majors in the subjects they teach or demonstrate knowledge of that subject. Teachers who were employed on January 8, 2002, when NCLB was enacted, must have at least a bachelor's degree, licensure and /or certification by 2005. Teachers who are working under license or certification waivers are not highly qualified teachers. (20 U. S. C. § 6319)

An exception involves teachers in public charter schools who must meet the certification or licensing requirements in their state public charter school laws.

PARENT INVOLVEMENT AND EMPOWERMENT

If the school district accepts Title I funds, the staff must consult with parents to develop a parent involvement policy to improve student academic performance. The district must evaluate the effectiveness of this parental involvement policy every year. The school must distribute this parent involvement policy to all parents and make the policy available to the community. (20 U. S. C. § 6318)

The school must hold a meeting every year to tell parents about the parent involvement policy and their right to be involved in their children's education. Title I funds are available for childcare and transportation so you can be involved. (20 U. S. C. § 6318)

You have a right to frequent reports about your child's progress, access to teachers, opportunities to volunteer and participate in your child's class, and to observe classroom activities.

PARENT'S RIGHT-TO-KNOW

Parents whose children attend Title I schools have more options than parents of children who attend schools that do not receive Title I funds. At the beginning of each school year, school districts that receive Title I funds must notify parents that they may request specific information about the qualifications of their children's teachers. At a minimum, you have a right to know–

- if the teacher is certified or licensed to teach the grade levels and subjects she is teaching
- if the teacher's certification or licensure was waived under an emergency or provisional status
- the teacher's college major and any graduate degree or certification
- if the child received services from a paraprofessional, the qualifications of that paraprofessional (20 U. S. C. § 6311)

If your child's school does not receive Title I funds, but is in a Title I school district, you will simply know if the school is improving at the required rate, and what subgroups the school is teaching successfully.

INSTRUCTIONAL MATERIALS _____

If your child attends a Title I school, you have a right to inspect instructional materials used in the curriculum. Instructional materials are print and audio-visual material. Instructional materials are also electronic and digital material, including information accessed through the Internet. Instructional materials do not include academic tests or assessments. (Title X, Section 1061)

TO PARENTS OF CHILDREN WITH SPECIAL EDUCATIONAL NEEDS _____

Parents of Children with Disabilities

NCLB defines the level of instruction that Title I schools must provide. "The purpose of this title is to ensure that all children have a fair, equal, and significant opportunity to obtain a high-quality education and reach, at a minimum, proficiency on challenging State academic achievement standards and state academic assessments." (20 U.S.C. § 6301)

The law gives the legal definitions of adequate teacher training, reading, adequate reading instruction, diagnostic reading assessment, and scientifically based research. The law sets the standard for academic performance. There is no longer any question about the minimum standards for an adequate reading program, student performance, teacher quality, or assessment.

For children with disabilities who are receiving services under the Individuals with Disabilities Education Act and have an Individualized Education Program, (IEP) the law mandates that the child will receive "the **reasonable adaptations and accommodations for students with disabilities** . . . necessary to measure the academic achievement of such students relative to State academic content and State student academic achievement standards."

The Individuals with Disabilities Education Act states that the child's Individualized Educational Program (IEP) shall include:

> (I) a statement of any individual modifications in the administration of State or districtwide assessments of student achievement that are needed in order for the child to participate in such assessment; and
> (II) if the IEP Team determines that the child will not participate in a particular State or districtwide assessment of student achievement (or part of such an assessment), a statement of
>> (aa) why that assessment is not appropriate for the child; and
>> (bb) how the child will be assessed." (20 U. S. C. § 1414(d)(1)(A)(v))

Adequate Yearly Progress reports relate to schools and school districts, not to individual children. The AYP calculations permit a school and school district to incorporate a percentage adjustment for children with severe cognitive disabilities so the school will not be adversely affected as the result of providing educational services to children with disabilities.

The timeline for teaching a child to read fluently has been set as the **end of grade three**.

You need to be familiar with the definitions of reading and the essential components of reading programs. These definitions apply to all programs, all schools, all children, all the time. These terms define and describe the minimum requirements for your child's reading program at school.

Parents of English Language Learners

No Child Left Behind includes specific requirements about how schools must educate children who are learning English. States and school districts must establish proficiency standards for speaking, listening, reading, and writing. School districts must use research-based language instruction curricula for English language learners that are effective with this population. (20 U. S. C. § 6823)

Schools must assess English language learners to measure the child's progress toward English proficiency and the child's comprehension, speaking, listening, reading, and writing skills in English. If the child has been in the United States for three or more years, the school must test the child in English every year. (20 U. S. C. § 6826)

School districts must provide research-based language instruction. Your child's language teachers must be fluent in English, including written and oral communication skills.

No Child Left Behind also requires schools to notify parents about their children's progress in the language program. Your child's school must notify you of:

- The reasons why they placed your child in a language instruction program
- Your child's English proficiency level, how the level was tested, and your child's academic achievement levels
- The method of instruction that the school will use in your child's language program
- How the school's language program meets your child's educational strengths and needs
- How the language program will help your child learn English, be promoted, and graduate from school
- If your child has a disability, how the language program meets the objectives in your child's IEP (20 U. S. C. § 7012)

The school must also provide you with information about your parental rights, including:

- Your right to remove your child from the language program immediately
- Your options if you decide not to enroll your child in the language program

You may remove your child from a language program at any time. (20 U. S. C. § 7012)

IN SUMMATION

In this chapter, you learned about key provisions of the No Child Left Behind Act that are of interest to parents. In the next chapter, you learn about provisions that are of interest to teachers, principals and paraprofessionals. These provisions include highly qualified teacher requirements, new requirements for paraprofessionals, parents' right to know the qualifications of their children's teachers, training and professional development, recruitment and retention, and teacher liability protection.

RESOURCES

You will find many excellent publications for parents in the *Wrightslaw: No Child Left Behind CD-ROM* and on the Internet. Here is a short list of recommended resources.

In the Wrightslaw No Child Left Behind CD-ROM

Report Cards: Non-Regulatory Guidance. Publication from the U. S. Department of Education answers frequently-asked questions about state and school district report cards.

No Child Left Behind: A Parent's Guide published by the U.S. Department of Education. Summarizes the main provisions of the law, answers common questions and provides information on where to find additional resources.

Public School Choice – Draft Non-Regulatory Guidance published by the U.S. Department of Education answers frequently asked questions about public school choice.

A Parent's Guide to Supplemental Services. This brochure from the U. S. Department of Education answers questions about how to obtain supplemental educational services.

Supplemental Educational Services – Draft Non Regulatory Guidance published by the U. S. Department of Education answers frequently asked questions about supplemental educational services.

Unsafe School Choice Option – Draft Non-Regulatory Guidance published by the U.S. Department of Education includes answers to frequently asked questions about school choice options for children who attend unsafe schools.

NCLB Fact Sheets. Fact sheets from the U. S. Department of Education about many topics, including reading, math, supplemental services, and good teachers.

On the Internet

➜ **BROKEN LINKS**: Internet links change often and many links are quickly outdated. If you find an article or publication is no longer available, use a search engine to find the document. Type the title of the article into the search box.

Parent Involvement Policies and the Law, What Parents Need to Know from National PTA.
URL: http://www.pta.org/parent involvement/helpchild/hc_piandlaw.asp

Reading Tips for Parents. Includes information about effective early reading programs and strategies for creating strong readers. In English and Spanish. http://www.ed.gov/

Put Reading First: Helping Your Child Learn to Read. Brochure describes kinds of early literacy activities that should take place at school and at home to help children learn to read successfully; based on findings of the National Reading Panel. http://www.nifl.gov/

Helping Your Child Become a Reader. This guide offers pointers on how to build the language skills of young children; includes a list of typical language accomplishments for different age groups, suggestions for children with reading problems or learning disabilities. (English and Spanish) http://www.ed.gov/

A New Wave of Evidence: The Impact of School, Family and Community Connections on Student Achievement published by the Southwest Educational Development Laboratory.
URL: http://www.sedl.org/connections/resources/evidence.pdf

An Action Guide for Community and Parent Leaders - Using NCLB to Improve Student Achievement by Public Education Network.
URL: http://www.publiceducation.org/pdf/NCLBBook.pdf

FOR YOUR NOTES

6 | NCLB FOR TEACHERS, PRINCIPALS AND PARAPROFESSIONALS

In this chapter, you learn about provisions in the No Child Left Behind Act that are of interest to teachers, principals and paraprofessionals. These provisions include highly qualified teacher requirements, new requirements for paraprofessionals, parents' right to know the qualifications of their children's teachers, training and professional development, recruitment and retention, and teacher liability protection.

According to the U. S. Department of Education:

- One-quarter of English teachers do not have a major or minor in English, literature, communications, or journalism

- One-third of life science teachers do not have a major or minor in biology or life science

- Fifty-six percent of physical science teachers do not have a major or minor in physics, chemistry, geology, or earth science

- More than half of history teachers do not have a major or minor in history

- Fifty-nine percent of math teachers do not have a major or minor in mathematics [7]

- More than four million students take physics, chemistry and history from teachers who are not prepared to teach these subjects [8]

No Child Left Behind calls for highly qualified teachers—teachers who demonstrate subject knowledge and skills in reading, writing, mathematics, and other basic subjects—to be in every classroom by the end of the 2005-06 school year.

HOW WILL NO CHILD LEFT BEHIND AFFECT YOU? ———————————————————

No Child Left Behind will affect everyone employed by schools and school districts. You should expect changes as your school and school district focus on teaching all students to higher levels of proficiency. Your state and school district must report their present levels of performance to parents and the public every year. These performance levels must increase steadily until all students are being educated to proficiency by 2014. (20 U. S. C. § 6301)

---

[7] Richard M. Ingersall, "The Problem of Underqualified Teachers in American Schools," *Educational Researcher* 28, no. 2 (March 1999) is available as an Appendix to *Improving Teacher Quality State Grants – Title II, Part A* in the *Wrightslaw NCLB CD-ROM.*
[8] U. S. Department of Education, "The Facts about . . . Good Teachers," http://www.ed.gov/nclb/methods/teachers/teachers.pdf

Chapter 6

K-3 Teachers

If you are a K-3 teacher, you must teach all your students to read. The law states that all children will be reading fluently by the end of grade 3. NCLB requires teachers to use research-based methods of reading instruction that include these essential components:

(A) phonemic awareness
(B) phonics
(C) vocabulary development
(D) reading fluency, including oral reading skills
(E) reading comprehension strategies (20 U. S. C. § 6368(5))

You must learn how to assess children and how to use test results to plan effective instruction. Diagnostic reading assessments based on scientific reading research will help you identify children's strengths and weaknesses so all children learn to read by the end of grade 3. (20 U. S. C. § 6368(7)) If a student is not making progress with one instructional method, you must select and use a different, more appropriate method.

Many teacher-training programs do not require students to learn research-based teaching methods. You may need to request additional training. Reading First grants include funds for teacher training. Reading First grants will not be available in all Title I schools. You may need to search for other training sources. The importance of early identification and intervention for reading problems cannot be overemphasized.

> ⏻ **TRAINING**: Contact your state branch of the International Dyslexia Association to locate training in research-based methods of reading instruction at www.interdys.org

> 📖 *Guidance for the Reading First Program* from the U.S. Department of Education answers frequently asked questions about Title I reading programs. This publication is available on the *Wrightslaw NCLB CD-ROM*.

Elementary School Teachers

If you are an upper elementary school teacher, you must teach math, reading, and science at higher levels of proficiency. As students exercise their school choice options and transfer from "needs improvement" schools to higher performing schools, you may need to teach students who are functioning at varying levels.

Middle School and High School Teachers

If you are a middle school or high school teacher, you must meet the highly qualified requirements for the core academic subjects you teach. Core academic subjects are English, reading or language arts, mathematics, science, foreign languages, civics and government, economics, arts, history, and geography. (20 U. S. C. § 7801(11))

Music, Gym, Foreign Language Teachers

If you are a music, gym, computer, or foreign language teacher, you will be affected by NCLB. If you teach in a "needs improvement" school, your school must offer public school choice and supplemental educational services. If many of your students transfer, you may find that the student population has reduced at your school and your services may no longer be needed.

Teachers of English-Language Learners

No Child Left Behind includes specific requirements about how schools must educate children who are learning English. School districts must provide research-based language instruction. Language teachers must be fluent in English, including written and oral communication skills. (20 U. S. C. § 6826)

If you teach a core academic subject, you must meet the highly qualified teacher requirements in that subject. Core academic subjects include English, reading or language arts, mathematics, science, foreign languages, civics and government, economics, arts, history, and geography.

States and school districts must establish proficiency standards for speaking, listening, reading, and writing. Schools must test English language learners every year to measure how well they are learning English and must notify parents of their child's progress. After three years, the child must be tested in English. If the child has an Individualized Educational Program (IEP), the ESL program must be coordinated with the IEP. (20 U. S. C. § 6311)

Special Education Teachers

Special education teachers must provide "specially designed instruction . . . to meet the unique needs of a child" (see the definition of special education in 20 U.S.C. § 1401(25)) and must teach their students to proficiency in reading, math, and science.

If you teach core academic subjects in middle school or high school, you must meet the highly qualified teacher requirements in these subjects. Core academic subjects include English, reading or language arts, mathematics, science, foreign languages, civics and government, economics, arts, history, and geography.

A student's IEP team decides if a student should take an alternative assessment. Alternate assessments must yield results for the grade in which the student is enrolled (at least in reading / language arts, mathematics, and, beginning in the 2007–2008 school year, science) if a child is to count as a child tested when calculating AYP. Some students have severe cognitive disabilities that prevent them from taking the annual state assessments, even with accommodations. The IEP team will decide if the child will take a grade level or out-of-level test and whether the child requires accommodations and modifications. (20 U. S. C. § 6311 and 20 U. S. C. § 1414(d))

Related Services Providers

If you are a speech pathologist, occupational therapist, physical therapist, or other therapist, you may have to work academics into your therapies. When students exercise their school choice options and transfer from unsuccessful schools, the need for related service providers may decline.

Paraprofessionals

If you are a paraprofessional who works in a Title I school, you may perform various duties, including:

- One-to-one tutoring, if tutoring is scheduled when a student would not receive instruction from a teacher
- Classroom management and organizing instructional materials
- Parent involvement activities
- Library and media center work
- Translating
- Instructional support

NCLB requires that you work "under the direct supervision of a teacher" and "in close and frequent proximity to the teacher." Your supervising teacher will prepare lessons, plan instructional support services for you to carry out, and evaluate student achievement.

If you provide physical assistance to children, act as a translator, conduct parent involvement activities, work in a cafeteria, help on the playground, or supervise school busses, you must have a high school diploma or equivalent. You do not have to meet the higher educational requirements listed for paraprofessionals. (20 U. S. C. § 6319)

Chapter 6

Principals

If you are a principal, you are the school instructional leader. You need to know about effective instructional curricula. You must ensure your staff uses research-based strategies and methods. You need to understand assessment instruments and how to use student achievement data to make instructional decisions.

You are accountable for ensuring that all students and all subgroups of students make acceptable progress, as defined by your state. You must ensure that all new teachers in your school meet the highly qualified requirement. You will attest annually in writing if your school complies with the highly qualified teacher requirements. (20 U. S. C. § 6319(i))

When your school and school district report cards are published, you may need to deal with staff stress and morale problems. If you improve your school's effectiveness, you should prepare for sudden increases in your student population.

NCLB offers resources to increase the effectiveness of principals and school superintendents. Your state may use Title II funds to recruit and retain principals. Some states have created leadership academies, mentoring programs for new principals, changed salary schedules, and compensation policies.

> **TIP:** A searchable database of teacher and principal grant opportunities is available at the U. S. Department of Education site: http://www.ed.gov/offices/OESE/TPR/index.html.

HIGHLY QUALIFIED TEACHER REQUIREMENTS

Since teachers with strong academic backgrounds boost the academic performance of their students, No Child Left Behind requires highly qualified teachers in every classroom by the end of the 2005-2006 school year.

The highly qualified teacher requirements apply to elementary school, middle school and high school teachers who teach core academic subjects. Core academic subjects are English, reading or language arts, mathematics, science, foreign languages, civics and government, economics, arts, history, and geography. If you teach more than one core academic subject, you must demonstrate competence in each subject. (20 U. S. C. § 7801(11))

The term "**highly qualified**" describes the minimum educational requirements you must meet. You must:

- Be certified by your state, **or**
- Pass your state teacher examination, **and**
- Have a bachelor's degree with training in your subject area, **and**
- Hold a license to teach in your State. (20 U. S. C. § 7801(23))

You may **not** be working under an emergency, temporary or provisional waiver.

The law includes other requirements that apply to new and veteran teachers, and to elementary, middle and secondary school teachers. If you were hired before January 8, 2002, you have until 2005 to meet the highly qualified teacher requirements **unless** you work in a school that receives Title I funds. If you work in a Title I school, you must meet these minimum standards now.

If You Are a Newly Hired Teacher

If you are a new elementary school teacher, "highly qualified" means

- You hold at least a bachelor's degree, **and**
- You passed a state test of knowledge and skills in reading, writing, mathematics, and other curriculum areas

If you are a new middle school or high school teacher, "highly qualified" means:

- You hold at least a bachelor's degree, **and**
- You have a major or advanced degree in the academic subjects you teach, **or**
- You passed an academic subject test in each academic subject you teach. (20 U. S. C. § 7801(23))

If You Are Not a Newly Hired Teacher

If you are a teacher who is not new to the profession, "highly qualified teacher" means:

- You hold at least a bachelor's degree, **and**
- You demonstrated competence in your academic subjects by passing an objective evaluation administered by your state. (20 U. S. C. § 7801(23))

If you are a special education teacher or ESL teacher and you teach core academic subjects, you must meet the highly qualified teacher requirements in those subjects.

If you are a vocational education teacher who also teaches core academic subjects, you must meet the definition of a highly qualified teacher in the subjects you teach. Core academic subjects are English, reading or language arts, mathematics, science, foreign languages, civics and government, economics, arts, history, and geography. (20 U. S. C. § 7801(11))

> 📖 *Improving Teacher Quality: Non-Regulatory Guidance*. This publication answers questions about requirements for highly qualified teachers, certification, alternative routes to teaching, subject area competency, which teachers must be highly qualified, high-quality professional development, and other issues. This publication is available on the *Wrightslaw NCLB CD-ROM*.

If You Are a Charter School Teacher

If you teach in a charter school, you must meet the certification or licensure provisions in your state's charter school law. If your state does not require charter school teachers to be licensed or certified, these requirements may not apply to you.

If you teach a core academic subject, the highly qualified teacher requirements apply to you. You must have a four-year college degree and demonstrate competence in the core academic areas that you teach.

If You Are a Paraprofessional

If you work as a paraprofessional in a Title I school, you must have a high school diploma or equivalent. If you provide instructional support, you must complete two years of post secondary education, have an associate degree or higher, or pass a state test. The test should test the equivalent of two years of college. You must demonstrate the ability to support teachers in reading, writing, and math instruction. (20 U. S. C. § 6603(4))

If you were employed as a paraprofessional when No Child Left Behind was enacted in January 2002, you must meet these new educational requirements by 2006. If you work in a school that does not receive Title I funds, you are not required to meet these educational standards.

If you are a paraprofessional who does not provide instructional support (i.e., you work as a playground monitor, in parent involvement activities or as translators), you must have a high school diploma, but are not required to meet the new educational requirements. (20 U. S. C. § 6319) Paraprofessionals in non-Title I school district do not need to meet these standards.

Federal funds to educate and train paraprofessionals are available through Titles I, II, III, V, and VII of the No Child Left Behind Act.

📖 *Title I Paraprofessionals - Draft Non-Regulatory Guidance* published by the U. S. Department of Education includes answers to questions about paraprofessionals. This publication is on the *Wrightslaw NCLB CD-ROM*.

PARENT'S RIGHT TO KNOW TEACHER'S QUALIFICATIONS

At the beginning of each school year, school districts that receive Title I funds must notify parents that they can request information about their children's teachers, including:

- if you meet State requirements for licensure and certification for the grade levels and subjects you teach
- if you are teaching under an emergency or provisional status in which licensing criteria have been waived
- your college major and graduate certification or degrees, and the discipline of your certification or degree
- if the child receives services from paraprofessionals, their qualifications (20 U. S. C. § 6311(d))

ADEQUATE YEARLY PROGRESS

If you work in a "needs improvement" school, your school may adopt a new curriculum as part of a corrective action plan. Teachers and parents will work with district personnel to select a research-based curriculum that addresses the problems that led to corrective action. (20 U. S. C. § 6312)

"Needs improvement" schools may experience fluctuations in population as parents exercise their public school choice option and transfer their children to better-performing schools.

ANNUAL PROFICIENCY TESTING

No Child Left Behind requires schools and districts to use annual proficiency testing to determine if schools and school districts are educating students. Schools must test students in reading and math in grades 3-8. Beginning in 2007, schools must also test science.

Your school must test at least 95 percent of all students. If more than 5 percent of students in a school are not tested, the school will not meet its Adequate Yearly Progress goals. (20 U. S. C. § 6311(b))

TRAINING AND PROFESSIONAL DEVELOPMENT

The highly qualified teacher requirements come with funds for training and professional development. Professional development programs must meet specific standards:

- be high quality, sustained, intensive, and classroom-focused
- have a positive, lasting impact on classroom instruction and performance
- evaluate impact on teacher effectiveness and student academic achievement (20 U. S. C. § 6622)

Professional development and training funded by No Child Left Behind may **not** be one-day or short-term workshops or conferences. Acceptable professional development programs:

- increase teachers' knowledge of the academic subjects they teach
- teach educators to implement a new curriculum
- instruct teachers in classroom management skills
- teach educators to use proven instructional strategies to increase student achievement
- teach educators to use effective research-based language programs for English language learners
- train teachers to improve teaching and learning with technology
- instruct teachers in research based methods for students with special educational needs
- teach educators how to use data from assessments in classroom practice
- teach school personnel how to work effectively with parents (20 U. S. C. § 6623)

⌐🖰 **TIP:** A searchable database of teacher and principal grant opportunities is available at the U. S. Department of Education site at http://www.ed.gov/offices/OESE/TPR/index.html.

If You Teach in a Private School

If you teach in a private school in a school district that accepts funds under Part A of Title II, you are eligible to participate in professional development programs. NCLB requires school districts to provide private school children, teachers, and educational personnel with educational services on an equitable basis. The school district is required to consult with private school officials to design, develop, and implement professional development programs. (20 U. S. C. § 7881)

TEACHER RETENTION AND RECRUITMENT

To help school districts recruit and retain highly qualified teachers, NCLB provides funds for:

- teacher mentoring
- team teaching
- reduced class schedules
- intensive professional development
- leadership academies (20 U. S. C. § 6622)

Alternate Career Paths for Teachers

Under NCLB, funds are available to:

- reform teacher certification requirements
- establish alternate routes to teaching
- reform tenure systems
- create teacher advancement programs
- create multiple career paths for teachers
- develop programs that encourage men to become elementary school teachers (20 U. S. C. § 6651)

Alternate Routes to Teaching

NCLB creates alternate routes to teaching for recent college graduates, mid-career professionals, and members of the Armed Forces who want to teach and have strong backgrounds in their subject areas. When these teachers enter high-need schools, they can receive on-the-job training, mentoring, and support.

In the **Troops-to-Teachers** program, members of the Armed Forces who become highly qualified teachers in high-need schools are eligible for bonuses and stipends. (20 U. S. C. § 6673)

The **Transition to Teacher** Program recruits qualified mid-career professionals to work as teachers in high-need schools. Individuals who sign a commitment to work in high-need schools are eligible for scholarships, stipends, bonuses, and other financial incentives. (20 U. S. C. § 6683)

Financial Incentives for Teachers and Principals

Funds are available for signing bonuses, differential pay, and other financial incentives to recruit and retain highly qualified teachers. If you teach a high need subject like reading, mathematics, or science in a high poverty school, you may be eligible for bonuses and other financial incentives. If you teach an academic subject that has a shortage of highly qualified teachers, you may be eligible for bonuses and scholarships. (20 U. S. C. § 6651)

Performance incentives, stipends, and scholarships are available to recruit mathematics, engineering, and science majors into teaching. Financial incentives are also available for principals who act as mentors to new principals. (20 U. S. C. § 6623)

TEACHER LIABILITY PROTECTION

To help schools maintain order and control, Congress added Teacher Liability Protection provisions in NCLB. The purpose of this statute is to protect teachers, principals, and other school personnel from liability if they are acting within the scope of their employment and do not violate Federal, State, and local laws.

Punitive damages will not be awarded unless a claimant establishes by clear and convincing evidence that the harm was caused by an act or omission that constitutes willful or criminal misconduct, or a conscious, flagrant indifference to the rights or safety of the individual harmed. (20 U. S. C. § 6732)

MEETING THE CHALLENGES

In the face of these changes and challenges, some people will fare better than others. If the requirements of your job or qualifications have changed in a manner that has an adverse impact on you, search for training that will prepare you to meet the challenges of No Child Left Behind Act.

IN SUMMATION

In this chapter, you learned about provisions in No Child Left Behind that are of interest to teachers, principals and paraprofessionals.

In the next chapter, you learn about provisions that of interest to attorneys and advocates for children. These provisions include new requirements about reading instruction and assessments, highly qualified teachers, public school choice and supplemental educational services, educational programs for immigrant children and English language learners, report cards and notices to parents, privacy, and parental right to inspect instructional materials.

RESOURCES

You will find many excellent publications in the *Wrightslaw: No Child Left Behind CD-ROM* and on the Internet. Here is a short list of recommended resources.

In the Wrightslaw No Child Left Behind CD-ROM

Early Reading First Guidance published by the U. S. Department of Education answers frequently asked questions about Early Reading First.

Impact of Title I on Charter Schools published by the U.S. Department of Education offers guidance about changes in Title that affect charter schools.

Improving Teacher Quality: Non-Regulatory Guidance. Answers frequently asked questions about requirements for highly qualified teachers, certification, alternative routes to teaching, subject area competency, which teachers must be highly qualified, "high-quality professional development."

No Child Left Behind Deskbook published by the U. S. Department of Education provides a detailed roadmap to the No Child Left Behind Act of 2001.

No Child Left Behind: A Toolkit for Teachers. Describes requirements for highly qualified teachers by subject and grade; answers frequently asked questions about teacher quality, accountability, testing, reading, scientifically based research, and safe schools. Includes resources and information about programs for ESL teachers, Reading First funds to improve reading skills of young children (K-3), and math achievement; includes a list of publications

Paraprofessional Non-Regulatory Guidance published by the U.S. Department of Education includes questions and answers about requirements for paraprofessionals, paraprofessional assessment, related issues, and funding issues.

Reading First Guidance published by the U.S. Department of Education answers frequently asked questions about reading and reading programs.

Supplemental Educational Services – Draft Non Regulatory Guidance published by the U. S. Department of Education answers frequently asked questions about supplemental educational services.

Using Data to Influence Classroom Decisions. This two-page brochure describes standardized assessments, dynamic assessments and screening assessments, gives classroom examples of each.

On the Internet

No Child Left Behind Act of 2001, Implications for Special Education Policy and Practice, Selected Sections of Title I and Title II published by the Council for Exceptional Children.
URL: http://www.cec.sped.org/pp/side-by-side09_04_02.pdf

A New Wave of Evidence: The Impact of School, Family and Community Connections on Student Achievement published by Southwest Educational Development Laboratory.
URL: http://www.sedl.org/connections/resources/evidence.pdf

Put Reading First: The Research building Blocks for Teaching Children to Read. This booklet from the U. S. Department of Education summarizes what researchers have learned about how to teach children to read: phonemic awareness; phonics; fluency; vocabulary; and text comprehension.
URL: http://www.nifl.gov/partnershipforreading/publications/PFRbookletBW.pdf

FOR YOUR NOTES

7 | NCLB FOR ATTORNEYS AND ADVOCATES

This chapter is an overview of No Child Left Behind provisions that will be of interest to legal practitioners. These provisions include legal requirements about reading, reading instruction and reading assessments, highly qualified teachers, public school choice and supplemental educational services, educational programs for immigrant children and English language learners, report cards and notices to parents, privacy, and parental right to inspect instructional materials. Each section concludes with a list questions.

The No Child Left Behind Act (NCLB) defines the standard of education that applies to all children who attend public schools. This standard expressly includes children with disabilities, limited English proficient children, migratory children, Indian children, neglected or delinquent children, homeless children, and young children in need of reading assistance.

The "Statement of Purpose" describes the intent of the law:

> The purpose of this title is to ensure that all children have a fair, equal, and significant opportunity to obtain a high-quality education and reach, at a minimum, proficiency on challenging State academic achievement standards and state academic assessments . . .
>
> closing the achievement gap between high- and low-performing children, especially the achievement gaps between minority and nonminority students, and between disadvantaged children and their more advantaged peers . . .
>
> holding schools, local educational agencies, and States accountable for improving the academic achievement of all students . . ." (20 U. S. C. § 6301)

The *Wrightslaw: No Child Left Behind CD-ROM* included with this book includes the *No Child Left Behind Deskbook* and guidance publications from the U. S. Department of Education about assessment, teacher quality, transfers from low-performing and unsafe schools, supplemental educational services from providers selected by parents, and other issues. These publications will help you master this complex statute and provide authority you may attach to legal briefs.

READING, INSTRUCTION, RESEARCH, AND ASSESSMENTS

Too often, the attorney represents a child who has severely deficient reading skills. Research has found a high correlation between poor reading skills, learning disabilities, and juvenile delinquency. Sadly, schools often use reading programs that are not effective in teaching children with disabilities, English language learners, migratory children, Native American children, neglected children, delinquent children, and homeless children to read.

A primary focus of this law is the requirement that school districts and individual schools use effective, research-based reading remediation programs so all children are reading at grade level by the end of third grade.

The law authorizes funds:

> To provide assistance to State educational agencies and local educational agencies in establishing reading programs for students in kindergarten through grade 3 that are based on scientifically based reading research, to ensure that **every student can read at grade level or above not later than the end of grade 3.** (emphasis added) (20 U. S. C. § 6361)

Attorneys, hearing officers, administrative law judges, and child advocates will find that the No Child Left Behind Act includes legal definitions of reading, reading instruction, and reading research.

Reading is defined as:

> a complex system of deriving meaning from print that requires all of the following:
>
> > skills and knowledge to understand how phonemes or speech sounds are connected to print,
> > the ability to decode unfamiliar words,
> > the ability to read fluently,
> > sufficient background information and vocabulary to foster reading comprehension,
> > the development of appropriate active strategies to construct meaning from print, and
> > the development and maintenance of a motivation to read. (20 U. S. C. § 6368(5))

The statute defines the **essential components of reading instruction** as:

> explicit and systematic instruction in (A) phonemic awareness; (B) phonics; (C) vocabulary development; (D) reading fluency, including oral reading skills; and (E) reading comprehension strategies. (20 U. S. C. § 6368(3))

No Child Left Behind defines **scientifically based reading research** as:

> (A) applies rigorous, systematic, and objective procedures to obtain valid knowledge relevant to reading development, reading instruction, and reading difficulties; and
> (B) includes research that
> > (i) employs systematic, empirical methods that draw on observation or experiment;
> > (ii) involves rigorous data analyses that are adequate to test the stated hypotheses and justify the general conclusions drawn;
> > (iii) relies on measurements or observational methods that provide valid data across evaluators and observers and across multiple measurements and observations; and
> > (iv) has been accepted by a peer-reviewed journal or approved by a panel of independent experts through a comparably rigorous, objective, and scientific review. (20 U. S. C. § 6368(6))

The more generic term, **scientifically based research**, appears seventy-nine times in the statute. The statute explains that "scientifically based research:"

> (A) means research that involves the application of rigorous, systematic, and objective procedures to obtain reliable and valid knowledge relevant to education activities and programs; and
> (B) includes research that
> > (i) employs systematic, empirical methods that draw on observation or experiment;
> > (ii) involves rigorous data analyses that are adequate to test the stated hypotheses and justify the general conclusions drawn;
> > (iii) relies on measurements or observational methods that provide reliable and valid data across evaluators and observers, across multiple measurements and observations, and across studies by the same or different investigators;
> > (iv) is evaluated using experimental or quasi-experimental designs in which individuals, entities, programs, or activities are assigned to different conditions and with appropriate controls to evaluate

the effects of the condition of interest, with a preference for random-assignment experiments, or other designs to the extent that those designs contain within-condition or across-condition controls; (v) ensures that experimental studies are presented in sufficient detail and clarity to allow for replication or, at a minimum, offer the opportunity to build systematically on their findings; and (vi) has been accepted by a peer-reviewed journal or approved by a panel of independent experts through a comparably rigorous, objective, and scientific review. (20 U. S. C. § 7801(37))

No Child Left Behind describes three types of reading assessments: screening assessments, diagnostic assessments, and classroom-based instructional reading assessments.

A **screening reading assessment** is a "brief procedure designed as a first step" to identify children "at high risk for delayed development or academic failure and in need of further diagnosis . . ." (20 U. S. C. § 6368(7)(B))

A **diagnostic reading assessment** (i.e., the "further diagnosis) is based on research and is used for the purposes of "identifying a child's specific areas of strengths and weaknesses so that the child has learned to read by the end of grade 3; determining any difficulties that a child may have in learning to read and the potential cause of such difficulties; and helping to determine possible reading intervention strategies and related special needs." (20 U. S. C. § 6368(7)(C))

A **classroom based instructional reading assessment** consists of classroom-based observations of the child performing academic tasks. (20 U. S. C. § 6368(7)(D))

If a school district receives Title I funds, the district is required to submit a plan to the state that describes assessments that will be used "to effectively identify students who may be at risk for reading failures or are having difficulty reading." The district's plan must describe how the district "will provide additional educational assistance to individual students assessed as needing help" to meet state academic standards. (20 U. S. C. § 6312(b))

Questions for the Attorney and Advocate

- Is the child proficient in reading?
- Is the child proficient in auditory processing?
- Does the child have phonemic awareness?
- What is the child's grade equivalent level when reading aloud as measured by the Gray Oral Reading Test?
- What is the child's grade equivalent level when reading silently as measured by the Woodcock Reading Mastery Tests Revised or other measures of reading comprehension?
- If the child is not proficient in reading, what steps has the school taken to bring the child to proficiency?
- Has the school administered a screener? If so, what were the findings?
- Has the school administered a diagnostic reading test? If so, what were the findings?
- What reading program is the school using to teach the child to read?
- Is this program a research-based reading program? Does this reading program include the "essential components" listed in 20 U. S. C. § 6368(3)?
- What research supports the use of this program?
- What assessments does the district use to identify children who may be at risk for reading failure or difficulty learning to read? Has the district used such an assessment with this child? What were the findings?
- What "additional educational assistance" is the district providing to this child?
- Is the child's teacher qualified to teach reading?

HIGHLY QUALIFIED TEACHERS

Our clients often attend low-income, low-achieving schools, where they are taught by unqualified teachers and paraprofessionals. NCLB requires that all teachers meet new highly qualified requirements by 2005. The legal definition of "highly qualified teacher" is in Title IX, 20 U. S. C. § 7801(23).

A **highly qualified teacher** has obtained full State certification as a teacher, or passed the State teacher licensing examination, and holds a license to teach in such State. For a teacher in public charter schools, the term means the teacher meets the requirements set out in the State's public charter school law and has not had certification waived on an emergency, temporary, or provisional basis.

The principal "must attest annually in writing as to whether such school is in compliance" with these highly qualified teacher requirements. This information "shall be available to any member of the general public on request." (20 U. S. C. § 6319(i))

A new elementary school teacher must have a bachelor's degree and demonstrate, "by passing a rigorous State test, subject knowledge and teaching skills in reading, writing, mathematics, and other areas of the basic elementary school curriculum..."

A new middle or secondary school teacher must have a bachelor's degree and must demonstrate "a high level of competency in each of the academic subjects in which the teacher teaches by either passing a rigorous State academic subject test in each of the academic subjects in which the teacher teaches . . . or successful completion..." of specific academic coursework such as an undergraduate major or graduate degree in that academic field.

An elementary, middle, or secondary school teacher who is not new to the profession, must have a bachelor's degree and must meet the requirements of a new teacher or demonstrate "competence in all the academic subjects in which the teacher teaches based on a high objective uniform State standard of evaluation." (20 U. S. C. § 7801(23))

All **paraprofessionals**, regardless of hiring date, must have a high school diploma. If hired after January 8, 2002, the paraprofessional who works in a Title I program must have completed two years of college, obtained an associates degree, or passed an assessment test. If the paraprofessional was hired before January 8, 2002, the person must meet the above criteria within four years. (20 U. S. C. § 6319(c) and (d))

Paraprofessionals who do not provide instructional support (i.e., work as a playground monitor, in parent involvement activities or as translators), must have a high school diploma, but are not required to meet the new educational requirements. An "instructional support" paraprofessional may provide one-on-one tutoring if the tutoring is scheduled at a time when a student would not otherwise receive instruction from a teacher. (20 U. S. C. § 6319)

At the beginning of each school year, schools that receive Title I funds must notify parents of their right to request information about the education, training and qualifications of their child's teachers and paraprofessionals. Schools must also notify parents if the child is taught by a teacher who is not "highly qualified" for four consecutive weeks. (20 U. S. C. § 6311)

Questions for the Attorney and Advocate

- Are all the child's teachers highly qualified?
- Does the child receive services from a paraprofessional?
- Does the child receive tutoring or one-on-one educational services from a paraprofessional?
- Does the child receive tutoring from a paraprofessional at a time when the child would otherwise receive instruction from a teacher?

- What are the paraprofessional's duties?
- Does the paraprofessional meet the new educational requirements?
- Has a teacher who is not highly qualified taught the child for more than four weeks?
- Has a substitute teacher who is not highly qualified taught the child for more than four weeks?
- If the child attends a Title I school, did the parents receive notice of their right to request information about the teachers' qualifications?

ADEQUATE YEARLY PROGRESS (AYP)

States, school districts, and schools are required to submit reports to comply with accountability provisions of NCLB. These reports can be used as evidence in litigation against school districts. NCLB does not define Adequate Yearly Progress (AYP) for state departments of education (SEAs). Adequate Yearly Progress (AYP) for a school district (LEA) that receives Title I funds "shall be defined by the State in a manner that"

(i) applies the same high standards of academic achievement to all public elementary school and secondary school students in the State;
(ii) is statistically valid and reliable;
(iii) results in continuous and substantial academic improvement for all students;
(iv) measures the progress of public elementary schools, secondary schools and local educational agencies and the State based primarily on the academic assessments described in paragraph (3);
(v) includes separate measurable annual objectives for continuous and substantial improvement . . .
(20 U. S. C. § 6311(b)(2)(C))

The state department of education (SEA) shall identify for improvement a school district that fails to make AYP for two consecutive years and mandate a corrective action plan. (20 U. S. C. § 6311(b)(2)(B)) The school district shall promptly notify the parents of every child who attends a school in "need of improvement" about the results of the review, the reasons why the school has been identified, and how parents can help to improve the quality of the school.

When a Title I school consistently fails to achieve "Adequate Yearly Progress," the child can transfer to a better school or receive supplemental educational services, including private tutoring and other remedial services.

Public School Choice

Before the beginning of the school year, each school district shall identify all schools that fail to make Adequate Yearly Progress for two consecutive years. The district shall "provide all students enrolled in the school with the option to transfer to another public school" served by LEA, which may include a public charter school. Priority for the option to transfer to a different school shall be given to the lowest achieving children from low-income families. (20 U. S. C. § 6316(b)(1)(E))

The school district shall provide transportation to the new school. (20 U. S. C. § 6316(b)(9))

Supplemental Educational Services

If the school in need of improvement fails to improve by the following year, the district must also make "supplemental educational services" available to the students. These services, described at 20 U. S. C. § 6316(e)(12)(C) may include individualized tutoring or other academic services obtained from individuals and entities in the private and commercial sectors.

Corrective action may include replacing staff and/or extending the school day or school year. The corrective action shall be published and disseminated to the public.

If the "needs improvement" school continues to fail, the school may be reopened as a public charter school, all or most of the staff may be replaced, or operation of the school may be given to a private management company or the State. (20 U. S. C. § 6316(b)(8))

Questions for the Attorney and Advocate

- Does the child attend a school that is on the "needs improvement" list?
- Has the school offered to transfer the child to a better performing school?
- Has the school offered to provide supplemental educational services?
- Have the parents received a list of supplemental service providers?

IMMIGRANT CHILDREN AND ENGLISH-LANGUAGE LEARNERS

No Child Left Behind includes specific requirements about how schools must educate children who are learning English. States and school districts must establish proficiency standards for speaking, listening, reading, and writing. School districts must use research-based language instruction curricula for English language learners that are effective with this population. (20 U. S. C. § 6825(c)(1))

Schools must assess English language learners to measure the child's progress toward English proficiency and the child's comprehension, speaking, listening, reading, and writing skills in English every year. (20 U. S. C. § 6311(b)(3)(C)(7).

If the child has been in the United States for three or more years, the school must test the child in English every year. (20 U. S. C. § 6826)

School districts must provide research-based language instruction. Language teachers must be fluent in English and have written and oral communication skills. (20 U. S. C. § 6826(c))

No Child Left Behind also requires schools to notify parents about their children's progress in the language program. The school must notify parents of:

- The reasons why they placed the child in the language instruction program;
- The child's English proficiency level, how the level was tested, and the child's academic achievement levels;
- The method of instruction that the school will use in the child's language program;
- How the school's language program meets the child's educational strengths and needs;
- How the language program will help the child learn English, be promoted, and graduate from school;
- If the child has a disability, how the language program meets the objectives in the child's IEP. (20 U. S. C. § 6312(g), 20 U. S. C. § 7012)

The school must also provide parents with information about their parental rights, including:

- Their right to remove their child from the language program immediately; and
- Their options if they decide not to enroll the child in the language program.

Parents may remove their child from a language program at any time. (20 U. S. C. § 7012)

Questions for the Attorney and Advocate

- Is the child enrolled in a language program?
- Does the program use research-based language instruction curricula?

- Has the school assessed the child's progress toward English proficiency?
- Has the school assessed the child's comprehension, speaking, listening, reading, and writing skills in English?
- Is the child's language teacher fluent in English? Does the teacher have written and oral communication skills?
- Did the school advise the parents of their rights as specified in 20 U. S. C. § 7012?

REPORT CARDS AND NOTICES TO PARENTS

The school and school district **Report Cards** and the **Parents Right-to-Know** mandated in the State Plan (20 U. S. C. § 6311(h) provide an excellent source of evidence for the child's attorney.

A school district that receives Title I funds shall "prepare and disseminate an annual local educational agency report card" that provides information about "the number and percentage of schools identified for school improvement . . . how long the schools have been so identified" and information about the LEA's results on the "statewide academic assessments" and whether a particular school "has been identified for school improvement."

The district shall publicly disseminate the report card "information . . . to all parents of students attending those schools . . . and make the information widely available through public means, such as posting on the Internet . . ." (20 U. S. C. § 6311(h)(2))

"At the beginning of each school year" the school district "shall notify the parents of each student attending any school receiving funds under this part that the parents may request, and the agency will provide the parents on request (and in a timely manner), information regarding the professional qualifications of the student's classroom teachers, including, at a minimum, the following:

(i) Whether the teacher has met State qualification and licensing criteria for the grade levels and subject areas in which the teacher provides instruction.

(ii) Whether the teacher is teaching under emergency or other provisional status through which State qualification or licensing criteria have been waived.

(iii) The baccalaureate degree major of the teacher and any other graduate certification or degree held by the teacher, and the field of discipline of the certification or degree.

(iv) Whether the child is provided services by paraprofessionals and, if so, their qualifications." (20 U. S. C. § 6311)

In addition, the school "shall provide to each individual parent (i) information on the level of achievement of the parent's child in each of the State academic assessments as required under this part; and (ii) timely notice that the parent's child has been assigned, or has been taught for four or more consecutive weeks by, a teacher who is not highly qualified." (20 U. S. C. § 6311(h)(6))

TRANSFERS FROM UNSAFE SCHOOLS

Under No Child Left Behind, no child is required to attend a persistently dangerous school. The state must identify persistently dangerous schools every year and make this information available to the public. If a child attends a persistently dangerous school, the school district must notify the parents of their right to transfer the child to a safe school in the district. Transfers should take place within **30 days.**

If the child is the victim of a violent crime while in or on the grounds of a public school, the parents can transfer the child to a safe school in the district within **10 days** of the incident. (20 U. S. C. § 7912)

PRIVACY AND INSTRUCTIONAL MATERIALS

The statute about privacy and parent access to information is in Title X, Section 1061. If the child attends a Title I school, parents have a right to inspect instructional materials used in the curriculum. Instructional materials are print and audio-visual material, and electronic and digital material, including information accessed through the Internet. Instructional materials do not include academic tests or assessments.

PENALTY FOR NON-COMPLIANCE

Many of the purportedly new deadlines in the Act were established when The Elementary and Secondary Education Act of 1965 was reauthorized in 1994.

The Act clearly states that no waivers will be given for failure to comply with the 1994 deadlines. For any failure to meet the requirements of "this section" (the state plan), "then the Secretary may withhold funds for State administration under this part until the Secretary determines that the State has fulfilled those requirements." (20 U. S. C. § 6311(g))

PRIVATE CAUSE OF ACTION

Whether individual parents and others will have a private cause of action to sue because of a state or school district's violation of the substantive or procedural requirements of No Child Left Behind is presently unclear. Some courts may hold that the Act provides an individual right of action and other courts may hold that the sole remedy is for the U. S. Department of Education to withhold funds.

Loss of Educational Opportunity

Assume a parent, acting on behalf of their child, files suit against a state or school district or both, alleging a violation of a right granted by No Child Left Behind. The attorney should be prepared to prove, as a matter of evidence, that the child suffered a loss of an educational opportunity and that the loss has damaged the child. This reasoning is consistent with the evolving case law about school district violations of the procedural requirements of the Individuals with Disabilities Education Act (IDEA).

Discrimination

Some states and school districts may deliberately withhold educational services or refuse to comply with NCLB in a consistent manner. For example, a school district may comply with the "school choice" provisions for some students, but not all students. This inconsistency may be based on race, disability, or other variables.

If the child has a right to be free from discrimination, and the inconsistency reflects an illegal pattern or practice of misconduct, then the child and parent may have a right to an individual cause of action under a civil rights statute such as Section 504 of the Rehabilitation Act.

For information about the Individuals with Disabilities Education Act, Section 504 of the Rehabilitation Act and U. S. Supreme Court IDEA caselaw, see *Wrightslaw: Special Education Law*.

Tactics and Strategies

For information about tactics and strategies in education litigation, how to organize the child's file, how to interpret educational, psychological, and state assessment data, and how to use letters as evidence, see *Wrightslaw: From Emotions to Advocacy*.

IN SUMMATION

In this chapter, you learned about provisions in No Child Left Behind that are of interest to attorneys and advocates. The next chapter, *No Child Left Behind for School Leaders and Academics*, focuses on accountability, adequate yearly progress for specific subgroups of children, proficiency, supplemental services providers, equitable services to private school students and teachers, research based instruction, and data collection.

RESOURCES

You will find many excellent publications in the *Wrightslaw: No Child Left Behind CD-ROM* and on the Internet. Here is a short list of recommended resources.

In the Wrightslaw No Child Left Behind CD-ROM

Guidance for the Reading First Program published by the U.S. Department of Education answers frequently asked questions about reading and reading programs.

Improving Teacher Quality: Non-Regulatory Guidance. Answers frequently asked questions about requirements for highly qualified teachers, certification, alternative routes to teaching, subject area competency, which teachers must be highly qualified, "high-quality professional development."

No Child Left Behind Deskbook published by the U. S. Department of Education provides a detailed roadmap to the No Child Left Behind Act of 2001.

Public School Choice: Draft Non-Regulatory Guidance published by the U.S. Department of Education answers frequently asked questions about public school choice.

Supplemental Educational Services: Draft Non-Regulatory Guidance published by the U. S. Department of Education answers frequently asked questions about supplemental educational services.

Unsafe School Choice Option: Draft Non-Regulatory Guidance published by the U.S. Department of Education includes answers to frequently asked questions about school choice options for children who attend unsafe schools.

On the Internet

Major Changes to ESEA in the No Child Left Behind Act published by the Learning First Alliance (2003). URL:
http://www.learningfirst.org/publications/nclb/

No Child Left Behind Act: A Description of State Responsibilities published by the Council of Chief State School Officers. URL:
http://www.ccsso.org/publications/index.cfm

No State Left Behind: The Challenges and Opportunities of ESEA 2001 published by Education Commission of the States.
URL: http://www.ecs.org/ecsmain.asp?page=/html/special/ESEA_main.htm

The No Child Left Behind Act: Notification and Reporting Requirements for Local School Boards (Resource Document #3) published by the National School Boards Association (2002).
URL: http://www.nsba.org/site/docs/5400/5367.pdf

FOR YOUR NOTES

8 | NCLB FOR SCHOOL LEADERS AND ACADEMICS

In this chapter, you learn that the No Child Left Behind Act emphasizes accountability, assessment, parent options, better-trained teachers, and research-based teaching methods. You learn about accountability, adequate yearly progress, proficiency, parent options, supplemental services providers, equitable services to private school students and teachers, research based instruction, and data collection and analysis.

The law requires schools to teach all children to proficiency in reading, math and science by 2014. The key requirements of the law—annual proficiency testing in grades 3-8, highly qualified teachers in every classroom, research based instruction, increased parental rights, public school choice, and state, district and school report cards—are strategies to accomplish this goal.

NCLB applies differently to Title I schools than to schools that do not receive Title I grants. One way or another, this law covers all public schools in all states.

ACCOUNTABILITY AND ASSESSMENTS

State Accountability

States must set proficiency levels on their reading and math tests that indicate grade-level performance. These proficiency levels must reflect state academic standards.

States must also determine the percentage of students overall and the percentage of students in specific groups who are expected to reach proficiency each year. States set specific increments that they will meet between now and 2014. The goals will be raised each year so all students and all subgroups of students will be performing at grade level by 2014. (20 U. S. C. § 6311(b))

School districts and states must make steady Adequate Yearly Progress (AYP) towards this goal. To measure progress, states must begin testing all students in grades 3 through 8 annually in reading and math during the 2005-2006 school year. They must begin testing students in grades 10 through 12 at least once in these subjects. By 2007-08, states must test students in science at least once during grades 3-8, grades 6-9, and grades 10-12. These test scores determine if your school is making Adequate Yearly Progress (AYP) towards the goal of proficiency for all children by the 2013-2014 deadline. (20 U. S. C. § 6311(c))

States that wish to avoid sanctions under the law must improve student test scores immediately. Clear communication between the governor's office, legislators, state department of education, the state board of education, and the state university system is essential to accomplishing this goal.

States need to evaluate where they stand, where they need to be, how they will get there, and identify problems that stand in the way. Without a thorough knowledge of this law and honest examination of the education issues in your state, you are likely to waste valuable time. This will result in expensive corrections in later years.

Chapter 8

School District Accountability

To make Adequate Yearly Progress, school districts must demonstrate annually that all students, including subgroups, meet state standards for grade-level work. Schools and districts will not make AYP if any subgroup misses the performance goal. (20 U. S. C. § 6312)

Since NCLB requires that all children be at the proficient level on state testing by 2014, states are given more flexibility in combining federal grants and expenditures.

Adequate Yearly Progress of Subgroups

In addition to reporting their overall progress, schools and school districts must report their progress in educating subgroups of children, including:

- children with disabilities
- English language learners
- racial minorities
- children from low-income families. (20 U. S. C. § 6311)

If a subgroup does not meet the AYP goals, the school or district will move into the "needs improvement" category. The school must test at least 95 percent of students in all subgroups. If the school does not test these students, the school will not meet its annual Adequate Yearly Progress (AYP) goal and will move into the "needs improvement" category. (20 U. S. C. § 6311(b)(2)(I))

States were required to include all children in their statewide testing programs before No Child Left Behind was enacted. At that time, less than half of the states met this requirement. The individual "Decision Letters on each State's Final Assessment System" from the U. S. Department of Education are on the Internet. The letters explain the basis for the non-approval of the state's assessment process.

　🖑 **Decision letters and States with Approved Title I Assessment Systems** at
　　http://www.ed.gov/admins/lead/account/finalassess/index.html.

These states set their Adequate Yearly Progress (AYP) figures based on performance information that is available. If states did not test all students, this information was not accurate.

Traditionally, children with disabilities and English language learners have often been excluded from proficiency testing. School leaders in states that have not included all children in statewide testing need to look at their test data histories to anticipate problems. When states begin testing all students, as required by law, they may find that state, school and school district AYP figures actually get worse.

Proficiency

Proficiency means the child is performing at an average grade level as determined by the state. NCLB requires states to develop achievement standards that "describe two levels of high achievement (proficient and advanced) that determine how well children are mastering the material in the State academic content standards; and describe a third level of achievement (basic) to provide complete information about the progress of the lower-achieving children toward mastering the proficient and advanced levels of achievement." (20 U. S. C. § 6311(b)(1)(D))

Not all states use the terms basic, proficient, and advanced as categories for their state testing. Some states use more than three categories. For example, Louisiana currently has five categories: Advanced, Mastery, Basic, Approaching Basic, and Unsatisfactory. According to the Louisiana State Plan, Advanced and Mastery is "Exceeding the Standard" while Basic is "Meeting the Standard."

The State NCLB Plan will tell you how the state will translate the score categories of its state testing to the terms of basic, proficient and advanced for NCLB accountability.

✍️ **All State NCLB Plans** are at: http://www.ed.gov/admins/lead/account/stateplans03/index.html

The purpose of the academic assessments required by NCLB is to improve educational outcomes. The assessments allow parents and the public to know if schools, districts and states reached their adequate yearly progress goals. In contrast to norm-referenced testing of children, this is similar to criterion-referenced testing that determines if a specific level or skill has been attained. The criteria used to determine mastery or achievement of the goal will fluctuate widely from one state to another.

PARENT OPTIONS

Public School Choice and Supplemental Services

When a school does not meet the AYP goals for two consecutive years, the school will fall into the "needs improvement" category. Students who attend the schools can transfer to better performing schools in the district.

When a school does not meet the AYP goals for three consecutive years, students from low-income families who attend the school can receive supplemental educational services from a provider selected by the parent. Supplemental educational services include tutoring, summer school programs, and after-school programs.

Supplemental Educational Services Providers

State departments of education must ensure that parents have an adequate list of providers from which to choose. Providers must be in place in all areas of the state.

Many individuals and organizations that are eligible to provide supplemental services may not be familiar with these provisions in the law. State departments of education are required to contact potential providers every year and encourage them to apply for inclusion on the state list of Supplemental Educational Service Providers.

Are you a provider? Have you been contacted by your state department of education? If not, consider sending an application to your state.

📖 The U.S. Department of Education has prepared several publications about supplemental educational services, including *Supplemental Educational Services-Draft Non-Regulatory Guidance* and *Toolkit for Faith-Based and Community Organizations to Provide Extra Academic Help*. These publications will answer many questions about these services and how to become a provider. These publications are available on the ***Wrightslaw NCLB CD-ROM***.

EQUITABLE SERVICES TO PRIVATE SCHOOL STUDENTS AND TEACHERS

Under Title I, participating school districts are required to provide eligible children who attend private elementary and secondary schools, their teachers, and their families with Title I services or benefits that are equitable to those provided to eligible public school children, teachers, and families.

These services must be developed in consultation with private school officials. Title I services provided to private schools by school districts are designed to meet their educational needs and supplement the educational services provided by the private school. (20 U. S. C. § 6320)

TEACHERS AND PARAPROFESSIONALS _____

Highly Qualified Teachers

State departments of education need to be knowledgeable about the highly qualified teacher requirements of No Child Left Behind because they must raise state teacher standards.

The U. S. Department of Education reports that only one state requires teachers to score above the 48th percentile on the Pre-professional Skills Test in Reading. Some states only required teachers to score above the 15th percentile on the skills test. In some states, elementary school teachers do not have to take any courses in how to teach reading. Raising these standards should lead to better results in the classroom.

📖 *Improving Teacher Quality: Non-Regulatory Guidance*. Answers frequently asked questions about requirements for highly qualified teachers, certification, alternative routes to teaching, subject area competency, which teachers must be highly qualified, "high-quality professional development." This publication is available on the *Wrightslaw NCLB CD-ROM*.

Paraprofessionals

Paraprofessionals who work in Title I schools must have a high school diploma or equivalent. Paraprofessionals who provide instructional support must complete two years of post secondary education, have an associate degree or higher, or pass a state or local test. Paraprofessionals who provide instructional support must demonstrate the ability to support teachers in reading, writing, and math instruction. (20 U. S. C. § 6319)

Paraprofessionals who were employed before January 8, 2002 must meet these new educational requirements by 2006. Paraprofessionals who do not work in a school that receives Title I funds are not required to meet these standards. Federal funds to educate and train paraprofessionals are available through Titles I, II, III, V, and VII of the No Child Left Behind Act.

A paraprofessional may be assigned to provide one-on-one tutoring for eligible students, if the tutoring is scheduled at a time when a student would not otherwise receive instruction from a teacher. (20 U. S. C. § 6319)

📖 *Title I Paraprofessionals - Draft Non-Regulatory Guidance* published by the U. S. Department of Education includes answers to questions about paraprofessionals. This publication is on the *Wrightslaw NCLB CD-ROM*.

RESEARCH-BASED INSTRUCTION_____

The term "**scientifically based research**" is used no less than seventy-nine times in the statute and is defined as follows:

The term "scientifically based research"

(A) means research that involves the application of rigorous, systematic, and objective procedures to obtain reliable and valid knowledge relevant to education activities and programs; and
(B) includes research that
(i) employs systematic, empirical methods that draw on observation or experiment;
(ii) involves rigorous data analyses that are adequate to test the stated hypotheses and justify the general conclusions drawn;
(iii) relies on measurements or observational methods that provide reliable and valid data across evaluators and observers, across multiple measurements and observations, and across studies by the same or different investigators;
(iv) is evaluated using experimental or quasi-experimental designs in which individuals, entities, programs, or activities are assigned to different conditions and with appropriate controls to evaluate

the effects of the condition of interest, with a preference for random-assignment experiments, or other designs to the extent that those designs contain within-condition or across-condition controls; (v) ensures that experimental studies are presented in sufficient detail and clarity to allow for replication or, at a minimum, offer the opportunity to build systematically on their findings; and (vi) has been accepted by a peer-reviewed journal or approved by a panel of independent experts through a comparably rigorous, objective, and scientific review. (20 U. S. C. § 7801(37), Section 9101 of NCLB Act)

Reading & Reading Instruction

No Child Left Behind includes the legal definition of **reading**:

Reading is a complex system of deriving meaning from print that requires all of the following:

(A) The skills and knowledge to understand how phonemes, or speech sounds, are connected to print
(B) The ability to decode unfamiliar words
(C) The ability to read fluently
(D) Sufficient background information and vocabulary to foster reading comprehension
(E) The development of appropriate active strategies to construct meaning from print
(F) The development and maintenance of a motivation to read

The statute lists five **essential components of reading instruction**

(A) phonemic awareness
(B) phonics
(C) vocabulary development
(D) reading fluency, including oral reading skills
(E) reading comprehension strategies

Some states have not identified a research-based reading curriculum that meets the Reading First requirements. These states may have limited personnel trained to implement these programs. Professional development funds are available to train teachers who will implement the new reading programs.

KNOWING THE RULES

Data Collection and Analysis

The U. S. Department of Education requires that state departments of education provide statistical information to comply with NCLB. Some states have not collected or reported data under past reauthorizations of the Elementary and Secondary Education Act. NCLB includes sanctions for states that do not comply with these reporting provisions. The U. S. Department of Education is withholding funds from states that are not in compliance.

States need to identify the information they need, who has it, how to get it, and ensure that local education agencies collect and transmit this data consistently, accurately and on time. States that spend money to train staff to do this job accurately and thoroughly will avoid future problems and sanctions.

Education funding makes up a large part of all state budgets. Compliance will be more efficient if governors and legislators, school boards, state boards of education, and state departments of education are knowledgeable about this law. If legislators, governors, and school leaders are not knowledgeable, they may unwittingly draft policies and pass budgets that trigger sanctions under the law. For example, the statute forbids cutting education budgets in anticipation of receiving NCLB funds. Time and effort will be used to undo legislative mistakes that could be avoided if the lawmakers knew the rules that accompany the NCLB funds they requested and received.

IN SUMMATION

In this chapter, you learned about provisions in the No Child Left Behind Act that are of interest to school leaders and academics. In the next chapter, you learn how to use tactics and strategy to obtain information and request action.

RESOURCES

You will find many excellent publications in the *Wrightslaw: No Child Left Behind CD-ROM* and on the Internet. Here is a short list of recommended resources.

In the Wrightslaw No Child Left Behind CD-ROM

Guidance for the Reading First Program published by the U.S. Department of Education answers frequently asked questions about reading and reading programs.

Improving Teacher Quality: Non-Regulatory Guidance. Answers frequently asked questions about requirements for highly qualified teachers, certification, alternative routes to teaching, subject area competency, which teachers must be highly qualified, "high-quality professional development."

No Child Left Behind Deskbook published by the U. S. Department of Education provides a detailed roadmap to the No Child Left Behind Act of 2001.

Public School Choice: Draft Non-Regulatory Guidance published by the U.S. Department of Education answers frequently asked questions about public school choice.

Standards and Assessments: Non-Regulatory Draft Guidance published by the U. S. Department of Education answers frequently asked questions about these topics.

Report Cards: Non-Regulatory Guidance. Publication from the U. S. Department of Education answers questions about state and school district (local educational agency) report cards.

Standards & Assessments: Non-Regulatory Draft Guidance. This publication about Standards and Assessment is written to assist States, districts, and schools in understanding and implementing The No Child Left Behind Act in the area of standards and assessments.

Supplemental Educational Services: Draft Non-Regulatory Guidance published by the U. S. Department of Education answers frequently asked questions about supplemental educational services.

Unsafe School Choice Option: Draft Non-Regulatory Guidance published by the U.S. Department of Education includes answers to frequently asked questions about school choice options for children who attend unsafe schools.

On the Internet

An Action Guide for Community and Parent Leaders - Using NCLB to Improve Student Achievement by Public Education Network.
URL: http://www.publiceducation.org/pdf/NCLBBook.pdf

A New Wave of Evidence: The Impact of School, Family and Community Connections on Student Achievement published by the Southwest Educational Development Laboratory.
URL: http://www.sedl.org/connections/resources/evidence.pdf

Major Changes to ESEA in the No Child Left Behind Act published by the Learning First Alliance (2003).
URL: http://www.learningfirst.org/publications/nclb/

Making Valid and Reliable Decisions in Determining Adequate Yearly Progress published by the Council of Chief State School Officers.
URL: http://www.ccsso.org/publications/index.cfm

No Child Left Behind Act: A Description of State Responsibilities published by the Council of Chief State School Officers.
URL: http://www.ccsso.org/publications/index.cfm

No State Left Behind: The Challenges and Opportunities of ESEA 2001 published by Education Commission of the States.
URL: http://www.ecs.org/ecsmain.asp?page=/html/special/ESEA_main.htm

The No Child Left Behind Act: Notification and Reporting Requirements for Local School Boards (Resource Document #3) published by the National School Boards Association (2002).

Using the No Child Left Behind Act to Improve Schools in Your State - A Toolkit for Business Leaders - Information Resources for Business Leadership to Increase Student Achievement under the "No Child Left Behind Act of 2002 published by the Business Roundtable.
URL: http://brt.org/toolkit/toolkit.html

FOR YOUR NOTES

9 | HOW TO OBTAIN INFORMATION AND REQUEST ACTION

In this chapter, you learn how to write effective letters to obtain information and request action. You will learn how to use the Freedom of Information Act and strategies to ensure that your letters accomplish their purpose.

As you read this chapter, refer to the sample letters in Chapter 11 (pages 99-116). You can adapt these letters to your circumstances.

WHY YOU WRITE LETTERS

You write letters to:

- Obtain information
- Request action
- Report a problem or file a complaint

You also use letters to build relationships, identify and solve problems, clarify decisions that are made or not made, and motivate people to take action. When you write a letter, be guided by your purpose. What do you want your letter to accomplish? Focus on one issue or two issues at most. Do not use one letter to accomplish several purposes. Long letters about several issues are confusing.

To Request Information

Most requests for information are straightforward. For example, you may write letters to:

- Request information about the qualifications of a child's teachers
- Request research about a child's reading program
- Request scientifically-based reading research about a child's reading program
- Request information about your school or school district report card
- Request school district's Reading First Application

To Request Action

When you write a letter to request action, your reader may be resistant. If you expect resistance, provide information that supports your request. For example, you may write letters to:

- Request that your child not be retained
- Request that your school board comply with NCLB
- Request that your state develop a comprehensive list of supplemental education service providers

Chapter 9

Using the Freedom of Information Act

The Freedom of Information Act is a federal law that makes virtually all government information available to the public. Each state has its own Open Records laws that vary slightly from state to state. These laws allow you to request information from state and federal agencies.

All applications, reports, plans, and evaluations that states, schools, and school districts are required to produce under NCLB are public records. You may want to read some of these reports. They will give you an idea of the strengths and weaknesses of your state or local education department. You may also wish to see reports produced by the U.S. Department of Education. You may want to see information that was collected but does not seem to appear in any report that has been prepared. If you are unable to find the data or a report that you wish to see, you may decide to file a Freedom of Information Act request to obtain it.

The Reporters Committee for Freedom of the Press publishes small books about how to use this law to obtain information. *How to Use the Federal FOI Act* contains the federal law, explains how the law works, and provides sample letters. The *Tapping Official's Secrets* books contain the Open Records and Open Meeting laws for every state. These books and the website will provide you with the information you need to use the Freedom of Information Act.

In many cases, a simple request letter will get you the information you want. If this is not successful, read about using the FOIA and Open Records laws and use the sample letters provided by the Reporters Committee for Freedom of the Press.

> ✍ **TIP:** The Reporters Committee for Freedom of the Press website is www.rcfp.org - it provides information about how to order *How to Use the Federal FOI Act* and *Tapping Officials' Secrets*. These two books can be ordered for about $15.

The editor of EducatonNews.org decided to use the Freedom of Information laws to obtain detailed information about the success of a school system. His approach will help you learn how to use this law.

> ✍ **FOI REQUEST**: This link will take you to Freedom of Information requests from the editor of EducationNews.org: www.educationnews.org/Academic-Preparation-&-Performance-Audits.htm

Strategies: Writing Good Letters

Before you write a letter, think about your purpose. If you are not an experienced letter-writer, ask a friend or co-worker to read your letter. Ask your reader to answer these questions.

- Why are you writing this letter?
- What is your purpose?
- What are you trying to accomplish?
- What do you want?

If your reader is unable to answer these questions without help from you, you need to revise your letter. If you follow these steps, you increase the odds that someone will read and respond to your letter.

> 📖 Read *Letter Writing Tips* at the end of this chapter. Also read Chapter 23, *How to Write Good Evidence Letters*, and Chapter 24, *Writing the Letter to the Stranger*, in *Wrightslaw: From Emotions to Advocacy*. This book is available in bookstores and on the Wrightslaw.com site at www.wrightslaw.com

Is Easy to Read

Use clear, everyday language. Avoid vague words, legal or educational jargon, and rambling sentences. Use short sentences (10 to 20 words) and short paragraphs (generally no more than six to eight lines). It is important to use short paragraphs because they are easier to read. When you use short sentences, short paragraphs, and simple language, your message is easier to understand. You create a favorable first impression.

Gets to the Point

If you are writing to request that your reader take action, get to the point. Tell the reader what you want in the first paragraph. Your readers are busy people. They are unlikely to finish your letter if you do not get to the point and tell them what you want them to do.

Should you **always** get to the point immediately? There are two exceptions to this rule: when you are writing to convey bad news or to persuade the reader to take action that he or she may not want to take. If you anticipate that getting to the point immediately may upset, anger, or alienate your reader, make an effort to maintain a good relationship with the reader. Be polite. You will learn how to write persuasive complaint letters in the next chapter.

Is Courteous

When you write a letter to obtain information or request action, treat your reader with courtesy and kindness. Do not demand that the reader take action. If you make demands, you ensure that your reader will look for reasons to deny, or delay, or not comply with your request. This is human nature.

If you need to provide the reader with suggestions or guidance, direct the reader with courtesy. Be sure to say "please" and "thank you."

Is Easy to Follow

Each paragraph of a letter should convey one idea that is expressed in the first sentence or two. Supporting information should follow the main idea. Do not make a reader slog through several paragraphs to discover your main idea.

Prompts the Reader to Act

At the beginning of a letter, explain why you are writing and what you want the reader to do. Your reader is more likely to remember the first and last thing read. In the last line of your letter, restate the action you want the reader to take.

Ends with Courtesy

Your reader will remember the final impression of your letter. Make sure you end your letter with courtesy. The decision to help is in the reader's hands. Convey your request as a request, not as a demand.

For example, you should write: "I would appreciate a prompt response" not, "I demand a response within ten days." You should write: "Please let me know when I can pick up this information" not, "I expect you to comply with my request immediately."

Gives Contact Information

Include a telephone number, fax number, or email address at the end of your letters. You may write, "If you have questions about my request for the documents, please call me at work (877-555-1212) or at home (877-555-1313) weekdays after 6 p.m." When you include contact information, the reader can contact you immediately with questions or answers.

LETTER WRITING TIPS

Image and Presentation

- First impressions are lasting impressions
- Use businesslike letters to create a good impression.
- Type letters or print from your computer.
- Use quality paper. Do not use cute stationery with flowers or little animals.
- Include contact information – phone number, fax number, and/or email.

Set the Right Tone

- Do not demand. Do not apologize. Do not threaten to sue.
- End your letter with courtesy.

Write to the Right Person

- Who can resolve your problem? Write your letter to this person.
- Address your letter to a real person. Use the person's name and job title. No one likes to receive letters addressed "To Whom It May Concern."

Delivery Options

- Deliver important letters by hand. Log in the time and date, identity of the person who received the letter, what the person told you, what they were wearing, what was happening at the time.
- Do not send certified or registered letters to the school.
- Do not mark letters "personal" or "confidential."

How Long?

- In general, keep your letters short, no more than one page.
- Get to the point in the first paragraph.

What to Include

- Tell the reader why you are writing the letter and what you want the reader to do.
- Cite facts that support your position or request. Be sure your facts are correct.

Deadlines

- Set a time limit for a reply. Two weeks is fair. (Do not make demands!)
- Write, call, write. Write a letter. Wait 10 days, then call.

What to Do if You Do Not Receive a Response

- If you do not receive a response, write a second letter, and include a copy of your first letter.
- If you get no response, set a short deadline before going higher. 10 days is reasonable.
- If you receive no response to the second letter, go higher in the chain of command.

IN SUMMATION

In this chapter, you learned how to write letters to obtain information and request action. You learned how to use the Freedom of Information Act to request information from state and federal agencies. You learned the qualities of good letters and strategies that will help you make a good impression. In Chapter 10, you learn how to report problems and file complaints.

10 | HOW TO REPORT A PROBLEM OR FILE A COMPLAINT

In this chapter, you learn how to write a persuasive complaint letter, use facts to present your case, and make a good first impression.

The No Child Left Behind Act does not include a formal complaint procedure. When you "file a complaint," you are alerting an individual who may have the power to fix a problem. The Secretary of the U. S. Department of Education appointed Regional Representatives for different regions in the country. These Regional Representatives are responsible for helping states comply with the law and for monitoring compliance in their region.

Regional Representatives are concerned with actions that indicate global problems with NCLB compliance. Before you "file a complaint" with your Regional Representative, make sure you have valid grounds for the complaint, you are familiar with the law, and you have a paper trail that shows deliberate non-compliance with the law.

Before you decide to file a complaint, you should answer these questions.

- Did you read the Guidance publications about this topic?
- Did you read your state accountability plan? Did the U. S. Department of Education approve the procedure you want to express concerns about?
- Did you express concerns to your school district or state department of education. Did you create a paper trail?
- Do you want to report a concern or request action?
- Should you express your concern to your state department of education? Should you express your concern to the Secretary's Regional Representative?

Suppose you are responsible for compiling assessment data for your state. You discovered problems with the accountability database. This may be an appropriate issue for your Regional Representative.

Suppose your school district did not test your child on the annual academic testing. If the school district did not report that your child was tested, there was no violation. If you have reason to believe the district reported false information, you may want to write a letter to your Regional Representative to advise her of the situation.

Remember, accountability follows money. Your state received Title I funds and allocated the funds to eligible school districts. Your state is responsible for ensuring that school districts comply with No Child Left Behind.

State and federal education authorities travel and may be away from the office for several days. If you call, expect to be referred to voicemail. Leave a short message about the problem, your name, phone number, and good times to contact you.

Although email is an alternate means of communication, email does not convey a serious purpose nor does email allow you to make a good first impression. If you want to file a complaint, write a letter. Provide facts and information that show:

- What the problem is
- Why you are concerned
- How the problem may affect state compliance

WRITING A PERSUASIVE COMPLAINT LETTER

Writing a good complaint letter is difficult. The Regional Representative who is responsible for No Child Left Behind compliance in several states does not have time to read long rambling letters. This person wants to know what the problem is, how the problem affects compliance, and how to reach you if she needs more information.

When you write a letter to file a complaint, keep the recipient in mind. This individual does not know you or your situation. Assume the person is conservative, fair, and open-minded. She will also visit three states in the next four days. When you describe your problem, get to the point. Provide facts that support your concerns.

Edit and Revise

The first letter you write is always a draft. After you write the first draft, put your letter away. Allow at least 24 to 48 hours before you edit the letter. Ask at least one cool-headed person to edit your letter. Choose a person who will tell you the truth and respect your confidentiality. Ask your editor to answer these questions:

- What is the purpose of my letter?
- What is my point?
- What do I want?
- Should I shorten the letter? Should I tone the letter down?

If your reader cannot answer the first three questions quickly, without explanations or prompting from you, your letter is not clear. When you edit a letter, you want to clarify, condense and strengthen your message. **Remove every unnecessary word.** Read your letter aloud to find spelling and grammar errors. Read "Letter Writing Tips" in Chapter 9.

Use Facts to Present Your Case

How you lay out facts in a letter is important. Select your facts carefully. Keep your opinions to a minimum. The Representative is not concerned about the background of the problem. She is concerned about violations of the state's No Child Left Behind plan. If you jump from one issue to another, the person will get confused, then frustrated. Your letter will not accomplish its purpose.

Make a Good Impression

When you write a complaint letter, you are writing to a person who has the power to solve your problem or complaint. In your letter, you introduce yourself to this decision-maker. When reading your letter, the person will form an impression of you. Do not blame or name-call. You have only one chance to make a good impression.

Speak to the Reader

Speak directly to the reader. Imagine you are talking about your problem. Use words like "you," "we," and "our" to make your letter more personal. When people read your letter, they will feel that your message is directed at them.

LETTER WRITING PITFALLS

People do not read long letters. You must capture the reader's interest and attention in the first few sentences. If you do not get the reader's interest quickly, the reader will skim the first paragraph or two, then put your letter aside.

People do not like angry letter-writers. Your letter is a personal statement about you. If you write an angry or demanding letter, you will not make a good impression. If you make a poor impression, the recipient may ignore subsequent communications from you because you sounded angry, unreasonable, or unreliable.

If you file a complaint with your Regional Representative, remember that this person's job is state compliance. Provide facts and information that support your complaint.

IN SUMMATION

In this chapter, you learned how to write letters to report a problem or file a complaint. The next chapter includes fifteen sample letters about No Child Left Behind issues. You can tailor these letters to your circumstances.

FOR YOUR NOTES

11 | SAMPLE LETTERS

This chapter includes fifteen sample letters about No Child Left Behind issues. The authors include parents, an attorney, a school board member, a retired teacher, and members of the Armed Forces.

Several letters focus on how to obtain information about a school or school district, including Title I status, reading research, state and school district report cards, and parental involvement policies.

A parent writes to object to the school's plan to retain her child. A retired teacher wants to learn how she can become a "Supplemental Service Provider." A school board member asks the state department of education for a suitable list of supplemental service providers. An individual in the Armed Forces expresses interest in becoming a teacher through the "Troops-to-Teachers" program. Two letters express different perspectives about access to student information by military recruiters.

In some cases, the purpose of the letter is not to request specific information, but to document that information is not readily available to the public, as required by NCLB. One letter will document the problem. A follow-up letter may be evidence of inaction and the failure to comply with the No Child Left Behind Act.

You can use these letters as templates and tailor them to your circumstances.

You should also read "How to Obtain Information and Request Act" (Chapter 9) about how to write effective letters and "How to Report a Problem or File a Complaint (Chapter 10).

SAMPLE LETTERS

#1. Sample Letter to Request Information about Teachers' Qualifications
#2. Sample Letter to Request Research about a Reading Program
#3. Sample Letter to Request Reading First Application
#4. Sample Letter Objecting to Retention of Child with a Disability
#5. Sample Letter from Attorney Using NCLB to Request Reading Research and File
#6. Sample Complaint Letter to USDOE Regarding SEA and LEA Failure to Provide Information about Report Cards
#7. Sample Complaint letter to USDOE Regarding SEA and LEA Failure to Provide Information about Title I Schools

#1. Sample Letter to Request Information about Teachers' Qualifications

MARY PARENT
17456 GENERAL PULLER HIGHWAY
DELTAVILLE, VIRGINIA 23043
899-555-1234

March 1, 2006

Dr. Charlotte Temple, Principal
Deltaville Middle School
1000 Main Street
Deltaville, Virginia 23043

    Re: Jennifer Parent (DOB: 01/01/91)
    School: Deltaville Middle School

Dear Dr. Temple:

My daughter Jennifer Parent is an eighth grade student at Deltaville Middle School. Jennifer has four teachers: Ms. Adams, Mr. Brown, Ms. Canady, and Ms. Davis, a substitute math teacher. Jennifer also receives tutoring from Ms. Evans, a paraprofessional.

When I read the USDOE's publication "Teacher Quality Guide Supports Parents' Right to Know" in the February 1 issue of *The Achiever: No Child Left Behind Newsletter*, I learned that I am entitled to information about Jennifer's teachers, including:

> (1) Whether the teacher has met State qualification and licensing criteria for the grade levels and subject areas in which the teacher provides instruction;
> (2) Whether the teacher is teaching under emergency or other provisional status through which State qualification or licensing criteria have been waived.
> (3) The baccalaureate degree major of the teacher and any other graduate certification or degree held by the teacher, and the field of discipline of the certification or degree.
> (4) Whether the child is provided services by paraprofessionals and, if so, their qualifications.

I am requesting this information about the qualifications of Jennifer's teachers and paraprofessional. I believe the information will help me work more effectively with her teachers. I am enclosing a copy of The Achiever. Some of the articles in this and future issues may be of interest to you and your staff.

If you have questions about my request, please call me at work (899-555-9876) or at home (899-555-1234) after 6 p.m., or you can email me at maryparent@deltavilleva.com. Thanks in advance for your help.

Sincerely,

Mary Parent

Enc: U. S. Department of Education publication, "Teacher Quality Guide Supports Parents Right to Know"
        from *The Achiever* (February 2, 2003)

#2. Sample Letter to Request Research about a Reading Program

MARY PARENT
17456 GENERAL PULLER HIGHWAY
DELTAVILLE, VIRGINIA 23043
899-555-1234

March 15, 2006

Dr. Charlotte Temple, Principal
Deltaville Middle School
1000 Main Street
Deltaville, Virginia 23043

      Re: Jennifer Parent (DOB: 01/01/91)
      School: Deltaville Middle School

Dear Dr. Temple:

My daughter Jennifer Parent is an eighth grade special education student at Deltaville Middle School. Ms. Adams has been using the One-Size Fits All reading program in her special education classes with my daughter. I would like to prepare for our upcoming IEP meeting by reading the research on that reading program.

Please send a copy of the research to me or tell me where it is available on a website so that I may be an informed participant at the meeting.

If you have questions about my request, please call me at work (899-555-9876) or at home (899-555-1234) after 6 p.m., or you can email me at maryparent@deltavilleva.com. Thank you in advance for your help.

Sincerely,

Mary Parent

#3. Sample Letter to Request Reading First Application

MARY PARENT
17456 GENERAL PULLER HIGHWAY
DELTAVILLE, VIRGINIA 23043
899-555-1234

April 1, 2006

Dr. Candace David, Superintendent
Hartfield County Public Schools
1000 Center Street
Hartfield, Virginia 23071

Re: Reading First Applications

Dear Dr. David:

I would appreciate a copy of the Reading First applications that were filed seeking grants and/or funds for the 2002-2003, 2003-2004, and 2004-2005 academic years.

If you need anything further from me to comply with this request, please call me at work (899-555-9876) or at home (899-555-1234) after 6 p.m., or you can email me at maryparent@deltavilleva.com.

Thank you in advance for your cooperation.

Sincerely,

Mary Parent

#4. Sample Letter Objecting to Retention of Child with a Disability

MARY PARENT

17456 GENERAL PULLER HIGHWAY
DELTAVILLE, VIRGINIA 23043
899-555-1234

May 1, 2006

Dr. Malcolm Higgins, Director
Special Education Services
Hartfield County Public Schools
1000 Center Street
Hartfield, Virginia 23071

Re: Jonathan Parent (DOB: 01/01/95)
School: Stingray Point Elementary School, Fourth Grade

Dear Dr. Higgins:

As you are aware, my son, Jonathan Parent, is a fourth grade student at Stingray Point Elementary School. Jonathan has been receiving special education services for his reading and writing problems since the first grade. At that time, he was reading at the beginning Kindergarten level. Now, as a fourth grade student, three years later, he has progressed barely one year in his reading grade equivalent level as measured by the diagnostic reading tests administered by your staff.

Yesterday we had another IEP meeting to discuss Jonathan's lack of progress. The staff told me that they believe that he has made a great deal of progress. Several members of the IEP team recommended that Jonathan repeat the fourth grade so that he can have more reading instruction before he attempts fifth grade work.

Recently we obtained private testing of Jonathan, which confirmed your districts own testing. Several copies of that report were given to the IEP Committee members. Jonathan has made less than a year's gain in reading over the past three years. The team says that Jonathan is making progress and yet is recommending retention.

My husband and I feel that retention is inappropriate. We understand that special education is a program designed to provide specialized instruction to meet Jonathan's unique needs. He needs to read at his age and grade level.

Retention is not a form of specialized instruction.

We are asking to meet again as a team to design a plan for specialized instruction that will teach Jonathan the reading skills that the school district requires fourth graders to learn so that they are prepared to enter the fifth grade.

We are available to meet on any Wednesday or Thursday for the next three weeks. Please call me at work (555-9876) or at home (555-1234) after 6 p.m., or you can email me at maryparent@deltavilleva.com to schedule the meeting. Thank you in advance for your help.

Sincerely,

Mary Parent

#5. Sample Letter from an Attorney Who Used NCLB to Request Reading Research and File

Peter W. D. Wright
ATTORNEY AT LAW

P. O. Box 1008
Deltaville, Virginia 23043-1008

(804) 776-7008
efax (202) 318-3239

June 12, 2006

Dr. Malcolm Higgins, Director
Special Education Services
Hartfield County Public Schools
1000 Center Street
Hartfield, Virginia 23071

Re: Jennifer Parent (DOB: 01/01/91)
School: Deltaville Middle School, Eighth Grade

Dear Dr. Higgins:

Jennifer's parents have consulted with me about their concerns regarding their daughter's inability to read. They advised that Jennifer has received several years of special education to address her reading and writing deficits. Despite your school system's best efforts, her reading has not improved and she is reading at the third grade level. The parents explained that her lack of progress appears directly related to the school district's rigid insistence on continuing to use the One Size Fits All educational reading program with Jennifer.

As you are aware, more than two years ago, Congress enacted the *No Child Left Behind Act*. One focus of the law is the requirement that schools use effective research based reading remediation programs. The "purpose" portion of the "Reading First" section of that statute states that it is:

> (1) To provide assistance to State educational agencies and local educational agencies in establishing reading programs for students in kindergarten through grade 3 that are based on scientifically based reading research, to ensure that every student can read at grade level or above not later than the end of grade 3. (20 U. S. C. § 6361)

The statute defines the essential components of reading instruction as follows:

> **(3) ESSENTIAL COMPONENTS OF READING INSTRUCTION**- The term 'essential components of reading instruction' means explicit and systematic instruction in —
>
> (A) phonemic awareness;
> (B) phonics;
> (C) vocabulary development;
> (D) reading fluency, including oral reading skills; and
> (E) reading comprehension strategies. (20 U. S. C. § 6368)

In subsection six of the same statute, *No Child Left Behind* describes Scientifically Based Reading Research.

> **(6) SCIENTIFICALLY BASED READING RESEARCH**- The term 'scientifically based reading research' means research that —
>
> (A) applies rigorous, systematic, and objective procedures to obtain valid knowledge relevant to reading development, reading instruction, and reading difficulties; and
>
> (B) includes research that —
>
> > (i) employs systematic, empirical methods that draw on observation or experiment;
> >
> > (ii) involves rigorous data analyses that are adequate to test the stated hypotheses and justify the general conclusions drawn;
> >
> > (iii) relies on measurements or observational methods that provide valid data across evaluators and observers and across multiple measurements and observations; and
> >
> > (iv) has been accepted by a peer-reviewed journal or approved by a panel of independent experts through a comparably rigorous, objective, and scientific review. (20 U. S. C. § 6368)

The parents advised me that they repeatedly shared their concerns about the One Size Fits All reading program with your staff. In light of their concerns, I would appreciate your providing me with the "scientifically based research" that was relied upon to support the continued use of the One Size Fits All reading program with Jennifer.

In addition to the preceding request for information, also enclosed is an Authorization for the Release of Records of Jennifer Parent. In addition to the research, please also send me a complete copy of Jennifer's educational records, including copies of all audio and video tape recordings and transcripts of any educational sessions and or educational meetings about Jennifer.

If there are any questions, please advise. Thanks.

Sincerely,

Peter W. D. Wright

cc: Mr. and Ms. Parent
Enc.   Authorization for the Release of Records of Jennifer Parent

#6. Sample Complaint Letter to U. S. Department of Education Regarding Failure of State and School District to Provide Information about Report Cards

MARY PARENT
17456 GENERAL PULLER HIGHWAY
DELTAVILLE, VIRGINIA 23043
899-555-1234

September 15, 2006

Robert Baker, Secretary's Regional Representative
U. S. Department of Education
The Wanamaker Building
100 Penn Square East-Suite 505
Philadelphia, PA 19107

Re: Deltaville Middle School
Hartfield County, Virginia

Dear Mr. Baker:

I am writing to you in your capacity as the "Regional Representative" for the Secretary of the U. S. Department of Education. I understand that you are the Secretary's Regional Representative who oversees the Commonwealth of Virginia.

I am trying to obtain copies of my school and school district report cards. I have looked on the Virginia Department of Education website and the Hartfield County school district website and cannot find this information. I sent an email to our Superintendent of Schools and requested the information. She did not reply. I sent a copy of that email to our State Commissioner of Education and requested that he provide this information. He did not reply. Enclosed are copies of these emails.

It is my understanding that the Virginia Department of Education is responsible for providing this information to the public. I would be most appreciative if you would provide me with a copy of the requested information. I am seeking a copy of the report cards for my school and my school district. My child attends Deltaville Middle School in Hartfield County, Virginia.

Please advise our State and school district that this information should be readily available to the public. If you or your designated representative write or email the Superintendent or State Commissioner, I would also appreciate your sending me a copy of that communication. My email address is maryparent@deltavilleva.com.

If you have questions about my request, please call me at work (899-555-9876) or at home (899-555-1234) after 6 p.m. I look forward to hearing from you. Thanks in advance for your help.

Sincerely,

Mary Parent

Enc.   Copy of email to Superintendent of Schools for Hartfield County
        Copy of email to Virginia Commissioner of Education

Chapter 11

#7. Sample Complaint letter to U. S. Department of Education about Failure to Provide Information about Title I Schools

MARY PARENT
17456 GENERAL PULLER HIGHWAY
DELTAVILLE, VIRGINIA 23043
899-555-1234

September 15, 2006

Robert Baker, Secretary's Regional Representative
The Wanamaker Building
100 Penn Square East-Suite 505
Philadelphia, PA 19107

      Re: Deltaville Middle School
             Hartfield County, Virginia

Dear Mr. Baker:

I am writing to you in your capacity as the Regional Representative for the Secretary of the U. S. Department of Education. From a web search of the U. S. Department of Education's website, I understand that you are the Secretary's Regional Representative who oversees the Commonwealth of Virginia.

I am trying to determine whether my child's school receives funds under Title I of the No Child Left Behind Act. I have looked on the Virginia Department of Education's website and Hartfield County's website and cannot find this information.

I then sent an email to our local Superintendent of Schools for Hartfield County and requested the information. She did not reply. I sent a copy of that email to our State Commissioner of Education and requested that he provide that information. He did not reply. Enclosed are copies of the emails.

It is my understanding that the Virginia Department of Education is responsible for providing this information to the public. I would be most appreciative if you would provide me with a copy of the requested information. Does Deltaville Middle School in Hartfield County, Virginia receive Title I funds?

I would also be most appreciative if you would instruct our State and our local school district that this information should be readily available to the public. If you or your designated representative write or email either the local Superintendent or State Commissioner, I would also be most appreciative if you would send me a copy of that communication. My email address is maryparent@deltavilleva.com.

If you have questions about my request, please call me at work (899-555-9876) or at home (899-555-1234) after 6 p.m. I look forward to hearing from you. Thanks in advance for your help.

Sincerely,

Mary Parent

#8. Sample Letter from School Board Chair to State Department of Education to Request Supplemental Service Providers

JEFFERSON A. GARDNER
4332 STINGRAY POINT LANE
DELTAVILLE, VIRGINIA 23043
899-555-0001

March 1, 2006

Sara Wright Murphy, Commissioner
Virginia Department of Education
P. O. Box 2120
Richmond, Virginia 23218

Dear Commissioner Murphy:

I am the Chair of the Hartfield County School Board. This year we were required to offer Supplemental Educational Services to the children in our school district who are from low-income families. We mailed a letter to all eligible families. We had a meeting at the school with the parents. We gave each family the list of state approved supplemental service providers.

We are concerned about the list that we provided to our parents. None of the providers is in or near our school district. I have read everything I can find on this requirement. I see that it is the state's responsibility to give school districts a list of approved supplemental service providers in their general geographic locations.

We are doing everything that is required of us to raise student achievement. We need your help. It must be obvious to you that a only a small handful of state-approved tutors are not sufficient to meet the needs of the Commonwealth of Virginia.

I am requesting that you provide us with a list of approved tutors who are within fifty miles of Deltaville. I look forward to hearing from you.

Sincerely,

Jefferson A. Gardner, Chair
Hartfield County School Board

#9. Sample Letter from School Board Chair to U. S. Department of Education about Inadequate State List of Supplemental Service Providers

JEFFERSON A. GARDNER
4332 STINGRAY POINT LANE
DELTAVILLE, VIRGINIA 23043
899-555-0001

April 1, 2006

Robert Baker, Secretary's Regional Representative
U. S. Department of Education
The Wanamaker Building
100 Penn Square East-Suite 505
Philadelphia, PA 19107

       Re: Hartfield County, Virginia

Dear Mr. Baker:

I am writing to you in your capacity as the "Regional Representative" for the Secretary of the U. S. Department of Education. From a search of the U. S. Department of Education's website, I understand that you are the Secretary's Regional Representative who oversees the Commonwealth of Virginia.

I am the Chair of the Hartfield County School Board. We are required to offer Supplemental Educational Services to children in our school district this year. We followed the requirements but have nothing to offer to these children. The state list of approved tutors is very short. None of the tutors on the list are anywhere near our school district.

Our Board has read the No Child Left Behind law and Guidance publications. We see that the Virginia Department of Education is responsible for contacting potential service providers annually. Our Board contacted a number of well-respected, qualified tutors located in Hartfield County and adjacent counties. We wanted to determine why their names were not on the state-approved list. The people we contacted said they had not heard of such a list and that they had not been contacted by anyone about such a list. We asked these people to contact the Virginia Department of Education in order to obtain and file an application to be a Supplemental Service Provider.

While we have taken these steps on our own, we are asking for your help. Our school district is over-burdened. Our staff should not have to undertake this task. Can you ensure that Virginia creates and maintains a reasonable and useful list of Supplemental Service Providers for our area, and that the list is updated annually?

Our school district is trying to comply with NCLB. We recognize that we must make improvements. We need the extra support these tutors will provide if we are to meet our Adequate Yearly Progress goals and avoid restructuring measures in our school district.

       Sincerely,

       Jefferson A. Gardner, Chair
       Hartfield County School Board

#10. Sample Letter to Request Improvements in Parental Information Policy

PENELOPE LADD
8730 EAGLE POINT LANE
DELTAVILLE, VIRGINIA 23043
899-555-4619

March 1, 2006

Jefferson Gardner, Chair
Hartfield County School Board
1000 Center Street
Hartfield, Virginia 23071

      Re: Parental Involvement Policy

Dear Mr. Gardner:

As you are aware, I am the Chair of the Parent-Teacher Association at Deltaville Elementary School. At the request of several members, I requested a copy of our school's No Child Left Behind "Parental Involvement Policy." When we compared this document with information from the U.S. Department of Education website about parental involvement policies, we realized that our policy needed to be changed and updated.

We formed a committee to revise our school's parent involvement policy to include the components required by the No Child Left Behind Act. As you know, we invited teachers and administrators from all Hartfield County schools to participate. Some school personnel were very receptive and provided useful input.

Enclosed is the parental involvement policy that our committee of teachers, parents, administrators and community members compiled. We request that the school board approve our revised Policy at the next meeting. Our members will be available at the meeting to answer questions. We will also bring copies of the documentation we used in designing this policy.

I look forward to hearing from you.

           Sincerely,

           Penelope Ladd
           President, Deltaville PTA

Enclosure: Draft parental involvement policy

#11. Sample Letter from Teacher to State Department of Education to Request Information and Application as Supplemental Educational Service Provider

LORI ASPEN SHERY
4332 JACKSON CREEK CIRCLE
DELTAVILLE, VIRGINIA 23043
804-555-5678

August 15, 2006

Sara Wright Murphy, Commissioner
Virginia Department of Education
P. O. Box 2120
Richmond, Virginia 23218

      Re: Supplemental Educational Service Provider

Dear Commissioner Murphy:

I am a public school teacher who retired last year after teaching for more than 25 years. During those years, I taught students at the elementary school, middle school and high school levels. I also provided one-to-one tutoring for children with special educational needs.

Since I retired, I am exploring the possibility of developing a tutoring business. I am interested in providing individualized tutoring in core academic subjects and/or providing remediation in the acquisition of reading, writing, spelling, and arithmetic skills.

I understand that the No Child Left Behind Act requires states to create a list of "Supplemental Educational Service Providers." I read the definition of these providers in the law at 20 U. S. C. § 6316(e)(12)(C). I also read the Guidance publication about Supplemental Education Services published by the U. S. Department of Education.

I believe I am qualified to be a provider, either as an individual with a sole "Schedule C" business, or in a partnership with another person, or perhaps as a for-profit or non-profit corporation. Please let me know this is correct.

I understand that if I am approved, I need to provide documentary evidence to establish that the children I serve are benefiting from my program. Is pre- and post-testing on individualized norm-referenced educational tests an appropriate method? Do you have suggestions about other ways to incorporate these measures?

Please send me an application, information and publications about Virginia's Supplemental Educational Service Provider program. I look forward to hearing from you.

                                    Sincerely,

                                    Lori Aspen Shery

#12. Sample Letter from Member of Armed Forces to Request Information about the Troops-to-Teacher Program

CHARLES S. COTTON
15 WINDMILL POINT LANE
DELTAVILLE, VIRGINIA 23043
804-555-6789

September 15, 2006

Robert Baker, Secretary's Regional Representative
The Wanamaker Building
100 Penn Square East-Suite 505
Philadelphia, PA 19107

Sara Wright Murphy, Commissioner
Virginia Department of Education
P. O. Box 2120
Richmond, Virginia 23218

Re: Troops-to-Teachers

Dear Mr. Baker and Ms. Wright:

I do not know if I should direct my letter to Mr. Baker or to Ms. Murphy. From a search of the U. S. Department of Education website, I learned that Mr. Baker is the Secretary's Regional Representative who oversees the Commonwealth of Virginia. I am also sending this letter to Ms. Murphy in her capacity as Commissioner of the Virginia Department of Education.

I have served in the Armed Forces for more than twenty years and will soon retire. My background and training is in mechanical engineering. My experience includes educating both new recruits and seasoned veterans in vocational and technical areas. I need 15 credit hours to earn a bachelor's degree.

I heard about a "Troops-to-Teachers" program that will allow me to work in a vocational or technical field with my present qualifications. I understand from reading the No Child Left Behind law at Title II, Subpart 1, Chapter A, beginning at 20 U. S. C. § 6671, that when I complete my bachelor's degree, I may be eligible to teach general education classes.

It appears that if I work with children with disabilities or from low-income families, I may also be eligible for a stipend of up to $5,000.00 or a bonus of up to $10,000.00. I am willing to relocate if necessary to teach under the "Troops-to-Teachers" program.

Please send me an application, information and other material that you have about this program.

Looking forward to hearing from you.

Sincerely,

Charles Stuart Cotton

#13. Sample Letter from a Conscientious Objector to a School Superintendent about Access to Student Information by Military Recruiters

WILLIAM DUNSTAN

51 STOVE POINT
DELTAVILLE, VIRGINIA 23043
804-555-6789

September 15, 2006

Dr. Candace David, Superintendent
Hartfield County Public Schools
1000 Center Street
Hartfield, Virginia 23071

Re: Information released to Military Recruiters

Dear Dr. David:

From radio talk shows and the newspaper, I understand that many public high schools in the country have a policy of releasing information about their graduates to universities and potential employers without the knowledge of their parents. I understand that there has been some controversy about the release of the same information to military recruiters. They all referred to the law, No Child Left Behind.

I just read 20 U. S. C. § 7908 of that law. The law mandates that schools: "shall provide military recruiters the same access to secondary school students as is provided generally to post secondary educational institutions or to prospective employers of those students." However, the law also says that parents may object to the release of this information.

I was a conscientious objector during the Vietnam War. I do not want any information about my son released to military recruiters. I realize that this request also prohibits you from releasing information to "post-secondary educational institutions" or "prospective employers" unless I sign a specific authorization for the release of information to a specific college or university.

Pursuant to 20 U. S. C. § 7908(a)(2), this letter is my **Notice** to you and our school district that release of information about my son is prohibited.

I understand that all parents in our school district should have been notified of their right to make such a request. I do not recall receiving such a notification. I request that you send me a copy of what was previously sent out to all parents. If parents have not been notified, please rectify this immediately.

Many thanks.

Sincerely,

William Dunstan

cc: Principal, Hartfield High School

#14. Sample Letter from a Military Veteran to a School Superintendent about Access to Student Information by Military Recruiters

RORY HARRISON
25678 GENERAL PULLER HWY
DELTAVILLE, VIRGINIA 23043
804-555-6789

September 15, 2006

Dr. Candace David, Superintendent
Hartfield County Public Schools
1000 Center Street
Hartfield, Virginia 23071

       Re: Information released to Military Recruiters

Dear Dr. David:

Yesterday I received a Form from my son's school explaining that I can prohibit the release of information about my son to "military recruiters," "post secondary educational institutions," and "prospective employers." The Form noted that the legal authority is based on the No Child Left Behind law and included a legal citation to 20 U. S. C. § 7908. I located and read that statute. From my reading, I understand that schools must provide military recruiters with access to the same information about students that schools have routinely provided to colleges and universities.

I graduated from the Naval Academy and have served the United States Navy with distinction for more than 20 years. Recruitment of qualified students for military service is a complex process. At one point, I served as a recruiter. I am writing to you as a parent who is also on active duty with the Navy.

I hope you will assure parents who contact you that the information you provide is limited and often consists of nothing more than the student's name, address, date of birth, class rank and expected graduation date. This allows the Armed Forces to send graduating seniors information about the benefits of military service. The information is not used for any other purpose than to help in recruitment efforts.

As a resident in this community for many years, I know many students and their parents. I would be happy to talk with your staff and the student body about the information that may be requested, how the information is used, and the benefits of service to our country.

Many thanks.

Sincerely,

Rory Harrison

cc: Principal, Hartfield High School

115

#15. Sample Letter to U. S. Department of Education about a School District's Failure to Test Children with Disabilities

STEPHANIE RICH
9823 TELSTAR CIRCLE
URBANNA, VIRGINIA 23175
899-555-1234

September 15, 2006

Robert Baker, Secretary's Regional Representative
U. S. Department of Education
The Wanamaker Building
100 Penn Square East-Suite 505
Philadelphia, PA 19107

    Re: Annual No Child Left Behind testing
             Hartfield County, Virginia

Dear Mr. Baker:

I am writing to you in your capacity as the Regional Representative for the Secretary of the U. S. Department of Education. From a search of the U. S. Department of Education website, I understand that you are the Secretary's Regional Representative who oversees the Commonwealth of Virginia.

I am writing about a possible problem that involves the failure to test some children in special education placements. A friend who works in the school district office advised me that when a child is placed in an out-of-district special education placement, the child is purposefully removed from the school district's database that is used to track students in the system. Because the school removes these students from the database, the families do not receive information that our district sends to families of students who attend public schools.

My niece is a child with a disability who was placed in an out-of-district placement. The school did not test my niece on the state proficiency tests last year. My friend advised me that none of the students with disabilities in out-of-district special education placements were tested. When our school district calculated their AYP figures, they tied these figures in to the student database. Since the district does not count students with disabilities who are in out-of-district placements, their calculations may not be accurate. Other parents have told me that they were strongly encouraged to keep their children with special educational needs home from school during the annual testing.

There may be a reasonable explanation for the methods of calculating AYP used by our school district. Their policy may be perfectly proper. However, my friend expressed concerns because the removal of students with disabilities from the database was conducted in a "hush-hush" manner so few people knew about it.

I would appreciate your looking into this matter and confirming that the administrators of Hartfield County Public Schools are accountable for educating all students and are reporting the results of the annual assessments in a legally proper manner. If my understanding of these requirements is incorrect, please clarify this for me.

Sincerely,

Stephanie Rich

12 | TABLE OF STATUTES

This Table of Statutes is a complete list of the United States Code sections cross-referenced with No Child Left Behind Act.

For example, the first entry is the United States Code at 20 U. S. C. Section (§) 6301. The citation is 20 U. S. C. § 6301 and is also Section 1001 of the No Child Left Behind Act. A few code sections are in Title 25 and are identified as 25 U. S. C. §.

20 United States Code Sections & Description	NCLB §§
TITLE I: Improving the Academic Achievement of the Disadvantaged	
§ 6301 Statement of Purpose	1001
§ 6302 Authorization of appropriations	1002
§ 6303 School improvement	1003
§ 6304 State administration	1004
Part A, Basic Program Requirements	
Subpart 1 - Basic Program Requirements	
§ 6311 State plans	1111
§ 6312 Local educational agency plans	1112
§ 6313 Eligible school attendance areas	1113
§ 6314 Schoolwide programs	1114
§ 6315 Targeted assistance schools	1115
§ 6316 Academic assessment and local educational agency and school improvement	1116
§ 6317 School support and recognition	1117
§ 6318 Parental involvement	1118
§ 6319 Qualifications for teachers and paraprofessionals	1119
§ 6320 Participation of children enrolled in private schools	1120
§ 6321 Fiscal requirements	1120A
§ 6322 Coordination requirements	1120B
Subpart 2 – Allocations	
§ 6331 Grants for the outlying areas and the Secretary of the Interior	1121
§ 6332 Allocations to States	1122
§ 6333 Basic grants to local educational agencies	1123
§ 6334 Concentration grants to local educational agencies	1124a
§ 6335 Targeted grants to local educational agencies	1125
§ 6336 Adequacy of funding of targeted grants to local educational agencies in fiscal years after fiscal year 2001	112AA

§ 6337 Education finance incentive grant program	1125A
§ 6338 Special allocation procedures	1126
§ 6339 Carryover and waiver	1127
Part B, Student Reading Skills Improvement Grants	
Subpart 1 - Reading First	
§ 6361 Purposes	1201
§ 6362 Formula grants to State educational agencies	1202
§ 6363 State formula grant applications	1203
§ 6364 Targeted assistance grants	1204
§ 6365 External evaluation	1205
§ 6366 National activities	1206
§ 6367 Information dissemination	1207
§ 6368 Definitions	1208
Subpart 2 - Early Reading First	
§ 6371 Purposes; definitions	1221
§ 6372 Local Early Reading First grants	1222
§ 6373 Federal administration	1223
§ 6374 Information dissemination	1224
§ 6375 Reporting requirements	1225
§ 6376 Evaluation	1226
Subpart 3 - William F Goodling Even Start Family Literacy Programs	
§ 6381 Statement of purpose	1231
§ 6381a Program authorized	1232
§ 6381b State educational agency programs	1233
§ 6381c Uses of funds	1234
§ 6381d Program elements	1235
§ 6381e Eligible participants	1236
§ 6381f Applications	1237
§ 6381g Award of subgrants	1238
§ 6381h Evaluation	1239
§ 6381i Indicators of program quality	1240
§ 6381j Research	1241
§ 6381k Construction	1242
Subpart 4—Improving Literacy Through School Libraries	
§ 6383 Improving literacy through school libraries	1251
Part C, Education of Migratory Children	
§ 6391 Program purpose	1301
§ 6392 Program authorized	1302
§ 6393 State allocations	1303
§ 6394 State applications; services	1304
§ 6395 Secretarial approval; peer review	1305
§ 6396 Comprehensive needs assessment and service-delivery plan; authorized activities	1306
§ 6397 Bypass	1307
§ 6398 Coordination of migrant education activities	1308
§ 6399 Definitions	1309

Part D, Prevention and Intervention Programs for Children and Youth who are Neglected, Delinquent, or At-Risk	
§ 6421 Purpose and program authorization	1401
§ 6422 Payments for programs under this Part	1402
Subpart 1 - State Agency Programs	
§ 6431 Eligibility	1411
§ 6432 Allocation of funds	1412
§ 6433 State reallocation of funds	1413
§ 6434 State plan and State agency applications	1414
§ 6435 Use of funds	1415
§ 6436 Institution-wide projects	1416
§ 6437 Three-year programs or projects	1417
§ 6438 Transition services	1418
§ 6439 Evaluation; technical assistance; annual model program	1419
Subpart 2 - Local Agency Programs	
§ 6451 Purpose	1421
§ 6452 Programs operated by local educational agencies	1422
§ 6453 Local educational agency applications	1423
§ 6454 Uses of funds	1424
§ 6455 Program requirements for correctional facilities receiving funds under this section	1425
§ 6456 Accountability	1426
Subpart 3 - General Provisions	
§ 6471 Program evaluations	1431
§ 6472 Definitions	1432
Part E - National Assessment of Title I	
§ 6491 Evaluations	1501
§ 6492 Demonstrations of innovative practices	1502
§ 6493 Assessment evaluation	1503
§ 6494 Close Up fellowship program	1504
Part F - Comprehensive School Reform	
§ 6511 Purpose	1601
§ 6512 Program authorization	1602
§ 6513 State applications	
§ 6514 State use of funds	1603
§ 6515 Local applications	1604
§ 6516 Local use of funds	1605
§ 6517 Evaluation and reports	1606
§ 6518 Quality initiatives	1607
Part G - Advanced Placement Programs	
§ 6531 Short title	1701
§ 6532 Purposes	1702
§ 6533 Funding distribution rule	1703
§ 6534 Advanced placement test fee program	1704

§ 6821 Formula grants to States	3111
§ 6822 Native American and Alaska Native children in school	3112
§ 6823 State and specially qualified agency plans	3113
§ 6824 Within-State allocations	3114
§ 6825 Subgrants to eligible entities	3115
§ 6826 Local plans	3116
Subpart 2 – Accountability and Administration	
§ 6841 Evaluations	3121
§ 6842 Achievement objectives and accountability	3122
§ 6843 Reporting requirements	3123
§ 6844 Coordination with related programs	3124
§ 6845 Rules of construction	3125
§ 6846 Legal authority under State law	3126
§ 6847 Civil rights	3127
§ 6848 Programs for Native Americans and Puerto Rico	3128
§ 6849 Prohibition	3129
Subpart 3 – National Activities	
§ 6861 National professional development project	3131
Subpart 4 – Definitions	
§ 6871 Eligible entity	3141
Part B - Improving Language Instruction Educational Programs	
§ 6891 Short title	3201
§ 6892 Purpose	3202
§ 6893 Native American children in school	3203
§ 6894 Residents of the territories and freely associated states	3204
Subpart 1 – Program Development and Enhancement	
§ 6911 Financial assistance for language instruction educational programs	3211
§ 6912 Program enhancement activities	3212
§ 6913 Comprehensive school and systemwide improvement activities	3213
§ 6914 Applications	3214
§ 6915 Capacity building	3215
§ 6916 Programs for Native Americans and Puerto Rico	3216
§ 6917 Evaluations	3217
§ 6918 Construction	3218
Subpart 2 – Research, Evaluation, and Dissemination	
§ 6931 Authority	3221
§ 6932 Research	3222
§ 6933 Academic excellence awards	3223
§ 6934 State grant program	3224
§ 6935 Instruction materials development	3225
Subpart 3 – Professional Development	
§ 6951 Professional development grants	3231

Subpart 4 – Emergency Immigrant Education Program	
§ 6961 Purpose	3241
§ 6962 State administrative costs	3242
§ 6963 Withholding	3243
§ 6964 State allotments	3244
§ 6965 State applications	3245
§ 6966 Administrative provisions	3246
§ 6967 Uses of funds	3247
§ 6968 Reports	3248
Subpart 5 – Administration	
§ 6981 Release time	3251
§ 6982 Notification	3252
§ 6983 Coordination and reporting requirements	3253
Part C - General Provisions	
§ 7011 Definitions	3301
§ 7012 Parental notification	3302
§ 7013 National Clearinghouse	3303
§ 7014 Regulations	3304
TITLE IV – 21st Century Schools	
Part A – Safe and Drug-Free Schools and Communities	
§ 7101 Short title	4001
§ 7102 Purpose	4002
§ 7103 Authorization of appropriations	4003
Subpart 1 - State Grants	
§ 7111 Reservations and allotments	4111
§ 7112 Reservation of State funds for safe and drug-free schools	4112
§ 7113 State application	4113
§ 7114 Local educational agency program	4114
§ 7115 Authorized activities	4115
§ 7116 Reporting	4116
§ 7117 Programs for Native Hawaiians	4117
Subpart 2 - National Programs	
§ 7131 Federal activities	4121
§ 7132 Impact evaluation	4122
§ 7133 Hate crime prevention	4123
§ 7134 Safe and Drug-Free Schools and Communities Advisory Committee	4124
§ 7135 National coordinator program	4125
§ 7136 Community service grant program	4126
§ 7137 School Security Technology and Resource Center	4127
§ 7138 National Center for School and Youth Safety	4128
§ 7139 Grants to reduce alcohol abuse	4129
§ 7140 Mentoring programs	4130
Subpart 3 - Gun Possession	

Subpart 1 - Charter School Programs	
§ 7221 Purpose	5201
§ 7221a Program authorized	5202
§ 7221b Applications	5203
§ 7221c Administration	5204
§ 7221d National activities	5205
§ 7221e Federal formula allocation during first year and for successive enrollment expansions	5206
§ 7221f Solicitation of input from charter school operators	5207
§ 7221g Records transfer	5208
§ 7221h Paperwork reduction	5209
§ 7221i Definitions	5210
§ 7221j Authorization of appropriations	5211
Subpart 2 - Credit Enhancement Initiatives To Assist Charter School Facility Acquisition, Construction, and Renovation	
§ 7223 Purpose	5221
§ 7223a Grants to eligible entities	5222
§ 7223b Applications	5223
§ 7223c Charter school objectives	5224
§ 7223d Reserve account	5225
§ 7223e Limitation on administrative costs	5226
§ 7223f Audits and reports	5227
§ 7223g No full faith and credit for grantee obligations	5228
§ 7223h Recovery of funds	5229
§ 7223i Definitions	5230
§ 7223j Authorization of appropriations	5231
Subpart 3 — Voluntary Public School Choice Programs	
§ 7225 Grants	5241
§ 7225a Uses of funds	5242
§ 7225b Applications	5243
§ 7225c Priorities	5244
§ 7225d Requirements and voluntary participation	5245
§ 7225e Evaluations	5246
§ 7225f Definitions	5247
§ 7225g Authorization of appropriations	5248
Part 3 – Magnet Schools Assistance	
§7231 Findings and purpose	5301
§7231a Definition	5302
§7231b Program authorized	5303
§7231c Eligibility	5304
§7231d Applications and requirements	5305
§7231e Priority	5306
§7231f Use of funds	5307
§7231g Prohibition	5308
§7231h Limitations	5309
§7231i Evaluations	5310
§7231j Authorization of appropriations; reservation	5311

Part D - Fund for the Improvement of Education	
§7241j Authorization of appropriations; reservation	5401
Subpart 1 - Fund for the Improvement of Education	
§ 7243 Programs authorized	5411
§ 7243a Applications	5412
§ 7243b Program requirements	5413
§ 7243c Studies of national significance	5414
Subpart 2 - Elementary and Secondary School Counseling Programs	
§ 7245 Elementary and secondary school counseling programs	5421
Subpart 3 - Partnerships in Character Education	
§ 7247 Partnerships in Character Education program	5431
Subpart 4 – Smaller Learning Communities	
§ 7249 Smaller learning communities	5441
Subpart 5 – Reading Is Fundamental	
§ 7251 Inexpensive book distribution program for reading motivation	5451
Subpart 6 - Gifted and Talented Students	
§ 7253 Short title	5461
§ 7253a Purpose	5462
§ 7253b Rule of construction	5463
§ 7253c Authorized programs	5464
§ 7253d Program priorities	5465
§ 7253e General provisions	5466
Subpart 7 - Star Schools Program	
§ 7255 Short title	5471
§ 7255a Purposes	5472
§ 7255b Grant program authorized	5473
§ 7255c Applications	5474
§ 7255d Other grant assistance	5475
§ 7255e Administrative provisions	5476
§ 7255f Definitions	5477
Subpart 8 - Ready to Teach	
§ 7257 Grants	5481
§ 7257a Application required	5482
§ 7257b Reports and evaluation	5483
§ 7257c Digital educational programming grants	5484
§ 7257d Administrative costs	5485
Subpart 9 – Foreign Language Assistance Program	
§ 7259 Short title	5491
§ 7259a Program authorized	5492
§ 7259b Applications	5493
§ 7259c Elementary school foreign language incentive program	5494

Subpart 10 - Physical Education	
§ 7261 Short title	5501
§ 7261a Purpose	5502
§ 7261b Program authorized	5503
§ 7261c Applications	5504
§ 7261d Requirements	5505
§ 7261e Administrative provisions	5506
§ 7261f Supplement, not supplant	5507
Subpart 11 - Community Technology Centers	
§ 7263 Purpose and program authorization	5511
§ 7263a Eligibility and application requirements	5512
§ 7263b Uses of funds	5513
Subpart 12 - Educational, Cultural, Apprenticeship, and Exchange Programs for Alaska Natives, Native Hawaiians, and Their Historical Whaling and Trading Partners in Massachusetts	
§ 7265 Short title	5521
§ 7265a Findings and purposes	5522
§ 7265b Program authorization	5523
§ 7265c Administrative provisions	5524
§ 7265d Availability of funds	5525
§ 7265e Definitions	5526
Subpart 13 - Excellence in Economic Education	
§ 7267 Short title	5531
§ 7267a Purpose and goals	5532
§ 7267b Grant program authorized	5533
§ 7267c Applications	5534
§ 7267d Requirements	5535
§ 7267e Administrative provisions	5536
§ 7267f Supplement, not supplant	5537
Subpart 14 - Grants to Improve the Mental Health of Children	
§ 7269 Grants for the integration of schools and mental health systems	5541
§ 7269a Promotion of school readiness through early childhood emotional and social development	5542
Subpart 15 - Arts in Education	
§ 7271 Assistance for arts education	5551
Subpart 16 - Parental Assistance and Local Family Information Centers	
§ 7273 Purposes	5561
§ 7273a Grants authorized	5562
§ 7273b Applications	5563
§ 7273c Uses of funds	5564
§ 7273d Administrative provisions	5565
§ 7273e Local family information centers	5567

Subpart 17 - Combating Domestic Violence	
§ 7275 Grants to combat the impact of experiencing or witnessing domestic violence on elementary and secondary school children	5571
Subpart 18 - Healthy, High-Performance Schools	
§ 7277 Grant program authorized	5581
§ 7277a State uses of funds	5582
§ 7277b Local uses of funds	5583
§ 7277c Report to Congress	5584
§ 7277d Limitations	5585
§ 7277e Healthy, high-performance school building defined	5586
Subpart 19 - Grants for Capital Expenses of Providing Equitable Services for Private School Students	
§ 7279 Grant program authorized	5591
§ 7279a Uses of funds	5592
§ 7279b Allotments to States	5593
§ 7279c Subgrants to local educational agencies	5594
§ 7279d Capital expenses defined	5595
§ 7279e Termination	5596
Subpart 20 - Additional Assistance for Certain Local Educational Agencies Impacted by Federal Property Acquisition	
§ 7281 Reservation	5601
§ 7281a Eligibility	5602
§ 7281b Maximum amount	5603
Subpart 21 - Women's Educational Equity Act	
§ 7283 Short title and findings	5611
§ 7283a Statement of purpose	5612
§ 7283b Programs authorized	5613
§ 7283c Applications	5614
§ 7283d Criteria and priorities	5615
§ 7283e Report	5616
§ 7283f Administration	5617
§ 7283g Amount	5618
TITLE VI — Flexibility and Accountability	
Part A - Improving Academic Achievement	
Subpart 1 - Accountability	
§ 7301 Grants for State assessments and related activities	6111
§ 7301a Grants for enhanced assessment instruments	6112
§ 7301b Funding	6113
Subpart 2 - Funding Transferability for State and Local Educational Agencies	
§ 7305 Short title	6121
§ 7305a Purpose	6122
§ 7305b Transferability of funds	6123

TITLE VII – Indian, Native Hawaiian, and Alaska Native Education	
Part A - Indian Education	
§ 7401 Statement of policy	7101
§ 7402 Purpose	7102
Subpart 1 - Formula Grants to Local Educational Agencies	
§ 7421 Purpose	7111
§ 7422 Grants to local educational agencies and tribes	7112
§ 7423 Amount of grants	7113
§ 7424 Applications	7114
§ 7425 Authorized services and activities	7115
§ 7426 Integration of services authorized	7116
§ 7427 Student eligibility forms	7117
§ 7428 Payments	7118
§ 7429 State educational agency review	7119
Subpart 2 - Special Programs and Projects To Improve Educational Opportunities for Indian Children	
§ 7441 Improvement of educational opportunities for Indian children	7121
§ 7442 Professional development for teachers and education professionals	7122
Subpart 3 - National Activities	
§ 7451 National research activities	7131
§ 7452 In-service training for teachers of Indian children	7132
§ 7453 Fellowships for Indian students	7133
§ 7454 Gifted and talented Indian students	7134
§ 7455 Grants to tribes for education administrative planning and development	7135
§ 7456 Improvement of educational opportunities for adult Indians	7136
Subpart 4 - Federal Administration	
§ 7471 National Advisory Council on Indian Education	7141
§ 7472 Peer review	7142
§ 7473 Preference for Indian applicants	7143
§ 7474 Minimum grant criteria	7144
Subpart 5 - Definitions; Authorizations of Appropriations	
§ 7491 Definitions	7151
§ 7492 Authorizations of appropriations	7152
Part B - Native Hawaiian Education	
§ 7511 Short title	7201
§ 7512 Findings	7202
§ 7513 Purposes	7203
§ 7514 Native Hawaiian Education Council and island councils	7204
§ 7515 Program authorized	7205
§ 7516 Administrative provisions	7206
§ 7517 Definitions	7207
Part C - Alaska Native Education	

§ 7541 Short title	7301
§ 7542 Findings	7302
§ 7543 Purposes	7303
§ 7544 Program authorized	7304
§ 7545 Administrative provisions	7305
§ 7546 Definitions	7306
NCLB § 702 - Conforming Amendments	702
NCLB § 703 - Savings Provisions	703
TITLE VIII - Impact Aid Program	
§ 7702 - Payments relating to federal acquisition of real property	801 (8001)
§ 7703 - Payments for eligible federally connected children	802 (8003)
§ 7707 - Construction	803 (8007)
§ 7709 - State consideration of payments in providing state aid	804 (8009)
§ 7714 - Authorization of appropriations	805 (8014)
TITLE IX – General Provisions	
Part A - Definitions	
§ 7801 Definitions	9101
§ 7802 Applicability of title	9102
§ 7803 Applicability to Bureau of Indian Affairs operated schools	9103
Part B - Flexibility in Use of Funds	
§ 7821 Consolidation of State administrative funds for elementary and secondary education programs	9201
§ 7822 Single local educational agency States	9202
§ 7823 Consolidation of funds for local administration	9203
§ 7824 Consolidated set-aside for Department of the Interior funds	9204
Part C - Coordination of Programs; Consolidated State and Local Plans and Applications	
§ 7841 Purpose	9301
§ 7842 Optional consolidated State plans or applications	9302
§ 7843 Consolidated reporting	9303
§ 7844 General applicability of State educational agency assurances	9304
§ 7845 Consolidated local plans or applications	9305
§ 7846 Other general assurances	9306
Part D - Waivers	
§ 7861 Waivers of statutory and regulatory requirements	9401
Part E - Uniform Provisions	
Subpart 1- Private Schools	
§ 7881 Participation by private school children and teachers	9501
§ 7882 Standards for by-pass	9502

§ 7883 Complaint process for participation of private school children	9503
§ 7884 By-pass determination process	9504
§ 7885 Prohibition against funds for religious worship or instruction	9505
§ 7886 Private, religious, and home schools	9506
Subpart 2 - Other Provisions	
§ 7901 Maintenance of effort	9521
§ 7902 Prohibition regarding State aid	9522
§ 7903 Privacy of assessment results	9523
§ 7904 School prayer	9524
§ 7905 Equal access to public school facilities	9525
§ 7906 General prohibitions	9526
§ 7907 Prohibitions on Federal Government and use of Federal funds	9527
§ 7908 Armed Forces recruiter access to students and student recruiting information	9528
§ 7909 Prohibition on federally sponsored testing	9529
§ 7910 Limitations on national testing or certification for teachers	9530
§ 7911 Prohibition on nationwide database	9531
§ 7912 Unsafe school choice option	9532
§ 7913 Prohibition on discrimination	9533
§ 7914 Civil rights	9534
§ 7915 Rulemaking	9535
§ 7916 Severability	9536
Part F - Evaluations	
§ 7941 Evaluations	9601
TITLE X — Repeals, Redesignations, and Amendments to Other Statutes	
Part A - Repeals	
NCLB § 1011 Repeals	
NCLB § 1012 Conforming clerical and technical amendments	
Part B - Redesignations	
NCLB § 1021 Comprehensive Regional Assistance Centers (Repealed)	
NCLB § 1022 National Diffusion Network (Repealed)	
NCLB § 1023 Eisenhower Regional Mathematics and Science Consortia (Repealed)	
NCLB § 1024 Technology-based technical assistance (Repealed)	
NCLB § 1025 Conforming amendments	
Part C - Homeless Education	
NCLB § 1031 Short title	
NCLB § 1032 Education for Homeless Children and Youths	
42 U.S.C. § 11431 Statement of policy	1032
42 U.S.C. § 11432 Grants for state and local activities for the education of homeless children and youths	1032
42 U.S.C. § 11433 Local educational agency subgrants for the education of homeless children and youths	1032
42 U.S.C. § 11434 Secretarial responsibilities	1032
42 U.S.C. § 11434a Definitions	1032
42 U.S.C. § 11435 Authorization of appropriations	1032

Part F – General Education Provisions Act	
NCLB § 1061 Student privacy, parental access to information, and administration of certain physical examinations to minors	1061
NCLB § 1062 Technical corrections	1062
Part G - Miscellaneous Other Statutes	
NCLB § 1071 Title 5 of the United States Code	1071
NCLB § 1072 Department of Education Organization Act	1072
NCLB § 1073 Education Flexibility Partnership Act of 1999	1073
NCLB § 1074 Educational Research, Development, Dissemination, and Improvement Act of 1994	
20 U. S. C. § 6052 Continuation of awards	1074
NCLB § 1075 National Child Protection Act of 1993	1075
NCLB § 1076 Technical and conforming amendments	1076

END OF TABLE OF STATUTES FOR THE NO CHILD LEFT BEHIND ACT

FOR YOUR NOTES

13 | Title I: No Child Left Behind

TITLE I: IMPROVING THE ACADEMIC ACHIEVEMENT OF THE DISADVANTAGED

➔ **OVERVIEW OF TITLE I:** The first four code sections of Title I set the stage for the No Child Left Behind Act.

20 U. S. C. § 6301. Statement of Purpose.
20 U. S. C. § 6302. Authorization of appropriations.
20 U. S. C. § 6303. School improvement
20 U. S. C. § 6304. State administration.

Title I has nine Parts:

Part A: Improving Basic Programs Operated by Local Educational Agencies
Part B: Student Reading Skills Improvement Grants
Part C: Education of Migratory Children
Part D: Prevention and Intervention Programs for Children and Youth who are Neglected, Delinquent, or At-risk
Part E: National Assessment of Title I
Part F: Comprehensive School Reform
Part G: Advanced Placement Programs
Part H: School Dropout Prevention
Part I: General Provisions

20 U. S. C. § 6301. Statement of Purpose.

➔ **OVERVIEW:** The Statement of Purpose is the most important statute in No Child Left Behind because it describes the overall purpose of the law: "that all children will have a fair, equal, and significant opportunity to receive a high-quality education" and reach "at a minimum, proficiency on challenging State academic achievement standards and state academic assessments."

Section 6301 lists twelve steps to accomplish these purposes. The law seeks to close the gap between low and high achieving students by holding states, local school districts, and schools accountable for improving the academic achievement of all students. The law requires schools to meet the educational needs of poor children, children with disabilities, children with limited English proficiency, minority and migratory children, and other neglected groups of children, and to publicly report their progress in educating these children every year.

If you are confused about a statute in No Child Left Behind, re-read this Statement of Purpose to see how a particular statute fits into the overall purpose of No Child Left Behind.

The purpose of this title is to ensure that **all children** have a fair, equal, and significant opportunity to obtain a **high-quality education** and reach, **at a minimum, proficiency** on **challenging State academic achievement standards and state academic assessments.** This purpose can be accomplished by —

(1) ensuring that **high-quality academic assessments, accountability systems, teacher preparation** and training, curriculum, and instructional materials are aligned with challenging State academic standards so that students, teachers, parents, and administrators **can measure progress against common expectations for student academic achievement;**

(2) **meeting the educational needs of low-achieving children** in our Nation's highest-poverty schools, limited English proficient children, migratory children, children with disabilities, Indian children, neglected or delinquent children, and young children in need of reading assistance;

(3) **closing the achievement gap** between high- and low-performing children, especially the achievement gaps between minority and nonminority students, and between disadvantaged children and their more advantaged peers;

(4) **holding schools, local educational agencies, and States accountable for improving the academic achievement of all students,** and identifying and turning around low-performing schools that have failed to provide a high-quality education to their students, while **providing alternatives to students in such schools** to enable the students to receive a high-quality education;

(5) distributing and targeting resources sufficiently to make a difference to local educational agencies and schools where needs are greatest;

(6) improving and **strengthening accountability, teaching, and learning** by using State assessment systems designed to ensure that students are meeting challenging State academic achievement and content standards and increasing achievement overall, but especially for the disadvantaged;

(7) providing **greater decisionmaking authority and flexibility** to schools and teachers in exchange for **greater responsibility for student performance;**

(8) providing children an **enriched and accelerated educational program,** including the use of schoolwide programs or additional services that **increase the amount and quality of instructional time;**

(9) **promoting schoolwide reform** and ensuring the access of children to **effective, scientifically based instructional strategies and challenging academic content;**

(10) significantly elevating the quality of instruction by providing staff in participating schools with substantial opportunities for professional development;

(11) coordinating services under all parts of this title with each other, with other educational services, and, to the extent feasible, with other agencies providing services to youth, children, and families; and

(12) affording **parents substantial and meaningful opportunities to participate in the education of their children.** (Section 1001 of the NCLB Act)

20 U. S. C. § 6302. Authorization of appropriations.

➡ **OVERVIEW:** Section 6302 authorizes appropriations to local school districts (local educational agencies) for Reading First, Early Reading First programs, Education of Migratory Children, School Reform, Advanced Placement, Dropout Prevention, and other programs.

(a) LOCAL EDUCATIONAL AGENCY GRANTS - For the purpose of carrying out part A, there are authorized to be appropriated —

(1) $13,500,000,000 for fiscal year 2002;

(2) $16,000,000,000 for fiscal year 2003;

(3) $18,500,000,000 for fiscal year 2004;

(4) $20,500,000,000 for fiscal year 2005;

(5) $22,750,000,000 for fiscal year 2006; and

(6) $25,000,000,000 for fiscal year 2007.

(b) READING FIRST -

(1) READING FIRST - For the purpose of carrying out subpart 1 of part B, there are authorized to be appropriated $900,000,000 for fiscal year 2002 and such sums as may be necessary for each of the 5 succeeding fiscal years.

(2) EARLY READING FIRST - For the purpose of carrying out subpart 2 of part B, there are authorized to be appropriated $75,000,000 for fiscal year 2002 and such sums as may be necessary for each of the 5 succeeding fiscal years.

(3) EVEN START - For the purpose of carrying out subpart 3 of part B, there are authorized to be appropriated $260,000,000 for fiscal year 2002 and such sums as may be necessary for each of the 5 succeeding fiscal years.

(4) IMPROVING LITERACY THROUGH SCHOOL LIBRARIES - For the purpose of carrying out subpart 4 of part B, there are authorized to be appropriated $250,000,000 for fiscal year 2002 and such sums as may be necessary for each of the 5 succeeding fiscal years.

(c) EDUCATION OF MIGRATORY CHILDREN - For the purpose of carrying out part C, there are authorized to be appropriated $410,000,000 for fiscal year 2002 and such sums as may be necessary for each of the 5 succeeding fiscal years.

(d) PREVENTION AND INTERVENTION PROGRAMS FOR YOUTH WHO ARE NEGLECTED, DELINQUENT, OR AT RISK - For the purpose of carrying out part D, there are authorized to be appropriated $50,000,000 for fiscal year 2002 and such sums as may be necessary for each of the 5 succeeding fiscal years.

(e) FEDERAL ACTIVITIES -

(1) SECTIONS 1501 AND 1502 - For the purpose of carrying out sections 1501 and 1502, there are authorized to be appropriated such sums as may be necessary for fiscal year 2002 and each of the 5 succeeding fiscal years.

📁 Section 1501 and Section 1502 of the NCLB Act refer to the National Assessment of Title I. For the corresponding United States Code reference to §§ 1501 and 1502 of the NCLB Act, please see 20 U. S. C. § 6491, 6492.

(2) SECTION 1504 -

(A) IN GENERAL - For the purpose of carrying out section 1504, (author's note, see 20 U. S. C. § 6494) there are authorized to be appropriated such sums as may be necessary for fiscal year 2002 and for each of the 5 succeeding fiscal years.

(B) SPECIAL RULE - Of the funds appropriated pursuant to subparagraph (A), not more than 30 percent may be used for teachers associated with students participating in the programs described in subsections (a)(1), (b)(1), and (c)(1).

(f) COMPREHENSIVE SCHOOL REFORM - For the purpose of carrying out part F, there are authorized to be appropriated such sums as may be necessary for fiscal year 2002 and each of the 5 succeeding fiscal years.

(g) ADVANCED PLACEMENT - For the purposes of carrying out part G, there are authorized to be appropriated such sums for fiscal year 2002 and each 5 succeeding fiscal year.

(h) SCHOOL DROPOUT PREVENTION - For the purpose of carrying out part H, there are authorized to be appropriated $125,000,000 for fiscal year 2002 and such sums as may be necessary for each of the 5 succeeding fiscal years, of which —

(1) up to 10 percent shall be available to carry out subpart 1 of part H for each fiscal year; and

(2) the remainder shall be available to carry out subpart 2 of part H for each fiscal year.

(i) SCHOOL IMPROVEMENT - For the purpose of carrying out section 1003(g), there are authorized to be appropriated $500,000,000 for fiscal year 2002 and such sums as may be necessary for each of the 5 succeeding fiscal years. (Section 1002 of the NCLB Act)

> 📁 Subsection (b) of 6302 lists the appropriations for Reading First programs. Subsection (c) of 6302 authorizes appropriations for migratory children. Subsection 6302(d) authorizes appropriations for neglected, delinquent and at risk children. The remaining subsections appropriate funds for research, school reform, advanced placement, drop-out prevention, and school improvements.

20 U. S. C. § 6303. School improvement.

> ➡️ **OVERVIEW:** Section 6303 requires states to set aside NCLB funds for school districts (LEAs) to use for schools identified for improvement, corrective action, and restructuring, or to provide direct or contracted services by the state. NCLB gives priority to districts that serve the lowest-achieving schools that demonstrate the greatest need. State Departments of Education must publicize the schools that receive funds or services under this subsection.

(a) STATE RESERVATIONS - Each State shall reserve 2 percent of the amount the State receives under subpart 2 of part A for fiscal years 2002 and 2003, and 4 percent of the amount received under such subpart for fiscal years 2004 through 2007, to carry out subsection (b) and to carry out the State's responsibilities under sections 1116 and 1117, including carrying out the State educational agency's statewide system of technical assistance and support for local educational agencies.

> 📁 In this and several other statutes are references to Sections 1116 and 1117 of the NCLB Act. These are in the United States Code at 20 U. S. C. § 6316 and 6317.

(b) USES - Of the amount reserved under subsection (a) for any fiscal year, the State educational agency —

(1) shall allocate not less than 95 percent of that amount directly to local educational agencies for schools identified for school improvement, corrective action, and restructuring, for activities under section 1116(b); or

(2) may, with the approval of the local educational agency, directly provide for these activities or arrange for their provision through other entities such as school support teams or educational service agencies.

(c) PRIORITY - The State educational agency, in allocating funds to local educational agencies under this section, shall give **priority to local educational agencies that** —

(1) serve the **lowest-achieving schools;**

(2) demonstrate the **greatest need** for such funds; and

(3) **demonstrate the strongest commitment** to ensuring that such funds are used to enable the lowest-achieving schools to **meet the progress goals** in school improvement plans under section 1116 (b)(3)(A)(v).

➡ **COMMENT:** If a school with very low state-wide test scores for its ESL students or students with disabilities then institutes an excellent ESL or research-based remedial reading program with teacher training, the school would have a better chance of obtaining a larger portion of these funds.

(d) UNUSED FUNDS - If, after consultation with local educational agencies in the State, the State educational agency determines that the amount of funds reserved to carry out subsection (b) is greater than the amount needed to provide the assistance described in that subsection, the State educational agency shall allocate the excess amount to local educational agencies in accordance with —

(1) the relative allocations the State educational agency made to those agencies for that fiscal year under subpart 2 of part A; or

(2) section 1126(c).

(e) SPECIAL RULE - Notwithstanding any other provision of this section, the amount of funds reserved by the State educational agency under subsection (a) in any fiscal year shall not decrease the amount of funds each local educational agency receives under subpart 2 below the amount received by such local educational agency under such subpart for the preceding fiscal year.

(f) REPORTING - The State educational agency **shall make publicly available** a list of those schools that have received funds or services pursuant to subsection (b) and the percentage of students from each school from families with incomes below the poverty line.

(g) ASSISTANCE FOR LOCAL SCHOOL IMPROVEMENT -

(1) PROGRAM AUTHORIZED - The Secretary shall award grants to States to enable the States to provide subgrants to local educational agencies for the purpose of providing assistance for school improvement consistent with section 1116.

(2) STATE ALLOTMENTS - Such grants shall be allotted among States, the Bureau of Indian Affairs, and the outlying areas, in proportion to the funds received by the States, the Bureau of Indian Affairs, and the outlying areas, respectively, for the fiscal year under parts A, C, and D of this title. The Secretary shall expeditiously allot a portion of such funds to States for the purpose of assisting local educational agencies and schools that were in school improvement status on the date preceding the date of enactment of the No Child Left Behind Act of 2001.

(3) REALLOCATIONS - If a State does not receive funds under this subsection, the Secretary shall reallocate such funds to other States in the same proportion funds are allocated under paragraph (2).

(4) STATE APPLICATIONS - Each State educational agency that desires to receive funds under this subsection shall submit an application to the Secretary at such time, and containing such information, as the Secretary shall reasonably require, except that such requirement shall be waived if a State educational agency submitted such information as part of its State plan under this part. Each State application shall describe how the State educational agency will allocate such funds in order to assist the State educational agency and local educational agencies in complying with school improvement, corrective action, and restructuring requirements of section 1116.

(5) **LOCAL EDUCATIONAL AGENCY GRANTS** - A grant to a local educational agency under this subsection shall be —

(A) of sufficient size and scope to support the activities required under sections 1116 and 1117, but not less than $50,000 and not more than $500,000 for each participating school;

(B) integrated with other funds awarded by the State under this Act; and

(C) **renewable for two additional 1-year periods if schools are meeting the goals in their school improvement plans** developed under section 1116.

(6) **PRIORITY** - The State, in awarding such grants, shall give priority to local educational agencies with the lowest-achieving schools that demonstrate —

(A) the greatest need for such funds; and

(B) the strongest commitment to ensuring that such funds are used to provide adequate resources to enable the lowest-achieving schools to meet the goals under school and local educational agency improvement, corrective action, and restructuring plans under section 1116.

(7) **ALLOCATION** - State educational agency that receives a grant under this subsection shall allocate at least 95 percent of the grant funds directly to local educational agencies for schools identified for school improvement, corrective action, or restructuring to carry out activities under section 1116(b), or may, with the approval of the local educational agency, directly provide for these activities or arrange for their provision through other entities such as school support teams or educational service agencies.

(8) **ADMINISTRATIVE COSTS** - A State educational agency that receives a grant award under this subsection may reserve not more than 5 percent of such grant funds for administration, evaluation, and technical assistance expenses.

(9) **LOCAL AWARDS** - Each local educational agency that applies for assistance under this subsection shall describe how it will provide the lowest-achieving schools the resources necessary to meet goals under school and local educational agency improvement, corrective action, and restructuring plans under section 1116. (Section 1003 of the NCLB Act)

20 U. S. C. § 6304. State administration.

➔ **SECTION OVERVIEW:** Section 6304 explains that funds may be reserved to carry out administrative duties under Parts A, C, and D of Title I.

(a) IN GENERAL - Except as provided in subsection (b), to carry out administrative duties assigned under parts A, C, and D of this title, each State may reserve the greater of —

(1) 1 percent of the amounts received under such parts; or

(2) $400,000 ($50,000 in the case of each outlying area).

(b) EXCEPTION - If the sum of the amounts appropriated for parts A, C, and D of this title is equal to or greater than $14,000,000,000, then the reservation described in subsection (a)(1) shall not exceed 1 percent of the amount the State would receive, if $14,000,000,000 were allocated among the States for parts A, C, and D of this title. (Section 1004 of the NCLB Act)

➡ **COMMENT:** In Part A, the United States Code (referred to as 20 U. S. C.) jumps from Section 6304 (20 U. S. C. § 6304) to Section 6311 (20 U. S. C. § 6311). In the NCLB statute, you will find many instances where a statute stops, then begins a new content section with another series of code sections, i.e., statutes, starting with a "00" or "01" or "11".

PART A - IMPROVING BASIC PROGRAMS OPERATED BY LOCAL EDUCATIONAL AGENCIES
SUBPART 1 - BASIC PROGRAM REQUIREMENTS

➔ **OVERVIEW:** Part A has two subparts:

Subpart 1 - Basic Program Requirements (Section 6311 through Section 6322)
Subpart 2 – Allocations (Section 6331 through Section 6339)

Subpart 1 includes requirements about state plans, local educational agency plans, eligible school attendance areas, schoolwide programs, targeted assistance schools, annual academic assessments, school districts and schools in need of improvement, school support and recognition, parental involvement, new requirements about qualifications of teachers and paraprofessionals, and participation of children enrolled in private schools.

Subpart 2 includes detailed information about grants and allocation formulas.

Part A, Basic Program Requirements, includes the following subparts and sections.

Subpart 1 - Basic Program Requirements

20 U. S. C. § 6311. State plans.
20 U. S. C. § 6312. Local educational agency plans.
20 U. S. C. § 6313. Eligible school attendance areas.
20 U. S. C. § 6314. Schoolwide programs.
20 U. S. C. § 6315. Targeted assistance schools.
20 U. S. C. § 6316. Academic assessment and local educational agency and school improvement.
20 U. S. C. § 6317. School support and recognition.
20 U. S. C. § 6318. Parental involvement.
20 U. S. C. § 6319. Qualifications for teachers and paraprofessionals.
20 U. S. C. § 6320. Participation of children enrolled in private schools.
20 U. S. C. § 6321. Fiscal requirements.
20 U. S. C. § 6322. Coordination requirements.

Subpart 2 - Allocations

20 U. S. C. § 6331. Grants for the outlying areas and the Secretary of the Interior.
20 U. S. C. § 6332. Allocations to States.
20 U. S. C. § 6333. Basic grants to local educational agencies.
20 U. S. C. § 6334. Concentration grants to local educational agencies.
20 U. S. C. § 6335. Targeted grants to local educational agencies.
20 U. S. C. § 6336. Adequacy of funding of targeted grants to local educational agencies in fiscal years after fiscal year 2001.
20 U. S. C. § 6337. Education finance incentive grant program.
20 U. S. C. § 6338. Special allocation procedures.
20 U. S. C. § 6339. Carryover and waiver.

📖 *Standards and Assessments: Non-Regulatory Draft Guidance*, published by the U. S. Department of Education includes frequently asked questions about academic standards, academic assessments, issues related to special populations and standards and assessments. This publication is available on the *Wrightslaw NCLB CD-ROM*.

20 U. S. C. § 6311. State plans.

➡ **OVERVIEW:** Section 6311 is one of the most important statutes in No Child Left Behind. This statute describes requirements for state plans, challenging state academic standards, and annual testing.

Section 6311(a) explains that states must submit State Plans before they can receive No Child Left Behind funds. State Plans must be developed in consultation with school districts, teachers, principals, administrators, and parents, and must be coordinated with other programs and statutes.

Section 6311(b) describes requirements about **academic standards and academic assessments and accountability**. Section 6311(b)(1) requires states to enact challenging standards in mathematics, reading/language arts, and science that describe the knowledge, skills, and achievement levels expected of all students. This section describes two levels of high achievement (proficient and advanced) and one level of low achievement (basic) to measure student mastery of academic skills and material.

Section 6311(b)(2) is about **accountability**. Each State is required to implement a single accountability system under which all schools make adequate yearly progress (AYP). This section includes the definition of **annual yearly progress (AYP)**, timelines, deadlines, measurable objectives, and goals.

Section 6311(c) requires each state to implement high-quality **annual academic assessments** in three areas (mathematics, reading/or language arts, and science) and to use the results of these assessments to measure the progress of school districts. This section includes detailed requirements for these assessments of proficiency.

Section 6311(h)(6) requires school districts to notify parents of their right to request information about the **professional qualifications of their child's teachers and paraprofessionals**. Parents are entitled to know if a teacher has met state licensing requirements, the teacher's major, field of discipline, and any graduate degree. If the child is receiving services from paraprofessionals, the parents are entitled to know their qualifications too.

(a) PLANS REQUIRED -

(1) **IN GENERAL** - For any State desiring to receive a grant under this part, the State educational agency **shall submit** to the Secretary a plan, developed by the State educational agency, in consultation with local educational agencies, teachers, principals, pupil services personnel, administrators (including administrators of programs described in other parts of this title), other staff, **and parents**, that satisfies the requirements of this section and that is coordinated with other programs under this Act, the Individuals with Disabilities Education Act, the Carl D. Perkins Vocational and Technical Education Act of 1998, the Head Start Act, the Adult Education and Family Literacy Act, and the McKinney-Vento Homeless Assistance Act.

(2) **CONSOLIDATED PLAN** - A State plan submitted under paragraph (1) may be submitted as part of a consolidated plan under section 9302.

(b) ACADEMIC STANDARDS, ACADEMIC ASSESSMENTS, AND ACCOUNTABILITY -

(1) CHALLENGING ACADEMIC ASSESSMENTS -

(A) **IN GENERAL** - Each State plan shall demonstrate that the State has adopted challenging academic content standards and challenging student academic achievement standards that will be used by the State, its local educational agencies, and its schools to carry out this part, except that a State shall not be required to submit such standards to the Secretary.

(B) **SAME STANDARDS** - The academic standards required by subparagraph (A) **shall be the same academic standards that the State applies to all schools and children in the State.**

(C) **SUBJECTS** - The State **shall** have such academic standards for all public elementary school and secondary school children, including children served under this part, in subjects determined by the State, but including **at least mathematics, reading or language arts, and (beginning in the 2005-2006 school year) science**, which **shall include the same knowledge, skills, and levels of achievement expected of all children.**

📖 *The Facts about State Standards* is a two-page fact sheet published by the U. S. Department of Education and available on the *Wrightslaw NCLB CD-ROM*.

(D) **CHALLENGING ACADEMIC STANDARDS** - Standards under this paragraph shall include —

(i) challenging **academic content standards** in academic subjects that —
(I) specify what children are expected to know and be able to do;
(II) contain coherent and rigorous content; and
(III) encourage the teaching of advanced skills; and
(ii) challenging student academic achievement standards that —
(I) are aligned with the State's academic content standards;
(II) **describe two levels of high achievement (proficient and advanced)** that determine how well children are mastering the material in the State academic content standards; and
(III) **describe a third level of achievement (basic)** to provide complete information about the progress of the lower-achieving children toward mastering the proficient and advanced levels of achievement.

➡️ **COMMENT:** The NCLB statute describes two levels of high achievement (proficient and advanced) and a third level of achievement (basic) that will measure the progress of low-achieving children toward the proficient and advanced levels.

(E) **INFORMATION** - For the subjects in which students will be served under this part, but for which a State is not required by subparagraphs (A), (B), and (C) to develop, and has not otherwise developed, such academic standards, the State plan shall describe a strategy for ensuring that students are taught the same knowledge and skills in such subjects and held to the same expectations as are all children.

(F) **EXISTING STANDARDS** - Nothing in this part shall prohibit a State from revising, consistent with this section, any standard adopted under this part before or after the date of enactment of the No Child Left Behind Act of 2001.

(2) **ACCOUNTABILITY** –

(A) **IN GENERAL** - Each State plan shall demonstrate that the State has developed and is implementing a single, statewide State accountability system that will be effective in ensuring that all local educational agencies, public elementary schools, and public secondary schools make adequate yearly progress as defined under this paragraph. Each State accountability system **shall** —
(i) be based on the academic standards and academic assessments adopted under paragraphs (1) and (3), and other academic indicators consistent with subparagraph (C)(vi) and (vii), and shall take into account the achievement of all public elementary school and secondary school students;
(ii) be the same accountability system the State uses for all public elementary schools and secondary schools or all local educational agencies in the State, except that public elementary schools, secondary schools, and local educational agencies not participating under this part are not subject to the requirements of section 1116; and
(iii) **include sanctions and rewards**, such as bonuses and recognition, the State will use to **hold** local educational agencies and public elementary schools and secondary schools **accountable** for student achievement and for ensuring that they make adequate yearly progress in accordance with the State's definition under subparagraphs (B) and (C).

(B) **ADEQUATE YEARLY PROGRESS** - Each State plan shall demonstrate, based on academic assessments described in paragraph (3), and in accordance with this paragraph, what constitutes adequate yearly progress of the State, and of all public elementary schools, secondary schools, and local educational agencies in the State, toward **enabling all public elementary school and secondary school students to meet the State's student academic achievement standards**, while working toward the goal of **narrowing the achievement gaps** in the State, local educational agencies, and schools.

(C) DEFINITION – "**Adequate yearly progress**" shall be defined by the State in. a manner that —

(i) applies the same high standards of academic achievement to all public elementary school and secondary school students in the State;

(ii) is **statistically valid and reliable**;

(iii) results in **continuous and substantial academic improvement for all students**;

(iv) measures the progress of public elementary schools, secondary schools and local educational agencies and the State based primarily on the academic assessments described in paragraph (3);

(v) includes **separate measurable annual objectives** for continuous and substantial improvement for each of the following:

(I) The achievement of all public elementary school and secondary school students.

(II) The achievement of

(aa) **economically disadvantaged students**;

(bb) students from **major racial and ethnic groups**;

(cc) students with **disabilities**; and

(dd) students with **limited English proficiency**; except that **disaggregation** of data under subclause (II) **shall not be required** in a case in which the **number of students in a category is insufficient** to yield statistically reliable information or the results would reveal personally identifiable information about an individual student;

(vi) in accordance with subparagraph (D), **includes graduation rates** for public secondary school students (defined as the percentage of students who graduate from secondary school with a regular diploma in the standard number of years) and at least one other academic indicator, as determined by the State for all public elementary school students; and

(vii) in accordance with subparagraph (D), at the State's discretion, may also include other academic indicators, as determined by the State for all public school students, measured separately for each group described in clause (v), such as achievement on additional State or locally administered assessments, **decreases in grade-to-grade retention rates**, attendance rates, and changes in the percentages of students completing gifted and talented, advanced placement, and college preparatory courses.

📖 *State Education Indicators with a Focus on Title I: 1999-2000* published by the U. S. Department of Education, Planning and Evaluation Service, and available on the *Wrightslaw NCLB CD-ROM*. This report tracks the progress of state Title I programs every year and includes State Profiles with information about demographics, accountability, the number of Title I schools that met AYP goals, and the number of Title I schools identified for school improvement. These State Profiles include state achievement test results for students in different groups (i.e., race/ethnicity, gender, low-income, limited-English proficient, disabled, migrant).

➔ **CHECK YOUR STATE'S PROFICIENCY BY SUBGROUP** To see the percentage of students in different subgroups that meet or exceed your state's definition of "proficient," look at the "Student Achievement Trend" in your State Profile. Your state is required to report two other measures of student outcomes: the high school dropout rate and the percentage of high school graduates who enroll in higher education.

(D) REQUIREMENTS FOR OTHER INDICATORS - In carrying out subparagraph (C)(vi) and (vii), the State —

(i) shall ensure that the indicators described in those provisions are valid and reliable, and are consistent with relevant, nationally recognized professional and technical standards, if any; and

(ii) except as provided in subparagraph (I)(i), may not use those indicators to reduce the number of, or change, the schools that would otherwise be subject to school improvement, corrective action, or restructuring under section 1116 if those additional indicators were not used, but may use them to identify additional schools for school improvement or in need of corrective action or restructuring.

(E) STARTING POINT - Each State, using data for the 2001-2002 school year, shall establish the starting point for measuring, under subparagraphs (G) and (H), the percentage of students **meeting or exceeding the State's proficient level of academic achievement** on the State assessments under paragraph (3) and pursuant to the timeline described in subparagraph (F). The starting point shall be, at a minimum, based on the higher of the percentage of students at the proficient level who are in —

(i) the State's lowest achieving group of students described in subparagraph (C)(v)(II); or
(ii) the school at the 20th percentile in the State, based on enrollment, among all schools ranked by the percentage of students at the proficient level.

(F) TIMELINE - Each State shall establish a **timeline for adequate yearly progress**. The timeline shall ensure that **not later than 12 years** after the end of the 2001-2002 school year, **all students in each group** described in subparagraph (C)(v) **will meet or exceed the State's proficient level of academic achievement on the State assessments** under paragraph (3).

(G) MEASURABLE OBJECTIVES - Each State shall establish **statewide annual measurable objectives**, pursuant to subparagraph (C)(v), for meeting the requirements of this paragraph, and which —

(i) shall be set separately for the assessments of mathematics and reading or language arts under subsection (a)(3);
(ii) shall be the same for all schools and local educational agencies in the State;
(iii) shall identify a single minimum percentage of students who are required to meet or exceed the proficient level on the academic assessments that applies separately to each group of students described in subparagraph (C)(v);
(iv) shall ensure that all students will meet or exceed the State's proficient level of academic achievement on the State assessments within the State's timeline under subparagraph (F); and
(v) may be the same for more than 1 year, subject to the requirements of subparagraph (H).

(H) INTERMEDIATE GOALS FOR ANNUAL YEARLY PROGRESS - Each State shall establish **intermediate goals for meeting the requirements**, including the measurable objectives in subparagraph (G), of this paragraph and that shall —

(i) increase in equal increments over the period covered by the State's timeline under subparagraph (F);
(ii) provide for the first increase to occur in not more than 2 years; and
(iii) provide for each following increase to occur in not more than 3 years.

(I) ANNUAL IMPROVEMENT FOR SCHOOLS - Each year, **for a school to make adequate yearly progress** under this paragraph —

(i) each group of students described in subparagraph (C)(v) **must meet or exceed the objectives set by the State** under subparagraph (G), except that if any group described in subparagraph (C)(v) does not meet those objectives in any particular year, the school shall be considered to have made adequate yearly progress if the percentage of students in that group who did not meet or exceed the proficient level of academic achievement on the State assessments under paragraph (3) for that year decreased by 10 percent of that percentage from the preceding school year and that group made progress on one or more of the academic indicators described in subparagraph (C)(vi) or (vii); and
(ii) **not less than 95 percent of each group of students** described in subparagraph (C)(v) who are enrolled in the school **are required to take the assessments**, consistent with paragraph (3)(C)(xi) **and with accommodations, guidelines, and alternative assessments provided in the same manner**

as those provided under section 612(a)(17)(A) of the Individuals with Disabilities Education Act and paragraph (3), on which adequate yearly progress is based (except that the 95 percent requirement described in this clause shall not apply in a case in which the number of students in a category is insufficient to yield statistically reliable information or the results would reveal personally identifiable information about an individual student).

→ **COMMENT:** Section (b)(2)(I) states that schools must test **at least 95 percent of all students** who are enrolled, including students with disabilities and students with limited English proficiency and must provide accommodations. On December 9, 2003, the U. S. Department of Education issued new regulations about allowing states and school districts to use alternate assessments to test students with severe cognitive impairments. These regulations are on the *Wrightslaw NCLB CD-ROM*.
On March 20, 2003 in Volume 68 of the Federal Register beginning at page 13796, et. seq. (68 FR 13796), the U.S. Department of Education published a notice that they were seeking comments on a proposed regulation to allow states and districts to use alternate assessments to assess no more than 1 percent of students with the most severe cognitive impairments. Students with severe cognitive impairments were described as "students whose intellectual functioning and adaptive behavior are three or more standard deviations below the mean." (See the chapters about understanding standardized test data in *Wrightslaw: From Emotions to Advocacy*.) For updates on NCLB regulations, visit the Wrightslaw NCLB site at www.wrightslaw.com/nclb/index.htm or search the Federal Register.

📂 Section 612(a)(17)(A) of IDEA 1997 is located in 20 U. S. C. § 1412(a)(17)(A) in the publication *Wrightslaw: Special Education Law*.

(J) **UNIFORM AVERAGING PROCEDURE** - For the purpose of determining whether schools are making adequate yearly progress, the State may establish a uniform procedure for averaging data which includes one or more of the following:

(i) The State may average data from the school year for which the determination is made with data from one or two school years immediately preceding that school year.
(ii) Until the assessments described in paragraph (3) are administered in such manner and time to allow for the implementation of the uniform procedure for averaging data described in clause (i), the State may use the academic assessments that were required under paragraph (3) as that paragraph was in effect on the day preceding the date of enactment of the No Child Left Behind Act of 2001, provided that nothing in this clause shall be construed to undermine or delay the determination of adequate yearly progress, the requirements of section 1116, or the implementation of assessments under this section.
(iii) The State may use data across grades in a school.

(K) **ACCOUNTABILITY FOR CHARTER SCHOOLS** - The accountability provisions under this Act shall be overseen for charter schools in accordance with State charter school law.

(3) **ACADEMIC ASSESSMENTS** -

📖 *The Facts: Measuring Progress* is a two-page fact sheet published by the U. S. Department of Education. *Measuring Progress* describes why children in grades three through eight must be tested every year and how annual testing will ensure that all children are learning and "no child is left behind." Objective testing provides information about what students know and can do, and allows teachers, parents and principals to know if each student is making substantial annual progress every year in every class. This fact sheet is available on the *Wrightslaw NCLB CD-ROM*.

(A) **IN GENERAL** - Each State plan shall demonstrate that the State educational agency, in consultation with local educational agencies, has implemented a set of **high-quality, yearly student academic assessments** that include, **at a minimum, academic assessments in mathematics, reading or language arts, and science** that will be used as the primary means of determining the yearly performance of the State and of each local educational agency and school in the State in enabling all children to meet the State's challenging student academic achievement standards, except that no State shall be required to meet the requirements of this part relating to science assessments until the beginning of the 2007-2008 school year.

(B) **USE OF ASSESSMENTS** - Each State educational agency may incorporate the data from the assessments under this paragraph into a State-developed longitudinal data system that links student test scores, length of enrollment, and graduation records over time.

(C) **REQUIREMENTS** - Such assessments shall —

(i) be the **same academic assessments used to measure the achievement of all children;**

(ii) be aligned with the State's challenging academic content and student academic achievement standards, and provide **coherent information about student attainment of such standards;**

(iii) **be used for purposes for which such assessments are valid and reliable, and be consistent with relevant, nationally recognized professional and technical standards;**

(iv) be used **only if** the State educational agency provides to the Secretary **evidence from the test publisher** or other relevant sources that the assessments used are of adequate technical quality for each purpose required under this Act and are consistent with the requirements of this section, and such evidence is made public by the Secretary upon request;

(v)

    (I) except as otherwise provided for grades 3 through 8 under clause vii, **measure the proficiency of students in, at a minimum, mathematics and reading or language arts**, and be administered not less than once during —
        (aa) grades 3 through 5;
        (bb) grades 6 through 9; and
        (cc) grades 10 through 12;

    (II) beginning not later than school year 2007-2008, **measure the proficiency of all students in science** and be administered not less than one time during —
        (aa) grades 3 through 5;
        (bb) grades 6 through 9; and
        (cc) grades 10 through 12;

(vi) involve multiple up-to-date measures of student academic achievement, including measures that assess higher-order thinking skills and understanding;

(vii) beginning **not later than school year 2005-2006**, measure the achievement of students against the challenging State academic content and student academic achievement standards **in each of grades 3 through 8 in, at a minimum, mathematics, and reading or language arts**, except that the Secretary may provide the State 1 additional year if the State demonstrates that exceptional or uncontrollable circumstances, such as a natural disaster or a precipitous and unforeseen decline in the financial resources of the State, prevented full implementation of the academic assessments by that deadline and that the State will complete implementation within the additional 1-year period;

(viii) at the discretion of the State, measure the proficiency of students in academic subjects not described in clauses (v), (vi), (vii) in which the State has adopted challenging academic content and academic achievement standards;

(ix) provide for—

    (I) the participation in such **assessments of all students;**

    (II) the **reasonable adaptations and accommodations for students with disabilities** (as defined under section 602(3) of the Individuals with Disabilities Education Act) necessary to measure the academic achievement of such students relative to State academic content and State student academic achievement standards; and

    (III) **the inclusion of limited English proficient students**, who shall be assessed in a valid and reliable manner and **provided reasonable accommodations on assessments** administered to such students under this paragraph, including, to the extent practicable, assessments in the language and form most likely to yield accurate data on what such students know and can do in academic content areas, until such students have achieved English language proficiency as determined under paragraph (7);

(x) notwithstanding subclause (III), the **academic assessment (using tests written in English) of reading or language arts of any student who has attended school in the United States** (not including Puerto Rico) **for three or more consecutive school years**, except that if the local educational agency determines, on a case-by-case individual basis, that academic assessments in another language or form would likely yield more accurate and reliable information on what such student knows and can do, the local educational agency may make a determination to assess such student in the appropriate language other than English for a period that does not exceed two additional consecutive years, provided that such student has not yet reached a level of English language proficiency sufficient to yield valid and reliable information on what such student knows and can do on tests (written in English) of reading or language arts;

(xi) include students who have attended schools in a local educational agency for a full academic year but have not attended a single school for a full academic year, except that the performance of students who have attended more than 1 school in the local educational agency in any academic year shall be used only in determining the progress of the local educational agency;

(xii) produce **individual student interpretive, descriptive, and diagnostic reports, consistent with clause (iii) that allow parents, teachers, and principals to understand and address the specific academic needs of students**, and include information regarding achievement on academic assessments aligned with State academic achievement standards, and that are **provided to parents, teachers, and principals**, as soon as is practicably possible after the assessment is given, **in an understandable and uniform format**, and to the extent practicable, **in a language that parents can understand**;

(xiii) enable results to be disaggregated within each State, local educational agency, and school by gender, by each major racial and ethnic group, by English proficiency status, by migrant status, by students with disabilities as compared to nondisabled students, and by economically disadvantaged students as compared to students who are not economically disadvantaged, except that, in the case of a local educational agency or a school, such disaggregation shall not be required in a case in which the number of students in a category is insufficient to yield statistically reliable information or the results would reveal personally identifiable information about an individual student;

(xiv) **be consistent with widely accepted professional testing standards, objectively measure academic achievement, knowledge, and skills**, and be tests that do not evaluate or assess personal or family beliefs and attitudes, or publicly disclose personally identifiable information; and

(xv) **enable itemized score analyses to be produced and reported**, consistent with clause (iii), to local educational agencies and schools, so that parents, teachers, principals, and administrators can interpret and address the specific academic needs of students as indicated by the students' achievement on assessment items.

(D) DEFERRAL - A State may defer the commencement, or suspend the administration, but not cease the development, of the assessments described in this paragraph, that were not required prior to the date of enactment of the No Child Left Behind Act of 2001, for 1 year for each year for which the amount appropriated for grants under section 6113(a)(2) is less than—

(i) $370,000,000 for fiscal year 2002;
(ii) $380,000,000 for fiscal year 2003;
(iii) $390,000,000 for fiscal year 2004; and(iv) $400,000,000 for fiscal years 2005 through 2007.

(4) SPECIAL RULE - Academic assessment measures in addition to those in paragraph (3) that do not meet the requirements of such paragraph may be included in the assessment under paragraph (3) as additional measures, but may not be used in lieu of the academic assessments required under paragraph (3). Such additional assessment measures may not be used to reduce the number of or change, the schools that would otherwise be subject to school improvement, corrective action, or restructuring under section 1116 if such additional indicators were not used, but may be used to identify additional schools for school improvement or in need of corrective action or restructuring except as provided in paragraph (2)(I)(i).

(5) STATE AUTHORITY - If a State educational agency provides evidence, which is satisfactory to the Secretary, that neither the State educational agency nor any other State government official, agency, or entity has sufficient authority, under State law, to adopt curriculum content and student academic achievement standards, and academic assessments aligned with such academic standards, which will be applicable to all students enrolled in the State's public elementary schools and secondary schools, then the State educational agency may meet the requirements of this subsection by—

(A) adopting academic standards and academic assessments that meet the requirements of this subsection, on a statewide basis, and limiting their applicability to students served under this part; or

(B) adopting and implementing policies that ensure that each local educational agency in the State that receives grants under this part will adopt curriculum content and student academic achievement standards, and academic assessments aligned with such standards, which—

(i) meet all of the criteria in this subsection and any regulations regarding such standards and assessments that the Secretary may publish; and
(ii) are applicable to all students served by each such local educational agency.

(6) LANGUAGE ASSESSMENTS - Each State plan shall identify the **languages other than English that are present in the participating student population** and indicate the languages for which yearly student academic assessments are not available and are needed. The State shall make every effort to **develop such assessments** and may request assistance from the Secretary if linguistically accessible academic assessment measures are needed. Upon request, the Secretary shall assist with the identification of appropriate academic assessment measures in the needed languages, but shall not mandate a specific academic assessment or mode of instruction.

(7) ACADEMIC ASSESSMENTS OF ENGLISH LANGUAGE PROFICIENCY - Each State plan shall demonstrate that local educational agencies in the State will, beginning not later than school year 2002-2003, provide for an **annual assessment of English proficiency (measuring students' oral language, reading, and writing skills in English) of all students with limited English proficiency** in the schools served by the State educational agency, except that the Secretary may provide the State 1 additional year if the State demonstrates that exceptional or uncontrollable circumstances, such as a natural disaster or a precipitous and unforeseen decline in the financial resources of the State, prevented full implementation of this paragraph by that deadline and that the State will complete implementation within the additional 1-year period.

(8) REQUIREMENT - Each State plan **shall describe**—

(A) how the State educational agency will assist each local educational agency and school affected by the State plan to develop the capacity to comply with each of the requirements of sections 1112(c)(1)(D), 1114(b), and 1115(c) that is applicable to such agency or school;

(B) how the State educational agency will assist each local educational agency and school affected by the State plan to provide additional educational assistance to individual students assessed as needing help to achieve the State's challenging academic achievement standards;

(C) the **specific steps** the State educational agency will take to ensure that both schoolwide programs and targeted assistance schools **provide instruction by highly qualified instructional staff** as required by sections 1114(b)(1)(C) and 1115(c)(1)(E), including steps that the State educational agency will take **to ensure that poor and minority children are not taught at higher rates than other children by inexperienced, unqualified, or out-of-field teachers**, and the measures that the State educational agency will use to evaluate and publicly report the progress of the State educational agency with respect to such steps;

(D) **an assurance** that the State educational agency will assist local educational agencies in **developing or identifying high-quality effective curricula aligned with State academic achievement standards** and how the State educational agency will disseminate such curricula to each local educational agency and school within the State; and

(E) such other factors the State educational agency determines appropriate to provide students an opportunity to achieve the knowledge and skills described in the challenging academic content standards adopted by the State.

(9) FACTORS AFFECTING STUDENT ACHIEVEMENT - Each State plan shall include an assurance that the State educational agency will coordinate and collaborate, to the extent feasible and necessary as determined by the State educational agency, with agencies providing services to children, youth, and families, with respect to local educational agencies within the State that are identified under section 1116 and that request assistance with addressing major factors that have significantly affected the academic achievement of students in the local educational agency or schools served by such agency.

(10) USE OF ACADEMIC ASSESSMENT RESULTS TO IMPROVE STUDENT ACADEMIC ACHIEVEMENT - Each State plan shall describe how the State educational agency will ensure that the results of the State assessments described in paragraph (3)—

(A) will be promptly provided to local educational agencies, schools, and teachers in a manner that is clear and easy to understand, **but not later than before the beginning of the next school year**; and

(B) be used by those local educational agencies, schools, and teachers **to improve the educational achievement of individual students.**

(c) OTHER PROVISIONS TO SUPPORT TEACHING AND LEARNING - Each State plan shall contain assurances that—

(1) the State educational agency will meet the requirements of subsection (h)(1) and, beginning with the 2002-2003 school year, will **produce the annual State report cards** described in such subsection, except that the Secretary may provide the State educational agency 1 additional year if the State educational agency demonstrates that exceptional or uncontrollable circumstances, such as a natural disaster or a precipitous and unforeseen decline in the financial resources of the State, prevented full implementation of this paragraph by that deadline and that the State will complete implementation within the additional 1-year period;

(2) the State will, beginning in school year 2002-2003, participate in **biennial State academic assessments of 4th and 8th grade reading and mathematics under the National Assessment of Educational Progress** carried out under section 411(b)(2) of the National Education Statistics Act of 1994 if the Secretary pays the costs of administering such assessments;

(3) the State educational agency, in consultation with the Governor, will include, as a component of the State plan, a plan to carry out the responsibilities of the State under sections 1116 and 1117, including carrying out the State educational agency's statewide system of technical assistance and support for local educational agencies;

(4) the State educational agency will work with other agencies, including educational service agencies or other

local consortia, and institutions to provide technical assistance to local educational agencies and schools, including technical assistance in providing professional development under section 1119, technical assistance under section 1117, and technical assistance relating to **parental involvement** under section 1118;

(5)

(A) where educational service agencies exist, the State educational agency will consider providing professional development and technical assistance through such agencies; and

(B) where educational service agencies do not exist, the State educational agency will consider providing professional development and technical assistance through other cooperative agreements such as through a consortium of local educational agencies;

(6) the State educational agency will notify local educational agencies and the public of the content and student academic achievement standards and academic assessments developed under this section, and of the authority to operate schoolwide programs, and will fulfill the State educational agency's responsibilities regarding local educational agency improvement and school improvement under section 1116, including such corrective actions as are necessary;

(7) the State educational agency will provide the least restrictive and burdensome regulations for local educational agencies and individual schools participating in a program assisted under this part;

(8) the State educational agency will inform the Secretary and the public of how Federal laws, if at all, hinder the ability of States to hold local educational agencies and schools accountable for student academic achievement;

(9) the State educational agency will encourage schools to consolidate funds from other Federal, State, and local sources for schoolwide reform in schoolwide programs under section 1114;

(10) the State educational agency will modify or eliminate State fiscal and accounting barriers so that schools can easily consolidate funds from other Federal, State, and local sources for schoolwide programs under section 1114;

(11) the State educational agency has involved the **committee of practitioners** established under section 1903(b)

(12) the State educational agency will inform local educational agencies in the State of the local educational agency's authority to transfer funds under title VI, to obtain waivers under part D of title IX, and, if the State is an Ed-Flex Partnership State, to obtain waivers under the Education Flexibility Partnership Act of 1999;

(13) the State educational agency will coordinate activities funded under this part with other Federal activities as appropriate; and

(14) the State educational agency will encourage local educational agencies and individual schools participating in a program assisted under this part to **offer family literacy services (using funds under this part)**, if the agency or school determines that a substantial number of students served under this part by the agency or school have parents who do not have a secondary school diploma or its recognized equivalent or who have low levels of literacy.

(d) **PARENTAL INVOLVEMENT** - Each State plan shall describe **how the State educational agency will support** the collection and dissemination to local educational agencies and schools of **effective parental involvement practices**. Such practices shall—

(1) be based on the most current research that meets the highest professional and technical standards, on effective parental involvement that fosters achievement to high standards for all children; and

(2) **be geared toward lowering barriers to greater participation by parents in school planning, review, and improvement experienced.**

(e) PEER REVIEW AND SECRETARIAL APPROVAL -

(1) SECRETARIAL DUTIES - The Secretary shall—

(A) establish a peer-review process to assist in the review of State plans;

(B) appoint individuals to the peer-review process who are representative of parents, teachers, State educational agencies, and local educational agencies, and who are familiar with educational standards, assessments, accountability, the needs of low-performing schools, and other educational needs of students;

(C) approve a State plan within 120 days of its submission unless the Secretary determines that the plan does not meet the requirements of this section;

(D) if the Secretary determines that the State plan does not meet the requirements of subsection (a), (b), or (c), immediately notify the State of such determination and the reasons for such determination;

(E) not decline to approve a State's plan before—

(i) offering the State an opportunity to revise its plan;
(ii) providing technical assistance in order to assist the State to meet the requirements of subsections (a), (b), and (c); and
(iii) providing a hearing; and

(F) have the authority to disapprove a State plan for not meeting the requirements of this part, but shall not have the authority to require a State, as a condition of approval of the State plan, to include in, or delete from, such plan one or more specific elements of the State's academic content standards or to use specific academic assessment instruments or items.

(2) STATE REVISIONS - A State plan shall be revised by the State educational agency if it is necessary to satisfy the requirements of this section.

➡ **COMMENT:** Subsection 6311(e) establishes a peer-review process for State plans. Peer reviewers must be familiar with educational standards, assessments, accountability, the needs of low-performing schools, and the educational needs of students.

(f) DURATION OF THE PLAN -

(1) IN GENERAL - Each State plan shall—

(A) remain in effect for the duration of the State's participation under this part; and

(B) be periodically reviewed and revised as necessary by the State educational agency to reflect changes in the State's strategies and programs under this part.

(2) ADDITIONAL INFORMATION - If significant changes are made to a State's plan, such as the adoption of new State academic content standards and State student achievement standards, new academic assessments, or a new definition of adequate yearly progress, such information shall be submitted to the Secretary.

➡ **COMMENT:** According to subsection 6311(f), State Plans must be reviewed and revised periodically to reflect new academic standards, new academic assessments, or a new definition of adequate yearly progress.

(g) PENALTIES -

(1) FAILURE TO MEET DEADLINES ENACTED IN 1994 -

(A) IN GENERAL - **If a State fails to meet the deadlines** established by the Improving America's Schools Act of 1994 (or under any waiver granted by the Secretary or under any compliance agreement with the Secretary) for demonstrating that the State has in place **challenging academic content standards and student achievement standards, and a system for measuring and monitoring adequate yearly progress, the Secretary shall withhold 25 percent of the funds** that would otherwise be available to the State for State administration and activities under this part in each year until the Secretary determines that the State meets those requirements.

(B) NO EXTENSION - Notwithstanding any other provision of law, 90 days after the date of enactment of the No Child Left Behind Act of 2001 the Secretary shall not grant any additional waivers of, or enter into any additional compliance agreements to extend, the deadlines described in subparagraph (A) for any State.

(2) FAILURE TO MEET REQUIREMENTS ENACTED IN 2001 - If a State fails to meet any of the requirements of this section, other than the requirements described in paragraph (1), then the Secretary may withhold funds for State administration under this part until the Secretary determines that the State has fulfilled those requirements.

➡ **COMMENT:** Subsection 6311(g) establishes that 90 days after NCLB became law (January 8, 2002), waivers would no longer be granted to states. If a state fails to meet deadlines established in 1994, funds may be withheld.

(h) REPORTS -

(1) ANNUAL STATE REPORT CARD -

(A) IN GENERAL - Not later than the beginning of the **2002-2003 school year**, unless the State has received a 1-year extension pursuant to subsection (c)(1), a State that receives assistance under this part shall prepare and disseminate an annual State report card.

(B) IMPLEMENTATION - The State report card shall be—
(i) concise; and
(ii) presented in an understandable and uniform format and, to the extent practicable, provided in a language that the parents can understand.

(C) REQUIRED INFORMATION - The State **shall** include in its annual State report card—

(i) information, in the aggregate, on student achievement at each proficiency level on the State academic assessments described in subsection (b)(3) (disaggregated by race, ethnicity, gender, disability status, migrant status, English proficiency, and status as economically disadvantaged, except that such disaggregation shall not be required in a case in which the number of students in a category is insufficient to yield statistically reliable information or the results would reveal personally identifiable information about an individual student);
(ii) information that provides a comparison between the actual achievement levels of each group of students described in subsection (b)(2)(C)(v) and the State's annual measurable objectives for each such group of students on each of the academic assessments required under this part;
(iii) the percentage of students not tested (disaggregated by the same categories and subject to the

same exception described in clause (i));

(iv) the most recent 2-year trend in student achievement in each subject area, and for each grade level, for which assessments under this section are required;

(v) aggregate information on any other indicators used by the State to determine the adequate yearly progress of students in achieving State academic achievement standards;

(vi) graduation rates for secondary school students consistent with subsection (b)(2)(C)(vi);

(vii) information on the performance of local educational agencies in the State regarding making adequate yearly progress, including the number and names of each school identified for school improvement under section 1116; and

(viii) the professional qualifications of teachers in the State, the percentage of such teachers teaching with emergency or provisional credentials, and the percentage of classes in the State not taught by highly qualified teachers, in the aggregate and disaggregated by high-poverty compared to low-poverty schools which, for the purpose of this clause, means schools in the top quartile of poverty and the bottom quartile of poverty in the State.

(D) OPTIONAL INFORMATION - The State may include in its annual State report card such other information as the State believes will best provide parents, students, and other members of the public with information regarding the progress of each of the State's public elementary schools and public secondary schools. Such information may include information regarding—

(i) school attendance rates;

(ii) average class size in each grade;

(iii) academic achievement and gains in English proficiency of limited English proficient students;

(iv) the incidence of school violence, drug abuse, alcohol abuse, student suspensions, and student expulsions;

(v) the extent and type of parental involvement in the schools;

(vi) the percentage of students completing advanced placement courses, and the rate of passing of advanced placement tests; and

(vii) a clear and concise description of the State's accountability system, including a description of the criteria by which the State evaluates school performance, and the criteria that the State has established, consistent with subsection (b)(2), to determine the status of schools regarding school improvement, corrective action, and restructuring.

(2) ANNUAL LOCAL EDUCATIONAL AGENCY REPORT CARDS -

(A) REPORT CARDS -

(i) IN GENERAL - Not later than the beginning of the **2002-2003 school year**, a local educational agency that receives assistance under this part **shall prepare and disseminate an annual local educational agency report card**, except that the State educational agency may provide the local educational agency 1 additional year if the local educational agency demonstrates that exceptional or uncontrollable circumstances, such as a natural disaster or a precipitous and unforeseen decline in the financial resources of the local educational agency, prevented full implementation of this paragraph by that deadline and that the local educational agency will complete implementation within the additional 1-year period.

(ii) SPECIAL RULE - If a State educational agency has received an extension pursuant to subsection (c)(1), then a local educational agency within that State shall not be required to include the information required under paragraph (1)(C) in such report card during such extension.

(B) MINIMUM REQUIREMENTS - The State educational agency shall ensure that each local educational agency collects appropriate data and includes in the local educational agency's annual report the information described in paragraph (1)(C) as applied to the local educational agency and each school served by the local educational agency, and—

(i) in the case of a local educational agency—
　　(I) the number and percentage of schools identified for school improvement under section 1116(c) and how long the schools have been so identified; and
　　(II) information that shows how students served by the local educational agency achieved on the statewide academic assessment compared to students in the State as a whole; and
(ii) in the case of a school—
　　(I) whether the school has been identified for school improvement; and
　　(II) information that shows how the school's students achievement on the statewide academic assessments and other indicators of adequate yearly progress compared to students in the local educational agency and the State as a whole.

(C) OTHER INFORMATION - A local educational agency may include in its annual local educational agency report card any other appropriate information, whether or not such information is included in the annual State report card.

(D) DATA - A local educational agency or school shall only include in its annual local educational agency report card data that are sufficient to yield statistically reliable information, as determined by the State, and that do not reveal personally identifiable information about an individual student.

(E) PUBLIC DISSEMINATION - The local educational agency shall, not later than the beginning of the 2002-2003 school year, unless the local educational agency has received a 1-year extension pursuant to subparagraph (A), **publicly disseminate** the information described in this paragraph **to all schools** in the school district served by the local educational agency **and to all parents** of students attending those schools in **an understandable and uniform format** and, to the extent practicable, provided in a language that the parents can understand, and make the information **widely available through public means**, such as **posting on the Internet, distribution to the media**, and distribution through public agencies, except that if a local educational agency issues a report card for all students, the local educational agency may include the information under this section as part of such report.

(3) PREEXISTING REPORT CARDS - A State educational agency or local educational agency that was providing public report cards on the performance of students, schools, local educational agencies, or the State prior to the enactment of the No Child Left Behind Act of 2001 may use those report cards for the purpose of this subsection, so long as any such report card is modified, as may be needed, to contain the information required by this subsection.

(4) ANNUAL STATE REPORT TO THE SECRETARY - Each State educational agency receiving assistance under this part shall report annually to the Secretary, and make widely available within the State—

(A) beginning with school year 2002-2003, information on the State's progress in developing and implementing the academic assessments described in subsection (b)(3);

(B) beginning not later than school year 2002-2003, information on the achievement of students on the academic assessments required by subsection (b)(3), including the disaggregated results for the categories of students identified in subsection (b)(2)(C)(v);

(C) in any year before the State begins to provide the information described in subparagraph (B), information on the results of student academic assessments (including disaggregated results) required under this section;

(D) beginning not later than school year 2002-2003, unless the State has received an extension pursuant to subsection (c)(1), information on the acquisition of English proficiency by children with limited English proficiency;

(E) the number and names of each school identified for school improvement under section 1116(c), the reason why each school was so identified, and the measures taken to address the achievement problems of such schools;

(F) the number of students and schools that participated in public school choice and supplemental service programs and activities under this title; and

(G) beginning not later than the 2002-2003 school year, information on the quality of teachers and the percentage of classes being taught by highly qualified teachers in the State, local educational agency, and school.

(5) REPORT TO CONGRESS - The Secretary shall transmit **annually** to the Committee on Education and the Workforce of the House of Representatives and the Committee on Health, Education, Labor, and Pensions of the Senate a report that provides national and State-level data on the information collected under paragraph (4).

(6) PARENTS RIGHT-TO-KNOW -

(A) QUALIFICATIONS - At the beginning of each school year, a local educational agency that receives funds under this part **shall notify the parents** of each student attending any school receiving funds under this part **that the parents may request, and the agency will provide** the parents on request (and in a timely manner), **information regarding the professional qualifications of the student's classroom teachers**, including, **at a minimum**, the following:

(i) Whether the teacher has met State **qualification and licensing criteria** for the grade levels and subject areas in which the teacher provides instruction.
(ii) Whether the teacher is **teaching under emergency or other provisional status** through which State qualification or licensing criteria have been waived.
(iii) The baccalaureate **degree major** of the teacher and any other graduate certification or degree held by the teacher, and the field of discipline of the certification or degree.
(iv) Whether the child is provided services by **paraprofessionals and, if so, their qualifications.**

(B) ADDITIONAL INFORMATION - In addition to the information that parents may request under subparagraph (A), **a school** that receives funds under this part **shall provide to each individual parent—**

(i) information on the **level of achievement of the parent's child in each of the State academic assessments** as required under this part; and
(ii) **timely notice that the parent's child has been assigned, or has been taught for four or more consecutive weeks by, a teacher who is not highly qualified.**

(C) FORMAT - The notice and information provided to parents under this paragraph shall be in an understandable and uniform format and, to the extent practicable, provided in a language that the parents can understand.

(i) PRIVACY - Information collected under this section shall be collected and disseminated in a manner that protects the privacy of individuals.

(j) TECHNICAL ASSISTANCE - The Secretary shall provide a State educational agency, at the State educational agency's request, technical assistance in meeting the requirements of this section, including the provision of advice by experts in the development of high-quality academic assessments, the setting of State standards, the development of measures of adequate yearly progress that are valid and reliable, and other relevant areas.

(k) VOLUNTARY PARTNERSHIPS - A State may enter into a voluntary partnership with another State to develop and implement the academic assessments and standards required under this section.

(l) CONSTRUCTION - Nothing in this part shall be construed to prescribe the use of the academic assessments described in this part for student promotion or graduation purposes.

(m) SPECIAL RULE WITH RESPECT TO BUREAU-FUNDED SCHOOLS - In determining the assessments to be used by each operated or funded by BIA school receiving funds under this part, the following shall apply:

(1) Each such school that is accredited by the State in which it is operating shall use the assessments the State has developed and implemented to meet the requirements of this section, or such other appropriate assessment as approved by the Secretary of the Interior.

(2) Each such school that is accredited by a regional accrediting organization shall adopt an appropriate assessment, in consultation with and with the approval of, the Secretary of the Interior and consistent with assessments adopted by other schools in the same State or region, that meets the requirements of this section.

(3) Each such school that is accredited by a tribal accrediting agency or tribal division of education shall use an assessment developed by such agency or division, except that the Secretary of the Interior shall ensure that such assessment meets the requirements of this section. (Section 1111 of the NCLB Act)

➡ **COMMENT:** Contrary to common misunderstandings about high stakes testing, grade retention, and NCLB, subsection 6311(l) states, "Nothing in this part shall be construed to prescribe the use of the academic assessments described in this part for student promotion or graduation purposes."

20 U. S. C. § 6312. Local educational agency plans.

➡ **OVERVIEW:** Section 6312, a key statute in No Child Left Behind, includes the requirements for school district/local education agency (LEA) Plans. Before a district can receive funds under NCLB, the district must file a plan with the State. The plan must describe high-quality academic assessments, how the district will help students who are having academic difficulties, criteria for poverty, services for homeless children, parental involvement, and other requirements, and must include assurances that the LEA will work with public schools and private schools.

Section 6312(b) requires plans to describe how the district will implement public school choice and supplemental services, and how the district will provide after school and school year extension programs. Section 6312(c) is about assurances. School districts must use academic assessments to review the progress of each school every year so all students are proficient twelve years after the 2001-2002 school year. Districts must ensure that parents receive the results of academic testing promptly and that this information is in an "understandable and uniform format."

Section 6312(g) requires schools to notify parents of children with Limited English Proficiency about the child's level of English proficiency, how the level was assessed, the child's academic achievement levels, the methods being used to teach the child, how the program will help the child learn English, and when the child is expected to complete the program.

📂 These plans are public records that may be obtained by anyone. (see Using the Freedom of Information Act (page 92)

📖 Read "*Public School Choice: Draft Non-Regulatory Guidance*" and "*Supplemental Educational Services: Non-Regulatory Guidance*" from the U. S. Department of Education for frequently asked questions and answers about these subjects. Both publications are available on the Wrightslaw NCLB CD-ROM.

(a) PLANS REQUIRED -

(1) **SUBGRANTS** - A local educational agency may receive a subgrant under this part for any fiscal year only if such agency has on file with the State educational agency a plan, approved by the State educational agency, that is coordinated with other programs under this Act, the Individuals with Disabilities Education Act, the Carl D. Perkins Vocational and Technical Education Act of 1998, the McKinney-Vento Homeless Assistance

Act, and other Acts, as appropriate.

(2) CONSOLIDATED APPLICATION - The plan may be submitted as part of a consolidated application under section 9305.

(b) PLAN PROVISIONS -

(1) IN GENERAL - In order to help low-achieving children meet challenging achievement academic standards, each local educational agency plan shall include —

(A) a **description of high-quality student academic assessments, if any, that are in addition to the academic assessments described in the State plan under section 1111(b)(3), that the local educational agency and schools served under this part will use** —

(i) to determine the success of children served under this part in meeting the State student academic achievement standards, and **to provide information to teachers, parents, and students on the progress being made toward meeting the State student academic achievement standards** described in section 1111(b)(1)(D)(ii);
(ii) to **assist in diagnosis, teaching, and learning in the classroom** in ways that best enable low-achieving children served under this part to meet State student achievement academic standards and do well in the local curriculum;
(iii) to determine what revisions are needed to projects under this part so that such children meet the State student academic achievement standards; and
(iv) **to identify effectively students who may be at risk for reading failure or who are having difficulty reading**, through the use of screening, diagnostic, and classroom-based instructional reading assessments, as defined under section 1208;

(B) at the local educational agency's discretion, a description of any other indicators that will be used in addition to the academic indicators described in section 1111 for the uses described in such section;

(C) a description of how the local educational agency will provide **additional educational assistance to individual students assessed as needing help** in meeting the State's challenging student academic achievement standards;

(D) a description of the strategy the local educational agency will use to coordinate programs under this part with programs under title II to provide professional development for teachers and principals, and, if appropriate, pupil services personnel, administrators, parents and other staff, including local educational agency level staff in accordance with sections 1118 and 1119;

(E) a description of how the local educational agency will coordinate and integrate services provided under this part with other educational services at the local educational agency or individual school level, such as —

(i) Even Start, Head Start, Reading First, Early Reading First, and other preschool programs, including plans for the transition of participants in such programs to local elementary school programs; and
(ii) services for children with limited English proficiency, children with disabilities, migratory children, neglected or delinquent youth, Indian children served under part A of title VII, homeless children, and immigrant children in order to increase program effectiveness, eliminate duplication, and reduce fragmentation of the instructional program;

(F) an assurance that the local educational agency will participate, if selected, in the State National Assessment of Educational Progress in 4th and 8th grade reading and mathematics carried out under section 411(b)(2) of the National Education Statistics Act of 1994;

(G) a description of the **poverty criteria** that will be used to select school attendance areas under section 1113;

(H) a description of **how teachers**, in consultation with parents, administrators, and pupil services personnel, in targeted assistance schools under section 1115, **will identify the eligible children most in need of services** under this part;

(I) a general description of the nature of the programs to be conducted by such agency's schools under sections 1114 and 1115 and, where appropriate, educational services outside such schools for children living in local institutions for **neglected or delinquent children**, and for neglected and delinquent children in community day school programs;

(J) a description of how the local educational agency will ensure that **migratory children** and formerly migratory children who are eligible to receive services under this part are selected to receive such services on the same basis as other children who are selected to receive services under this part;

(K) if appropriate, a description of how the local educational agency will use funds under this part to support **preschool programs** for children, particularly children participating in Early Reading First, or in a Head Start or Even Start program, which services may be provided directly by the local educational agency or through a subcontract with the local Head Start agency designated by the Secretary of Health and Human Services under section 641 of the Head Start Act, or an agency operating an Even Start program, an Early Reading First program, or another comparable public early childhood development program;

(L) a description of the actions the local educational agency will take to assist its low-achieving schools identified under section 1116 as in need of improvement;

(M) a description of the actions the local educational agency will take to implement **public school choice and supplemental services**, consistent with the requirements of section 1116;

(N) a description of how the local educational agency will meet the requirements of section 1119;

(O) a description of the services the local educational agency will provide **homeless children**, including services provided with funds reserved under section 1113(c)(3)(A);

(P) a description of the strategy the local educational agency will use to implement effective **parental involvement** under section 1118; and

(Q) where appropriate, a description of how the local educational agency will use funds under this part to support **after school** (including before school and summer school) and **school-year extension** programs.

(2) EXCEPTION - The academic assessments and indicators described in subparagraphs (A) and (B) of paragraph (1) shall not be used —

(A) in lieu of the academic assessments required under section 1111(b)(3) and other State academic indicators under section 1111(b)(2); or

(B) to reduce the number of, or change which, schools would otherwise be subject to school improvement, corrective action, or restructuring under section 1116, if such additional assessments or indicators described in such subparagraphs were not used, but such assessments and indicators may be used to identify additional schools for school improvement or in need of corrective action or restructuring.

(c) ASSURANCES -

(1) IN GENERAL - Each local educational agency plan shall provide assurances that the local educational agency will —

(A) inform eligible schools and parents of schoolwide program authority and the ability of such schools to consolidate funds from Federal, State, and local sources;

(B) provide technical assistance and support to schoolwide programs;

(C) work in consultation with schools as the schools develop the schools' plans pursuant to section 1114 and assist schools as the schools implement such plans or undertake activities pursuant to section 1115 so that each school can make adequate yearly progress toward meeting the State student academic achievement standards;

(D) fulfill such agency's school improvement responsibilities under section 1116, including taking actions under paragraphs (7) and (8) of section 1116(b);

(E) provide services to **eligible children attending private elementary schools and secondary schools** in accordance with section 1120, and timely and meaningful consultation with private school officials regarding such services;

(F) take into account the experience of model programs for the educationally disadvantaged, and the **findings of relevant scientifically based research** indicating that services may be most effective if focused on students in the earliest grades at schools that receive funds under this part;

(G) in the case of a local educational agency that chooses to use funds under this part to provide early childhood development services to low-income children below the age of compulsory school attendance, ensure that such services comply with the performance standards established under section 641A(a) of the Head Start Act;

(H) work in consultation with schools as the schools develop and implement their plans or activities under sections 1118 and 1119;

(I) comply with the requirements of section 1119 regarding the qualifications of teachers and paraprofessionals and professional development;

(J) inform eligible schools of the local educational agency's authority to obtain waivers on the school's behalf under title IX and, if the State is an Ed-Flex Partnership State, to obtain waivers under the Education Flexibility Partnership Act of 1999;

(K) coordinate and collaborate, to the extent feasible and necessary as determined by the local educational agency, with the State educational agency and other agencies providing services to children, youth, and families with respect to a school in school improvement, corrective action, or restructuring under section 1116 if such a school requests assistance from the local educational agency in addressing major factors that have significantly affected student achievement at the school;

(L) ensure, through incentives for voluntary transfers, the provision of professional development, recruitment programs, or other effective strategies, that **low-income students and minority students are not taught at higher rates than other students by unqualified, out-of-field, or inexperienced teachers;**

(M) **use the results of the student academic assessments** required under section 1111(b)(3), and other measures or indicators available to the agency, **to review annually the progress of each school** served by the agency and receiving funds under this part **to determine whether all of the schools are making the** progress necessary to ensure that **all students will meet the State's proficient level of achievement** on the State academic assessments described in section 1111(b)(3) **within 12 years from the end of the 2001-2002 school year;**

(N) ensure that the **results from the academic assessments** required under section 1111(b)(3) will be **provided to parents and teachers as soon as is practicably possible** after the test is taken, in an understandable and uniform format and, to the extent practicable, provided in a language that the parents can understand; and

(O) assist each school served by the agency and assisted under this part in developing or identifying examples of high-quality, effective curricula consistent with section 1111(b)(8)(D).

(2) SPECIAL RULE - In carrying out subparagraph (G) of paragraph (1), the Secretary —

(A) shall consult with the Secretary of Health and Human Services and shall establish procedures (taking into consideration existing State and local laws, and local teacher contracts) to assist local educational agencies to comply with such subparagraph; and

(B) shall disseminate to local educational agencies the Head Start performance standards as in effect under section 641A(a) of the Head Start Act, and such agencies affected by such subparagraph shall plan for the implementation of such subparagraph (taking into consideration existing State and local laws, and local teacher contracts), including pursuing the availability of other Federal, State, and local funding sources to assist in compliance with such subparagraph.

(3) INAPPLICABILITY - Paragraph (1)(G) of this subsection shall not apply to preschool programs using the Even Start model or to Even Start programs that are expanded through the use of funds under this part.

(d) PLAN DEVELOPMENT AND DURATION -

(1) CONSULTATION - Each local educational agency plan shall be developed in consultation with teachers, principals, administrators (including administrators of programs described in other parts of this title), and other appropriate school personnel, and with parents of children in schools served under this part.

(2) DURATION - Each such plan shall be submitted for the first year for which this part is in effect following the date of enactment of the No Child Left Behind Act of 2001 and shall remain in effect for the duration of the agency's participation under this part.

(3) REVIEW - Each local educational agency shall periodically review and, as necessary, revise its plan.

(e) STATE APPROVAL -

(1) IN GENERAL - Each local educational agency plan shall be filed according to a schedule established by the State educational agency.

(2) APPROVAL - The State educational agency shall approve a local educational agency's plan **only if** the State educational agency determines that the local educational agency's plan —
(A) enables schools served under this part to substantially help children served under this part meet the academic standards expected of all children described in section 1111(b)(1); and
(B) meets the requirements of this section.

(3) REVIEW - The State educational agency shall review the local educational agency's plan to determine if such agencies activities are in accordance with sections 1118 and 1119.

(f) PROGRAM RESPONSIBILITY - The local educational agency plan shall reflect the shared responsibility of schools, teachers, and the local educational agency in making decisions regarding activities under sections 1114 and 1115.

(g) PARENTAL NOTIFICATION -

> ➔ **COMMENT:** The school must advise the parents of children with disabilities how a language instruction program meets the child's IEP goals and objectives. Parents have the right to remove their child from a language program, or chose a different language program, if available. The Title III, Part C reference below is to the legal definition of a "language instruction educational program" in Title III at 20 U. S. C. § 7011(8). Title III is in the ***Wrightslaw NCLB CD-ROM.***

(1) IN GENERAL -

(A) NOTICE - Each local educational agency using funds under this part to provide a **language instruction educational program** as determined in Part C of Title III **shall**, not later than 30 days after the beginning of the school year, **inform a parent** or parents of a limited English proficient child identified for participation or participating in, such a program of —

(i) the **reasons for the identification** of their child as limited English proficient and in need of placement in a language instruction educational program;

(ii) the child's **level of English proficiency, how such level was assessed**, and the status of the **child's academic achievement**;

(iii) the **methods of instruction** used in the program in which their child is, or will be participating, and the methods of instruction used in other available programs, including how such programs differ in content, instructional goals, and the use of English and a native language in instruction;

(iv) how the program in which their child is, or will be participating, will **meet the educational strengths and needs** of their child;

(v) **how such program will specifically help their child learn English**, and meet age-appropriate academic achievement standards for grade promotion and graduation;

(vi) the **specific exit requirements** for the program, including the **expected rate of transition** from such program into classrooms that are not tailored for limited English proficient children, and the **expected rate of graduation** from secondary school for such program if funds under this part are used for children in secondary schools;

(vii) in the case of a **child with a disability**, how such program **meets the objectives of the individualized education program** of the child;

(viii) information pertaining to **parental rights** that includes written guidance —
    (I) detailing —
        (aa) **the right that parents have to have their child immediately removed from such program upon their request**; and
        (bb) the options that parents have **to decline to enroll** their child in such program **or to choose another program** or method of instruction, if available; and
    (II) assisting parents in selecting among various programs and methods of instruction, if more than one program or method is offered by the eligible entity.

(B) SEPARATE NOTIFICATION - In addition to providing the information required to be provided under paragraph (1), each eligible entity that is using funds provided under this part to provide a language instruction educational program, and that has failed to make progress on the **annual measurable achievement objectives** described in section 3122 for any fiscal year for which part A is in effect, **shall separately** inform a parent or the parents of a child identified for participation in such program, or participating in such program, **of such failure not later than 30 days after such failure occurs.**

(2) NOTICE - The notice and information provided in paragraph (1) to a parent or parents of a child identified for participation in a language instruction educational program for limited English proficient children **shall be in an understandable and uniform format** and, to the extent practicable, provided **in a language that the parents can understand.**

(3) SPECIAL RULE APPLICABLE DURING THE SCHOOL YEAR - For those children who have not been identified as limited English proficient prior to the beginning of the school year the local educational agency shall notify parents within the first 2 weeks of the child being placed in a language instruction educational program consistent with paragraphs (1) and (2).

(4) PARENTAL PARTICIPATION - Each local educational agency receiving funds under this part shall implement an effective means of **outreach to parents of limited English proficient students** to inform the parents regarding how the parents can be involved in the education of their children, and be active participants in assisting their children to attain English proficiency, achieve at high levels in core academic subjects, and meet challenging State academic achievement standards and State academic content standards expected of all students, including holding, and sending notice of opportunities for, regular meetings for the purpose of formulating and responding to recommendations from parents of students assisted under this part.

(5) BASIS FOR ADMISSION OR EXCLUSION - A student shall not be admitted to, or excluded from, any federally assisted education program on the basis of a surname or language-minority status. (Section 1112 of the NCLB Act)

20 U. S. C. § 6313. Eligible school attendance areas.

➔ **OVERVIEW:** School districts, known as local educational agencies (LEAs) are required to use Part A funds in "eligible school attendance areas." If funds are not sufficient to serve all eligible areas, a rank order system shall be used. If 35 percent of children in a school are from low-income families, the LEA may designate that area or school as eligible.

(1) IN GENERAL - A local educational agency shall use funds received under this part only in eligible school attendance areas.

(2) ELIGIBLE SCHOOL ATTENDANCE AREAS - For the purposes of this part —

(A) the term **'school attendance area'** means, in relation to a particular school, the geographical area in which the children who are normally served by that school reside; and

(B) the term **'eligible school attendance area'** means a school attendance area in which the percentage of children from low-income families is at least as high as the percentage of children from low-income families served by the local educational agency as a whole.

(3) RANKING ORDER - If funds allocated in accordance with subsection (c) are insufficient to serve all eligible school attendance areas, a local educational agency shall —

(A) annually rank, without regard to grade spans, such agency's eligible school attendance areas in which the concentration of children from low-income families exceeds 75 percent from highest to lowest according to the percentage of children from low-income families; and

(B) serve such eligible school attendance areas in rank order.

(4) REMAINING FUNDS - If funds remain after serving all eligible school attendance areas under paragraph (3), a local educational agency shall —

(A) annually rank such agency's remaining eligible school attendance areas from highest to lowest either by grade span or for the entire local educational agency according to the percentage of children from low-income families; and

(B) serve such eligible school attendance areas in rank order either within each grade-span grouping or within the local educational agency as a whole.

(5) MEASURES - The local educational agency shall use the same **measure of poverty,** which measure shall be the number of children ages 5 through 17 in poverty counted in the most recent census data approved by the Secretary, the number of children eligible for free and reduced priced lunches under the Richard B. Russell National School Lunch Act, the number of children in families receiving assistance under the State program funded under part A of title IV of the Social Security Act, or the number of children eligible to receive medical assistance under the Medicaid program, or a composite of such indicators, with respect to all school attendance areas in the local educational agency —

(A) to identify eligible school attendance areas;

(B) to determine the ranking of each area; and

(C) to determine allocations under subsection (c).

(6) EXCEPTION - This subsection shall not apply to a local educational agency with a total enrollment of less than 1,000 children.

(7) WAIVER FOR DESEGREGATION PLANS - The Secretary may approve a local educational agency's written request for a waiver of the requirements of subsections (a) and (c), and permit such agency to treat as eligible, and serve, any school that children attend with a State-ordered, court-ordered school desegregation plan or a plan that continues to be implemented in accordance with a State-ordered or court-ordered desegregation plan, if —

(A) the number of economically disadvantaged children enrolled in the school is at least 25 percent of the school's total enrollment; and

(B) the Secretary determines on the basis of a written request from such agency and in accordance with such criteria as the Secretary establishes, that approval of that request would further the purposes of this part.

(b) LOCAL EDUCATIONAL AGENCY DISCRETION -

(1) IN GENERAL - Notwithstanding subsection (a)(2), a local educational agency may —

(A) designate as eligible any school attendance area or school in which **at least 35 percent of the children are from low-income families;**

(B) use funds received under this part in a school that is not in an eligible school attendance area, if the percentage of children from low-income families enrolled in the school is equal to or greater than the percentage of such children in a participating school attendance area of such agency;

(C) designate and serve a school attendance area or school that is not eligible under this section, but that was eligible and that was served in the preceding fiscal year, but only for 1 additional fiscal year; and

(D) elect not to serve an eligible school attendance area or eligible school that has a higher percentage of children from low-income families if —

(i) the school meets the comparability requirements of section 1120A(c);
(ii) the school is receiving supplemental funds from other State or local sources that are spent

according to the requirements of section 1114 or 1115; and

(iii) the funds expended from such other sources equal or exceed the amount that would be provided under this part.

(2) SPECIAL RULE - Notwithstanding paragraph (1)(D), the number of children attending private elementary schools and secondary schools who are to receive services, and the assistance such children are to receive under this part, shall be determined without regard to whether the public school attendance area in which such children reside is assisted under subparagraph (A).

(c) ALLOCATIONS -

(1) IN GENERAL - A local educational agency shall allocate funds received under this part to eligible school attendance areas or eligible schools, identified under subsections (a) and (b), in rank order, on the basis of the total number of children from low-income families in each area or school.

(2) SPECIAL RULE -

(A) IN GENERAL - Except as provided in subparagraph (B), the per-pupil amount of funds allocated to each school attendance area or school under paragraph (1) shall be at least 125 percent of the per-pupil amount of funds a local educational agency received for that year under the poverty criteria described by the local educational agency in the plan submitted under section 1112, except that this paragraph shall not apply to a local educational agency that only serves schools in which the percentage of such children is 35 percent or greater.

(B) EXCEPTION - A local educational agency may reduce the amount of funds allocated under subparagraph (A) for a school attendance area or school by the amount of any supplemental State and local funds expended in that school attendance area or school for programs that meet the requirements of section 1114 or 1115.

(3) RESERVATION - A local educational agency shall reserve such funds as are necessary under this part to provide services comparable to those provided to children in schools funded under this part to serve —

(A) homeless children who do not attend participating schools, including providing educationally related support services to children in shelters and other locations where children may live;

(B) children in local institutions for neglected children; and

(C) if appropriate, children in local institutions for delinquent children, and neglected or delinquent children in community day school programs.

(4) FINANCIAL INCENTIVES AND REWARDS RESERVATION - A local educational agency may reserve such funds as are necessary from those funds received by the local educational agency under title II, and not more than 5 percent of those funds received by the local educational agency under subpart 2, to provide **financial incentives and rewards to teachers** who serve in schools eligible under this section and identified for school improvement, corrective action, and restructuring under section 1116(b) for the **purpose of attracting and retaining qualified and effective teachers.** (Section 1113 of the NCLB Act)

20 U. S. C. § 6314. Schoolwide programs.

➡ **OVERVIEW:** Section 6314(b) describes the components of schoolwide programs, including a needs assessment, strategies to enable all children to meet proficient and advanced levels of academic achievement, and instructional strategies and methods that are based on scientific research. Section 6314(b)(1) states that students must receive instruction from highly qualified teachers. Schoolwide programs include high quality professional development programs for teachers and other school staff.

Schoolwide programs must identify struggling students' difficulties in a timely manner and must develop effective programs to help these students master knowledge and skills at proficient or advanced levels. Strategies include increasing the amount and quality of learning with extended school year, before- and after-school programs, and summer programs. The schoolwide plan must involve parents, members of the community, and individuals who will carry out the plan. If the plan relates to a secondary school, students must also be involved.

(a) USE OF FUNDS FOR SCHOOLWIDE PROGRAMS -

(1) IN GENERAL - A local educational agency may consolidate and use funds under this part, together with other Federal, State, and local funds, in order to upgrade the entire educational program of a school that serves an eligible school attendance area in which not less than 40 percent of the children are from low-income families, or not less than 40 percent of the children enrolled in the school are from such families.

(2) IDENTIFICATION OF STUDENTS NOT REQUIRED -

 (A) IN GENERAL - No school participating in a schoolwide program shall be required —

  (i) to identify particular children under this part as eligible to participate in a schoolwide program; or
  (ii) to provide services to such children that are supplementary, as otherwise required by section 1120A(b).

 (B) SUPPLEMENTAL FUNDS - A school participating in a schoolwide program shall use funds available to carry out this section **only to supplement** the amount of funds that would, in the absence of funds under this part, be made available from non-Federal sources for the school, including funds needed to provide services that are required by law for children with disabilities and children with limited English proficiency.

(3) EXEMPTION FROM STATUTORY AND REGULATORY REQUIREMENTS -

 (A) EXEMPTION - Except as provided in subsection (b), the Secretary may, through publication of a notice in the Federal Register, exempt schoolwide programs under this section from statutory or regulatory provisions of any other noncompetitive formula grant program administered by the Secretary (other than formula or discretionary grant programs under the Individuals with Disabilities Education Act, except as provided in section 613(a)(2)(D) of such Act), or any discretionary grant program administered by the Secretary, to support schoolwide programs if the intent and purposes of such other programs are met.

 (B) REQUIREMENTS - A school that chooses to use funds from such other programs shall not be relieved of the requirements relating to health, safety, civil rights, student and parental participation and involvement, services to private school children, maintenance of effort, comparability of services, uses of Federal funds to supplement, not supplant non-Federal funds, or the distribution of funds to State educational agencies or local educational agencies that apply to the receipt of funds from such programs.

 (C) RECORDS - A school that consolidates and uses funds from different Federal programs under this section **shall not be required to maintain separate fiscal accounting records, by program,** that identify the specific activities supported by those particular funds **as long as the school maintains records that demonstrate that the schoolwide program, considered as a whole, addresses the intent and purposes of each of the Federal programs** that were consolidated to support the schoolwide program.

(4) PROFESSIONAL DEVELOPMENT - Each school receiving funds under this part for any fiscal year shall devote sufficient resources to effectively carry out the activities described in subsection (b)(1)(D) in accordance with section 1119 for such fiscal year, except that **a school may enter into a consortium with another school to carry out such activities.**

(b) COMPONENTS OF A SCHOOLWIDE PROGRAM -

(1) IN GENERAL - A schoolwide program **shall** include the following components:

(A) A **comprehensive needs assessment of the entire school** (including taking into account the needs of migratory children as defined in section 1309(2)) that is based on information which includes the achievement of children in relation to the State academic content standards and the State student academic achievement standards described in section 1111(b)(1).

(B) **Schoolwide reform strategies** that —

(i) provide opportunities for all children to meet the State's **proficient and advanced levels of student academic achievement** described in section 1111(b)(1)(D);
(ii) use effective **methods and instructional strategies that are based on scientifically based research** that —
(I) strengthen the core academic program in the school;
(II) increase the amount and quality of learning time, such as providing an extended school year and before - and after-school and summer programs and opportunities, and help provide an enriched and accelerated curriculum; and
(III) include strategies for meeting the educational needs of historically underserved populations;
(iii)
(I) include strategies to address the needs of all children in the school, but **particularly the needs of low-achieving children and those at risk of not meeting the State student academic achievement standards** who are members of the target population of any program that is included in the schoolwide program, which may include —
(aa) counseling, pupil services, and mentoring services;
(bb) college and career awareness and preparation, such as college and career guidance, personal finance education, and innovative teaching methods, which may include applied learning and team-teaching strategies; and
(cc) the integration of vocational and technical education programs; and
(II) address how the school will determine if such needs have been met; and
(iv) are consistent with, and are designed to implement, the State and local improvement plans, if any.

(C) **Instruction by highly qualified teachers.**

(D) In accordance with section 1119 and subsection (a)(4), **high-quality and ongoing professional development for teachers, principals, and paraprofessionals** and, if appropriate, **pupil services personnel, parents, and other staff** to enable all children in the school to meet the State's student academic achievement standards.

(E) Strategies to **attract high-quality highly qualified teachers** to high-need schools.

(F) Strategies to **increase parental involvement** in accordance with section 1118, such as family literary services.

(G) Plans for assisting preschool children in the transition from early childhood programs, such as Head Start, Even Start, Early Reading First, or a State-run preschool program, to local elementary school programs.

(H) Measures to include teachers in the decisions regarding the use of academic assessments described in section 1111(b)(3) in order to provide information on, and to improve, the achievement of individual students and the overall instructional program.

(I) Activities to ensure that **students who experience difficulty** mastering the proficient or advanced levels of academic achievement standards required by section 1111(b)(1) **shall be provided with effective, timely additional assistance** which **shall include measures to ensure that students' difficulties are identified on a timely basis** and to provide **sufficient information on which to base effective assistance.**

(J) Coordination and integration of Federal, State, and local services and programs, including programs supported under this Act, violence prevention programs, nutrition programs, housing programs, Head Start, adult education, vocational and technical education, and job training.

(2) PLAN -

(A) IN GENERAL - Any eligible school that desires to operate a schoolwide program shall first develop (or amend a plan for such a program that was in existence on the day before the date of enactment of the No Child Left Behind Act of 2001), in consultation with the local educational agency and its school support team or other technical assistance provider under section 1117, a comprehensive plan for reforming the total instructional program in the school that —

(i) describes how the school will implement the components described in paragraph (1);
(ii) describes how the school will use resources under this part and from other sources to implement those components;
(iii) includes a list of State educational agency and local educational agency programs and other Federal programs under subsection (a)(3) that will be consolidated in the schoolwide program; and
(iv) describes how the school will provide individual student academic assessment results in a language the parents can understand, including an interpretation of those results, to the parents of a child who participates in the academic assessments required by section 1111(b)(3).

(B) PLAN DEVELOPMENT - The comprehensive plan shall be —

(i) developed during a one-year period, unless —
    (I) the local educational agency, after considering the recommendation of the technical assistance providers under section 1117, determines that less time is needed to develop and implement the schoolwide program; or
    (II) the school is operating a schoolwide program on the day preceding the date of enactment of the No Child Left Behind Act of 2001, in which case such school may continue to operate such program, but shall develop amendments to its existing plan during the first year of assistance after that date to reflect the provisions of this section;
(ii) developed with the involvement of parents and other members of the community to be served and individuals who will carry out such plan, including teachers, principals, and administrators (including administrators of programs described in other parts of this title), and, if appropriate, pupil services personnel, technical assistance providers, school staff, and, if the plan relates to a secondary school, students from such school;
(iii) in effect for the duration of the school's participation under this part and reviewed and revised, as necessary, by the school;
(iv) available to the local educational agency, parents, and the public, and the information contained in such plan shall be in an understandable and uniform format and, to the extent practicable, provided in a language that the parents can understand; and
(v) if appropriate, developed in coordination with programs under Reading First, Early Reading First, Even Start, Carl D. Perkins Vocational and Technical Education Act of 1998, and the Head Start Act.

(c) PREKINDERGARTEN PROGRAM - A school that is eligible for a schoolwide program under this section may use funds made available under this part to establish or enhance prekindergarten programs for children below the age of 6, such as Even Start programs or Early Reading First programs. (Section 1114 of the NCLB Act)

20 U. S. C. § 6315. Targeted assistance schools.

➡ **OVERVIEW:** If a school does not operate a schoolwide program, Title I funds may be used for eligible children who are identified as having the greatest need for assistance. Eligible children are those identified as failing, or at risk of failing to meet the State's academic achievement standards. This category includes economically disadvantaged children, children with disabilities, migrant children, limited English proficient children, Head Start, Even Start, and Early Reading First Children, children in institutions, and homeless children.

Targeted assistance schools must use effective methods and instructional strategies based on scientifically based research. Other strategies include extended school year programs, before- and after-school programs, and summer programs. Instruction shall be provided by highly qualified teachers.

(a) IN GENERAL - In all schools selected to receive funds under section 1113(c) that are **ineligible for a schoolwide program** under section 1114, or that choose not to operate such a schoolwide program, a local educational agency serving such school may use funds received under this part only for programs that provide services to eligible children under subsection (b) identified as having the greatest need for special assistance.

(b) ELIGIBLE CHILDREN -

(1) ELIGIBLE POPULATION -

(A) IN GENERAL - The eligible population for services under this section is —

(i) children not older than age 21 who are entitled to a free public education through grade 12; and
(ii) children who are not yet at a grade level at which the local educational agency provides a free public education.

(B) ELIGIBLE CHILDREN FROM ELIGIBLE POPULATION - From the population described in subparagraph (A), eligible children are children identified by the school as failing, or most at risk of failing, to meet the State's challenging student academic achievement standards on the basis of multiple, educationally related, objective criteria established by the local educational agency and supplemented by the school, except that children from preschool through grade 2 shall be selected solely on the basis of such criteria as teacher judgment, interviews with parents, and developmentally appropriate measures.

(2) CHILDREN INCLUDED -

(A) IN GENERAL - Children who are **economically disadvantaged, children with disabilities, migrant children or limited English proficient children,** are eligible for services under this part on the same basis as other children selected to receive services under this part.

(B) HEAD START, EVEN START, OR EARLY READING FIRST CHILDREN - A child who, at any time in the 2 years preceding the year for which the determination is made, participated in a Head Start, Even Start, or Early Reading First program, or in preschool services under this title, is eligible for services under this part.

(C) PART C CHILDREN - A child who, at any time in the 2 years preceding the year for which the determination is made, received services under part C is eligible for services under this part.

(D) NEGLECTED OR DELINQUENT CHILDREN - A child in a local institution for neglected or delinquent children and youth or attending a community day program for such children is eligible for services under this part.

(E) HOMELESS CHILDREN - A child who is homeless and attending any school served by the local educational agency is eligible for services under this part.

(3) SPECIAL RULE - Funds received under this part may not be used to provide services that are otherwise required by law to be made available to children described in paragraph (2) but may be used to coordinate or supplement such services.

(c) COMPONENTS OF A TARGETED ASSISTANCE SCHOOL PROGRAM -

(1) IN GENERAL - To assist targeted assistance schools and local educational agencies to meet their responsibility to provide for all their students served under this part the opportunity to meet the State's challenging student academic achievement standards in subjects as determined by the State, each targeted assistance program under this section **shall** —

(A) use such program's resources under this part to help participating children meet such State's challenging student academic achievement standards expected for all children;

(B) ensure that planning for students served under this part is incorporated into existing school planning;

(C) use **effective methods and instructional strategies** that are **based on scientifically based research** that strengthens the core academic program of the school and that —

(i) **give primary consideration to providing extended learning time, such as an extended school year, before - and after-school, and summer programs and opportunities;**
(ii) help provide an accelerated, high-quality curriculum, including applied learning; and
(iii) minimize removing children from the regular classroom during regular school hours for instruction provided under this part;

(D) coordinate with and support the regular education program, which may include services to assist preschool children in the transition from early childhood programs such as Head Start, Even Start, Early Reading First or State-run preschool programs to elementary school programs;

(E) provide **instruction by highly qualified teachers;**

(F) in accordance with subsection (e)(3) and section 1119, provide **opportunities for professional development** with resources provided under this part, and, to the extent practicable, from other sources, for teachers, principals, and paraprofessionals, including, if appropriate, pupil services personnel, parents, and other staff, who work with participating children in programs under this section or in the regular education program;

(G) **provide strategies to increase parental involvement** in accordance with section 1118, such as family literacy services; and

(H) coordinate and integrate Federal, State, and local services and programs, including programs supported under this Act, violence prevention programs, nutrition programs, housing programs, Head Start, adult education, vocational and technical education, and job training.

(2) REQUIREMENTS - Each school conducting a program under this section shall assist participating children selected in accordance with subsection (b) to meet the State's proficient and advanced levels of achievement by —

(A) the coordinating of resources provided under this part with other resources; and

(B) reviewing, on an ongoing basis, the progress of participating children and revising the targeted assistance program, if necessary, to provide additional assistance to enable such children to meet the State's challenging student academic achievement standards, such as an extended school year, before - and after-school, and summer programs and opportunities, training for teachers regarding how to identify students who need additional assistance, and training for teachers regarding how to implement student academic achievement standards in the classroom.

(d) INTEGRATION OF PROFESSIONAL DEVELOPMENT - To promote the integration of staff supported with funds under this part into the regular school program and overall school planning and improvement efforts, public school personnel who are paid with funds received under this part may —

(1) participate in general professional development and school planning activities; and

(2) assume limited duties that are assigned to similar personnel who are not so paid, including duties beyond classroom instruction or that do not benefit participating children, so long as the amount of time spent on such duties is the same proportion of total work time as prevails with respect to similar personnel at the same school.

(e) SPECIAL RULES -

(1) SIMULTANEOUS SERVICE - Nothing in this section shall be construed to prohibit a school from serving students under this section simultaneously with students with similar educational needs, in the same educational settings where appropriate.

(2) COMPREHENSIVE SERVICES - If —

(A) health, nutrition, and other social **services are not otherwise available** to eligible children in a targeted assistance school and such school, if appropriate, has engaged in a comprehensive needs assessment and established a collaborative partnership with local service providers; and

(B) **funds are not reasonably available** from other public or private sources to provide such services, then a portion of the **funds** provided under this part **may be used as a last resort to provide** such services, including —

(i) the provision of **basic medical equipment**, such as eyeglasses and hearing aids;
(ii) **compensation** of a coordinator; and
(iii) **professional development** necessary to assist teachers, pupil services personnel, other staff, and parents in identifying and meeting the comprehensive needs of eligible children.

(3) PROFESSIONAL DEVELOPMENT - Each school receiving funds under this part for any fiscal year shall devote sufficient resources to carry out effectively the professional development activities described in subparagraph (F) of subsection (c)(1) in accordance with section 1119 for such fiscal year, and a school may enter into a consortium with another school to carry out such activities. (Section 1115 of NCLB Act)

20 U. S. C. § 6316. Academic assessment and local educational agency and school improvement.

➡ **OVERVIEW:** The statute about academic assessment and school district improvement is a key statute. This statute includes requirements about schools in need of improvement, school plans, public school choice, and supplemental educational services.

School districts must use the results of state academic assessments to review the progress of each Title I school every year to determine if the school is making adequate yearly progress. School districts must identify elementary and secondary schools that fail to make adequate yearly progress for two consecutive years as in need of improvement, corrective action, or restructuring, and must publicize and disseminate this information to parents, teachers, principals, schools, and the community.

Each school identified for school improvement must develop a plan to address the identified deficiencies. The plan must include strategies based on scientifically based research that will strengthen academics and address the specific deficiencies that caused the school to be identified. The plan must establish specific annual, measurable objectives for continuous, substantial progress by each group of students. The plan must also describe how the school will provide written notice to parents.

Students who are enrolled in failing schools can transfer to another public school that is not a failing school or receive supplemental educational services at no cost to the parents.

Compare subsection 20 U. S. C. § 6316(b)(1) with the next subsection, 20 U. S. C. § 6316(c)(1) which requires States to identify failing school districts (i.e., LEAs).

(a) LOCAL REVIEW -

(1) IN GENERAL - Each **local educational agency** receiving funds under this part **shall** —

(A) **use the State academic assessments** and other indicators described in the State plan **to review annually the progress of each school** served under this part **to determine whether the school is making adequate yearly progress** as defined in section 1111(b)(2);

(B) at the local educational agency's discretion, use any academic assessments or any other academic indicators described in the local educational agency's plan under section 1112(b)(1)(A) and (B) to review annually the progress of each school served under this part to determine whether the school is making adequate yearly progress as defined in section 1111(b)(2), except that the local educational agency may not use such indicators (other than as provided for in section 1111(b)(2)(I)) if the indicators reduce the number or change the schools that would otherwise be subject to school improvement, corrective action, or restructuring under section 1116 if such additional indicators were not used, but may identify additional schools for school improvement or in need of corrective action or restructuring;

(C) **publicize and disseminate** the results of the local annual review described in paragraph (1) **to parents, teachers, principals, schools, and the community** so that the teachers, principals, other staff, and schools can continually refine, in an instructionally useful manner, the program of instruction to help all children served under this part meet the challenging State student academic achievement standards established under section 1111(b)(1); and

(D) review the effectiveness of the actions and activities the schools are carrying out under this part with respect to parental involvement, professional development, and other activities assisted under this part.

(2) AVAILABLE RESULTS - The State educational agency shall ensure that the **results** of State academic assessments administered in that school year **are available** to the local educational agency before the beginning of the next school year.

(b) SCHOOL IMPROVEMENT -

(1) GENERAL REQUIREMENTS -

(A) **IDENTIFICATION** - Subject to subparagraph (C), a **local educational agency shall identify for school improvement any elementary school or secondary school served under this part that fails, for 2 consecutive years, to make adequate yearly progress** as defined in the State's plan under section 1111(b)(2).

(B) DEADLINE - The identification described in subparagraph (A) shall take place **before the beginning of the school year following such failure to make adequate yearly progress.**

(C) APPLICATION - Subparagraph (A) shall not apply to a school if almost every student in each group specified in section 1111(b)(2)(C)(v) enrolled in such school is meeting or exceeding the State's proficient level of academic achievement.

(D) TARGETED ASSISTANCE SCHOOLS - To determine if an elementary school or a secondary school that is conducting a targeted assistance program under section 1115 should be identified for school improvement, corrective action, or restructuring under this section, a local educational agency may choose to review the progress of only the students in the school who are served, or are eligible for services, under this part.

(E) PUBLIC SCHOOL CHOICE -

(i) IN GENERAL - In the case of a school identified for school improvement under this paragraph, the local educational agency **shall**, not later than the first day of the school year following such identification, **provide all students enrolled in the school with the option to transfer to another public school** served by the local educational agency, which **may include a public charter school, that has not been identified for school improvement** under this paragraph, unless such an option is prohibited by State law.
(ii) RULE - In providing students the option to transfer to another public school, the local educational agency shall give **priority** to the lowest achieving children from low-income families, as determined by the local educational agency for purposes of allocating funds to schools under section 1113(c)(1).

(F) TRANSFER - **Students who use the option to transfer** under subparagraph (E) and paragraph (5)(A), (7)(C)(i), or (8)(A)(i) or subsection (c)(10)(C)(vii) **shall be enrolled in classes and other activities in the public school to which the students transfer in the same manner as all other children at the public school.**

(2) OPPORTUNITY TO REVIEW AND PRESENT EVIDENCE; TIME LIMIT -

(A) IDENTIFICATION - Before identifying an elementary school or a secondary school for school improvement under paragraphs (1) or (5)(A), for corrective action under paragraph (7), or for restructuring under paragraph (8), the local educational agency **shall** provide the school with an opportunity to review the school-level data, including academic assessment data, on which the proposed identification is based.

(B) EVIDENCE - If the principal of a school proposed for identification under paragraph (1), (5)(A), (7), or (8) believes, or a majority of the parents of the students enrolled in such school believe, that the proposed identification is in error for statistical or other substantive reasons, the principal may provide supporting evidence to the local educational agency, which **shall** consider that evidence before making a final determination.

(C) FINAL DETERMINATION - Not later than 30 days after a local educational agency provides the school with the opportunity to review such school-level data, the local educational agency **shall make public** a final determination on the status of the school with respect to the identification.

(3) SCHOOL PLAN -

(A) REVISED PLAN - After the resolution of a review under paragraph (2), each school identified under paragraph (1) for school improvement shall, not later than 3 months after being so identified, develop or revise a school plan, in consultation with parents, school staff, the local educational agency serving the school, and outside experts, for approval by such local educational agency. The school plan shall cover a 2-year period and —

(i) **incorporate strategies based on scientifically based research that will strengthen the core academic subjects in the school and address the specific academic issues that caused the school to be identified for school improvement**, and may include a strategy for the implementation of a comprehensive school reform model that includes each of the components described in part F;

(ii) adopt policies and practices concerning the school's core academic subjects that have the greatest likelihood of ensuring that **all groups of students** specified in section 1111(b)(2)(C)(v) and enrolled in the school **will meet the State's proficient level** of achievement on the State academic assessment described in section 1111(b)(3) not later than 12 years after the end of the 2001-2002 school year;

(iii) provide an assurance that the school will spend not less than 10 percent of the funds made available to the school under section 1113 for each fiscal year that the school is in school improvement status, for the purpose of providing to the school's teachers and principal high-quality professional development that —

(I) **directly addresses the academic achievement problem that caused the school to be identified for school improvement;**

(II) meets the requirements for **professional development** activities under section 1119; and

(III) is provided in a manner that affords increased opportunity for participating in that professional development;

(iv) **specify how the funds** described in clause (iii) **will be used** to remove the school from school improvement status;

(v) **establish specific annual, measurable objectives for continuous and substantial progress by each group of students** specified in section 1111(b)(2)(C)(v) and enrolled in the school that will ensure that all such groups of students will, in accordance with adequate yearly progress as defined in section 1111(b)(2), meet the State's proficient level of achievement on the State academic assessment described in section 1111(b)(3) not later than 12 years after the end of the 2001-2002 school year;

(vi) describe how the **school will provide written notice about the identification to parents of each student enrolled in such school**, in a format and, to the extent practicable, in a language that the parents can understand;

(vii) specify the responsibilities of the school, the local educational agency, and the State educational agency serving the school under the plan, including the technical assistance to be provided by the local educational agency under paragraph (4) and the local educational agency's responsibilities under section 1120A;

(viii) include **strategies to promote effective parental involvement in the school;**

(ix) incorporate, as appropriate, **activities before school, after school, during the summer, and during any extension of the school year;** and

(x) incorporate a teacher mentoring program.

(B) CONDITIONAL APPROVAL - The local educational agency may condition approval of a school plan under this paragraph on —

(i) inclusion of one or more of the corrective actions specified in paragraph (7)(C)(iv); or

(ii) feedback on the school improvement plan from parents and community leaders.

(C) PLAN IMPLEMENTATION - Except as provided in subparagraph (D), a school shall implement the school plan (including a revised plan) expeditiously, **but not later than the beginning of the next full school year** following the identification under paragraph (1).

(D) PLAN APPROVED DURING SCHOOL YEAR - Notwithstanding subparagraph (C), if a plan is not approved prior to the beginning of a school year, such plan shall be implemented immediately upon approval.

(E) LOCAL EDUCATIONAL AGENCY APPROVAL - The local educational agency, within 45 days of receiving a school plan, shall —

(i) establish a peer review process to assist with review of the school plan; and
(ii) promptly review the school plan, work with the school as necessary, and approve the school plan if the plan meets the requirements of this paragraph.

(4) TECHNICAL ASSISTANCE -

(A) IN GENERAL - For each school identified for school improvement under paragraph (1), the local educational agency serving the school shall ensure the provision of technical assistance as the school develops and implements the school plan under paragraph (3) throughout the plan's duration.

(B) SPECIFIC ASSISTANCE - Such technical assistance —

(i) shall include assistance in analyzing data from the assessments required under section 1111(b)(3), and other examples of student work, to identify and address problems in instruction, and problems if any, in implementing the parental involvement requirements described in section 1118, the professional development requirements described in section 1119, and the responsibilities of the school and local educational agency under the school plan, and to identify and address solutions to such problems;
(ii) shall include assistance in identifying and implementing **professional development, instructional strategies, and methods of instruction that are based on scientifically based research and that have proven effective in addressing the specific instructional issues that caused the school to be identified for school improvement;**
(iii) shall include assistance in analyzing and revising the school's budget so that **the school's resources are more effectively allocated to the activities most likely to increase student academic achievement and to remove the school from school improvement status;** and
(iv) may be provided —
    (I) by the local educational agency, through mechanisms authorized under section 1117; or
    (II) by the State educational agency, an institution of higher education (that is in full compliance with all the reporting provisions of title II of the Higher Education Act of 1965), a private not-for-profit organization or for-profit organization, an educational service agency, or another entity with experience in helping schools improve academic achievement.

(C) SCIENTIFICALLY BASED RESEARCH - **Technical assistance** provided under this section by a local educational agency or an entity approved by that agency **shall be based on scientifically based research.**

(5) FAILURE TO MAKE ADEQUATE YEARLY PROGRESS AFTER IDENTIFICATION - In the case of **any school** served under this part **that fails to make adequate yearly progress**, as set out in the State's plan under section 1111(b)(2), by the end of the first full school year after identification under paragraph (1), the local educational agency serving such school —

(A) **shall continue to provide all students enrolled in the school with the option to transfer to another public school** served by the local educational agency in accordance with subparagraphs (E) and (F);

(B) **shall make supplemental educational services available** consistent with subsection (e)(1); and

(C) shall continue to provide technical assistance.

🗁 The definition of supplemental educational services is at 20 U. S. C. § 6316(e)(12)(C).

📖 *Supplemental Educational Services: Non-Regulatory Guidance* published by the U. S. Department of Education. This publication includes frequently-asked questions and answers about supplemental educational services including identification and approval of providers and monitoring requirements, school district requirements to arrange for supplemental educational services, the role of parents, monitoring, funding, and definitions. Available on the Wrightslaw NCLB CD-ROM.

(6) NOTICE TO PARENTS - A local educational agency **shall promptly** provide to a parent or parents (in an understandable and uniform format and, to the extent practicable, in a language the parents can understand) **of each student enrolled in an elementary school or a secondary school identified for school improvement** under paragraph (1), for corrective action under paragraph (7), **or for restructuring** under paragraph (8) —

(A) **an explanation of what the identification means**, and **how the school compares** in terms of academic achievement to other elementary schools or secondary schools served by the local educational agency and the State educational agency involved;

(B) the **reasons** for the identification;

(C) an **explanation** of what the school identified for school improvement **is doing to address the problem of low achievement;**

(D) an explanation of what the local educational agency or State educational agency is doing to help the school address the achievement problem;

(E) an explanation of **how the parents can become involved** in addressing the academic issues that caused the school to be identified for school improvement; and

(F) an explanation of the **parents' option to transfer their child to another public school** under paragraphs (1)(E), (5)(A), (7)(C)(i), (8)(A)(i), and subsection (c)(10)(C)(vii) (with **transportation provided by the agency** when required by paragraph (9)) **or to obtain supplemental educational services for the child**, in accordance with subsection (e).

(7) CORRECTIVE ACTION -

(A) IN GENERAL - In this subsection, the term **'corrective action'** means action, consistent with State law, that —

  (i) substantially and directly responds to —
     (I) the **consistent academic failure of a school** that caused the local educational agency to take such action; and
     (II) any underlying **staffing, curriculum, or other problems in the school;** and
  (ii) is designed to increase substantially the likelihood that **each group of students** described in 1111(b)(2)(C) enrolled in the school identified for corrective action **will meet or exceed the State's proficient levels of achievement on the State academic assessments** described in section 1111(b)(3).

(B) SYSTEM - In order to help students served under this part meet challenging State student academic achievement standards, each local educational agency shall implement a system of corrective action in accordance with subparagraphs (C) through (E).

(C) ROLE OF LOCAL EDUCATIONAL AGENCY - In the case of any school served by a local educational agency under this part that **fails to make adequate yearly progress**, as defined by the State under section 1111(b)(2), **by the end of the second full school year** after the identification under paragraph (1), the local educational agency **shall** —

(i) continue to **provide all students enrolled in the school with the option to transfer** to another public school served by the local educational agency, in accordance with paragraph (1)(E) and (F);
(ii) continue to provide technical assistance consistent with paragraph (4) while instituting any corrective action under clause (iv);
(iii) continue to **make supplemental educational services available,** in accordance with subsection (e), to children who remain in the school; and
(iv) identify the school for corrective action and **take at least one of the following corrective actions:**

    (I) Replace the school staff who are relevant to the failure to make adequate yearly progress.
    (II) Institute and **fully implement a new curriculum,** including providing appropriate professional development for all relevant staff, that is based on scientifically based research and offers substantial promise of improving educational achievement for low-achieving students and enabling the school to make adequate yearly progress.
    (III) Significantly **decrease management authority** at the school level.
    (IV) **Appoint an outside expert** to advise the school on its progress toward making adequate yearly progress, based on its school plan under paragraph (3).
    (V) **Extend the school year or school day for the school.**
    (VI) **Restructure the internal organizational structure of the school.**

➡ **COMMENT:** When schools continue to fail, the school district must take at least one of several corrective actions: replace the staff, restructure the school, extend the school day, appoint an outside expert, decrease management authority, and/or implement a new curriculum.

(D) DELAY - Notwithstanding any other provision of this paragraph, the local educational agency may delay, for a period not to exceed 1 year, implementation of the requirements under paragraph (5), corrective action under this paragraph, or restructuring under paragraph (8) if the school makes adequate yearly progress for 1 year or if its failure to make adequate yearly progress is **due to exceptional or uncontrollable circumstances,** such as a natural disaster or a precipitous and unforeseen decline in the financial resources of the local educational agency or school. No such period shall be taken into account in determining the number of consecutive years of failure to make adequate yearly progress.

    (E) PUBLICATION AND DISSEMINATION - The local educational agency **shall publish and disseminate information regarding any corrective action** the local educational agency takes under this paragraph at a school—

        (i) **to the public and to the parents of each student** enrolled in the school subject to corrective action;
        (ii) in an understandable and uniform format and, to the extent practicable, provided in a language that the parents can understand; and
        (iii) through such means as the Internet, the media, and public agencies.

    (8) RESTRUCTURING -

    (A) FAILURE TO MAKE ADEQUATE YEARLY PROGRESS - If, **after 1 full school year of corrective action under paragraph (7),** a school subject to such corrective action **continues to fail** to make adequate yearly progress, then the local educational agency **shall**—

        (i) continue to provide all students enrolled in the school with **the option to transfer to another public school** served by the local educational agency, in accordance with paragraph (1)(E) and (F);
        (ii) continue to make **supplemental educational services** available, in accordance with subsection (e), to children who remain in the school; and(iii) prepare a plan and make necessary arrangements to carry out subparagraph (B).

    (B) ALTERNATIVE GOVERNANCE - Not later than the beginning of the school year following the year in which the local educational agency implements subparagraph (A), the local educational agency **shall**

implement one of the following alternative governance arrangements for the school consistent with State law:

(i) **Reopening the school as a public charter school.**

(ii) **Replacing all or most of the school staff** (which may include the principal) who are relevant to the failure to make adequate yearly progress.

(iii) Entering into a contract with an entity, such as a **private management company**, with a demonstrated record of effectiveness, to operate the public school.

(iv) Turning the operation of the school over to the **State educational agency**, if permitted under State law and agreed to by the State.

(v) Any other major restructuring of the school's governance arrangement that makes **fundamental reforms,** such as significant changes in the school's staffing and governance, to improve student academic achievement in the school and that has substantial promise of enabling the school to make adequate yearly progress as defined in the State plan under section 1111(b)(2). In the case of a rural local educational agency with a total of less than 600 students in average daily attendance at the schools that are served by the agency and all of whose schools have a School Locale Code of 7 or 8, as determined by the Secretary, the Secretary shall, at such agency's request, provide technical assistance to such agency for the purpose of implementing this clause.

(C) PROMPT NOTICE - The local educational agency shall—

(i) **provide prompt notice to teachers and parents** whenever subparagraph (A) or (B) applies; and

(ii) **provide the teachers and parents with an adequate opportunity to—**
    (I) **comment before taking any action** under those subparagraphs; and
    (II) **participate in developing any plan** under subparagraph (A)(iii).

➡ **COMMENT:** If a school continues to fail, the school district may re-open the school as a charter school, replace the staff, turn the school over to the State, or implement other fundamental reforms.

(9) TRANSPORTATION - In any case described in paragraph (1)(E) for schools described in paragraphs (1)(A), (5), (7)(C)(i), and (8)(A), and subsection (c)(10)(C)(vii), the local educational agency **shall provide, or shall pay for the provision of, transportation for the student to the public school the student attends.**

(10) FUNDS FOR TRANSPORTATION AND SUPPLEMENTAL EDUCATIONAL SERVICES -

(A) IN GENERAL- Unless a lesser amount is needed to comply with paragraph (9) and to satisfy all requests for supplemental educational services under subsection (e), a local educational agency shall spend an amount equal to 20 percent of its allocation under subpart 2, from which the agency shall spend—

(i) an amount equal to 5 percent of its allocation under subpart 2 to provide, or pay for, transportation under paragraph (9);

(ii) an amount equal to 5 percent of its allocation under subpart 2 to provide supplemental educational services under subsection (e); and(iii) an amount equal to the remaining 10 percent of its allocation under subpart 2 for transportation under paragraph (9), supplemental educational services under subsection (e), or both, as the agency determines.

(B) TOTAL AMOUNT - The total amount described in subparagraph (A)(ii) is the maximum amount the local educational agency shall be required to spend under this part on supplemental educational services described in subsection (e).

(C) INSUFFICIENT FUNDS - If the amount of funds described in subparagraph (A)(ii) or (iii) and available to provide services under this subsection is **insufficient to provide supplemental educational services to each child whose parents request the services, the local educational agency shall give**

priority to providing the services to the lowest-achieving children.

➡️ **COMMENT:** This does not say "offer it to the lowest-achieving children first." The offer must be made to all children. Then, within the group that requested the services, start choosing children from the bottom up, until funds run out.

(D) PROHIBITION - A local educational agency shall not, as a result of the application of this paragraph, reduce by more than 15 percent the total amount made available under section 1113(c) to a school described in paragraph (7)(C) or (8)(A) of subsection (b).

(11) COOPERATIVE AGREEMENT - In any case described in paragraph (1)(E), (5)(A), (7)(C)(i), or (8)(A)(i), or subsection (c)(10)(C)(vii) if all public schools served by the local educational agency to which a child may transfer are identified for school improvement, corrective action or restructuring, the agency **shall, to the extent practicable, establish a cooperative agreement with other local educational agencies in the area for a transfer.**

(12) DURATION - If any school identified for school improvement, corrective action, or restructuring makes **adequate yearly progress for two consecutive school years,** the local educational agency shall no longer subject the school to the requirements of school improvement, corrective action, or restructuring or identify the school for school improvement for the succeeding school year.

(13) SPECIAL RULE - A local educational agency **shall permit a child who transferred to another school under this subsection to remain in that school until the child has completed the highest grade in that school.** The obligation of the local educational agency to provide, or to provide for, transportation for the child ends at the end of a school year if the local educational agency determines that the school from which the child transferred is no longer identified for school improvement or subject to corrective action or restructuring.

(14) STATE EDUCATIONAL AGENCY RESPONSIBILITIES - The State educational agency **shall**—

(A) make technical assistance under section 1117 available to schools identified for school improvement, corrective action, or restructuring under this subsection consistent with section 1117(a)(2);

(B) if the State educational agency determines that a local educational agency failed to carry out its responsibilities under this subsection, take such corrective actions as the State educational agency determines to be appropriate and in compliance with State law;

(C) ensure that academic assessment results under this part are provided to schools before any identification of a school may take place under this subsection; and

(D) for local educational agencies or schools identified for improvement under this subsection, notify the Secretary of **major factors** that were brought to the attention of the State educational agency under section 1111(b)(9) that have significantly affected student academic achievement.

➡️ **COMMENT:** The burden is on the State to ensure that local school districts take corrective action.

(c) STATE REVIEW AND LOCAL EDUCATIONAL AGENCY IMPROVEMENT -

(1) IN GENERAL - A State **shall**—

(A) **annually review the progress of each local educational agency** receiving funds under this part to determine whether schools receiving assistance under this part are making adequate yearly progress as defined in section 1111(b)(2) toward meeting the State's student academic achievement standards and to determine if each local educational agency is carrying out its responsibilities under this section and sections 1117, 1118, and 1119; and

(B) **publicize** and disseminate to local educational agencies, teachers and other staff, parents, students, and the community the results of the State review, including statistically sound disaggregated results, as required by section 1111(b)(2).

(2) REWARDS - In the case of a local educational agency that, for 2 consecutive years, has **exceeded adequate yearly progress** as defined in the State plan under section 1111(b)(2), the State may make rewards of the kinds described under section 1117 to the agency.

(3) **IDENTIFICATION OF LOCAL EDUCATIONAL AGENCY FOR IMPROVEMENT** - A State shall **identify for improvement any local educational agency that, for 2 consecutive years**, including the period immediately prior to the date of enactment of the No Child Left Behind Act of 2001, **failed to make adequate yearly progress** as defined in the State's plan under section 1111(b)(2).

➡ **COMMENT:** The State is ultimately responsible for ensuring that local school districts make adequate yearly progress.

(4) **TARGETED ASSISTANCE SCHOOLS** - When reviewing targeted assistance schools served by a local educational agency, a State educational agency **may choose to review** the progress of only the students in such schools who are served, or are eligible for services, under this part.

(5) **OPPORTUNITY TO REVIEW AND PRESENT EVIDENCE** -

(A) **REVIEW** - Before identifying a local educational agency for improvement under paragraph (3) or corrective action under paragraph (10), a State educational agency **shall** provide the local educational agency with an opportunity to review the data, including academic assessment data, on which the proposed identification is based.

(B) **EVIDENCE** - If the local educational agency believes that the proposed identification is in error for statistical or other substantive reasons, the agency may provide supporting evidence to the State educational agency, which **shall consider** the evidence before making a final determination not later than 30 days after the State educational agency provides the local educational agency with the opportunity to review such data under subparagraph (A).

(6) **NOTIFICATION TO PARENTS** - The State educational agency **shall promptly provide to the parents** (in a format and, to the extent practicable, in a language the parents can understand) **of each student enrolled in a school** served by a local educational agency **identified for improvement, the results of the review** under paragraph (1) and, if the agency is identified for improvement, the reasons for that identification and how parents can participate in upgrading the quality of the local educational agency.

(7) **LOCAL EDUCATIONAL AGENCY REVISIONS** -

(A) **PLAN** - Each local educational agency identified under paragraph (3) **shall, not later than 3 months** after being so identified, develop or revise a local educational agency plan, **in consultation with parents, school staff, and others.** Such plan **shall**—

(i) **incorporate scientifically based research strategies** that strengthen the core academic program in schools served by the local educational agency;
(ii) identify actions that have the greatest likelihood of improving the achievement of participating children in meeting the State's student academic achievement standards;
(iii) address the **professional development needs** of the instructional staff serving the agency by committing to **spend not less than 10 percent** of the funds received by the local educational agency under subpart 2 for each fiscal year in which the agency is identified for improvement **for**

professional development (including funds reserved for professional development under subsection (b)(3)(A)(iii)), but excluding funds reserved for professional development under section 1119;

(iv) **include specific measurable achievement goals and targets for each of the groups of students identified in the disaggregated data** pursuant to section 1111(b)(2)(C)(v), consistent with adequate yearly progress as defined under section 1111(b)(2);

(v) address the **fundamental teaching and learning needs** in the schools of that agency, and the specific academic problems of low–achieving students, **including a determination of why the local educational agency's prior plan failed** to bring about increased student academic achievement;

(vi) incorporate, as appropriate, **activities before school, after school, during the summer, and during an extension of the school year;**

(vii) **specify the responsibilities of the State educational agency and the local educational agency under the plan**, including specifying the technical assistance to be provided by the State educational agency under paragraph (9) and the local educational agency's responsibilities under section 1120A; and

(viii) include strategies to promote **effective parental involvement** in the school.

(B) IMPLEMENTATION - The local educational agency shall implement the plan (including a revised plan) **expeditiously,** but **not later than the beginning of the next school year** after the school year in which the agency was identified for improvement.

(8) ➔ COMMENT: There is no subsection 8 in No Child Left Behind. Apparently, this is a typographical error in the original Act.)

(9) STATE EDUCATIONAL AGENCY RESPONSIBILITY -

(A) TECHNICAL OR OTHER ASSISTANCE - For each local educational agency identified under paragraph (3), the State educational agency shall provide technical or other assistance if requested, as authorized under section 1117, to better enable the local educational agency to—

(i) develop and implement the local educational agency's plan; and
(ii) work with schools needing improvement.

(B) METHODS AND STRATEGIES - Technical assistance provided under this section by the State educational agency or an entity authorized by such agency shall be supported by effective methods and instructional strategies based on scientifically based research. Such technical assistance shall address problems, if any, in implementing the parental involvement activities described in section 1118 and the professional development activities described in section 1119.

(10) CORRECTIVE ACTION - In order to help students served under this part meet challenging State student academic achievement standards, each State shall implement a system of corrective action in accordance with the following:

(A) DEFINITION - As used in this paragraph, the term **'corrective action'** means action, consistent with State law, that—

(i) substantially and directly **responds to the consistent academic failure** that caused the State to take such action and to any underlying staffing, curricular, or other problems in the agency; and
(ii) is **designed to meet the goal of having all students served under this part achieve at the proficient and advanced student academic achievement levels.**

(B) GENERAL REQUIREMENTS - After providing technical assistance under paragraph (9) and subject to subparagraph (E), the State—

(i) **may take corrective action at any time** with respect to a local educational agency that has been identified under paragraph (3);

(ii) **shall take corrective action** with respect to any local educational agency that fails to make adequate yearly progress, as defined by the State, by the end of the second full school year after the identification of the agency under paragraph (3); and

(iii) shall continue to provide technical assistance while instituting any corrective action under clause (i) or (ii).

(C) CERTAIN CORRECTIVE ACTIONS REQUIRED - In the case of a local educational agency identified for corrective action, **the State educational agency shall take at least one of the following corrective actions:**

(i) Deferring programmatic **funds** or reducing administrative funds.

(ii) Instituting and **fully implementing a new curriculum** that is based on State and local academic content and achievement standards, including **providing appropriate professional development based on scientifically based research** for all relevant staff, that offers substantial promise of improving educational achievement for low-achieving students.

(iii) **Replacing the local educational agency personnel** who are relevant to the failure to make adequate yearly progress.

(iv) **Removing particular schools from the jurisdiction of the local educational agency** and establishing alternative arrangements for public governance and supervision of such schools.

(v) **Appointing**, through the State educational agency, **a receiver or trustee** to administer the affairs of the local educational agency in place of the superintendent and school board.

(vi) **Abolishing or restructuring the local educational agency.**

(vii) **Authorizing students to transfer** from a school operated by the local educational agency **to a higher-performing public school operated by another local educational agency** in accordance with subsections (b)(1)(E) and (F), **and providing to such students transportation** (or the costs of transportation) to such schools consistent with subsection (b)(9), in conjunction with carrying out not less than one additional action described under this subparagraph.

→ **COMMENT:** NCLB requires states to take at least one of the seven corrective actions listed in Section 6316(c)(10) above. States also have the power to abolish school districts (local educational agencies).

(D) HEARING - Prior to implementing any corrective action under this paragraph, the State educational agency shall provide notice and a hearing to the affected local educational agency, if State law provides for such notice and hearing. The hearing shall take place **not later than 45 days following the decision to implement corrective action.**

(E) NOTICE TO PARENTS - The State educational agency **shall publish, and disseminate to parents and the public, information on any corrective action** the State educational agency takes under this paragraph **through such means as the Internet, the media, and public agencies.**

(F) DELAY - Notwithstanding subparagraph (B)(ii), a State educational agency **may delay, for a period not to exceed 1 year, implementation of corrective action** under this paragraph if the local educational agency makes adequate yearly progress for 1 year or its failure to make adequate yearly progress is due to **exceptional or uncontrollable circumstances**, such as a natural disaster or a precipitous and unforeseen decline in the financial resources of the local educational agency. No such period shall be taken into account in determining the number of consecutive years of failure to make adequate yearly progress.

(11) SPECIAL RULE - If a local educational agency **makes adequate yearly progress for two consecutive school years** beginning after the date of identification of the agency under paragraph (3), the State educational agency need no longer identify the local educational agency for improvement or subject the local educational agency to corrective action for the succeeding school year.

(d) CONSTRUCTION - Nothing in this section shall be construed to alter or otherwise affect the rights, remedies, and procedures afforded school or school district employees under Federal, State, or local laws (including applicable regulations or court orders) or under the terms of collective bargaining agreements, memoranda of understanding, or other agreements between such employees and their employers.

(e) SUPPLEMENTAL EDUCATIONAL SERVICES -

(1) SUPPLEMENTAL EDUCATIONAL SERVICES - In the case of any school described in paragraph (5), (7), or (8) of subsection (b), the local educational agency serving such school **shall**, subject to this subsection, arrange for the provision of **supplemental educational services** to eligible children in the school from **a provider with a demonstrated record of effectiveness**, that is **selected by the parents** and approved for that purpose by the State educational agency in accordance with reasonable criteria, consistent with paragraph (5), that the State educational agency shall adopt.

(2) LOCAL EDUCATIONAL AGENCY RESPONSIBILITIES - Each local educational agency subject to this subsection shall—

(A) provide, at a minimum, **annual notice to parents** (in an understandable and uniform format and, to the extent practicable, in a language the parents can understand) of—

(i) the **availability of services** under this subsection;
(ii) the **identity of approved providers** of those services that are within the local educational agency or whose services are reasonably available in neighboring local educational agencies; and
(iii) a brief **description of the services, qualifications, and demonstrated effectiveness of each such provider;**

(B) if requested, **assist parents in choosing a provider** from the list of approved providers maintained by the State;

(C) apply fair and equitable procedures for serving students if the number of spaces at approved providers is not sufficient to serve all students; and

(D) not disclose to the public the identity of any student who is eligible for, or receiving, supplemental educational services under this subsection **without the written permission of the parents of the student.**

(3) AGREEMENT - In the case of the **selection of an approved provider by a parent**, the local educational agency **shall enter into an agreement** with such provider. Such agreement shall—

(A) require the local educational agency to develop, in consultation with parents (and the provider chosen by the parents), **a statement of specific achievement goals for the student, how the student's progress will be measured**, and a **timetable** for improving achievement that, in the case of a student with disabilities, is consistent with the student's **individualized education program** under section 614(d) of the Individuals with Disabilities Education Act;

📁 Section 614(d) of IDEA is codified at 20 U. S. C. § 1414(d).

📖 The full text of the Individuals with Disabilities Education Act, implementing regulations and commentary is in *Wrightslaw: Special Education Law* (ISBN 1-892320-03-7) published by Harbor House Law Press. *Wrightslaw: Special Education Law* and the companion book, *Wrightslaw: From Emotions to Advocacy* are available at most bookstores and on the Wrightslaw.com site at www.wrightslaw.com

(B) describe how the student's **parents and** the student's **teacher or teachers will be regularly informed of the student's progress;**

(C) provide for the termination of such agreement if the provider is unable to meet such goals and timetables;

(D) contain provisions with respect to the **making of payments to the provider** by the local educational agency; and

(E) prohibit the provider from disclosing to the public the identity of any student eligible for, or receiving, supplemental educational services under this subsection without the **written permission of the parents** of such student.

(4) STATE EDUCATIONAL AGENCY RESPONSIBILITIES - A **State educational agency shall—**

(A) in consultation with local educational agencies, parents, teachers, and other interested members of the public, **promote maximum participation by providers** to ensure, to the extent practicable, that parents have as many choices as possible;

(B) develop and apply **objective criteria**, consistent with paragraph (5), to potential providers that are based on a **demonstrated record of effectiveness in increasing the academic proficiency** of students in subjects relevant to meeting the State academic content and student achievement standards adopted under section 1111(b)(1);

(C) **maintain an updated list of approved providers** across the State, by school district, from which parents may select;

(D) develop, implement, and **publicly report on standards and techniques** for monitoring the quality and effectiveness of the services offered by approved providers under this subsection, and for withdrawing approval from providers that fail, for 2 consecutive years, to contribute to increasing the academic proficiency of students served under this subsection as described in subparagraph (B); and

(E) **provide annual notice to potential providers of supplemental educational services** of the opportunity to provide services under this subsection and of the applicable procedures for obtaining approval from the State educational agency to be an approved provider of those services.

(5) CRITERIA FOR PROVIDERS - In order for a provider to be included on the State list under paragraph (4)(C), a provider shall agree to carry out the following:

(A) **Provide** parents of children receiving supplemental educational services under this subsection and the appropriate local educational agency with **information on the progress of the children** in increasing achievement, in a format and, to the extent practicable, a language that such parents can understand.

(B) Ensure that **instruction provided and content used by the provider** are consistent with the instruction provided and content used by the local educational agency and State, and are **aligned with State student academic achievement standards.**

(C) Meet all applicable Federal, State, and local health, safety, and **civil rights** laws.

(D) Ensure that all instruction and content under this subsection are secular, neutral, and nonideological.

➡ **COMMENT:** This statement about civil rights means providers must comply with Section 504 of the Rehabilitation Act of 1973. The Section 504 statute and regulations are in *Wrightslaw: Special Education Law* (ISBN 1-892320-03-7) published by Harbor House Law Press.

📖 For information about supplemental educational services and how supplemental services providers will be identified and approved, read *Supplemental Educational Services: Non-Regulatory Guidance* published by the U. S. Department of Education. The publication is on the Wrightslaw NCLB CD-ROM.

(6) AMOUNTS FOR SUPPLEMENTAL EDUCATIONAL SERVICES - The amount that a local educational agency shall make available for supplemental educational services for each child receiving those services under this subsection shall be the lesser of—

(A) the amount of the agency's allocation under subpart 2, divided by the number of children from families below the poverty level counted under section 1124(c)(1)(A); or

(B) the actual costs of the supplemental educational services received by the child.

(7) FUNDS PROVIDED BY STATE EDUCATIONAL AGENCY - Each State educational agency may use funds that the agency reserves under this part, and part A of title V, to assist local educational agencies that do not have sufficient funds to provide services under this subsection for all eligible students requesting such services.

(8) DURATION - The local educational agency shall continue to provide supplemental educational services to a child receiving such services under this subsection **until the end of the school year in which such services were first received.**

➡️ **COMMENT:** Parents do not have to wait for the school to help them choose a provider. The choice of a provider is made by the parent. Once the parent chooses a provider from the state-approved list, the parent may enroll the child for services with the provider. The provider bills the school district directly. The earlier the parent enrolls the child when the child becomes eligible, the more instruction the child will receive before the end of the school year.

(9) PROHIBITION - Nothing contained in this subsection shall permit the making of any payment for religious worship or instruction.

(10) WAIVER -

(A) **REQUIREMENT** - At the request of a local educational agency, a **State educational agency may waive, in whole or in part, the requirement of this subsection to provide supplemental educational services** if the State educational agency determines that —

(i) none of the providers of those services on the list approved by the State educational agency under paragraph (4)(C) makes those services available in the area served by the local educational agency or within a reasonable distance of that area; and
(ii) the local educational agency provides evidence that it is not able to provide those services.

(B) **NOTIFICATION** - The State educational agency shall notify the local educational agency, within 30 days of receiving the local educational agency's request for a waiver under subparagraph (A), whether the request is approved or disapproved and, if disapproved, the reasons for the disapproval, in writing.

(11) SPECIAL RULE - If State law prohibits a State educational agency from carrying out one or more of its responsibilities under paragraph (4) with respect to those who provide, or seek approval to provide, supplemental educational services, **each local educational agency in the State shall carry out those responsibilities** with respect to its students who are eligible for those services.

(12) DEFINITIONS - In this subsection—

(A) the term **'eligible child'** means a child from a low-income family, as determined by the local educational agency for purposes of allocating funds to schools under section 1113(c)(1);

(B) the term **'provider'** means a **non-profit entity**, a **for-profit** entity, or a local educational agency that—

(i) has a demonstrated record of effectiveness in increasing student academic achievement;

(ii) is capable of providing supplemental educational services that are consistent with the instructional program of the local educational agency and the academic standards described under section 1111; and

(iii) is financially sound; and

(C) the term '**supplemental educational services**' means **tutoring** and other supplemental academic enrichment services that are—

(i) in **addition to instruction provided during the school day**; and

(ii) are of **high quality, research–based**, and specifically **designed to increase the academic achievement of eligible children on the academic assessments** required under section 1111 and attain proficiency in meeting the State's academic achievement standards.

➡ **COMMENT:** Decisions about supplemental educational services and public school choice will be made by the child's parent. Supplemental services may be less disruptive to the child than transferring to another school.

(f) SCHOOLS AND LEAS PREVIOUSLY IDENTIFIED FOR IMPROVEMENT OR CORRECTIVE ACTION -

(1) SCHOOLS -

(A) SCHOOL IMPROVEMENT -

(i) SCHOOLS IN SCHOOL-IMPROVEMENT STATUS BEFORE DATE OF ENACTMENT - Any school that was in the first year of school improvement status under this section on the day preceding the date of enactment of the No Child Left Behind Act of 2001 (as this section was in effect on such day) shall be treated by the local educational agency as a school that is in the first year of school improvement status under paragraph (1).

(ii) SCHOOLS IN SCHOOL-IMPROVEMENT STATUS FOR 2 OR MORE YEARS BEFORE DATE OF ENACTMENT - Any school that was in **school improvement status under this section for two or more consecutive school years preceding the date of enactment** of the No Child Left Behind Act of 2001 (as this section was in effect on such day) shall be treated by the local educational agency as a school described in subsection (b)(5).

(B) CORRECTIVE ACTION - Any school that was in corrective action status under this section on the day preceding the date of enactment of the No Child Left Behind Act of 2001 (as this section was in effect on such day) shall be treated by the local educational agency as a school described in paragraph (7).

(2) LEAS -

(A) LEA IMPROVEMENT - A State shall identify for improvement under subsection (c)(3) any local educational agency that was in improvement status under this section as this section was in effect on the day preceding the date of enactment of the No Child Left Behind Act of 2001.

(B) CORRECTIVE ACTION - A State shall identify for corrective action under subsection (c)(10) any local educational agency that was in corrective action status under this section as this section was in effect on the day preceding the date of enactment of the No Child Left Behind Act of 2001.

(C) SPECIAL RULE - For the schools and other local educational agencies described under paragraphs (1) and (2), as required, the State shall ensure that public school choice in accordance with subparagraphs (b)(1)(E) and (F) and supplemental education services in accordance with subsection (e) are **provided not later than the first day of the 2002-2003 school year.**

(D) TRANSITION - With respect to a determination that a local educational agency has for 2 consecutive years failed to make adequate yearly progress as defined in the State plan under section 1111(b)(2), such determination shall include in such 2-year period any continuous period of time immediately preceding the date of enactment of the No Child Left Behind Act of 2001 during which the agency has failed to make such progress.

(g) SCHOOLS FUNDED BY THE BUREAU OF INDIAN AFFAIRS -

(1) ADEQUATE YEARLY PROGRESS FOR BUREAU FUNDED SCHOOLS -

(A) DEVELOPMENT OF DEFINITION -

(i) DEFINITION - The Secretary of the Interior, in consultation with the Secretary if the Secretary of Interior requests the consultation, using the process set out in section 1138(b) of the Education Amendments of 1978, shall **define adequate yearly progress**, consistent with section 1111(b), for the schools funded by the Bureau of Indian Affairs **on a regional or tribal basis**, as appropriate, taking into account the **unique circumstances and needs of such schools and the students** served by such schools.

(ii) USE OF DEFINITION - The Secretary of the Interior, consistent with clause (i), may use the definition of adequate yearly progress that the State in which the school that is funded by the Bureau is located uses consistent with section 1111(b), or in the case of schools that are located in more than one State, the Secretary of the Interior may use whichever State definition of adequate yearly progress that best meets the unique circumstances and needs of such school or schools and the students the schools serve.

(B) WAIVER - The tribal governing body or **school board of a school funded by the Bureau of Indian Affairs may waive, in part or in whole, the definition of adequate yearly progress** established pursuant to paragraph (A) where such definition is determined by such body or school board to be inappropriate. If such definition is waived, the tribal governing body or school board **shall**, within 60 days thereafter, submit to the Secretary of Interior a proposal for **an alternative definition of adequate yearly progress**, consistent with section 1111(b), that takes into account the unique circumstances and needs of such school or schools and the students served. The Secretary of the Interior, in consultation with the Secretary if the Secretary of Interior requests the consultation, shall approve such alternative definition unless the Secretary determines that the definition does not meet the requirements of section 1111(b), taking into account the unique circumstances and needs of such school or schools and the students served.

(C) TECHNICAL ASSISTANCE - The Secretary of Interior shall, in consultation with the Secretary if the Secretary of Interior requests the consultation, either directly or through a contract, provide technical assistance, upon request, to a tribal governing body or school board of a school funded by the Bureau of Indian Affairs that seeks to develop an alternative definition of adequate yearly progress.

(2) ACCOUNTABILITY FOR BIA SCHOOLS - For the purposes of this section, **schools funded by the Bureau of Indian Affairs** shall be considered schools subject to subsection (b), as specifically provided for in this subsection, except that such schools **shall not be subject to subsection (c), or the requirements to provide public school choice and supplemental educational services under subsections (b) and (e).**

(3) SCHOOL IMPROVEMENT FOR BUREAU SCHOOLS -

(A) CONTRACT AND GRANT SCHOOLS - For a school **funded** by the Bureau of Indian Affairs which is operated under a **contract** issued by the Secretary of the Interior pursuant to the Indian Self-Determination Act (25 U.S.C. 450 et seq.) or under a grant issued by the Secretary of the Interior pursuant to the Tribally Controlled Schools Act of 1988 (25 U.S.C. 2501 et seq.), the school board of such school shall be responsible for meeting the requirements of subsection (b) relating to development and subsection (b)(5), other than subsection (b)(1)(E). The Bureau of Indian Affairs shall be responsible for meeting the requirements of subsection (b)(4) relating to technical assistance.

(B) BUREAU OPERATED SCHOOLS - For schools **operated** by the Bureau of Indian Affairs, the Bureau shall be responsible for meeting the requirements of subsection (b) relating to development and implementation of any school improvement plan as described in subsections (b)(1) through (b)(5), other than subsection (b)(1)(E).

(4) CORRECTIVE ACTION AND RESTRUCTURING FOR BUREAU–FUNDED SCHOOLS -

(A) CONTRACT AND GRANT SCHOOLS - For a school **funded by the Bureau of Indian Affairs** which is operated under a **contract** issued by the Secretary of the Interior pursuant to the Indian Self-Determination Act (25 U.S.C. 450 et seq.) or under a grant issued by the Secretary of the Interior pursuant to the Tribally Controlled Schools Act of 1988 (25 U.S.C. 2501 et seq.), the school board of such school shall be responsible for meeting the requirements of subsection (b) relating to corrective action and restructuring as described in subsection (b)(7) and (b)(8). Any action taken by such school board under subsection (b)(7) or (b)(8) shall take into account the unique circumstances and structure of the Bureau of Indian Affairs-funded school system and the laws governing that system.

(B) BUREAU OPERATED SCHOOLS - For schools **operated by the Bureau of Indian Affairs**, the Bureau shall be responsible for meeting the requirements of subsection (b) relating to corrective action and restructuring as described in subsection (b)(7) and (b)(8). Any action taken by the Bureau under subsection (b)(7) or (b)(8) shall take into account the unique circumstances and structure of the Bureau of Indian Affairs-funded school system and the laws governing that system.

➡ **COMMENT:** It appears that schools funded or operated by the Bureau of Indian Affairs schools are not required to adhere to the accountability provisions of NCLB. BIA schools are not required to offer public school choice or supplemental educational services. The result of lower expectations may be lower standards.

(5) ANNUAL REPORT - On an annual basis, the Secretary of the Interior shall report to the Secretary of Education and to the appropriate committees of Congress regarding any schools funded by the Bureau of Indian Affairs which have been identified for school improvement. Such report shall include—

(A) the **identity of each school**;

(B) a **statement from each affected school board** regarding the factors that lead to such identification; and

(C) an analysis by the Secretary of the Interior, in consultation with the Secretary if the Secretary of Interior requests the consultation, as to whether sufficient resources were available to enable such school to achieve adequate yearly progress.

(h) OTHER AGENCIES - After receiving the notice described in subsection (b)(14)(D), the Secretary may notify, to the extent feasible and necessary as determined by the Secretary, other relevant Federal agencies regarding the **major factors** that were determined by the State educational agency to have significantly affected student academic achievement. (Section 1116 of the NCLB Act)

20 U. S. C. § 6317. School support and recognition.

➡ **OVERVIEW:** In addition to sanctions for poor performance, No Child Left Behind includes rewards for schools that meet or exceed their goals. Section 6317(a) describes priorities for assisting schools in corrective action and schools in need of improvement, including the roles of regional centers and school support teams.

Section 6317(b) describes state recognition programs, including the academic achievement award program, distinguished schools, and awards for teachers. **Financial awards are available to individual teachers and schools** that have the greatest gains in closing the achievement gap and/or exceed their adequate yearly progress goals.

(a) SYSTEM FOR SUPPORT -

(1) IN GENERAL - Each State **shall establish a statewide system of intensive and sustained support** and improvement for local educational agencies and schools receiving funds under this part, in order to increase the opportunity for all students served by those agencies and schools to meet the State's academic content standards and student academic achievement standards.

(2) PRIORITIES - In carrying out this subsection, a State shall —

(A) **first**, provide support and assistance to local educational agencies with **schools subject to corrective** action under section 1116 and assist those schools, in accordance with section 1116(b)(11), for which a local educational agency has failed to carry out its responsibilities under paragraphs (7) and (8) of section 1116(b);

(B) **second**, provide support and assistance to other local educational agencies with schools **identified as in need of improvement** under section 1116(b); and

(C) **third**, provide support and assistance to other local educational agencies and schools participating under this part that need that support and assistance in order to achieve the purpose of this part.

(3) REGIONAL CENTERS - Such a statewide system shall, to the extent practicable, work with and receive support and assistance from the comprehensive regional technical assistance centers and the regional educational laboratories under section 941(h) of the Educational Research, Development, Dissemination, and Improvement Act of 1994, or other providers of technical assistance.

(4) STATEWIDE SYSTEM -

(A) In order to achieve the purpose described in paragraph (1), the statewide system **shall include, at a minimum**, the following approaches:

(i) Establishing school support teams in accordance with subparagraph (C) for assignment to, and working in, schools in the State that are described in paragraph (2).
(ii) Providing such support as the State educational agency determines necessary and available in order to ensure the effectiveness of such teams.
(iii) Designating and using distinguished teachers and principals who are chosen from schools served under this part that have been especially successful in improving academic achievement.
(iv) Devising additional approaches to providing the assistance described in paragraph (1), such as providing assistance through institutions of higher education and educational service agencies or other local consortia, and private providers of scientifically based technical assistance.

(B) PRIORITY - The State educational agency shall give priority to the approach described in clause (i) of subparagraph (A).

(5) SCHOOL SUPPORT TEAMS -

(A) COMPOSITION - **Each school support team** established under this section **shall be composed of persons knowledgeable about scientifically based research and practice on teaching and learning** and about successful schoolwide projects, school reform, **and improving educational opportunities for low-achieving students**, including —

(i) highly qualified or distinguished teachers and principals;
(ii) pupil services personnel;
(iii) parents;
(iv) representatives of institutions of higher education;
(v) representatives of regional educational laboratories or comprehensive regional technical assistance centers;
(vi) representatives of outside consultant groups; or
(vii) other individuals as the State educational agency, in consultation with the local educational agency, may determine appropriate.

(B) FUNCTIONS - Each school support team assigned to a school under this section **shall** —

(i) review and **analyze all facets of the school's operation**, including the design and operation of the instructional program, and assist the school in developing recommendations for improving student performance in that school;
(ii) collaborate with parents and school staff and the local educational agency serving the school in the design, implementation, and monitoring of a plan that, if fully implemented, can reasonably be expected to improve student performance and help the school meet its goals for improvement, including adequate yearly progress under section 1111(b)(2)(B);
(iii) **evaluate, at least semiannually, the effectiveness of school personnel assigned to the school**, including identifying outstanding teachers and principals, and make findings and recommendations to the school, the local educational agency, and, where appropriate, the State educational agency; and
(iv) make additional recommendations as the school implements the plan described in clause (ii) to the local educational agency and the State educational agency concerning additional assistance that is needed by the school or the school support team.

(C) CONTINUATION OF ASSISTANCE - After one school year, from the beginning of the activities, such school support team, in consultation with the local educational agency, may recommend that the school support team continue to provide assistance to the school, or that the local educational agency or the State educational agency, as appropriate, take alternative actions with regard to the school.

(b) STATE RECOGNITION -

(1) ACADEMIC ACHIEVEMENT AWARDS PROGRAM -

(A) IN GENERAL - Each State receiving a grant under this part —

(i) shall establish a program for making academic achievement awards to recognize schools that meet the criteria described in subparagraph (B); and
(ii) as appropriate and as funds are available under subsection (c)(2)(A), **may financially reward schools** served under this part that meet the criteria described in clause (ii).

(B) CRITERIA - The criteria referred to in subparagraph (A) are that a school —
(i) **significantly closed the achievement gap** between the groups of students described in section 1111(b)(2); **or**
(ii) **exceeded their adequate yearly progress**, consistent with section 1111(b)(2), for 2 or more consecutive years.

(2) DISTINGUISHED SCHOOLS - Of those schools meeting the criteria described in paragraph (2), **each State shall designate as distinguished schools those schools that have made the greatest gains in closing the achievement gap** as described in subparagraph (B)(i) or exceeding adequate yearly progress as described in subparagraph (B)(ii). Such distinguished schools may serve as models for and provide support to other schools, especially schools identified for improvement under section 1116, to assist such schools in meeting the State's academic content standards and student academic achievement standards.

(3) AWARDS TO TEACHERS - A State program under paragraph (1) may also **recognize and provide financial awards to teachers** teaching in a school described in such paragraph that consistently makes significant gains in academic achievement in the areas in which the teacher provides instruction, or to teachers or principals designated as distinguished under subsection (a)(4)(A)(iii).

(c) FUNDING -

(1) IN GENERAL - Each State —

(A) shall use funds reserved under section 1003(a) and may use funds made available under section 1003(g) for the approaches described under subsection (a)(4)(A); and

(B) shall use State administrative funds authorized under section 1004(a) to establish the statewide system of support described under subsection (a).

(2) RESERVATIONS OF FUNDS BY STATE -

(A) AWARDS PROGRAM - For the purpose of carrying out subsection (b)(1), each State receiving a grant under this part may reserve, from the amount (if any) by which the funds received by the State under subpart 2 for a fiscal year exceed the amount received by the State under that subpart for the preceding fiscal year, not more than 5 percent of such excess amount.

(B) TEACHER AWARDS - For the purpose of carrying out subsection (b)(3), a State educational agency may reserve such funds as necessary from funds made available under section 2113.

(3) USE WITHIN 3 YEARS - Notwithstanding any other provision of law, the amount reserved under subparagraph (A) by a State for each fiscal year shall remain available to the State until expended for a period not exceeding 3 years receipt of funds.

(4) SPECIAL ALLOCATION RULE FOR SCHOOLS IN HIGH-POVERTY AREAS -

(A) IN GENERAL - Each State shall distribute not less than 75 percent of any amount reserved under paragraph (2)(A) for each fiscal year **to schools** described in subparagraph (B), **or to teachers** in those schools consistent with subsection (b)(3).

(B) SCHOOL DESCRIBED - A school described in subparagraph (A) is a school whose student population is in the highest quartile of schools statewide in terms of the percentage of children from low income families. (Section 1117 of the NCLB Act)

20 U. S. C. § 6318. Parental involvement.

➜ **OVERVIEW:** This statute includes important requirements about parental involvement for schools and school districts that receive Title I funds. Each district that receives Title I funds must consult with parents to develop a parent involvement policy to improve student academic achievement and school performance. Districts must evaluate the effectiveness of their parental involvement policies every year.

Section 6318(b) requires each Title I school to jointly develop with parents a written parental involvement policy. This parental involvement policy must be distributed to parents and be made available to the community. Section 6318(c) includes requirements about how parental involvement policies will be developed and implemented, and how parents will be involved in school improvement plans and programs.

Section 6318(d) describes shared responsibilities for student academic achievement. Schools and parents are to develop a school-parent compact that describes the school's responsibility to provide high-quality curriculum and instruction in a supportive, effective learning environment, sets out requirements for communication between teachers and parents, including frequent progress reports. Parents shall have access to school staff, and opportunities to participate in their child's class and observe classroom activities.

Section 6318(e) describes strategies to ensure parental involvement and develop partnerships between parents, schools and the community. Schools can use Title I funds to pay for **transportation**, **child care**, and other costs to ensure parental participation.

(a) LOCAL EDUCATIONAL AGENCY POLICY -

(1) IN GENERAL - A local educational agency may receive funds under this part **only if such agency** implements programs, activities, and procedures for the involvement of parents in programs assisted under this part consistent with this section. Such programs, activities, and procedures **shall be planned and implemented with meaningful consultation with parents of participating children.**

(2) WRITTEN POLICY - Each local educational agency that receives funds under this part **shall develop jointly with, agree on with, and distribute to, parents of participating children a written parent involvement policy.** The policy shall be incorporated into the local educational agency's plan developed under section 1112, establish the agency's expectations for parent involvement, and describe how the agency will—

(A) **involve parents in the joint development of the plan** under section 1112, and the process of school review and improvement under section 1116;

(B) provide the coordination, technical assistance, and other support necessary to assist participating schools in planning and implementing effective parent involvement activities to improve student academic achievement and school performance;

(C) build the schools' and parents' capacity for strong parental involvement as described in subsection (e);

(D) coordinate and integrate parental involvement strategies under this part with parental involvement strategies under other programs, such as the Head Start program, Reading First program, Early Reading First program, Even Start program, Parents as Teachers program, and Home Instruction Program for Preschool Youngsters, and State-run preschool programs;

(E) conduct, with the involvement of parents, **an annual evaluation of the content and effectiveness of the parental involvement** policy in improving the academic quality of the schools served under this part, including identifying barriers to greater participation by parents in activities authorized by this section (**with particular attention to parents** who are economically disadvantaged, are disabled, have limited English proficiency, have limited literacy, or are of any racial or ethnic minority background), and use the findings of such evaluation to design strategies for more effective parental involvement, and to revise, if necessary, the parental involvement policies described in this section; and

(F) involve parents in the activities of the schools served under this part.

(3) RESERVATION -

(A) IN GENERAL - Each local educational agency shall reserve not less than 1 percent of such agency's allocation under subpart 2 of this part to carry out this section, including promoting family literacy and parenting skills, except that this paragraph shall not apply if 1 percent of such agency's allocation under subpart 2 of this part for the fiscal year for which the determination is made is $5,000 or less.

(B) PARENTAL INPUT - Parents of children receiving services under this part **shall be involved** in the decisions regarding how funds reserved under subparagraph (A) are allotted for parental involvement activities.

(C) DISTRIBUTION OF FUNDS - Not less than 95 percent of the funds reserved under subparagraph (A) shall be distributed to schools served under this part.

(b) SCHOOL PARENTAL INVOLVEMENT POLICY -

(1) IN GENERAL - **Each school** served under this part **shall** jointly develop with, and **distribute to, parents of participating children a written parental involvement policy**, agreed on by such parents, that shall describe the means for carrying out the requirements of subsections (c) through (f). Parents shall be notified of the policy in an understandable and uniform format and, to the extent practicable, provided in a language the parents can understand. **Such policy shall be made available to the local community and updated periodically to meet the changing needs of parents and the school.**

(2) SPECIAL RULE - If the school has a parental involvement policy that applies to all parents, such school may amend that policy, if necessary, to meet the requirements of this subsection.

(3) AMENDMENT - If the local educational agency involved has a school district-level parental involvement policy that applies to all parents, such agency may amend that policy, if necessary, to meet the requirements of this subsection.

(4) PARENTAL COMMENTS - If the plan under section 1112 **is not satisfactory to the parents of participating children**, the local educational agency **shall submit any parent comments with such plan** when such local educational agency submits the plan to the State.

(c) POLICY INVOLVEMENT - Each school served under this part **shall** —

(1) **convene an annual meeting**, at a convenient time, to which **all parents of participating children shall be invited and encouraged to attend**, to inform parents of their school's participation under this part and to explain the requirements of this part, and the right of the parents to be involved;

(2) **offer a flexible number of meetings**, such as meetings **in the morning or evening, and may provide**, with funds provided under this part, **transportation, child care, or home visits,** as such services relate to parental involvement;

(3) **involve parents, in an organized, ongoing, and timely way, in the planning, review, and improvement** of programs under this part, including the planning, review, and improvement of the school parental involvement policy and the joint development of the schoolwide program plan under section 1114(b)(2), except that if a school has in place a process for involving parents in the joint planning and design of the school's programs, the school may use that process, if such process includes an adequate representation of parents of participating children;

(4) **provide parents of participating children** —

(A) **timely information about programs** under this part;

(B) a description and explanation of the **curriculum** in use at the school, the **forms of academic assessment used to measure student progress**, and the **proficiency levels students are expected to meet**; and

(C) if requested by parents, opportunities for **regular meetings to formulate suggestions and to participate, as appropriate, in decisions relating to the education of their children,** and respond to any such suggestions as soon as practicably possible; and

(5) if the schoolwide program plan under section 1114(b)(2) is not satisfactory to the parents of participating children, submit any parent comments on the plan when the school makes the plan available to the local educational agency.

(d) SHARED RESPONSIBILITIES FOR HIGH STUDENT ACADEMIC ACHIEVEMENT - As a component of the school-level parental involvement policy developed under subsection (b), each school served under this part **shall jointly develop with parents** for all children served under this part a **school-parent compact** that outlines how parents, the entire school staff, and students will **share the responsibility for improved student academic achievement** and the means by which the school and parents will build and develop a partnership to help children achieve the State's high standards. Such compact shall —

(1) describe the school's **responsibility to provide high-quality curriculum and instruction in a supportive and effective learning environment** that enables the children served under this part to meet the State's student academic achievement standards, and the ways in which each **parent will be responsible for supporting their children's learning,** such as monitoring attendance, homework completion, and television watching; volunteering in their child's classroom; and participating, as appropriate, in decisions relating to the education of their children and positive use of extracurricular time; and

(2) address the importance of **communication between teachers and parents** on an ongoing basis through, **at a minimum—**

(A) parent-teacher conferences in elementary schools, at least annually, during which the compact shall be discussed as the compact relates to the **individual child's achievement;**

(B) frequent **reports to parents on their children's progress;** and

(C) reasonable access to staff, opportunities to volunteer and participate in their child's class, **and observation of classroom activities.**

➡ **CLASSROOM OBSERVATIONS:** Parents may observe their children in class, despite the attempts of some schools to prevent parent observations.

(e) BUILDING CAPACITY FOR INVOLVEMENT - To ensure effective involvement of parents and to support a partnership among the school involved, parents, and the community to improve student academic achievement, each school and local educational agency assisted under this part —

(1) **shall provide assistance to parents** of children served by the school or local educational agency, as appropriate, in understanding such topics as the State's academic content standards and State student academic achievement standards, State and local academic assessments, the requirements of this part, and **how to monitor a child's progress and work with educators** to improve the achievement of their children;

(2) **shall provide materials and training to help parents to work with their children to improve their children's achievement,** such as literacy training and using technology, as appropriate, to foster parental involvement;

(3) **shall educate teachers, pupil services personnel, principals, and other staff,** with the assistance of parents, in the value and utility of contributions of parents, and in how to reach out to, communicate with, and work with **parents as equal partners,** implement and coordinate parent programs, and build ties between parents and the school;

(4) **shall,** to the extent feasible and appropriate, **coordinate and integrate parent involvement programs** and activities with Head Start, Reading First, Early Reading First, Even Start, the Home Instruction Programs for

Preschool Youngsters, the Parents as Teachers Program, and public preschool and other programs, and conduct other activities, such as parent resource centers, that encourage and support parents in more fully participating in the education of their children;

(5) **shall ensure that information** related to school and parent programs, meetings, and other activities **is sent to the parents** of participating children in a format and, to the extent practicable, in a language the parents can understand;

(6) may **involve parents in the development of training** for teachers, principals, and other educators to improve the effectiveness of such training;

(7) may provide necessary literacy training from funds received under this part if the local educational agency has exhausted all other reasonably available sources of funding for such training;

(8) **may pay reasonable and necessary expenses associated with local parental involvement activities, including transportation and child care costs, to enable parents to participate in school-related meetings and training sessions;**

(9) may train parents to enhance the involvement of other parents;

(10) may arrange school meetings at a variety of times, or conduct in-home conferences between teachers or other educators, who work directly with participating children, with parents who are unable to attend such conferences at school, in order to maximize parental involvement and participation;

(11) may adopt and implement model approaches to improving parental involvement;

(12) may establish a districtwide parent advisory council to provide advice on all matters related to parental involvement in programs supported under this section;

(13) may develop appropriate roles for community-based organizations and businesses in parent involvement activities; and

(14) **shall provide** such other **reasonable support for parental involvement activities** under this section as parents may request.

➔ COMMENT: Parents may request support in setting up a program that encompasses items 6-13 above.

(f) ACCESSIBILITY - In carrying out the parental involvement requirements of this part, local educational agencies and schools, to the extent practicable, shall provide full opportunities for the participation of **parents with limited English proficiency, parents with disabilities, and parents of migratory children**, including providing information and school reports required under section 1111 in a format and, to the extent practicable, in a language such parents understand.

(g) INFORMATION FROM PARENTAL INFORMATION AND RESOURCE CENTERS - In a State where a parental information and resource center is established to provide training, information, and support to parents and individuals who work with local parents, local educational agencies, and schools receiving assistance under this part, each local educational agency or school that receives assistance under this part and is located in the State shall assist parents and parental organizations by informing such parents and organizations of the existence and purpose of such centers.

(h) REVIEW - The State educational agency shall review the local educational agency's parental involvement policies and practices to determine if the policies and practices meet the requirements of this section. (Section 1118 of the NCLB Act)

20 U. S. C. § 6319. Qualifications for teachers and paraprofessionals.

➜ **OVERVIEW:** Section 6319, new qualification requirements for teachers and paraprofessionals, is another key statute. According to Section (a), all teachers hired after No Child Left Behind was enacted in 2001 must be highly qualified! The state must ensure that all teachers in core academic subjects are highly qualified by the end of the 2005-2006 school year. Section (b) includes state and local reporting requirements.

Sections (c) through (g) include requirements about paraprofessionals. Section (c) states that all paraprofessionals hired after No Child Left Behind was enacted **must** have a high school diploma or equivalent, complete two years of study at a college or university, have an associate's degree (minimum), or take a rigorous skills test. Section (d) states that paraprofessionals who were employed at the time the law was passed must meet these requirements by January 8, 2006. Section (g) describes duties and limitations of paraprofessionals. Paraprofessionals may not provide instructional services to children unless they are working under the direct supervision of a teacher.

According to section (i), the principal must certify annually that the school is in compliance with this section. This information must be available to the public at the school and main office of the LEA.

(a) TEACHER QUALIFICATIONS AND MEASURABLE OBJECTIVES -

(1) IN GENERAL - Beginning with the first day of the first school year after the date of enactment of the No Child Left Behind Act of 2001, each local educational agency receiving assistance under this part **shall ensure that all teachers hired after such day and teaching in a program supported with funds under this part are highly qualified.**

(2) STATE PLAN - As part of the plan described in section 1111, each State educational agency receiving assistance under this part shall develop a plan to ensure that **all teachers teaching in core academic subjects within the State are highly qualified** not later than the end of the 2005-2006 school year. Such plan **shall establish annual measurable objectives for each local educational agency and school that, at a minimum**
—

(A) **shall include an annual increase in the percentage of highly qualified teachers** at each local educational agency and school, to ensure that **all teachers teaching in core academic subjects in each public elementary school and secondary school are highly qualified not later than the end of the 2005-2006 school year;**

(B) **shall include an annual increase in** the percentage of **teachers who are receiving high-quality professional development** to enable such teachers to become highly qualified and successful classroom teachers; and

(C) may include such other measures as the State educational agency determines to be appropriate to increase teacher qualifications.

(3) LOCAL PLAN - As part of the plan described in section 1112, each local educational agency receiving assistance under this part shall develop a plan to ensure that **all teachers teaching within the school district** served by the local educational agency **are highly qualified not later than the end of the 2005-2006 school year.**

🗁 The definition of "highly qualified teacher" is in Title IX at 20 U. S. C. § 7801(23). A "highly qualified teacher" has full State certification, holds a license to teach, and meets the State's requirements. Depending on whether the teacher is in an elementary, middle school or secondary school, the highly qualified teacher has a high degree of competency in all academic subjects taught. Existing teachers must have demonstrated competence in all the academic subjects taught, based on a high objective uniform State standard of evaluation. New teachers must hold at least a bachelor's degree and must pass a rigorous state test.

(b) REPORTS -

(1) ANNUAL STATE AND LOCAL REPORTS -

(A) LOCAL REPORTS - Each State educational agency described in subsection (a)(2) shall require each local educational agency receiving funds under this part to **publicly report, each year**, beginning with the 2002-2003 school year, **the annual progress of the local educational agency as a whole and of each of the schools** served by the agency, in meeting the measurable objectives described in subsection (a)(2).

(B) STATE REPORTS - Each State educational agency receiving assistance under this part shall prepare and submit each year, beginning with the 2002-2003 school year, a report to the Secretary, describing the State educational agency's progress in meeting the measurable objectives described in subsection (a)(2).

(C) INFORMATION FROM OTHER REPORTS - A State educational agency or local educational agency may submit information from the reports described in section 1111(h) for the purposes of this subsection, if such report is modified, as may be necessary, to contain the information required by this subsection, and may submit such information as a part of the reports required under section 1111(h).

(2) ANNUAL REPORTS BY THE SECRETARY - Each year, beginning with the 2002-2003 school year, the Secretary shall publicly report the annual progress of State educational agencies, local educational agencies, and schools, in meeting the measurable objectives described in subsection (a)(2).

(c) NEW PARAPROFESSIONALS -

📂 The definition of a highly qualified paraprofessional is in Title II, at 20 U. S. C. § 6602(4): "The term 'highly qualified paraprofessional' means a paraprofessional who has not less than 2 years of— (A) experience in a classroom; and (B) postsecondary education or demonstrated competence in a field or academic subject for which there is a significant shortage of qualified teachers."

📖 *Title I Paraprofessionals: Draft Non-Regulatory Guidance* published by the U. S. Department of Education includes frequently-asked questions and answers about requirements for paraprofessionals, assessment of paraprofessionals, and related issues. (available on the *Wrightslaw NCLB CD-ROM*.)

(1) IN GENERAL - Each local educational agency receiving assistance under this part shall ensure that **all paraprofessionals hired** after the date of enactment of the No Child Left Behind Act of 2001 and working in a program supported with funds under this part **shall have** —

(A) **completed at least 2 years of study at an institution of higher education;**

(B) **obtained an associate's (or higher) degree**; or

(C) met a rigorous standard of quality and can demonstrate, through a formal State or local **academic assessment** —

(i) knowledge of, and the ability to assist in instructing, reading, writing, and mathematics; or
(ii) knowledge of, and the ability to assist in instructing, reading readiness, writing readiness, and mathematics readiness, as appropriate.

(2) CLARIFICATION - The receipt of a secondary school diploma (or its recognized equivalent) shall be necessary but not sufficient to satisfy the requirements of paragraph (1)(C).

(d) EXISTING PARAPROFESSIONALS - Each local educational agency receiving assistance under this part shall ensure that **all paraprofessionals** hired before the date of enactment of the No Child Left Behind Act of 2001, and working in a program supported with funds under this part shall, not later than 4 years after the date of enactment **satisfy the requirements of subsection (c).**

(e) EXCEPTIONS FOR TRANSLATION AND PARENTAL INVOLVEMENT ACTIVITIES - Subsections (c) and (d) shall not apply to a paraprofessional—

(1) who is proficient in English and a language other than English and who provides services primarily to enhance the participation of children in programs under this part by acting as a translator; or

(2) whose duties consist solely of conducting parental involvement activities consistent with section 1118.

(f) GENERAL REQUIREMENT FOR ALL PARAPROFESSIONALS - Each local educational agency receiving assistance under this part shall ensure that all paraprofessionals working in a program supported with funds under this part, regardless of the paraprofessionals' hiring date, have earned a secondary school diploma or its recognized equivalent.

(g) DUTIES OF PARAPROFESSIONALS -

(1) IN GENERAL - Each local educational agency receiving assistance under this part shall ensure that a paraprofessional working in a program supported with funds under this part **is not assigned a duty inconsistent** with this subsection.

(2) RESPONSIBILITIES PARAPROFESSIONALS MAY BE ASSIGNED - A paraprofessional described in paragraph (1) may be assigned —

(A) to provide **one-on-one tutoring** for eligible students, **if the tutoring is scheduled at a time when a student would not otherwise receive instruction from a teacher;**

(B) to assist with classroom management, such as **organizing instructional and other materials;**

(C) to provide assistance in a computer laboratory;

(D) to conduct parental involvement activities;

(E) to provide support in a library or media center;

(F) to act as a translator; or

(G) to provide instructional services to students in accordance with paragraph (3).

(3) ADDITIONAL LIMITATIONS - A paraprofessional described in paragraph (1) —

(A) **may not provide any instructional service to a student unless the paraprofessional is working under the direct supervision of a teacher** consistent with section 1119; and

(B) may assume limited duties that are assigned to similar personnel who are not working in a program supported with funds under this part, including duties beyond classroom instruction or that do not benefit participating children, so long as the amount of time spent on such duties is the same proportion of total work time as prevails with respect to similar personnel at the same school.

(h) USE OF FUNDS - A local educational agency receiving funds under this part may use such funds to support ongoing training and professional development to assist teachers and paraprofessionals in satisfying the requirements of this section.

(i) VERIFICATION OF COMPLIANCE -

(1) IN GENERAL - In verifying compliance with this section, each local educational agency, **at a minimum, shall require that the principal of each school** operating a program under section 1114 or 1115 **attest annually in writing as to whether such school is in compliance with the requirements of this section.**

(2) AVAILABILITY OF INFORMATION - Copies of attestations under paragraph (1) —

(A) **shall be maintained at each school** operating a program under section 1114 or 1115 **and at the main office of the local educational agency; and**

(B) **shall be available to any member of the general public on request.**

(j) COMBINATIONS OF FUNDS - Funds provided under this part that are used for professional development purposes may be combined with funds provided under title II of this Act, other Acts, and other sources.

(k) SPECIAL RULE - Except as provided in subsection (l), no State educational agency shall require a school or a local educational agency to expend a specific amount of funds for professional development activities under this part, except that this paragraph shall not apply with respect to requirements under section 1116(c)(3).

(l) MINIMUM EXPENDITURES - Each local educational agency that receives funds under this part shall use not less than 5 percent, or more than 10 percent, of such funds for each of fiscal years 2002 and 2003, and not less than 5 percent of the funds for each subsequent fiscal year, for professional development activities to ensure that teachers who are not highly qualified become highly qualified not later than the end of the 2005-2006 school year. (Section 1119 of the NCLB Act)

20 U. S. C. § 6320. Participation of children enrolled in private schools.

➡ **OVERVIEW:** Section (a) requires schools to provide special educational services or other benefits to eligible children who are enrolled in private schools. Public school officials must consult with private school officials to develop programs. If the district disagrees with private school officials about providing services through a contract, the district must provide, in writing, an analysis of the reasons why the school district chose not to use a contractor. Section (c) requires school districts to calculate the number of children from low-income families who attend private schools and describes the complaint process.

(a) GENERAL REQUIREMENT -

(1) IN GENERAL - To the extent consistent with the number of eligible children identified under section 1115(b) in the school district served by a local educational agency who are enrolled in private elementary schools and secondary schools, a local educational agency **shall**, after timely and meaningful consultation with appropriate private school officials, **provide** such children, **on an equitable basis, special educational services or other benefits** under this part (such as **dual enrollment**, educational radio and television, computer equipment and materials, other technology, and mobile educational services and equipment) that address their needs, and shall ensure that **teachers and families of the children participate**, on an equitable basis, in services and activities developed pursuant to sections 1118 and 1119.

(2) SECULAR, NEUTRAL, NONIDEOLOGICAL - Such educational services or other benefits, including materials and equipment, shall be secular, neutral, and nonideological.

(3) EQUITY - Educational services and other benefits for such private school children shall be equitable in comparison to services and other benefits for public school children participating under this part, and shall be provided in a timely manner.

(4) EXPENDITURES - Expenditures for educational services and other benefits to eligible private school children shall be equal to the proportion of funds allocated to participating school attendance areas based on the number of children from low-income families who attend private schools, which the local educational agency may determine **each year or every 2 years.**

(5) PROVISION OF SERVICES - The local educational agency may provide services under this section directly or through contracts with public and private agencies, organizations, and institutions.

(b) CONSULTATION -

(1) IN GENERAL - To ensure timely and meaningful consultation, a local educational agency **shall consult** with appropriate private school officials during the design and development of such agency's programs under this part, on issues such as —

(A) how the children's needs will be identified;

(B) what services will be offered;

(C) how, where, and by whom the services will be provided;

(D) how the services will be academically assessed and how the results of that assessment will be used to improve those services;

(E) the size and scope of the equitable services to be provided to the eligible private school children, and the proportion of funds that is allocated under subsection (a)(4) for such services;

(F) the method or sources of data that are used under subsection (c) and section 1113(c)(1) to determine the number of children from low-income families in participating school attendance areas who attend private schools;

(G) how and when the agency will make decisions about the delivery of services to such children, including a thorough consideration and analysis of the views of the private school officials on the provision of services through a contract with potential third-party providers; and

(H) how, if the agency disagrees with the views of the private school officials on the provision of services through a contract, the local educational agency will provide in writing to such private school officials an analysis of the reasons why the local educational agency has chosen not to use a contractor.

(2) TIMING - Such consultation shall include meetings of agency and private school officials and shall occur before the local educational agency makes any decision that affects the opportunities of eligible private school children to participate in programs under this part. **Such meetings shall continue throughout implementation and assessment of services provided under this section.**

(3) DISCUSSION - Such consultation shall include a discussion of service delivery mechanisms a local educational agency can use to provide equitable services to eligible private school children.

(4) DOCUMENTATION - Each local educational agency **shall** maintain in the agency's records and provide to the State educational agency involved **a written affirmation signed by officials of each participating private school that the consultation required by this section has occurred.** If such officials do not provide such affirmation within a reasonable period of time, the local educational agency shall forward the documentation that such consultation has taken place to the State educational agency.

(5) COMPLIANCE -

(A) **IN GENERAL** - A private school official shall have **the right to complain to the State educational**

agency that the local educational agency did not engage in consultation that was meaningful and timely, or did not give due consideration to the views of the private school official.

(B) PROCEDURE - If the private school official wishes to complain, the official shall provide the basis of the noncompliance with this section by the local educational agency to the State educational agency, and the local educational agency shall forward the appropriate documentation to the State educational agency.

(c) ALLOCATION FOR EQUITABLE SERVICE TO PRIVATE SCHOOL STUDENTS -

(1) CALCULATION - A local educational agency **shall have the final authority**, consistent with this section, **to calculate the number of children**, ages 5 through 17, who are from low-income families and attend private schools **by** —

(A) using the same measure of low income used to count public school children;

(B) using the results of a survey that, to the extent possible, protects the identity of families of private school students, and allowing such survey results to be extrapolated if complete actual data are unavailable;

(C) applying the low-income percentage of each participating public school attendance area, determined pursuant to this section, to the number of private school children who reside in that school attendance area; or

(D) using an equated measure of low income correlated with the measure of low income used to count public school children.

(2) COMPLAINT PROCESS - Any dispute regarding low-income data for private school students **shall be subject to the complaint process** authorized in section 9505.

➡ **COMMENT:** It appears that Section 9505 in Title IX of NCLB is a typographical error in the original NCLB Act. It seems this should be characterized as Section 9503, which is the same as 20 U. S. C. § 7883, entitled "Complaint process for participation of private school children."

(d) PUBLIC CONTROL OF FUNDS -

(1) IN GENERAL - The control of funds provided under this part, and title to materials, equipment, and property purchased with such funds, shall be in a public agency, and a public agency shall administer such funds, materials, equipment, and property.

(2) PROVISION OF SERVICES -

(A) PROVIDER - The provision of services under this section shall be provided—

(i) by employees of a public agency; or
(ii) through contract by such public agency with an individual, association, agency, or organization.

(B) REQUIREMENT - In the provision of such services, such employee, individual, association, agency, or organization shall be independent of such private school and of any religious organization, and such employment or contract shall be under the control and supervision of such public agency.

(e) STANDARDS FOR A BYPASS - If a local educational agency **is prohibited** by law from providing for the participation in programs on an equitable basis of eligible children enrolled in private elementary schools and secondary schools, **or** if the Secretary **determines** that a local educational agency **has substantially failed or is**

unwilling, to provide for such participation, as required by this section, the Secretary **shall** —

(1) **waive the requirements of this section for such local educational agency;**

(2) arrange for the provision of services to such children through arrangements that shall be subject to the requirements of this section and sections 9503 and 9504; and

(3) in making the determination under this subsection, consider one or more factors, including the quality, size, scope, and location of the program and the opportunity of eligible children to participate. (Section 1120 of the NCLB Act)

20 U. S. C. § 6321. Fiscal requirements.

➜ **OVERVIEW:** This section describes funding, written assurances, procedures, records, and compliance.

(a) MAINTENANCE OF EFFORT - A local educational agency may receive funds under this part for any fiscal year only if the State educational agency involved finds that the local educational agency has maintained the agency's fiscal effort in accordance with section 9521.

(b) FEDERAL FUNDS TO SUPPLEMENT, NOT SUPPLANT, NON-FEDERAL FUNDS -

(1) IN GENERAL - A State educational agency or local educational agency shall use Federal funds received under this part **only to supplement the funds** that would, in the absence of such Federal funds, be made available from non-Federal sources for the education of pupils participating in programs assisted under this part, and not to supplant such funds.

(2) SPECIAL RULE - No local educational agency shall be required to provide services under this part through a **particular instructional method** or in a particular instructional setting in order to demonstrate such agency's compliance with paragraph (1).

(c) COMPARABILITY OF SERVICES -

(1) IN GENERAL -

(A) COMPARABLE SERVICES - Except as provided in paragraphs (4) and (5), a local educational agency may receive funds under this part only if State and local funds will be used in schools served under this part to provide services that, taken as a whole, are at least comparable to services in schools that are not receiving funds under this part.

(B) SUBSTANTIALLY COMPARABLE SERVICES - If the local educational agency is serving all of such agency's schools under this part, such agency may receive funds under this part only if such agency will use State and local funds to provide services that, taken as a whole, are substantially comparable in each school.

(C) BASIS - A local educational agency may meet the requirements of subparagraphs (A) and (B) on a grade-span by grade-span basis or a school-by-school basis.

(2) WRITTEN ASSURANCE -

(A) EQUIVALENCE - A local educational agency shall be considered to have met the requirements of paragraph (1) if such agency has filed with the State educational agency **a written assurance** that such agency has established and implemented —

(i) a local educational agency-wide salary schedule;

(ii) a policy to ensure equivalence among schools in teachers, administrators, and other staff; and

(iii) a policy to **ensure equivalence among schools** in the provision of **curriculum materials and instructional supplies**.

(B) DETERMINATIONS - For the purpose of this subsection, in the determination of expenditures per pupil from State and local funds, or instructional salaries per pupil from State and local funds, staff salary differentials for years of employment shall not be included in such determinations.

(C) EXCLUSIONS - A local educational agency need not include unpredictable changes in student enrollment or personnel assignments that occur after the beginning of a school year in determining comparability of services under this subsection.

(3) PROCEDURES AND RECORDS - Each local educational agency assisted under this part shall —

(A) develop procedures for compliance with this subsection; and

(B) **maintain records that are updated biennially** documenting such agency's compliance with this subsection.

(4) INAPPLICABILITY - This subsection shall not apply to a local educational agency that does not have more than one building for each grade span.

(5) COMPLIANCE - For the purpose of determining compliance with paragraph (1), a local educational agency may exclude State and local funds expended for —

(A) language instruction educational programs; and

(B) the excess costs of providing services to children with disabilities as determined by the local educational agency.

(d) EXCLUSION OF FUNDS - For the purpose of complying with subsections (b) and (c), a State educational agency or local educational agency may exclude supplemental State or local funds expended in any school attendance area or school for programs that meet the intent and purposes of this part. (Section 1120A of NCLB Act)

20 U. S. C. § 6322. Coordination requirements.

➡ **OVERVIEW:** This section describes requirements about coordinating services between school districts, Head Start and other early childhood development programs.

(a) IN GENERAL - Each local educational agency receiving assistance under this part shall carry out the activities described in subsection (b) with Head Start agencies and, if feasible, other entities carrying out early childhood development programs such as the Early Reading First program.

(b) ACTIVITIES - The activities referred to in subsection (a) are activities that increase coordination **between the local educational agency and a Head Start agency** and, if feasible, other entities carrying out early childhood development programs, such as the Early Reading First program, serving children who will attend the schools of the local educational agency, including —

(1) developing and implementing a systematic procedure for receiving records regarding such children, transferred with parental consent from a Head Start program or, where applicable, another early childhood development program such as the Early Reading First program;

(2) establishing channels of communication between school staff and their counterparts (including teachers,

social workers, and health staff) in such Head Start agencies or other entities carrying out early childhood development programs such as the Early Reading First program, as appropriate, to facilitate coordination of programs;

(3) conducting meetings involving parents, kindergarten or elementary school teachers, and Head Start teachers or, if appropriate, teachers from other early childhood development programs such as the Early Reading First program, to discuss the developmental and other needs of individual children;

(4) organizing and participating in joint transition-related training of school staff, Head Start program staff, Early Reading First program staff, and, where appropriate, other early childhood development program staff; and

(5) linking the educational services provided by such local educational agency with the services provided by local Head Start agencies and entities carrying out Early Reading First programs.

(c) COORDINATION OF REGULATIONS - The Secretary shall work with the Secretary of Health and Human Services to coordinate regulations promulgated under this part with regulations promulgated under the Head Start Act. (Section 1120B of NCLB Act)

SUBPART 2 - ALLOCATIONS

➜ **OVERVIEW:** Subpart 2 (Sections 6331 through 6339) about Allocations includes grants to outlying areas and states, concentration grants and targeted grants to LEAs, adequacy of funding, education finance incentive program, special allocation procedures, and rules about carryover and waivers.

20 U. S. C. § 6331. Grants for the outlying areas and the Secretary of the Interior.

➜ **OVERVIEW:** Outlying areas are the United States Virgin Islands, Guam, American Samoa, and the Commonwealth of the Northern Mariana Islands. 'Freely associated states' are the Marshall Islands, the Federated States of Micronesia, and the Republic of Palau. This section also refers to American Indians and the Department of Interior.

(a) RESERVATION OF FUNDS - From the amount appropriated for payments to States for any fiscal year under section 1002(a) and 1125A(f), the Secretary shall reserve a total of 1 percent to provide assistance to—

(1) the outlying areas in the amount determined in accordance with subsection (b); and

(2) the Secretary of the Interior in the amount necessary to make payments pursuant to subsection (d).

(b) ASSISTANCE TO OUTLYING AREAS -

(1) FUNDS RESERVED - From the amount made available for any fiscal year under subsection (a), the Secretary shall award grants to local educational agencies in the outlying areas.

(2) COMPETITIVE GRANTS - Until each appropriate outlying area enters into an agreement for extension of United States educational assistance under the Compact of Free Association after the date of enactment of the No Child Left Behind Act of 2001, the Secretary shall carry out the competition described in paragraph (3), except that the amount reserved to carry out such competition shall not exceed $5,000,000.

(3) LIMITATION FOR COMPETITIVE GRANTS -

(A) COMPETITIVE GRANTS - The Secretary shall use funds described in paragraph (2) to award grants to the outlying areas and freely associated States to carry out the purposes of this part.

(B) AWARD BASIS - The Secretary shall award grants under subparagraph (A) on a competitive basis, taking into consideration the recommendations of the Pacific Region Educational Laboratory in Honolulu, Hawaii.

(C) USES - Except as provided in subparagraph (D), grant funds awarded under this paragraph may be used only—

(i) for programs described in this Act, including teacher training, curriculum development, instructional materials, or general school improvement and reform; and
(ii) to provide direct educational services that assist all students with meeting challenging State academic content standards.

(D) ADMINISTRATIVE COSTS - The Secretary may provide not more than 5 percent of the amount reserved for grants under this paragraph to pay the administrative costs of the Pacific Region Educational Laboratory under subparagraph (B).

(4) SPECIAL RULE - The provisions of Public Law 95–134, permitting the consolidation of grants by the outlying areas, shall not apply to funds provided to the freely associated States under this section.

(c) DEFINITIONS - For the purpose of subsections (a) and (b)—

(1) the term **'freely associated states'** means the Republic of the Marshall Islands, the Federated States of Micronesia, and the Republic of Palau; and

(2) the term **'outlying area'** means the United States Virgin Islands, Guam, American Samoa, and the Commonwealth of the Northern Mariana Islands.

(d) ALLOTMENT TO THE SECRETARY OF THE INTERIOR -

(1) IN GENERAL - The amount allotted for payments to the Secretary of the Interior under subsection (a)(2) for any fiscal year shall be, as determined pursuant to criteria established by the Secretary, the amount necessary to meet the special educational needs of—

(A) Indian children on reservations served by elementary schools and secondary schools for Indian children operated or supported by the Department of the Interior; and

(B) out-of-State Indian children in elementary schools and secondary schools in local educational agencies under special contracts with the Department of the Interior.

(2) PAYMENTS - From the amount allotted for payments to the Secretary of the Interior under subsection (a)(2), the Secretary of the Interior shall make payments to local educational agencies, on such terms as the Secretary determines will best carry out the purposes of this part, with respect to out-of-State Indian children described in paragraph (1). The amount of such payment may not exceed, for each such child, the greater of—

(A) 40 percent of the average per-pupil expenditure in the State in which the agency is located; or

(B) 48 percent of such expenditure in the United States. (Section 1121 of NCLB Act)

20 U. S. C. § 6332. Allocations to States.

➡ **OVERVIEW:** This section refers to allocations for States which are the 50 States, the District of Columbia, and the Commonwealth of Puerto Rico.

(a) ALLOCATION FORMULA - Of the amount appropriated under section 1002(a) to carry out this part for each of fiscal years 2002– 2007 (referred to in this subsection as the current fiscal year)—

(1) an amount equal to the amount made available to carry out section 1124 for fiscal year 2001 shall be allocated in accordance with section 1124;

(2) an amount equal to the amount made available to carry out section 1124A for fiscal year 2001 shall be allocated in accordance with section 1124A; and

(3) an amount equal to 100 percent of the amount, if any, by which the amount made available to carry out sections 1124, 1124A, and 1125 for the current fiscal year for which the determination is made exceeds the amount available to carry out sections 1124 and 1124A for fiscal year 2001 shall be allocated in accordance with section 1125.

(b) ADJUSTMENTS WHERE NECESSITATED BY APPROPRIATIONS -

(1) IN GENERAL - If the sums available under this subpart for any fiscal year are insufficient to pay the full amounts that all local educational agencies in States are eligible to receive under sections 1124, 1124A, and 1125 for such year, the Secretary shall ratably reduce the allocations to such local educational agencies, subject to subsections (c) and (d) of this section.

(2) ADDITIONAL FUNDS - If additional funds become available for making payments under sections 1124, 1124A, and 1125 for such fiscal year, allocations that were reduced under paragraph (1) shall be increased on the same basis as they were reduced.

(c) HOLD-HARMLESS AMOUNTS -

(1) AMOUNTS FOR SECTIONS 1124, 1124A, AND 1125 - For each fiscal year, the amount made available to each local educational agency under each of sections 1124, 1124A, and 1125 shall be—

(A) not less than 95 percent of the amount made available for the preceding fiscal year if the number of children counted for grants under section 1124 is not less than 30 percent of the total number of children aged 5 to 17 years, inclusive, in the local educational agency;

(B) not less than 90 percent of the amount made available for the preceding fiscal year if the percentage described in subparagraph (A) is between 15 percent and 30 percent; and

(C) not less than 85 percent of the amount made available for the preceding fiscal year if the percentage described in subparagraph (A) is below 15 percent.

(2) PAYMENTS - If sufficient funds are appropriated, the amounts described in paragraph (1) shall be paid to all local educational agencies that received grants under section 1124A for the preceding fiscal year, regardless of whether the local educational agency meets the minimum eligibility criteria for that fiscal year described in section 1124A(a)(1)(A) except that a local educational agency that does not meet such minimum eligibility criteria for 4 consecutive years shall no longer be eligible to receive a hold harmless amount referred to in paragraph (1).

(3) APPLICABILITY - Notwithstanding any other provision of law, the Secretary shall not take into consideration the hold-harmless provisions of this subsection for any fiscal year for purposes of calculating State or local allocations for the fiscal year under any program administered by the Secretary other than a program authorized under this part.

(4) POPULATION DATA - For any fiscal year for which the Secretary calculates grants on the basis of population data for counties, the Secretary shall apply the hold-harmless percentages in paragraphs (1) and

(2) to counties and, if the Secretary's allocation for a county is not sufficient to meet the hold-harmless requirements of this subsection for every local educational agency within that county, the State educational agency shall reallocate funds proportionately from all other local educational agencies in the State that are receiving funds in excess of the hold-harmless amounts specified in this subsection.

(d) RATABLE REDUCTIONS -

(1) IN GENERAL - If the sums made available under this subpart for any fiscal year are insufficient to pay the full amounts that local educational agencies in all States are eligible to receive under subsection (c) for such year, the Secretary shall ratably reduce such amounts for such year.

(2) ADDITIONAL FUNDS - If additional funds become available for making payments under subsection (c) for such fiscal year, amounts that were reduced under paragraph (1) shall be increased on the same basis as such amounts were reduced.

(e) DEFINITION - For the purpose of this section and sections 1124, 1124A, 1125, and 1125A, the term 'State' means each of the 50 States, the District of Columbia, and the Commonwealth of Puerto Rico. (Section 1122 of NCLB Act)

20 U. S. C. § 6333. Basic grants to local educational agencies.

➡ **OVERVIEW:** This section describes basic grants to school districts / local educational agencies, criteria for poverty, and how the number of children below the poverty line will be established.

(a) AMOUNT OF GRANTS -

(1) GRANTS FOR LOCAL EDUCATIONAL AGENCIES AND PUERTO RICO - Except as provided in paragraph (4) and in section 1126, the grant that a local educational agency is eligible to receive under this section for a fiscal year is the amount determined by multiplying—

(A) the number of children counted under subsection (c); and

(B) 40 percent of the average per-pupil expenditure in the State, except that the amount determined under this subparagraph shall not be less than 32 percent, or more than 48 percent, of the average per-pupil expenditure in the United States.

(2) CALCULATION OF GRANTS -

(A) ALLOCATIONS TO LOCAL EDUCATIONAL AGENCIES - The Secretary shall calculate grants under this section on the basis of the number of children counted under subsection (c) for local educational agencies, unless the Secretary and the Secretary of Commerce determine that some or all of those data are unreliable or that their use would be otherwise inappropriate, in which case—
(i) the two Secretaries shall publicly disclose the reasons for their determination in detail; and
(ii) paragraph (3) shall apply.

(B) ALLOCATIONS TO LARGE AND SMALL LOCAL EDUCATIONAL AGENCIES -

(i) For any fiscal year to which this paragraph applies, the Secretary shall calculate grants under this section for each local educational agency.
(ii) The amount of a grant under this section for each large local educational agency shall be the amount determined under clause (i).
(iii) For small local educational agencies, the State educational agency may either—
(I) distribute grants under this section in amounts determined by the Secretary under clause (i); or

(II) use an alternative method approved by the Secretary to distribute the portion of the State's total grants under this section that is based on those small agencies.

(iv) An alternative method under clause (iii)(II) shall be based on population data that the State educational agency determines best reflect the current distribution of children in poor families among the State's small local educational agencies that meet the eligibility criteria of subsection (b).

(v) If a small local educational agency is dissatisfied with the determination of its grant by the State educational agency under clause (iii)(II), it may appeal that determination to the Secretary, who shall respond not later than 45 days after receipt of such appeal.

(vi) As used in this subparagraph—

> (I) the term **'large local educational agency'** means a local educational agency serving an area with a total population of 20,000 or more; and
>
> (II) the term **'small local educational agency'** means a local educational agency serving an area with a total population of less than 20,000.

(3) ALLOCATIONS TO COUNTIES -

(A) CALCULATION - For any fiscal year to which this paragraph applies, the Secretary shall calculate grants under this section on the basis of the number of children counted under subsection (c) for counties, and State educational agencies shall suballocate county amounts to local educational agencies, in accordance with regulations issued by the Secretary.

(B) DIRECT ALLOCATIONS - In any State in which a large number of local educational agencies overlap county boundaries, or for which the State believes it has data that would better target funds than allocating them by county, the State educational agency **may apply** to the Secretary for authority to make the allocations under this subpart for a particular fiscal year directly to local educational agencies without regard to counties.

(C) ALLOCATIONS TO LOCAL EDUCATIONAL AGENCIES - If the Secretary approves the State educational agency's application under subparagraph (B), the State educational agency shall provide the Secretary an assurance that such allocations shall be made—

> (i) using precisely the same factors for determining a grant as are used under this subpart; or
> (ii) using data that the State educational agency submits to the Secretary for approval that more accurately target poverty.

(D) APPEAL - The State educational agency shall provide the Secretary an assurance that it will establish a procedure through which a local educational agency that is dissatisfied with its determinations under subparagraph (B) may appeal directly to the Secretary for a final determination.

(4) PUERTO RICO -

(A) IN GENERAL - For each fiscal year, the grant that the Commonwealth of Puerto Rico shall be eligible to receive under this section shall be the amount determined by multiplying the number of children counted under subsection (c) for the Commonwealth of Puerto Rico by the product of—

> (i) subject to subparagraph (B), the percentage that the average per-pupil expenditure in the Commonwealth of Puerto Rico is of the lowest average per-pupil expenditure of any of the 50 States; and
> (ii) 32 percent of the average per-pupil expenditure in the United States.

(B) MINIMUM PERCENTAGE - The percentage in subparagraph (A)(i) shall not be less than—

> (i) for fiscal year 2002, 77.5 percent;
> (ii) for fiscal year 2003, 80.0 percent;

(iii) for fiscal year 2004, 82.5 percent;

(iv) for fiscal year 2005, 85.0 percent;

(v) for fiscal year 2006, 92.5 percent; and

(vi) for fiscal year 2007 and succeeding fiscal years, 100.0 percent.

(C) LIMITATION - If the application of subparagraph (B) would result in any of the 50 States or the District of Columbia receiving less under this subpart than it received under this subpart for the preceding fiscal year, the percentage in subparagraph (A) shall be the greater of—

(i) the percentage in subparagraph (A)(i);

(ii) the percentage specified in subparagraph (B) for the preceding fiscal year; or

(iii) the percentage used for the preceding fiscal year.

(b) MINIMUM NUMBER OF CHILDREN TO QUALIFY - A local educational agency is eligible for a basic grant under this section for any fiscal year only if the number of children counted under subsection (c) for that agency is both—

(1) 10 or more; and

(2) more than 2 percent of the total school-age population in the agency's jurisdiction.

(c) CHILDREN TO BE COUNTED -

(1) CATEGORIES OF CHILDREN - The number of children to be counted for purposes of this section is the aggregate of—

(A) the number of children aged 5 to 17, inclusive, in the school district of the local educational agency from families below the poverty level as determined under paragraph (2);

(B) the number of children (determined under paragraph (4) for either the preceding year as described in that paragraph, or for the second preceding year, as the Secretary finds appropriate) aged 5 to 17, inclusive, in the school district of such agency in institutions for neglected and delinquent children (other than such institutions operated by the United States), but not counted pursuant to subpart 1 of part D for the purposes of a grant to a State agency, or being supported in foster homes with public funds; and

(C) the number of children aged 5 to 17, inclusive, in the school district of such agency from families above the poverty level as determined under paragraph (4).

(2) DETERMINATION OF NUMBER OF CHILDREN - For the purposes of this section, the Secretary shall determine the number of children aged 5 to 17, inclusive, from families below the poverty level on the basis of the most recent satisfactory data, described in paragraph (3), available from the Department of Commerce. The District of Columbia and the Commonwealth of Puerto Rico shall be treated as individual local educational agencies. If a local educational agency contains two or more counties in their entirety, then each county will be treated as if such county were a separate local educational agency for purposes of calculating grants under this part. The total of grants for such counties shall be allocated to such a local educational agency, which local educational agency shall distribute to schools in each county within such agency a share of the local educational agency's total grant that is no less than the county's share of the population counts used to calculate the local educational agency's grant.

(3) POPULATION UPDATES -

(A) IN GENERAL - In fiscal year 2002 and each subsequent fiscal year, the Secretary shall use updated data on the number of children, aged 5 to 17, inclusive, from families below the poverty level for counties or local educational agencies, published by the Department of Commerce, unless the Secretary and the

Secretary of Commerce determine that the use of the updated population data would be inappropriate or unreliable. If appropriate and reliable data are not available annually, the Secretary shall use data which are updated every 2 years.

(B) INAPPROPRIATE OR UNRELIABLE DATA - If the Secretary and the Secretary of Commerce determine that some or all of the data referred to in subparagraph (A) are inappropriate or unreliable, the Secretary and the Secretary of Commerce shall publicly disclose their reasons.

(C) CRITERIA OF POVERTY - In determining the families that are below the poverty level, the Secretary shall use the criteria of poverty used by the Bureau of the Census in compiling the most recent decennial census, as the criteria have been updated by increases in the Consumer Price Index for All Urban Consumers, published by the Bureau of Labor Statistics.

(4) OTHER CHILDREN TO BE COUNTED -

(A) For the purpose of this section, the Secretary shall determine the number of children aged 5 to 17, inclusive, from families above the poverty level on the basis of the number of such children from families receiving an annual income, in excess of the current criteria of poverty, from payments under a State program funded under part A of title IV of the Social Security Act; and in making such determinations, the Secretary shall use the criteria of poverty used by the Bureau of the Census in compiling the most recent decennial census for a family of four in such form as those criteria have been updated by increases in the Consumer Price Index for All Urban Consumers, published by the Bureau of Labor Statistics.

(B) The Secretary shall determine the number of such children and the number of children aged 5 through 17 living in institutions for neglected or delinquent children, or being supported in foster homes with public funds, on the basis of the caseload data for the month of October of the preceding fiscal year (using, in the case of children described in the preceding sentence, the criteria of poverty and the form of such criteria required by such sentence which were determined for the calendar year preceding such month of October) or, to the extent that such data are not available to the Secretary before January of the calendar year in which the Secretary's determination is made, then on the basis of the most recent reliable data available to the Secretary at the time of such determination.

(C) Except for the data on children living in institutions for neglected or delinquent children, the Secretary of Health and Human Services shall collect and transmit the information required by this subparagraph to the Secretary not later than January 1 of each year.

(D) For the purpose of this section, the Secretary shall consider all children who are in correctional institutions to be living in institutions for delinquent children.

(5) ESTIMATE - When requested by the Secretary, the Secretary of Commerce shall make a special updated estimate of the number of children of such ages who are from families below the poverty level (as determined under paragraph (1)(A)) in each school district, and the Secretary is authorized to pay (either in advance or by way of reimbursement) the Secretary of Commerce the cost of making this special estimate. The Secretary of Commerce shall give consideration to any request of the chief executive of a State for the collection of additional census information.

(d) STATE MINIMUM - Notwithstanding section 1122, the aggregate amount allotted for all local educational agencies within a State may not be less than the lesser of—

(1) 0.25 percent of the total amount allocated to States under this section for fiscal year 2001, plus 0.35 percent of the total amount allocated to States under this section in excess of the amount allocated for fiscal year 2001; or

(2) the average of—

(A) the amount calculated in paragraph (1), above; and

(B) the number of children in such State counted under subsection (c) in the fiscal year multiplied by 150 percent of the national average per-pupil payment made with funds available under this section for that year. (Section 1124 of NCLB Act)

20 U. S. C. § 6334. Concentration grants to local educational agencies.

➡ **OVERVIEW:** This section describes additional grants and special rules for small states.

(a) ELIGIBILITY FOR AND AMOUNT OF GRANTS -

(1) IN GENERAL -

(A) Except as otherwise provided in this paragraph, each local educational agency which is eligible for a grant under section 1124 for any fiscal year is eligible for an additional grant under this section for that fiscal year if the number of children counted under section 1124(c) in the agency exceeds either—

(i) 6,500; or
(ii) 15 percent of the total number of children aged 5 through 17 in the agency.

(B) Notwithstanding section 1122, no State shall receive less than the lesser of—

(i) 0.25 percent of the total amount allocated to States under this section for fiscal year 2001, plus 0.35 percent of the total amount allocated to States under this section in excess of the amount allocated for fiscal year 2001; or
(ii) the average of—
(I) the amount calculated under clause (i); and
(II) the greater of—
(aa) $340,000; or
(bb) the number of children in such State counted for purposes of this section in that fiscal year multiplied by 150 percent of the national average per-pupil payment made with funds available under this section for that year.

(2) DETERMINATION - For each county or local educational agency eligible to receive an additional grant under this section for any fiscal year, the Secretary shall determine the product of—

(A) the number of children counted under section 1124(c) for that fiscal year; and

(B) the amount in section 1124(a)(1)(B) for each State except the Commonwealth of Puerto Rico, and the amount in section 1124(a)(4) for the Commonwealth of Puerto Rico.

(3) AMOUNT - The amount of the additional grant for which an eligible local educational agency or county is eligible under this section for any fiscal year shall be an amount which bears the same ratio to the amount available to carry out this section for that fiscal year as the product determined under paragraph (2) for such local educational agency for that fiscal year bears to the sum of such products for all local educational agencies in the United States for that fiscal year.

(4) LOCAL ALLOCATIONS -

(A) Grant amounts under this section shall be determined in accordance with section 1124(a)(2), (3), and (4).

(B) For any fiscal year for which the Secretary allocates funds under this section on the basis of counties, a State may reserve not more than 2 percent of its allocation under this section to make grants to local educational agencies that meet the criteria of paragraph (1)(A)(i) or (ii) and are in ineligible counties that do not meet these criteria.

(b) SMALL STATES - In any State for which on the date of enactment of the No Child Left Behind Act of 2001 the number of children counted under section 1124(c) is less than 0.25 percent of the number of those children counted for all States, the State educational agency shall allocate funds under this section among the local educational agencies in the State either—

(1) in accordance with paragraphs (2) and (4) of subsection (a); or

(2) based on their respective concentrations and numbers of children counted under section 1124(c), except that only those local educational agencies with concentrations or numbers of children counted under section 1124(c) that exceed the state-wide average percentage of such children or the statewide average number of such children shall receive any funds on the basis of this paragraph. (Section 1124A of NCLB Act)

20 U. S. C. § 6335. Targeted grants to local educational agencies.

➡ **OVERVIEW:** This section describes targeted grants that are available to school districts / local educational agencies.

(a) ELIGIBILITY OF LOCAL EDUCATIONAL AGENCIES -

(1) IN GENERAL - A local educational agency in a State is eligible to receive a **targeted grant** under this section for any fiscal year if—

(A) the number of children in the local educational agency counted under section 1124(c), before application of the weighted child count described in subsection (c), is at least 10; and

(B) if the number of children counted for grants under section 1124(c), before application of the weighted child count described in subsection (c), is at least 5 percent of the total number of children aged 5 to 17 years, inclusive, in the school district of the local educational agency.

(2) SPECIAL RULE - For any fiscal year for which the Secretary allocates funds under this section on the basis of counties, funds made available as a result of applying this subsection shall be reallocated by the State educational agency to other eligible local educational agencies in the State in proportion to the distribution of other funds under this section.

(b) GRANTS FOR LOCAL EDUCATIONAL AGENCIES, THE DISTRICT OF COLUMBIA, AND THE COMMONWEALTH OF PUERTO RICO -

(1) IN GENERAL - The amount of the grant that a local educational agency in a State (other than the Commonwealth of Puerto Rico) is eligible to receive under this section for any fiscal year shall be the product of—

(A) the weighted child count determined under subsection (c); and

(B) the amount determined under section 1124(a)(1)(B).

(2) PUERTO RICO - For each fiscal year, the amount of the grant the Commonwealth of Puerto Rico is eligible to receive under this section shall be equal to the number of children counted under subsection (c) for the Commonwealth of Puerto Rico, multiplied by the amount determined in section 1124(a)(4) for the Commonwealth of Puerto Rico.

(c) WEIGHTED CHILD COUNT -

(1) WEIGHTS FOR ALLOCATIONS TO COUNTIES -

(A) IN GENERAL - For each fiscal year for which the Secretary uses county population data to calculate grants, the weighted child count used to determine a county's allocation under this section is the larger of the two amounts determined under subparagraphs (B) and (C).

(B) BY PERCENTAGE OF CHILDREN - The amount referred to in subparagraph (A) is determined by adding—

(i) the number of children determined under section 1124(c) for that county who constitute not more than 15.00 percent, inclusive, of the county's total population aged 5 to 17, inclusive, multiplied by 1.0;
(ii) the number of such children who constitute more than 15.00 percent, but not more than 19.00 percent, of such population, multiplied by 1.75;
(iii) the number of such children who constitute more than 19.00 percent, but not more than 24.20 percent, of such population, multiplied by 2.5;
(iv) the number of such children who constitute more than 24.20 percent, but not more than 29.20 percent, of such population, multiplied by 3.25; and
(v) the number of such children who constitute more than 29.20 percent of such population, multiplied by 4.0.

(C) BY NUMBER OF CHILDREN - The amount referred to in subparagraph (A) is determined by adding—

(i) the number of children determined under section 1124(c) who constitute not more than 2,311, inclusive, of the county's total population aged 5 to 17, inclusive, multiplied by 1.0;
(ii) the number of such children between 2,312 and 7,913, inclusive, in such population, multiplied by 1.5;
(iii) the number of such children between 7,914 and 23,917, inclusive, in such population, multiplied by 2.0;
(iv) the number of such children between 23,918 and 93,810, inclusive, in such population, multiplied by 2.5; and
(v) the number of such children in excess of 93,811 in such population, multiplied by 3.0.

(D) PUERTO RICO - Notwithstanding subparagraph (A), the weighting factor for the Commonwealth of Puerto Rico under this paragraph shall not be greater than the total number of children counted under section 1124(c) multiplied by 1.82.

(2) WEIGHTS FOR ALLOCATIONS TO LOCAL EDUCATIONAL AGENCIES -

(A) IN GENERAL - For each fiscal year for which the Secretary uses local educational agency data, the weighted child count used to determine a local educational agency's grant under this section is the larger of the two amounts determined under subparagraphs (B) and (C).

(B) BY PERCENTAGE OF CHILDREN - The amount referred to in subparagraph (A) is determined by adding—

(i) the number of children determined under section 1124(c) for that local educational agency who constitute not more than 15.58 percent, inclusive, of the agency's total population aged 5 to 17, inclusive, multiplied by 1.0;
(ii) the number of such children who constitute more than 15.58 percent, but not more than 22.11

percent, of such population, multiplied by 1.75;

(iii) the number of such children who constitute more than 22.11 percent, but not more than 30.16 percent, of such population, multiplied by 2.5;

(iv) the number of such children who constitute more than 30.16 percent, but not more than 38.24 percent, of such population, multiplied by 3.25; and

(v) the number of such children who constitute more than 38.24 percent of such population, multiplied by 4.0.

(C) BY NUMBER OF CHILDREN - The amount referred to in subparagraph (A) is determined by adding—

(i) the number of children determined under section 1124(c) who constitute not more than 691, inclusive, of the agency's total population aged 5 to 17, inclusive, multiplied by 1.0;

(ii) the number of such children between 692 and 2,262, inclusive, in such population, multiplied by 1.5;

(iii) the number of such children between 2,263 and 7,851, inclusive, in such population, multiplied by 2.0;

(iv) the number of such children between 7,852 and 35,514, inclusive, in such population, multiplied by 2.5; and

(v) the number of such children in excess of 35,514 in such population, multiplied by 3.0.

(D) PUERTO RICO - Notwithstanding subparagraph (A), the weighting factor for the Commonwealth of Puerto Rico under this paragraph shall not be greater than the total number of children counted under section 1124(c) multiplied by 1.82.

(d) CALCULATION OF GRANT AMOUNTS - Grant amounts under this section shall be calculated in the same manner as grant amounts are calculated under section 1124(a)(2) and (3).

(e) STATE MINIMUM - Notwithstanding any other provision of this section or section 1122, from the total amount available for any fiscal year to carry out this section, each State shall be allotted at least the lesser of—

(1) 0.35 percent of the total amount available to carry out this section; or

(2) the average of—

(A) 0.35 percent of the total amount available to carry out this section; and

(B) 150 percent of the national average grant under this section per child described in section 1124(c), without application of a weighting factor, multiplied by the State's total number of children described in section 1124(c), with-out application of a weighting factor. (Section 1125 of NCLB Act)

20 U. S. C. § 6336. Adequacy of funding of targeted grants to local educational agencies in fiscal years after fiscal year 2001.

➡ **OVERVIEW:** Section 6336(a) includes Congressional Findings about economically disadvantaged students, poverty rates, the percentage of poor children in schools, and the need for adequate funding to educate disadvantaged children. If more than 2 percent of students live below the poverty level, the school district qualifies for funds. At the time of press, the U. S. Department of Education's No Child Left Behind website at www.nclb.gov stated that fifty-nine percent of schools and nine out of ten school districts receive Title I funds.

(a) FINDINGS - Congress makes the following findings:

(1) The current Basic Grant Formula for the distribution of funds under this part **often does not provide**

funds for the economically disadvantaged students for which such funds are targeted.

(2) Any school district in which **more than 2 percent of the students live below the poverty level** qualifies for funding under the Basic Grant Formula. As a result, **9 out of every 10 school districts** in the country receive some form of aid under the Formula.

(3) Fifty-eight percent of all schools receive at least some funding under this part, including many suburban schools **with predominantly well-off students.**

(4) **One out of every 5 schools** with concentrations of poor students between 50 and 75 percent receive no funding at all under this part.

(5) In passing the Improving America's Schools Act in 1994, Congress declared that grants under this part would more **sharply target high poverty schools** by using the Targeted Grant Formula, but annual appropriation Acts **have prevented the use** of that Formula.

(6) The advantage of the Targeted Grant Formula over other funding formulas under this part is that the Targeted Grant Formula provides increased grants per poor child as the percentage of economically disadvantaged children in a school district increases.

(7) Studies have found that the poverty of a child's family is much more likely to be associated with educational disadvantage if the family lives in an area with large concentrations of poor families.

(8) States with large populations of high poverty students would receive significantly more funding if more funds under this part were allocated through the Targeted Grant Formula.

(9) Congress has an obligation to allocate funds under this part so that such funds will positively affect the largest number of economically disadvantaged students.

(b) LIMITATION ON ALLOCATION OF TITLE I FUNDS CONTINGENT ON ADEQUATE FUNDING OF TARGETED GRANTS - Pursuant to section 1122, the total amount allocated in any fiscal year after fiscal year 2001 for programs and activities under this part shall not exceed the amount allocated in fiscal year 2001 for such programs and activities unless the amount available for targeted grants to local educational agencies under section 1125 in the applicable fiscal year meets the requirements of section 1122(a). (Section 1125AA of NCLB Act)

20 U. S. C. § 6337. Education finance incentive grant program.

➡ **OVERVIEW:** Section 6337 authorizes grants to states and describes how funds will be allocated to local school districts.

(a) GRANTS - From funds appropriated under subsection (f) the Secretary is authorized to make grants to States, from allotments under subsection (b), to carry out the programs and activities of this part.

(b) DISTRIBUTION BASED UPON FISCAL EFFORT AND EQUITY -

(1) IN GENERAL -

(A) IN GENERAL - Except as provided in subparagraph (B), funds appropriated pursuant to subsection (f) shall be allotted to each State based upon the number of children counted under section 1124(c) in such State multiplied by the product of—

(i) the amount in section 1124(a)(1)(B) for all States other than the Commonwealth of Puerto Rico, except that the amount determined under that subparagraph shall not be less that 34 percent or more than 46 percent of the average per pupil expenditure in the United States, and the amount in section 1124(a)(4) for the Commonwealth of Puerto Rico, except that the amount in section 1124(a)(4)(A)(ii) shall be 34 percent of the average per pupil expenditure in the United States; multiplied by

(ii) such State's effort factor described in paragraph (2); multiplied by

(iii) 1.30 minus such State's equity factor described in paragraph (3).

(B) STATE MINIMUM - Notwithstanding any other provision of this section or section 1122, from the total amount available for any fiscal year to carry out this section, each State shall be allotted at least the lesser of—

(i) 0.35 percent of total appropriations; or

(ii) the average of—

(I) 0.35 percent of the total amount available to carry out this section; and

(II) 150 percent of the national average grant under this section per child described in section 1124(c), without application of a weighting factor, multiplied by the State's total number of children described in section 1124(c), without application of a weighting factor.

(2) EFFORT FACTOR -

(A) IN GENERAL - Except as provided in subparagraph (B), the effort factor for a State shall be determined in accordance with the succeeding sentence, except that such factor shall not be less than 0.95 nor greater than 1.05. The effort factor determined under this sentence shall be a fraction the numerator of which is the product of the 3-year average per-pupil expenditure in the State multiplied by the 3-year average per capita income in the United States and the denominator of which is the product of the 3-year average per capita income in such State multiplied by the 3-year average per-pupil expenditure in the United States.

(B) COMMONWEALTH OF PUERTO RICO - The effort factor for the Commonwealth of Puerto Rico shall be equal to the lowest effort factor calculated under subparagraph (A) for any State.

(3) EQUITY FACTOR -

(A) DETERMINATION -

(i) IN GENERAL - Except as provided in subparagraph (B), the Secretary **shall determine the equity factor** under this section for each State in accordance with clause (ii).

(ii) COMPUTATION -

(I) **IN GENERAL** - For each State, the Secretary shall compute a weighted coefficient of variation for the per-pupil expenditures of local educational agencies in accordance with subclauses (II), (III), and (IV).

(II) **VARIATION** - In computing coefficients of variation, the Secretary shall weigh the variation between per-pupil expenditures in each local educational agency and the average per-pupil expenditures in the State according to the number of pupils served by the local educational agency.

(III) **NUMBER OF PUPILS** - In determining the number of pupils under this paragraph served by each local educational agency and in each State, the Secretary shall multiply the number of children counted under section 1124(c) by a factor of 1.4.

(IV) **ENROLLMENT REQUIREMENT** - In computing coefficients of variation, the Secretary shall include only those local educational agencies with an enrollment of more than 200 students.

(B) SPECIAL RULE - The equity factor for a State that meets the disparity standard described in section 222.162 of title 34, Code of Federal Regulations (as such section was in effect on the day preceding the date of enactment of the No Child Left Behind Act of 2001) or a State with only one local educational agency shall be not greater than 0.10.

(c) USE OF FUNDS; ELIGIBILITY OF LOCAL EDUCATIONAL AGENCIES - All funds awarded to each State under this section shall be allocated to local educational agencies under the following provisions. Within local educational agencies, funds allocated under this section shall be distributed to schools on a basis consistent with section 1113, and may only be used to carry out activities under this part. A local educational agency in a State is eligible to receive a targeted grant under this section for any fiscal year if—

(A) the number of children in the local educational agency counted under section 1124(c), before application of the weighted child count described in paragraph (3), is at least 10; and

(B) if the number of children counted for grants under section 1124(c), before application of the weighted child count described in paragraph (3), is at least 5 percent of the total number of children aged 5 to 17 years, inclusive, in the school district of the local educational agency. For any fiscal year for which the Secretary allocates funds under this section on the basis of counties, funds made available as a result of applying this subsection shall be reallocated by the State educational agency to other eligible local educational agencies in the State in proportion to the distribution of other funds under this section.

(d) ALLOCATION OF FUNDS TO ELIGIBLE LOCAL EDUCATIONAL AGENCIES - Funds received by States under this section shall be allocated within States to eligible local educational agencies on the basis of weighted child counts calculated in accordance with paragraph (1), (2), or (3), as appropriate for each State.

(1) STATES WITH AN EQUITY FACTOR LESS THAN .10 - In States with an equity factor less than .10, the weighted child counts referred to in subsection (d) shall be calculated as follows:

(A) WEIGHTS FOR ALLOCATIONS TO COUNTIES -

(i) IN GENERAL - For each fiscal year for which the Secretary uses county population data to calculate grants, the weighted child count used to determine a county's allocation under this section is the larger of the two amounts determined under clauses (ii) and (iii).
(ii) BY PERCENTAGE OF CHILDREN - The amount referred to in clause (i) is determined by adding—
(I) the number of children determined under section 1124(c) for that county who constitute not more than 15.00 percent, inclusive, of the county's total population aged 5 to 17, inclusive, multiplied by 1.0;
(II) the number of such children who constitute more than 15.00 percent, but not more than 19.00 percent, of such population, multiplied by 1.75;
(III) the number of such children who constitute more than 19.00 percent, but not more than 24.20 percent, of such population, multiplied by 2.5;
(IV) the number of such children who constitute more than 24.20 percent, but not more than 29.20 percent, of such population, multiplied by 3.25; and
(V) the number of such children who constitute more than 29.20 percent of such population, multiplied by 4.0.
(iii) BY NUMBER OF CHILDREN - The amount referred to in clause (i) is determined by adding
(I) the number of children determined under section 1124(c) who constitute not more than 2,311, inclusive, of the county's total population aged 5 to 17, inclusive, multiplied by 1.0;
(II) the number of such children between 2,312 and 7,913, inclusive, in such population, multiplied by 1.5;
(III) the number of such children between 7,914 and 23,917, inclusive, in such population, multiplied by 2.0;
(IV) the number of such children between 23,918 and 93,810, inclusive, in such population, multiplied by 2.5; and
(V) the number of such children in excess of 93,811 in such population, multiplied by 3.0.

(B) WEIGHTS FOR ALLOCATIONS TO LOCAL EDUCATIONAL AGENCIES -

(i) IN GENERAL - For each fiscal year for which the Secretary uses local educational agency data, the weighted child count used to determine a local educational agency's grant under this section is the larger of the two amounts determined under clauses (ii) and (iii).

(ii) BY PERCENTAGE OF CHILDREN - The amount referred to in clause (i) is determined by adding—

(I) the number of children determined under section 1124(c) for that local educational agency who constitute not more than 15.58 percent, inclusive, of the agency's total population aged 5 to 17, inclusive, multiplied by 1.0;

(II) the number of such children who constitute more than 15.58 percent, but not more than 22.11 percent, of such population, multiplied by 1.75;

(III) the number of such children who constitute more than 22.11 percent, but not more than 30.16 percent, of such population, multiplied by 2.5;

(IV) the number of such children who constitute more than 30.16 percent, but not more than 38.24 percent, of such population, multiplied by 3.25; and

(V) the number of such children who constitute more than 38.24 percent of such population, multiplied by 4.0.

(iii) BY NUMBER OF CHILDREN - The amount referred to in clause (i) is determined by adding—

(I) the number of children determined under section 1124(c) who constitute not more than 691, inclusive, of the agency's total population aged 5 to 17, inclusive, multiplied by 1.0;

(II) the number of such children between 692 and 2,262, inclusive, in such population, multiplied by 1.5;

(III) the number of such children between 2,263 and 7,851, inclusive, in such population, multiplied by 2.0;

(IV) the number of such children between 7,852 and 35,514, inclusive, in such population, multiplied by 2.5; and

(V) the number of such children in excess of 35,514 in such population, multiplied by 3.0.

(2) STATES WITH AN EQUITY FACTOR GREATER THAN OR EQUAL TO .10 AND LESS THAN .20 -
In States with an equity factor greater than or equal to .10 and less than .20, the weighted child counts referred to in subsection (d) shall be calculated as follows:

(A) WEIGHTS FOR ALLOCATIONS TO COUNTIES -

(i) IN GENERAL - For each fiscal year for which the Secretary uses county population data to calculate grants, the weighted child count used to determine a county's allocation under this section is the larger of the two amounts determined under clauses (ii) and (iii).

(ii) BY PERCENTAGE OF CHILDREN - The amount referred to in clause (i) is determined by adding—

(I) the number of children determined under section 1124(c) for that county who constitute not more than 15.00 percent, inclusive, of the county's total population aged 5 to 17, inclusive, multiplied by 1.0;

(II) the number of such children who constitute more than 15.00 percent, but not more than 19.00 percent, of such population, multiplied by 1.5;

(III) the number of such children who constitute more than 19.00 percent, but not more than 24.20 percent, of such population, multiplied by 3.0;

(IV) the number of such children who constitute more than 24.20 percent, but not more than 29.20 percent, of such population, multiplied by 4.5; and

(V) the number of such children who constitute more than 29.20 percent of such population, multiplied by 6.0.

(iii) BY NUMBER OF CHILDREN - The amount referred to in clause (i) is determined by adding—

(I) the number of children determined under section 1124(c) who constitute not more than

2,311, inclusive, of the county's total population aged 5 to 17, inclusive, multiplied by 1.0;

(II) the number of such children between 2,312 and 7,913, inclusive, in such population, multiplied by 1.5;

(III) the number of such children between 7,914 and 23,917, inclusive, in such population, multiplied by 2.25;

(IV) the number of such children between 23,918 and 93,810, inclusive, in such population, multiplied by 3.375; and

(V) the number of such children in excess of 93,811 in such population, multiplied by 4.5.

(B) WEIGHTS FOR ALLOCATIONS TO LOCAL EDUCATIONAL AGENCIES -

(i) IN GENERAL - For each fiscal year for which the Secretary uses local educational agency data, the weighted child count used to determine a local educational agency's grant under this section is the larger of the two amounts determined under clauses (ii) and (iii).

(ii) BY PERCENTAGE OF CHILDREN - The amount referred to in clause (i) is determined by adding—

(I) the number of children determined under section 1124(c) for that local educational agency who constitute not more than 15.58 percent, inclusive, of the agency's total population aged 5 to 17, inclusive, multiplied by 1.0;

(II) the number of such children who constitute more than 15.58 percent, but not more than 22.11 percent, of such population, multiplied by 1.5;

(III) the number of such children who constitute more than 22.11 percent, but not more than 30.16 percent, of such population, multiplied by 3.0;

(IV) the number of such children who constitute more than 30.16 percent, but not more than 38.24 percent, of such population, multiplied by 4.5; and

(V) the number of such children who constitute more than 38.24 percent of such population, multiplied by 6.0.

(iii) BY NUMBER OF CHILDREN - The amount referred to in clause (i) is determined by adding—

(I) the number of children determined under section 1124(c) who constitute not more than 691, inclusive, of the agency's total population aged 5 to 17, inclusive, multiplied by 1.0;

(II) the number of such children between 692 and 2,262, inclusive, in such population, multiplied by 1.5;

(III) the number of such children between 2,263 and 7,851, inclusive, in such population, multiplied by 2.25;

(IV) the number of such children between 7,852 and 35,514, inclusive, in such population, multiplied by 3.375; and

(V) the number of such children in excess of 35,514 in such population, multiplied by 4.5.

(3) STATES WITH AN EQUITY FACTOR GREATER THAN OR EQUAL TO .20 - In States with an equity factor greater than or equal to .20, the weighted child counts referred to in subsection (d) shall be calculated as follows:

(A) WEIGHTS FOR ALLOCATIONS TO COUNTIES -

(i) IN GENERAL - For each fiscal year for which the Secretary uses county population data to calculate grants, the weighted child count used to determine a county's allocation under this section is the larger of the two amounts determined under clauses (ii) and (iii).

(ii) BY PERCENTAGE OF CHILDREN - The amount referred to in clause (i) is determined by adding—

(I) the number of children determined under section 1124(c) for that county who constitute not more than 15.00 percent, inclusive, of the county's total population aged 5 to 17, inclusive, multiplied by 1.0;

(II) the number of such children who constitute more than 15.00 percent, but not more than 19.00 percent, of such population, multiplied by 2.0;

(III) the number of such children who constitute more than 19.00 percent, but not more than 24.20 percent, of such population, multiplied by 4.0;

(IV) the number of such children who constitute more than 24.20 percent, but not more than 29.20 percent, of such population, multiplied by 6.0; and

(V) the number of such children who constitute more than 29.20 percent of such population, multiplied by 8.0.

(iii) **BY NUMBER OF CHILDREN** - The amount referred to in clause (i) is determined by adding—

(I) the number of children determined under section 1124(c) who constitute not more than 2,311, inclusive, of the county's total population aged 5 to 17, inclusive, multiplied by 1.0;

(II) the number of such children between 2,312 and 7,913, inclusive, in such population, multiplied by 2.0;

(III) the number of such children between 7,914 and 23,917, inclusive, in such population, multiplied by 3.0;

(IV) the number of such children between 23,918 and 93,810, inclusive, in such population, multiplied by 4.5; and

(V) the number of such children in excess of 93,811 in such population, multiplied by 6.0.

(B) WEIGHTS FOR ALLOCATIONS TO LOCAL EDUCATIONAL AGENCIES -

(i) **IN GENERAL** - For each fiscal year for which the Secretary uses local educational agency data, the weighted child count used to determine a local educational agency's grant under this section is the larger of the two amounts determined under clauses (ii) and (iii).

(ii) **BY PERCENTAGE OF CHILDREN** - The amount referred to in clause (i) is determined by adding—

(I) the number of children determined under section 1124(c) for that local educational agency who constitute not more than 15.58 percent, inclusive, of the agency's total population aged 5 to 17, inclusive, multiplied by 1.0;

(II) the number of such children who constitute more than 15.58 percent, but not more than 22.11 percent, of such population, multiplied by 2.0;

(III) the number of such children who constitute more than 22.11 percent, but not more than 30.16 percent, of such population, multiplied by 4.0;

(IV) the number of such children who constitute more than 30.16 percent, but not more than 38.24 percent, of such population, multiplied by 6.0; and

(V) the number of such children who constitute more than 38.24 percent of such population, multiplied by 8.0.

(iii) **BY NUMBER OF CHILDREN** - The amount referred to in clause (i) is determined by adding—

(I) the number of children determined under section 1124(c) who constitute not more than 691, inclusive, of the agency's total population aged 5 to 17, inclusive, multiplied by 1.0;

(II) the number of such children between 692 and 2,262, inclusive, in such population, multiplied by 2.0;

(III) the number of such children between 2,263 and 7,851, inclusive, in such population, multiplied by 3.0;

(IV) the number of such children between 7,852 and 35,514, inclusive, in such population, multiplied by 4.5; and

(V) the number of such children in excess of 35,514 in such population, multiplied by 6.0.

(e) MAINTENANCE OF EFFORT -

(1) **IN GENERAL** - Except as provided in paragraph (2), a State is entitled to receive its full allotment of funds under this section for any fiscal year if the Secretary finds that either the combined fiscal effort per student or the aggregate expenditures within the State with respect to the provision of free public education for the fiscal year preceding the fiscal year for which the determination is made was not less than 90 percent of such combined fiscal effort or aggregate expenditures for the second fiscal year preceding the fiscal year for which the determination is made.

(2) REDUCTION OF FUNDS - The Secretary shall reduce the amount of funds awarded to any State under this section in any fiscal year in the exact proportion to which the State fails to meet the requirements of paragraph (1) by falling below 90 percent of both the fiscal effort per student and aggregate expenditures (using the measure most favorable to the State), and no such lesser amount shall be used for computing the effort required under paragraph (1) for subsequent years.

(3) WAIVERS - The Secretary may waive, for 1 fiscal year only, the requirements of this subsection if the Secretary determines that such a waiver would be equitable due to exceptional or uncontrollable circumstances such as a natural disaster or a precipitous and unforeseen decline in the financial resources of the State.

(f) AUTHORIZATION OF APPROPRIATIONS - There are authorized to be appropriated to carry out this section such sums as may be necessary for fiscal year 2002 and for each of the 5 succeeding fiscal years.

(g) ADJUSTMENTS WHERE NECESSITATED BY APPROPRIATIONS -

(1) IN GENERAL - If the sums available under this section for any fiscal year are insufficient to pay the full amounts that all local educational agencies in States are eligible to receive under this section for such year, the Secretary **shall ratably reduce the allocations to such local educational agencies**, subject to paragraphs (2) and (3).

(2) ADDITIONAL FUNDS - If additional funds become available for making payments under this section for such fiscal year, allocations that were reduced under paragraph (1) shall be increased on the same basis as they were reduced.

(3) HOLD-HARMLESS AMOUNTS - For each fiscal year, if sufficient funds are available, the amount made available to each local educational agency under this section shall be

(A) not less than 95 percent of the amount made available for the preceding fiscal year if the number of children counted for grants under section 1124 is not less than 30 percent of the total number of children aged 5 to 17 years, inclusive, in the local educational agency;

(B) not less than 90 percent of the amount made available for the preceding fiscal year if the percentage described in subparagraph (A) is between 15 percent and 30 percent; and

(C) not less than 85 percent of the amount made available for the preceding fiscal year if the percentage described in subparagraph (A) is below 15 percent.

(4) APPLICABILITY - Notwithstanding any other provision of law, the Secretary shall not take into consideration the hold-harmless provisions of this subsection for any fiscal year for purposes of calculating State or local allocations for the fiscal year under any program administered by the Secretary other than a program authorized under this part. (Section 1125A of NCLB Act)

20 U. S. C. § 6338. Special allocation procedures.

➡ **OVERVIEW:** If a local school district is unable or unwilling to provide for the special educational needs of neglected children who live in institutions, the state must assume responsibility for these children.

(a) ALLOCATIONS FOR NEGLECTED CHILDREN -

(1) IN GENERAL - If a State educational agency determines that a local educational agency in the State **is unable or unwilling to provide for the special educational needs of children who are living in institutions for neglected children** as described in section 1124(c)(1)(B), **the State educational agency shall**, if such agency assumes responsibility for the special educational needs of such children, **receive the portion of such local educational agency's allocation** under sections 1124, 1124A, 1125, and 1125A that is attributable to such children.

(2) SPECIAL RULE - If the State educational agency **does not assume such responsibility, any other State or local public agency that does assume such responsibility shall receive that portion of the local educational agency's allocation.**

(b) ALLOCATIONS AMONG LOCAL EDUCATIONAL AGENCIES - The State educational agency may allocate the amounts of grants under sections 1124, 1124A, 1125, and 1125A among the affected local educational agencies—

(1) if two or more local educational agencies serve, in whole or in part, the same geographical area;

(2) if a local educational agency provides free public education for children who reside in the school district of another local educational agency; or

(3) to reflect the merger, creation, or change of boundaries of one or more local educational agencies.

(c) REALLOCATION - If a State educational agency determines that the amount of a grant a local educational agency would receive under sections 1124, 1124A, 1125, and 1125A is more than such local educational agency will use, the State educational agency shall make the excess amount available to other local educational agencies in the State that need additional funds in accordance with criteria established by the State educational agency. (Section 1126 of NCLB Act)

20 U. S. C. § 6339. Carryover and waiver.

(a) LIMITATION ON CARRYOVER - Notwithstanding section 421(b) of the General Education Provisions Act or any other provision of law, not more than 15 percent of the funds allocated to a local educational agency for any fiscal year under this subpart (but not including funds received through any reallocation under this subpart) may remain available for obligation by such agency for one additional fiscal year.

(b) WAIVER - A State educational agency may, once every 3 years, waive the percentage limitation in subsection (a) if—

(1) the agency determines that the request of a local educational agency is reasonable and necessary; or
(2) supplemental appropriations for this subpart become available.

(c) EXCLUSION - The percentage limitation under subsection (a) shall not apply to any local educational agency that receives less than $50,000 under this subpart for any fiscal year. (Section 1127 of NCLB Act)

PART B - STUDENT READING SKILLS IMPROVEMENT GRANTS

➔ **OVERVIEW:** In the context of "Reading First, the U. S. Department of Education discussed the National Assessment for Educational Progress (NAEP) report issued in 2000. Over 85 percent of all fourth-graders in high-poverty schools scored below the proficient level in reading. Approximately 40 percent of students cannot read at a basic level. These children do not have fundamental reading skills. Average-performing students have made no progress in reading over the past 10 years. The lowest-performing readers have become even less successful. One goal of No Child Left Behind is that all children will learn to read well by the end of third grade.

Part B includes four subparts:
Subpart 1 - Reading First
Subpart 2 - Early Reading First

Subpart 3 - William F. Goodling Even Start Family Literacy Programs
Subpart 4 - Improving Literacy Through School Libraries.

Part B, Student Reading Skills Improvement Grants, includes the following four subparts and sections.

Subpart 1 - Reading First

20 U. S. C. § 6361. Purposes.
20 U. S. C. § 6362. Formula grants to State educational agencies.
20 U. S. C. § 6363. State formula grant applications.
20 U. S. C. § 6364. Targeted assistance grants.
20 U. S. C. § 6365. External evaluation.
20 U. S. C. § 6366. National activities.
20 U. S. C. § 6367. Information dissemination.
20 U. S. C. § 6368. Definitions.

Subpart 2 - Early Reading First

20 U. S. C. § 6371. Purposes; definitions.
20 U. S. C. § 6372. Local Early Reading First grants.
20 U. S. C. § 6373. Federal administration.
20 U. S. C. § 6374. Information dissemination
20 U. S. C. § 6375. Reporting requirements.
20 U. S. C. § 6376. Evaluation.

Subpart 3 - William F. Goodling Even Start Family Literacy Programs

20 U. S. C. § 6381. Statement of purpose.
20 U. S. C. § 6381a. Program authorized.
20 U. S. C. § 6381b. State educational agency programs.
20 U. S. C. § 6381c. Uses of funds.
20 U. S. C. § 6381d. Program elements.
20 U. S. C. § 6381e. Eligible participants.
20 U. S. C. § 6381f. Applications.
20 U. S. C. § 6381g. Award of subgrants.
20 U. S. C. § 6381h. Evaluation.
20 U. S. C. § 6381i. Indicators of program quality.
20 U. S. C. § 6381j. Research.
20 U. S. C. § 6381k. Construction.

Subpart 4—Improving Literacy Through School Libraries

20 U. S. C. § 6383. Improving literacy through school libraries.

SUBPART 1 - READING FIRST

➜ **OVERVIEW:** Reading First grants may be used on research-based programs for children in Kindergarten through third grade. States and school districts must use effective instructional materials, programs, learning systems, and strategies that are proven to teach reading. Reading First provides funding for screening, diagnostic, and classroom-based instructional reading assessments.

Reading First also provides professional development funds so all teachers have the skills to teach effectively. Reading First specifies that teachers' classroom instructional decisions must be informed by scientifically-based reading research. Reading First grants are available for state and local programs in which students are systematically and explicitly taught five key reading skills:

Phonemic awareness: the ability to hear, identify, and play with individual sounds - or phonemes - in spoken words
Phonics: the relationship between the letters of written language and the sounds of spoken language
Fluency: the capacity to read text accurately and quickly

Vocabulary: the words students must know to communicate effectively
Comprehension: the ability to understand and gain meaning from what has been read

📖 *Guidance for the Reading First Program* by the U. S. Department of Education includes frequently asked questions and answers about effective reading programs. (in the *Wrightslaw NCLB CD-ROM*)

20 U. S. C. § 6361. Purposes.

➜ **OVERVIEW:** Section 6361 is a key statute because it describes the purposes of Reading First.

The purposes of this subpart are as follows:

(1) To provide assistance to State educational agencies and local educational agencies in establishing **reading programs for students in kindergarten through grade 3** that are **based on scientifically based reading research, to ensure that every student can read at grade level or above not later than the end of grade 3.**

(2) To provide assistance to State educational agencies and local educational agencies in **preparing teachers, including special education teachers**, through professional development and other support, so the teachers can identify specific reading barriers facing their students and so the **teachers have the tools to effectively help their students learn to read.**

(3) To provide assistance to State educational agencies and local educational agencies in **selecting or administering screening, diagnostic, and classroom-based instructional reading assessments.**

(4) To provide assistance to State educational agencies and local educational agencies in **selecting or developing effective instructional materials** (including classroom-based materials to assist teachers in implementing the essential components of reading instruction), **programs, learning systems, and strategies** to implement **methods that have been proven to prevent or remediate reading failure** within a State.

(5) To strengthen coordination among schools, early literacy programs, and family literacy programs to improve reading achievement for all children. (Section 1201 of NCLB Act)

20 U. S. C. § 6362. Formula grants to State educational agencies.

➜ **OVERVIEW:** Section 6362 describes grants to states, subgrants to local school districts, limitations and priorities, how local funds can be used, reporting requirements, reviews and progress reports, and consequences to states for insufficient progress.

(a) IN GENERAL -

(1) **AUTHORIZATION TO MAKE GRANTS** - In the case of each State educational agency that in accordance with section 1203 submits to the Secretary an application for a 6-year period, the Secretary, from amounts appropriated under section 1002(b)(1) and subject to the application's approval, shall make a grant to the State educational agency for the uses specified in subsections (c) and (d). For each fiscal year, the funds provided under the grant shall equal the allotment determined for the State educational agency under subsection (b).

(2) **DURATION OF GRANTS** - Subject to subsection (e)(3), a grant under this section shall be awarded for a period of not more than 6 years.

(b) DETERMINATION OF AMOUNT OF ALLOTMENTS -

(1) **RESERVATIONS FROM APPROPRIATIONS** - From the total amount made available to carry out this subpart for a fiscal year, the Secretary —

(A) shall reserve one-half of 1 percent for allotments for the United States Virgin Islands, Guam, American Samoa, and the Commonwealth of the Northern Mariana Islands, to be distributed among these outlying areas on the basis of their relative need, as determined by the Secretary in accordance with the purposes of this subpart;

(B) shall reserve one-half of 1 percent for the Secretary of the Interior for programs under this subpart in schools operated or funded by the Bureau of Indian Affairs;

(C) may reserve not more than 2 1/2 percent or $25,000,000, whichever is less, to carry out section 1205 (relating to external evaluation) and section 1206 (relating to national activities);

(D) shall reserve $5,000,000 to carry out sections 1207 and 1224 (relating to information dissemination); and

(E) for any fiscal year, beginning with fiscal year 2004, for which the amount appropriated to carry out this subpart exceeds the amount appropriated for fiscal year 2003, shall reserve, to carry out section 1204, the lesser of —

    (i) $90,000,000; or
    (ii) 10 percent of such excess amount.

(2) STATE ALLOTMENTS - In accordance with paragraph (3), the Secretary shall allot among each of the States the total amount made available to carry out this subpart for any fiscal year and not reserved under paragraph (1).

(3) DETERMINATION OF STATE ALLOTMENT AMOUNTS -

(A) IN GENERAL - Subject to subparagraph (B), the Secretary shall allot the amount made available under paragraph (2) for a fiscal year among the States in proportion to the number of children, aged 5 to 17, who reside within the State and are from families with incomes below the poverty line for the most recent fiscal year for which satisfactory data are available, compared to the number of such individuals who reside in all such States for that fiscal year.

(B) EXCEPTIONS -

    (i) MINIMUM GRANT AMOUNT - Subject to clause (ii), no State receiving an allotment under subparagraph (A) may receive less than one-fourth of 1 percent of the total amount allotted under such subparagraph.
    (ii) PUERTO RICO - The percentage of the amount allotted under subparagraph (A) that is allotted to the Commonwealth of Puerto Rico for a fiscal year may not exceed the percentage that was received by the Commonwealth of Puerto Rico of the funds allocated to all States under subpart 2 of part A for the preceding fiscal year.

(4) DISTRIBUTION OF SUBGRANTS - The Secretary may make a grant to a State educational agency only if the State educational agency agrees to expend at least 80 percent of the amount of the funds provided under the grant for the purpose of making, in accordance with subsection (c), competitive subgrants to eligible local educational agencies.

(5) REALLOTMENT - If a State educational agency described in paragraph (2) does not apply for an allotment under this section for any fiscal year, or if the State educational agency's application is not approved, the Secretary shall reallot such amount to the remaining State educational agencies in accordance with paragraph (3).

(6) DEFINITION OF STATE - For purposes of this subsection, the term 'State' means each of the 50 States, the District of Columbia, and the Commonwealth of Puerto Rico.

(c) SUBGRANTS TO LOCAL EDUCATIONAL AGENCIES -

(1) AUTHORIZATION TO MAKE SUBGRANTS - In accordance with paragraph (2), a State educational agency that receives a grant under this section shall make competitive subgrants to eligible local educational agencies.

(2) ALLOCATION -

(A) MINIMUM SUBGRANT AMOUNT - In making subgrants under paragraph (1), a State educational agency shall allocate to each eligible local educational agency that receives such a subgrant, at a minimum, an amount that bears the same relation to the funds made available under subsection (b)(4) as the amount the eligible local educational agency received under part A for the preceding fiscal year bears to the amount all the local educational agencies in the State received under part A for the preceding fiscal year.

(B) PRIORITY - In making subgrants under paragraph (1), a State educational agency **shall give priority** to eligible local educational agencies in which at least —

(i) **15 percent** of the children served by the eligible local educational agency are from families with incomes **below the poverty line**; or
(ii) 6,500 children served by the eligible local educational agency are from families with incomes below the poverty line.

(3) NOTICE - A State educational agency receiving a grant under this section shall provide notice to all eligible local educational agencies in the State of the availability of competitive subgrants under this subsection and of the requirements for applying for the subgrants.

(4) LOCAL APPLICATION - To be eligible to receive a subgrant under this subsection, an eligible local educational agency shall submit an application to the State educational agency at such time, in such manner, and containing such information as the State educational agency may reasonably require.

(5) STATE REQUIREMENT - In distributing subgrant funds to eligible local educational agencies under this subsection, **a State educational agency shall —**

(A) **provide funds in sufficient size and scope to enable the eligible local educational agencies to improve reading instruction;** and

(B) **provide the funds** in amounts **related to the number or percentage of students in kindergarten through grade 3 who are reading below grade level.**

➡ **COMMENT:** This requirement prevents state departments of education from spreading the money so thinly across states that no school district has enough money to do an effective job. The state must give preference to the lowest performing school districts with the greatest chance of success for the largest number of children.

(6) LIMITATION TO CERTAIN SCHOOLS - In distributing subgrant funds under this subsection, an eligible local educational agency **shall provide funds only to schools that both —**

(A) are among the schools served by that eligible local educational agency with the highest percentages or numbers of students in kindergarten through grade 3 reading below grade level, based on the most currently available data; and

(B)

      (i) are identified for school improvement under section 1116(b); or

      (ii) have the highest percentages or numbers of children counted under section 1124(c).

(7) LOCAL USES OF FUNDS -

(A) REQUIRED USES - Subject to paragraph (8), an eligible local educational agency that receives a subgrant under this subsection **shall** use the funds provided under the subgrant to carry out the following activities:

    (i) Selecting and administering screening, diagnostic, and classroom-based instructional reading assessments.

    (ii) Selecting and implementing a learning system or program of reading instruction based on scientifically based reading research that —

      (I) **includes the essential components of reading instruction**; and

      (II) **provides such instruction to the children** in kindergarten through grade 3 in the schools served by the eligible local educational agency, including children who —

        (aa) may have **reading difficulties**;

        (bb) are at **risk of being referred to special education** based on these difficulties;

        (cc) have been evaluated under section 614 of the Individuals with Disabilities Education Act but, in accordance with section 614(b)(5) of that Act, have **not been identified** as being a child with a disability (as defined in section 602 of that Act); (Wrightslaw Note: See 20 U. S. C. § 1401, definitions and § 1414(a-c) about evaluations under IDEA.)

        (dd) are being served under such Act **primarily due to being identified as being a child with a specific learning disability** (as defined in section 602 of that Act) related to reading;

          📁 See 20 U. S. C. §1401(3) and §1401(26) for the definitions of "disability" and "specific learning disability."

        (ee) **are deficient in the essential components of reading skills**, as listed in subparagraphs (A) through (E) of section 1208(3); or

        (ff) are identified as having **limited English proficiency.**

    (iii) **Procuring** and implementing instructional materials, including education technology such as software and other digital curricula, that are based on **scientifically based reading research.**

    (iv) **Providing professional development for teachers of kindergarten through grade 3, and special education teachers of kindergarten through grade 12, that —**

      (I) **will prepare these teachers in all of the essential components of reading instruction**;

      (II) **shall** include —

        (aa) information on instructional materials, programs, strategies, and approaches **based on scientifically based reading research, including early intervention, classroom reading materials, and remedial programs and approaches**; and

        (bb) **instruction in the use of screening, diagnostic, and classroom-based instructional reading assessments** and other procedures that **effectively identify students who may be at risk for reading failure or who are having difficulty reading;**

      (III) **shall be provided by eligible professional development providers**; and

      (IV) **will assist teachers in becoming highly qualified in reading instruction** in accordance with the requirements of section 1119.

    (v) **Collecting and summarizing data** —

      (I) to document the effectiveness of activities carried out under this subpart in individual schools and in the local educational agency as a whole; and

      (II) to stimulate and accelerate improvement by identifying the schools that produce significant gains in reading achievement.

    (vi) **Reporting data** for all students and categories of students described in section 1111(b)(2)(C)(v)(II).

    (vii) Promoting reading and library programs that provide access to engaging reading material, including coordination with programs funded through grants received under subpart 4, where applicable.

(B) ADDITIONAL USES - Subject to paragraph (8), an eligible local educational agency that receives a subgrant under this subsection may use the funds provided under the subgrant to carry out the following activities:

(i) Humanities-based family literacy programs (which may be referred to as 'Prime Time Family Reading Time') that bond families around the acts of reading and using public libraries.
(ii) Providing training in the essential components of reading instruction to a parent or other individual who volunteers to be a student's reading tutor, to enable such parent or individual to support instructional practices that are based on scientifically based reading research and are being used by the student's teacher.
(iii) Assisting parents, through the use of materials and reading programs, strategies, and approaches (including family literacy services) that are based on scientifically based reading research, to encourage reading and support their child's reading development.

(8) LOCAL PLANNING AND ADMINISTRATION - An eligible local educational agency that receives a subgrant under this subsection **may use not more than 3.5 percent of the funds** provided under the subgrant **for planning and administration.**

(d) STATE USES OF FUNDS -

(1) IN GENERAL - A State educational agency that receives a grant under this section may expend not more than a total of 20 percent of the grant funds to carry out the activities described in paragraphs (3), (4), and (5).

(2) PRIORITY - A State educational agency shall give priority to carrying out the activities described in paragraphs (3), (4), and (5) for schools described in subsection (c)(6).

(3) PROFESSIONAL INSERVICE AND PRESERVICE DEVELOPMENT AND REVIEW - A State educational agency may expend **not more than 65 percent** of the amount of the funds made available under paragraph (1) —

(A) to develop and implement a program of **professional development for teachers, including special education teachers, of kindergarten through grade 3** that —

(i) will prepare these teachers in all the **essential components of reading instruction;**
(ii) shall include —
(I) information on instructional materials, programs, strategies, and approaches based on **scientifically based reading research,** including **early intervention and reading remediation materials, programs, and approaches;** and
(II) instruction in the use of **screening, diagnostic, and classroom-based instructional reading assessments and other scientifically based procedures** that effectively identify students who may be at risk for reading failure or who are having difficulty reading; and
(iii) shall be provided by eligible professional development providers;

(B) to strengthen and enhance preservice courses for students preparing, at **all public institutions of higher education in the State,** to teach kindergarten through grade 3 by —

(i) reviewing such courses to determine whether the courses' content is consistent with the findings of the **most current scientifically based reading research, including findings on the essential components of reading instruction;**
(ii) following up such reviews with recommendations to ensure that such institutions offer courses

that meet the highest standards; and

(iii) preparing a report on the **results of such reviews**, submitting the report to the reading and literacy partnership for the State established under section 1203(d), and **making the report available for public review by means of the Internet**; and

(C) to make recommendations on **how the State licensure and certification standards in the area of reading might be improved.**

(4) TECHNICAL ASSISTANCE FOR LOCAL EDUCATIONAL AGENCIES AND SCHOOLS - A State educational agency may expend not more than 25 percent of the amount of the funds made available under paragraph (1) for one or more of the following:

(A) Assisting local educational agencies in accomplishing the tasks required to design and implement a program under this subpart, including —

(i) selecting and implementing a program or programs of reading instruction based on scientifically based reading research;
(ii) selecting screening, diagnostic, and classroom-based instructional reading assessments; and
(iii) identifying eligible professional development providers to help prepare reading teachers to teach students using the programs and assessments described in clauses (i) and (ii).

(B) Providing expanded opportunities to students in kindergarten through grade 3 who are served by eligible local educational agencies for receiving reading assistance from alternative providers that includes —

(i) screening, diagnostic, and classroom-based instructional reading assessments; and
(ii) as need is indicated by the assessments under clause (i), instruction based on scientifically based reading research that includes the essential components of reading instruction.

(5) PLANNING, ADMINISTRATION, AND REPORTING -

(A) EXPENDITURE OF FUNDS - A State educational agency may expend **not more than 10 percent** of the amount of funds made available under paragraph (1) for the activities described in this paragraph.

(B) PLANNING AND ADMINISTRATION - A State educational agency that receives a grant under this section may expend funds made available under subparagraph (A) for planning and administration relating to the State uses of funds authorized under this subpart, including the following:

(i) Administering the distribution of competitive subgrants to eligible local educational agencies under subsection (c) and section 1204(d).
(ii) Assessing and evaluating, on a regular basis, eligible local educational agency activities assisted under this subpart, with respect to whether they have been effective in increasing the number of children in grades 1, 2, and 3 served under this subpart who can read at or above grade level.

(C) ANNUAL REPORTING -

(i) **IN GENERAL** - A State educational agency that receives a grant under this section shall expend funds made available under subparagraph (A) to provide the Secretary annually with a report on the implementation of this subpart.
(ii) **INFORMATION INCLUDED - Each report under this subparagraph shall include information on the following:**
(I) Evidence that the State educational agency is fulfilling its obligations under this subpart.
(II) Specific identification of those schools and local educational agencies that report the largest gains in reading achievement.
(III) The progress the State educational agency and local educational agencies within the State

are making in reducing the number of students served under this subpart in grades 1, 2, and 3 who are reading below grade level, as demonstrated by such information as teacher reports and school evaluations of mastery of the essential components of reading instruction.

(IV) Evidence on whether the State educational agency and local educational agencies within the State have significantly increased the number of students reading at grade level or above, significantly increased the percentages of students described in section 1111(b)(2)(C)(v)(II) who are reading at grade level or above, and successfully implemented this subpart.

(iii) PRIVACY PROTECTION - Data in the report shall be reported in a manner that protects the privacy of individuals.

(iv) CONTRACT - To the extent practicable, a State educational agency shall enter into a contract with an entity that conducts scientifically based reading research, under which contract the entity will assist the State educational agency in producing the reports required to be submitted under this subparagraph.

(e) REVIEW -

(1) PROGRESS REPORT -

(A) SUBMISSION - Not later than 60 days after the termination of the third year of the grant period, each State educational agency receiving a grant under this section shall submit a progress report to the Secretary.

(B) INFORMATION INCLUDED - The progress report shall include information on the progress the State educational agency and local educational agencies within the State are making in reducing the number of students served under this subpart in grades 1, 2, and 3 who are reading below grade level (as demonstrated by such information as teacher reports and school evaluations of mastery of the essential components of reading instruction). The report shall also include evidence from the State educational agency and local educational agencies within the State that the State educational agency and the local educational agencies have significantly increased the number of students reading at grade level or above, significantly increased the percentages of students described in section 1111(b)(2)(C)(v)(II) who are reading at grade level or above, and successfully implemented this subpart.

(2) PEER REVIEW - The progress report described in paragraph (1) shall be reviewed by the peer review panel convened under section 1203(c)(2).

(3) CONSEQUENCES OF INSUFFICIENT PROGRESS - After submission of the progress report described in paragraph (1), if the Secretary determines that the State educational agency is not making significant progress in meeting the purposes of this subpart, the Secretary **may withhold from the State educational agency, in whole or in part, further payments under this section** in accordance with section 455 of the General Education Provisions Act or take such other action authorized by law as the Secretary determines necessary, including **providing technical assistance upon request** of the State educational agency.

(f) FUNDS NOT USED FOR STATE LEVEL ACTIVITIES -

Any portion of funds described in subsection (d)(1) that a State educational agency does not expend in accordance with subsection (d)(1) shall be expended for the purpose of making subgrants in accordance with subsection (c). (Section 1202 of NCLB Act)

20 U. S. C. § 6363. State formula grant applications.

➡ **OVERVIEW:** State applications will be reviewed by a panel of experts chosen by the Secretary of Education, the National Institute for Literacy, the National Research Council of the National Academy of Sciences, and the National Institute of Child Health and Human Development of the National Institutes of Health. Members of the expert panel have training, expertise and experience in these areas:

Training teachers how to teach reading using methods based on scientific research;
Developing research-based curricula for effective reading instruction;
Developing research assessments;
Teaching reading in the early grades; and
Promoting research-based reading programs to policymakers on the local, state and national levels

(a) APPLICATIONS -

(1) IN GENERAL - A State educational agency that desires to receive a grant under section 1202 shall submit an application to the Secretary at such time and in such form as the Secretary may require. The application shall contain the information described in subsection (b).

(2) SPECIAL APPLICATION PROVISIONS - For those State educational agencies that have received a grant under part C of title II (as such part was in effect on the day before the date of enactment of the No Child Left Behind Act of 2001), the Secretary shall establish a modified set of requirements for an application under this section that takes into account the information already submitted and approved under that program and minimizes the duplication of effort on the part of such State educational agencies.

(b) CONTENTS - An application under this section shall contain the following:

(1) An assurance that the Governor of the State, in consultation with the State educational agency, has established a reading and literacy partnership described in subsection (d), and a description of how such partnership —

   (A) coordinated the development of the application; and

   (B) will assist in the oversight and evaluation of the State educational agency's activities under this subpart.

(2) A description, if applicable, of the State's strategy to expand, continue, or modify activities authorized under part C of title II (as such part was in effect on the day before the date of enactment of the No Child Left Behind Act of 2001).

(3) An assurance that the State educational agency, and any local educational agencies receiving a subgrant from that State educational agency under section 1202, will, if requested, participate in the external evaluation under section 1205.

(4) **A State educational agency plan containing a description of the following:**

   (A) How the State educational agency will assist local educational agencies in **identifying screening, diagnostic, and classroom-based instructional reading assessments.**

   (B) How the State educational agency will assist local educational agencies in **identifying instructional materials, programs, strategies, and approaches, based on scientifically based reading research, including early intervention and reading remediation materials, programs, and approaches.**

   (C) How the State educational agency **will ensure that professional development activities related to reading instruction** and provided under section 1202 **are** —

      (i) coordinated with other Federal, State, and local level funds, and used effectively to improve instructional practices for reading; and
      (ii) **based on scientifically based reading research.**

   (D) How the activities assisted under section 1202 will address the needs of teachers and other instructional staff in implementing the essential components of reading instruction.

(E) How subgrants made by the State educational agency under section 1202 will meet the requirements of section 1202, including how the State educational agency will ensure that eligible local educational agencies receiving subgrants under section 1202 **will use practices based on scientifically based reading research.**

(F) How the State educational agency will, to the extent practicable, make grants to eligible local educational agencies in both rural and urban areas.

(G) How the State educational agency will build on, and promote coordination among literacy programs in the State (including federally funded programs such as programs under the Adult Education and Family Literacy Act, the Individuals with Disabilities Education Act, and subpart 2), to increase the effectiveness of the programs in improving reading for adults and children and to avoid duplication of the efforts of the program.

(H) How the State educational agency **will assess and evaluate, on a regular basis**, eligible local educational agency activities assisted under section 1202, with respect to **whether the activities have been effective in achieving the purposes** of section 1202.

(I) Any other information that the Secretary may reasonably require.

(c) APPROVAL OF APPLICATIONS -

(1) IN GENERAL - The Secretary shall approve an application of a State educational agency under this section only if such application meets the requirements of this section.

(2) PEER REVIEW -

(A) IN GENERAL - The Secretary, in consultation with the National Institute for Literacy, shall convene a panel to evaluate applications under this section. At a minimum, the panel shall include —

(i) three individuals selected by the Secretary;
(ii) three individuals selected by the National Institute for Literacy;
(iii) three individuals selected by the National Research Council of the National Academy of Sciences; and
(iv) three individuals selected by the National Institute of Child Health and Human Development.

(B) EXPERTS - The panel shall include —

(i) experts who are competent, by virtue of their training, expertise, or experience, to evaluate applications under this section;
(ii) experts who provide professional development to individuals who teach reading to children and adults based on scientifically based reading research;
(iii) experts who provide professional development to other instructional staff based on scientifically based reading research; and
(iv) an individual who has expertise in screening, diagnostic, and classroom-based instructional reading assessments.

(C) RECOMMENDATIONS - The panel shall recommend grant applications from State educational agencies under this section to the Secretary for funding or for disapproval.

(d) READING AND LITERACY PARTNERSHIPS -

(1) IN GENERAL - For a State educational agency to receive a grant under section 1202, the Governor of the State, in consultation with the State educational agency, **shall establish a reading and literacy partnership**.

(2) REQUIRED PARTICIPANTS - The reading and literacy partnership shall include the following participants:

(A) The Governor of the State.

(B) The chief State school officer.

(C) The chairman and the ranking member of each committee of the State legislature that is responsible for education policy.

(D) A representative, selected jointly by the Governor and the chief State school officer, of at least one eligible local educational agency.

(E) A representative, selected jointly by the Governor and the chief State school officer, of a community-based organization working with children to improve their reading skills, particularly a community-based organization using tutors and scientifically based reading research.

(F) State directors of appropriate Federal or State programs with a strong reading component, selected jointly by the Governor and the chief State school officer.

(G) A parent of a public or private school student or a parent who educates the parent's child in the parent's home, selected jointly by the Governor and the chief State school officer.

(H) A teacher, who may be a special education teacher, who successfully teaches reading, and another instructional staff member, selected jointly by the Governor and the chief State school officer.

(I) A family literacy service provider selected jointly by the Governor and the chief State school officer.

(3) OPTIONAL PARTICIPANTS - The reading and literacy partnership may include additional participants, who shall be selected jointly by the Governor and the chief State school officer, and who may include a representative of —

(A) an institution of higher education operating a program of teacher preparation in the State that is based on scientifically based reading research;

(B) a local educational agency;

(C) a private nonprofit or for-profit eligible professional development provider providing instruction based on scientifically based reading research;

(D) an adult education provider;

(E) a volunteer organization that is involved in reading programs; or

(F) a school library or a public library that offers reading or literacy programs for children or families.

(4) PREEXISTING PARTNERSHIP - If, before the date of enactment of the No Child Left Behind Act of 2001, a State educational agency established a consortium, partnership, or any other similar body that was considered a reading and literacy partnership for purposes of part C of title II of this Act (as such part was in effect on the day before the date of enactment of No Child Left Behind Act of 2001), that consortium, partnership, or body may be considered a reading and literacy partnership for purposes of this subsection consistent with the provisions of this subpart. (Section 1203 of NCLB Act)

20 U. S. C. § 6364. Targeted assistance grants.

➔ **OVERVIEW:** Targeted assistance grants are awarded to states that have an increasing percentage of third graders who are proficient in reading. The state may make subgrants available to local school districts.

(a) ELIGIBILITY CRITERIA FOR AWARDING TARGETED ASSISTANCE GRANTS TO STATES - Beginning with fiscal year 2004, from funds appropriated under section 1202(b)(1)(E), the Secretary shall make grants, on a competitive basis, to those State educational agencies that —

(1) for each of 2 consecutive years, demonstrate that an increasing percentage of third graders in each of the groups described in section 1111(b)(2)(C)(v)(II) in the schools served by the local educational agencies receiving funds under section 1202 are reaching the proficient level in reading; and

(2) for each of the same such consecutive 2 years, demonstrate that schools receiving funds under section 1202 are improving the reading skills of students in grades 1, 2, and 3 based on screening, diagnostic, and classroom-based instructional reading assessments.

(b) CONTINUATION OF PERFORMANCE AWARDS - For any State educational agency that receives a competitive grant under this section, the Secretary shall make an award for each of the succeeding years that the State educational agency demonstrates it is continuing to meet the criteria described in subsection (a).

(c) DISTRIBUTION OF TARGETED ASSISTANCE GRANTS -

(1) IN GENERAL - The Secretary shall make a grant to each State educational agency with an application approved under this section in an amount that bears the same relation to the amount made available to carry out this section for a fiscal year as the number of children counted under section 1124(c) for the State bears to the number of such children so counted for all States with applications approved for that year.

(2) PEER REVIEW - The peer review panel convened under section 1203(c)(2) shall review the applications submitted under this subsection. The panel shall recommend such applications to the Secretary for funding or for disapproval.

(3) APPLICATION CONTENTS - A State educational agency that desires to receive a grant under this section shall submit an application to the Secretary at such time, in such manner, and accompanied by such information as the Secretary may require. Each such application shall include the following:

(A) Evidence that the State educational agency has carried out its obligations under section 1203.

(B) Evidence that the State educational agency has met the criteria described in subsection (a).

(C) The amount of funds requested by the State educational agency and a description of the criteria the State educational agency intends to use in distributing subgrants to eligible local educational agencies under this section to continue or expand activities under subsection (d)(5).

(D) Evidence that the State educational agency has increased significantly the percentage of students reading at grade level or above.

(E) Any additional evidence that demonstrates success in the implementation of this section.

(d) SUBGRANTS TO ELIGIBLE LOCAL EDUCATIONAL AGENCIES -

(1) IN GENERAL - The Secretary may make a grant to a State educational agency under this section only if the State educational agency agrees to **expend 100 percent** of the amount of the funds provided under the grant for the purpose of making competitive subgrants in accordance with this subsection to eligible local educational agencies.

(2) NOTICE - A State educational agency receiving a grant under this section shall provide notice to all local educational agencies in the State of the availability of competitive subgrants under this subsection and of the requirements for applying for the subgrants.

(3) APPLICATION - To be eligible to receive a subgrant under this subsection, an eligible local educational agency shall submit an application to the State educational agency at such time, in such manner, and containing such information as the State educational agency may reasonably require.

(4) DISTRIBUTION -

(A) IN GENERAL - A State educational agency shall distribute subgrants under this section through a competitive process based on relative need of eligible local educational agencies and the evidence described in this paragraph.

(B) EVIDENCE USED IN ALL YEARS - For all fiscal years, a State educational agency shall distribute subgrants under this section based on evidence that an eligible local educational agency —

(i) satisfies the requirements of section 1202(c)(4);
(ii) will carry out its obligations under this subpart;
(iii) will work with other local educational agencies in the State that have not received a subgrant under this subsection to assist such nonreceiving agencies in increasing the reading achievement of students; and
(iv) is meeting the criteria described in subsection (a).

(5) LOCAL USES OF FUNDS - An eligible local educational agency that receives a subgrant under this subsection —

(A) shall use the funds provided under the subgrant to carry out the activities described in section 1202(c)(7)(A); and

(B) may use such funds to carry out the activities described in section 1202(c)(7)(B). (Section 1204 of NCLB Act)

20 U. S. C. § 6365. External evaluation.

➜ **OVERVIEW:** This section authorizes the Secretary of Education to contract with an independent organization that will conduct a rigorous, scientifically valid evaluation of the Reading First program.

(a) IN GENERAL - From funds reserved under section 1202(b)(1)(C), **the Secretary shall contract with an independent organization outside of the Department for a 5-year, rigorous, scientifically valid, quantitative evaluation of this subpart.**

(b) PROCESS - The evaluation under subsection (a) shall be conducted by an organization that is capable of designing and carrying out an independent evaluation that identifies the effects of specific activities carried out by State educational agencies and local educational agencies under this subpart on improving reading instruction. Such evaluation shall take into account factors influencing student performance that are not controlled by teachers or education administrators.

(c) ANALYSIS - The evaluation under subsection (a) shall include the following:

(1) **An analysis of the relationship between each of the essential components of reading instruction and overall reading proficiency.**

(2) An analysis of **whether assessment tools used by State** educational agencies and local educational agencies **measure** the essential components of reading.

(3) An analysis of **how State reading standards correlate with the essential components of reading instruction.**

(4) An analysis of whether the receipt of a targeted assistance grant under section 1204 results in an increase in the number of children who read proficiently.

(5) A measurement of the **extent to which specific instructional materials improve reading proficiency.**

(6) A measurement of the **extent to which specific screening, diagnostic, and classroom-based instructional reading assessments assist teachers in identifying specific reading deficiencies.**

(7) A measurement of the **extent to which professional development programs** implemented by State educational agencies using funds received under this subpart **improve reading instruction.**

(8) A measurement of **how well students preparing to enter the teaching profession are prepared to teach the essential components of reading instruction.**

(9) An analysis of **changes in students' interest in reading** and **time spent reading outside of school.**

(10) Any other analysis or measurement pertinent to this subpart that is determined to be appropriate by the Secretary.

(d) PROGRAM IMPROVEMENT - The **findings of the evaluation** conducted under this section **shall be provided to State educational agencies and local educational agencies on a periodic basis** for use in **program improvement.** (Section 1205 of NCLB Act)

➔ **COMMENT:** This evaluation report is a public record.

20 U. S. C. § 6366. National activities.

➔ **OVERVIEW:** This section authorizes the Secretary of Education to evaluate the impact of Reading First on children who may be eligible for special education services because they are having difficulty learning to read.

From funds reserved under section 1202(b)(1)(C), the Secretary —

(1) may provide technical assistance in achieving the purposes of this subpart to State educational agencies, local educational agencies, and schools requesting such assistance;

(2) shall, at a minimum, evaluate the impact of services provided to children under this subpart with respect to their referral to, and eligibility for, **special education services** under the Individuals with Disabilities Education Act (**based on their difficulties learning to read**); and

(3) shall carry out the external evaluation as described in section 1205. (Section 1206 of NCLB Act)

20 U. S. C. § 6367. Information dissemination.

➡ **OVERVIEW:** Section 6367 describes an affirmative obligation to disseminate information about scientifically based research on effective reading programs.

(a) IN GENERAL - From funds reserved under section 1202(b)(1)(D), the **National Institute for Literacy**, in collaboration with **the Secretary of Education**, the **Secretary of Health and Human Services**, and the Director of the **National Institute for Child Health and Human Development shall** —

(1) **disseminate information on scientifically based reading research pertaining to children, youth, and adults;**

(2) identify and disseminate information about schools, local educational agencies, and State educational agencies that have effectively developed and implemented classroom reading programs that meet the requirements of this subpart, including those State educational agencies, local educational agencies, and schools that have been identified as effective through the evaluation and peer review provisions of this subpart; and

(3) support the continued identification and dissemination of information on reading programs that contain the essential components of reading instruction as supported by scientifically based reading research, that can lead to improved reading outcomes for children, youth, and adults.

(b) DISSEMINATION AND COORDINATION - **At a minimum**, the National Institute for Literacy shall disseminate the information described in subsection (a) to —

(1) recipients of Federal financial assistance under this title, title III, the Head Start Act, the Individuals with Disabilities Education Act, and the Adult Education and Family Literacy Act; and

(2) each Bureau funded school (as defined in section 1141 of the Education Amendments of 1978).

(c) USE OF EXISTING NETWORKS - In carrying out this section, the National Institute for Literacy shall, to the extent practicable, use existing information and dissemination networks developed and maintained through other public and private entities including through the Department and the National Center for Family Literacy.

(d) NATIONAL INSTITUTE FOR LITERACY - For purposes of funds reserved under section 1202(b)(1)(D) to carry out this section, the National Institute for Literacy shall administer such funds in accordance with section 242(b) of Public Law 105-220 (relating to the establishment and administration of the National Institute for Literacy). (Section 1207 of NCLB Act)

20 U. S. C. § 6368. Definitions.

➡ **OVERVIEW:** This is one of the more important definition sections in the entire NCLB statute. Section (3) describes the five **"essential components of reading instruction."** Section (5) is the **legal definition of reading** which is a complex system that requires the acquisition of six skills.
Section (6) defines **scientifically based reading research**. Section (7) defines **screening assessments, diagnostic reading assessments**, and classroom-based **instructional reading assessments**. A screening assessment is designed to identify children who may be at risk for academic failure and in need of "further diagnosis" of the child's need for special services or additional reading instruction. A diagnostic reading assessment identifies the child's strengths and weaknesses, causes of reading difficulties, and intervention strategies that are needed for the child to learn to read by the end of third grade.

Bookmark this section so you can find these definitions quickly.

(1) **ELIGIBLE LOCAL EDUCATIONAL AGENCY** - The term 'eligible local educational agency' means a local educational agency that —

(A) is among the local educational agencies in the State with the highest numbers or percentages of students in kindergarten through grade 3 reading below grade level, based on the most currently available data; and

(B) has —

(i) jurisdiction over a geographic area that includes an area designated as an empowerment zone, or an enterprise community, under part I of subchapter U of chapter 1 of the Internal Revenue Code of 1986;
(ii) jurisdiction over a significant number or percentage of schools that are identified for school improvement under section 1116(b); or
(iii) the highest numbers or percentages of children who are counted under section 1124(c), in comparison to other local educational agencies in the State.

(2) ELIGIBLE PROFESSIONAL DEVELOPMENT PROVIDER - The term 'eligible professional development provider' means a provider of professional development in reading instruction to teachers, including special education teachers, that is based on scientifically based reading research.

(3) ESSENTIAL COMPONENTS OF READING INSTRUCTION - The term 'essential components of reading instruction' means explicit and systematic instruction in —

(A) phonemic awareness;

(B) phonics;

(C) vocabulary development;

(D) reading fluency, including oral reading skills; and

(E) reading comprehension strategies.

(4) INSTRUCTIONAL STAFF - The term 'instructional staff' —

(A) means individuals who have responsibility for teaching children to read; and

(B) includes principals, teachers, supervisors of instruction, librarians, library school media specialists, teachers of academic subjects other than reading, and other individuals who have responsibility for assisting children to learn to read.

(5) READING - The term 'reading' means a complex system of deriving meaning from print that requires all of the following:

(A) The skills and knowledge to understand how phonemes, or speech sounds, are connected to print.

(B) The ability to decode unfamiliar words.

(C) The ability to read fluently.

(D) Sufficient background information and vocabulary to foster reading comprehension.

(E) The development of appropriate active strategies to construct meaning from print.

(F) The development and maintenance of a motivation to read.

(6) SCIENTIFICALLY BASED READING RESEARCH - The term 'scientifically based reading research' means research that —

(A) **applies rigorous, systematic, and objective procedures** to obtain valid knowledge relevant to reading development, reading instruction, and reading difficulties; and

(B) **includes research** that —

(i) employs systematic, empirical methods that draw on observation or experiment;
(ii) involves **rigorous data analyses** that are adequate to test the stated hypotheses and justify the general conclusions drawn;
(iii) relies on measurements or observational methods that **provide valid data across evaluators and observers and across multiple measurements and observations**; and
(iv) has been **accepted by a peer-reviewed journal or approved by a panel of independent experts** through a **comparably rigorous, objective, and scientific review.**

(7) SCREENING, DIAGNOSTIC, AND CLASSROOM-BASED INSTRUCTIONAL READING ASSESSMENTS -

(A) IN GENERAL - The term 'screening, diagnostic, and classroom-based instructional reading assessments' means —

(i) screening reading assessments;
(ii) diagnostic reading assessments; and
(iii) classroom-based instructional reading assessments.

(B) SCREENING READING ASSESSMENT - The term 'screening reading assessment' means an assessment that is —

(i) valid, reliable, and based on scientifically based reading research; and
(ii) a **brief** procedure designed as a **first step** in identifying children who may be at high risk for delayed development or academic failure and **in need of further diagnosis** of their need for special services or additional reading instruction.

(C) DIAGNOSTIC READING ASSESSMENT - The term 'diagnostic reading assessment' means an assessment that is —

(i) valid, reliable, and based on scientifically based reading research; and
(ii) used for the purpose of —
(I) identifying a child's **specific areas of strengths and weaknesses** so that the child has **learned to read by the end of grade 3;**
(II) determining any difficulties that a child may have in learning to read and the potential **cause of such difficulties;** and
(III) helping to **determine possible reading intervention strategies** and related special needs.

(D) CLASSROOM-BASED INSTRUCTIONAL READING ASSESSMENT - The term 'classroom-based instructional reading assessment' means an assessment that —

(i) evaluates children's learning based on systematic observations by teachers of children performing academic tasks that are part of their daily classroom experience; and
(ii) is used to improve instruction in reading, including classroom instruction. (Section 1208 of NCLB Act)

Subpart 2 - Early Reading First

→ **OVERVIEW:** Subpart 2 focuses on the need for **early identification of reading problems and early intervention** to remediate these problems. Section 6371 describes the purposes of Early Reading First: to enhance language development and literacy of preschool children by using methods based on scientifically based reading research when teaching preschool children to read. Applicants may be school districts or public or private agencies that serve preschool age children.

20 U. S. C. § 6371. Purposes; definitions.

(a) PURPOSES - The purposes of this subpart are as follows:

(1) To support local efforts to enhance the **early language, literacy, and prereading development** of preschool age children, particularly those from low-income families, through strategies and professional development that are based on **scientifically based reading research.**

(2) To provide preschool age children with **cognitive learning opportunities** in high-quality language and literature-rich environments, so that the children can attain the fundamental **knowledge and skills necessary for optimal reading development** in kindergarten and beyond.

(3) To demonstrate language and literacy activities based on **scientifically based reading research** that supports the age-appropriate development of—

(A) recognition, leading to automatic recognition, of letters of the alphabet;

(B) knowledge of letter sounds, the blending of sounds, and the use of increasingly complex vocabulary;

(C) an understanding that written language is composed of phonemes and letters each representing one or more speech sounds that in combination make up syllables, words, and sentences;

(D) spoken language, including vocabulary and oral comprehension abilities; and

(E) knowledge of the purposes and conventions of print.

(4) To use screening assessments to **effectively identify preschool age children** who **may be at risk for reading failure.**

(5) To integrate such scientific reading research-based instructional materials and literacy activities with existing programs of preschools, child care agencies and programs, Head Start centers, and family literacy services.

(b) DEFINITIONS - For purposes of this subpart:

(1) ELIGIBLE APPLICANT - The term **'eligible applicant'** means—

(A) one or more **local educational agencies** that are eligible to receive a subgrant under subpart 1;

(B) one or more **public or private organizations or agencies**, acting on behalf of one or more programs that serve preschool age children (such as a program at a Head Start center, a child care program, or a family literacy program), which organizations or agencies shall be located in a community served by a local educational agency described in subparagraph (A); or

(C) one or more local educational agencies described in subparagraph (A) in collaboration with one or more organizations or agencies described in subparagraph (B).

➔ **COMMENT:** An applicant for a grant to teach reading to preschool children need not be just an LEA, but can also be a private organization or agency.

(2) SCIENTIFICALLY BASED READING RESEARCH - The term **'scientifically based reading research'** has the same meaning given to that term in section 1208.

(3) SCREENING READING ASSESSMENT - The term **'screening reading assessment'** has the same meaning given to that term in section 1208. (Section 1221 of NCLB Act)

20 U. S. C. § 6372. Local Early Reading First grants.

➔ **OVERVIEW:** Section 6372 spells out required components of preschool language programs that are eligible for grants.

(a) PROGRAM AUTHORIZED - From amounts appropriated under section 1002(b)(2), **the Secretary shall award grants**, on a competitive basis, for periods of not more than 6 years, to eligible applicants to enable the eligible applicants to carry out the authorized activities described in subsection (d).

(b) APPLICATIONS - An eligible applicant that desires to receive a grant under this section **shall submit an application** to the Secretary, which shall **include** a description of—

(1) the programs to be served by the proposed project, including demographic and socioeconomic information on the preschool age children enrolled in the programs;

(2) how the proposed project will enhance the school readiness of preschool age children in high-quality oral language and literature-rich environments;

(3) how the proposed project will prepare and provide ongoing assistance to staff in the programs, through professional development and other support, to provide high-quality language, literacy, and prereading activities using scientifically based reading research, for preschool age children;

(4) how the proposed project will provide services and use instructional materials that are **based on scientifically based reading research on early language acquisition, prereading activities, and the development of spoken vocabulary skills;**

(5) how the proposed project will help staff in the programs to meet more effectively the diverse needs of preschool age children in the community, including such children with limited English proficiency, disabilities, or other special needs;

(6) how the proposed project will integrate such instructional materials and literacy activities with existing preschool programs and family literacy services;

(7) how the proposed project will help children, particularly **children experiencing difficulty with spoken language, prereading, and early reading skills,** to **make the transition from preschool** to formal classroom instruction in school;

(8) if the eligible applicant has received a subgrant under subpart 1, how the activities conducted under this subpart will be coordinated with the eligible applicant's activities under subpart 1 at the kindergarten through grade 3 level;

(9) how the proposed project will **evaluate the success** of the activities supported under this subpart in enhancing the early language, literacy, and prereading development of preschool age children served by the project; and

(10) such other information as the Secretary may require.

(c) APPROVAL OF LOCAL APPLICATIONS - The Secretary shall select applicants for funding under this subpart based on the quality of the applications and the recommendations of a peer review panel convened under section 1203(c)(2), that includes, at a minimum, three individuals, selected from the entities described in clauses (ii), (iii), and (iv) of section 1203(c)(2)(A), who are experts in early reading development and early childhood development.

(d) AUTHORIZED ACTIVITIES - An eligible applicant that receives a grant under this subpart shall use the funds provided under the grant to carry out the following activities:

(1) Providing preschool age children with high-quality oral language and literature-rich environments in which to acquire language and prereading skills.

(2) Providing **professional development** that is **based on scientifically based reading research knowledge of early language and reading development for the staff** of the eligible applicant and that will assist in developing the preschool age children's—

(A) recognition, leading to automatic recognition, of letters of the alphabet, knowledge of letters, sounds, blending of letter sounds, and increasingly complex vocabulary;

(B) understanding that written language is composed of phonemes and letters each representing one or more speech sounds that in combination make up syllables, words, and sentences;

(C) spoken language, including vocabulary and oral comprehension abilities; and

(D) knowledge of the purposes and conventions of print.

(3) Identifying and providing activities and instructional materials that are **based on scientifically based reading research** for use in developing the skills and abilities described in paragraph (2).

(4) Acquiring, providing training for, and implementing screening reading assessments or other appropriate measures that are based on scientifically based reading research to determine whether preschool age children are developing the skills described in this subsection.

(5) Integrating such instructional materials, activities, tools, and measures into the programs offered by the eligible applicant.

(e) AWARD AMOUNTS - The Secretary may establish a maximum award amount, or ranges of award amounts, for grants under this subpart. (Section 1222 of NCLB Act)

20 U. S. C. § 6373. Federal administration.

The Secretary shall consult with the Secretary of Health and Human Services to coordinate the activities under this subpart with preschool age programs administered by the **Department of Health and Human Services**. (Section 1223 of NCLB Act)

20 U. S. C. § 6374. Information dissemination

From the funds the National Institute for Literacy receives under section 1202(b)(1)(D), the National Institute for Literacy, in consultation with the Secretary, shall disseminate information regarding projects assisted under this subpart that have proven effective. (Section 1224 of NCLB Act)

20 U. S. C. § 6375. Reporting requirements.

Each eligible applicant receiving a grant under this subpart shall report annually to the Secretary regarding the eligible applicant's progress in addressing the purposes of this subpart. Such report shall include, at a minimum, a description of—

(1) the **research-based instruction, materials, and activities** being used in the programs funded under the grant;

(2) the types of programs funded under the grant and the ages of children served by such programs;

(3) the **qualifications of the program staff** who provide early literacy instruction under such programs and the type of ongoing professional development provided to such staff; and

(4) the results of the evaluation described in section 1222(b)(9). (Section 1225 of NCLB Act)

20 U. S. C. § 6376. Evaluation.

➡ **OVERVIEW:** Section 6376 authorizes the Secretary of Education to conduct an independent evaluation of the effectiveness of **Early Reading First**.

(a) IN GENERAL - From the total amount made available under section 1002(b)(2) for the period beginning October 1, 2002, and ending September 30, 2006, the Secretary shall reserve not more than $3,000,000 to conduct **an independent evaluation** of the effectiveness of this subpart.

(b) REPORTS -

(1) INTERIM REPORT - Not later than October 1, 2004, **the Secretary shall submit an interim report** to the Committee on Education and the Workforce of the House of Representatives and the Committee on Health, Education, Labor, and Pensions of the Senate.

(2) FINAL REPORT - Not later than September 30, 2006, the Secretary shall submit **a final report** to the committees described in paragraph (1).

(c) CONTENTS - The reports submitted under subsection (b) shall include information on the following:

(1) How the grant recipients under this subpart are **improving the prereading skills of preschool children.**

(2) The **effectiveness of the professional development program** assisted under this subpart.

(3) How early childhood **teachers are being prepared with scientifically based reading research** on early reading development.

(4) What activities and instructional practices are **most effective.**

(5) How prereading instructional materials and literacy activities based on scientifically based reading research are being integrated into preschools, child care agencies and programs, programs carried out under the Head Start Act, and family literacy programs.

(6) Any recommendations on strengthening or modifying this subpart. (Section 1226 of NCLB Act)

SUBPART 3 - WILLIAM F. GOODLING EVEN START FAMILY LITERACY PROGRAMS

➡️ **OVERVIEW:** Even Start provides funding for family literacy programs that include adult education, childhood education, parenting education, and interactive literacy activities. Family literacy programs must use instructional programs based on scientifically based reading research. Parents and children are eligible to receive testing, counseling, related services, and other developmental and support services.

20 U. S. C. § 6381. Statement of purpose.

➡️ **OVERVIEW:** The purpose of Subpart 3 is to break the cycle of poverty and illiteracy by ensuring that children and adults learn to read.

It is the **purpose** of this subpart to help **break the cycle of poverty and illiteracy** by—

(1) improving the educational opportunities of the Nation's low-income families by integrating early childhood education, adult literacy or adult basic education, and parenting education into a unified family literacy program, to be referred to as 'Even Start'; and

(2) establishing a program that shall—

(A) be implemented through cooperative projects that build on high-quality existing community resources to create a new range of services

(B) promote the academic achievement of children and adults;

(C) assist children and adults from low-income families to achieve to challenging State content standards and challenging State student achievement standards; and

(D) use instructional programs based on scientifically based reading research and addressing the prevention of reading difficulties for children and adults, to the extent such research is available. (Section 1231 of NCLB Act)

20 U. S. C. § 6381a. Program authorized.

➡️ **OVERVIEW:** Section (a) authorizes funds for programs for children of migrant workers, outlying areas, and Indian tribes and tribal organizations. Section (b) reserves funds for evaluation, technical assistance, program improvement, and research.

➡️ **CITATION NOTE:** The citation of this statute, **20 U. S. C. §6381a** is different from what you have encountered so far in that the citation is **6381a,** not **6381(a)**. Almost all statutes that have subsections start the first subsection with (a) then (b), etc. For example, jump back two statutes to 20 U. S. C. § 6376 and you will see that the main subsections are listed as (a), (b), and (c). That is the normal usual format. However, in this instance, immediately below, the next subsection is correctly reported as 20 U. S. C. § 6381a(a). This use of the lower case alphabet following a numerical section number only occurs in one other instance in Title I beginning at 20 U. S. C. § 6561a.

(a) RESERVATION FOR MIGRANT PROGRAMS, OUTLYING AREAS, AND INDIAN TRIBES -

(1) IN GENERAL - For each fiscal year, the Secretary shall reserve 5 percent of the amount appropriated under section 1002(b)(3) (or, if such appropriated amount exceeds $200,000,000, 6 percent of such amount) for programs, under such terms and conditions as the Secretary shall establish, that are consistent with the purpose of this subpart, and according to their relative needs, for—

(A) children of migratory workers;

(B) the outlying areas; and

(C) Indian tribes and tribal organizations.

(2) SPECIAL RULE - After December 21, 2000, the Secretary shall award a grant, on a competitive basis, of sufficient size and for a period of sufficient duration to demonstrate the effectiveness of a family literacy program in a prison that houses women and their preschool age children and that has the capability of developing a program of high quality.

(3) COORDINATION OF PROGRAMS FOR AMERICAN INDIANS - The Secretary shall ensure that programs under paragraph (1)(C) are coordinated with family literacy programs operated by the Bureau of Indian Affairs in order to avoid duplication and to encourage the dissemination of information on high-quality family literacy programs serving American Indians.

(b) RESERVATION FOR FEDERAL ACTIVITIES -

(1) EVALUATION, TECHNICAL ASSISTANCE, PROGRAM IMPROVEMENT, AND REPLICATION ACTIVITIES - Subject to paragraph (2), from amounts appropriated under section 1002(b)(3), the Secretary may reserve not more than 3 percent of such amounts for purposes of—

(A) carrying out the evaluation required by section 1239; and

(B) providing, through grants or contracts with eligible organizations, technical assistance, program improvement, and replication activities.

(2) RESEARCH - In any fiscal year, if the amount appropriated under section 1002(b)(3) for such year—

(A) is equal to or less than the amount appropriated for the preceding fiscal year, the Secretary may reserve from such amount only the amount necessary to continue multi-year activities carried out pursuant to section 1241(b) that began during or prior to the fiscal year preceding the fiscal year for which the determination is made; or

(B) exceeds the amount appropriated for the preceding fiscal year, then the Secretary shall reserve from such excess amount $2,000,000 or 50 percent, whichever is less, to carry out section 1241(b).

(c) RESERVATION FOR GRANTS -

(1) GRANTS AUTHORIZED -

(A) IN GENERAL - For any fiscal year for which at least one State educational agency applies and submits an application that meets the requirements and goals of this subsection and for which the amount appropriated under section 1002(b)(3) exceeds the amount appropriated under that section for the preceding fiscal year, the Secretary shall reserve, from the amount of the excess remaining after the application of subsection (b)(2), the amount of the remainder or $1,000,000, whichever is less, to award grants, on a competitive basis, to State educational agencies to enable them to plan and implement statewide family literacy initiatives to coordinate and, where appropriate, integrate existing Federal, State, and local literacy resources consistent with the purposes of this subpart.

(B) COORDINATION AND INTEGRATION - The coordination and integration described in subparagraph (A) shall include coordination and integration of funds available under the Adult Education and Family Literacy Act, the Head Start Act, this subpart, part A of this title, and part A of title IV of the Social Security Act.

(C) RESTRICTION - No State educational agency may receive more than one grant under this subsection.

(2) CONSORTIA -

(A) ESTABLISHMENT - To receive a grant under this subsection, a State educational agency shall establish a consortium of State-level programs under the following provisions of laws:

(i) This title (other than part D).
(ii) The Head Start Act.
(iii) The Adult Education and Family Literacy Act.
(iv) All other State-funded preschool programs and programs providing literacy services to adults.

(B) PLAN - To receive a grant under this subsection, the consortium established by a State educational agency shall create a plan to use a portion of the State educational agency's resources, derived from the programs referred to in subparagraph (A), to strengthen and expand family literacy services in the State.

(C) COORDINATION WITH SUBPART 1 - The consortium shall coordinate its activities under this paragraph with the activities of the reading and literacy partnership for the State educational agency established under section 1203(d), if the State educational agency receives a grant under section 1202.

(3) READING INSTRUCTION - Statewide family literacy initiatives implemented under this subsection **shall base reading instruction on scientifically based reading research**.

(4) TECHNICAL ASSISTANCE - The Secretary shall provide, directly or through a grant or contract with an organization with experience in the development and operation of successful family literacy services, technical assistance to State educational agencies receiving a grant under this subsection.

(5) MATCHING REQUIREMENT - The Secretary shall not make a grant to a State educational agency under this subsection unless the State educational agency agrees that, with respect to the costs to be incurred by the eligible consortium in carrying out the activities for which the grant was awarded, the State educational agency will make available non-Federal contributions in an amount equal to not less than the Federal funds provided under the grant.

(d) STATE EDUCATIONAL AGENCY ALLOCATION -

(1) IN GENERAL - From amounts appropriated under section 1002(b)(3) and not reserved under subsection (a), (b), or (c), the Secretary shall make grants to State educational agencies from allocations under paragraph (2)

(2) ALLOCATIONS - Except as provided in paragraph (3), from the total amount available under paragraph (1) for allocation to State educational agencies in any fiscal year, each State educational agency shall be eligible to receive a grant under paragraph (1) in an amount that bears the same ratio to the total amount as the amount allocated under part A to that State educational agency bears to the total amount allocated under that part to all State educational agencies.

(3) MINIMUM - No State educational agency shall receive a grant under paragraph (1) in any fiscal year in an amount that is less than $250,000, or one-half of 1 percent of the amount appropriated under section 1002(b)(3) and not reserved under subsections (a), (b), and (c) for such year, whichever is greater.

(e) DEFINITIONS - For the purpose of this subpart—

(1) the term **'eligible entity'** means a partnership composed of—

(A) a **local educational agency**; and

(B) a **nonprofit community-based organization**, a **public agency** other than a local educational agency, an institution of higher education, or a **public or private non-profit organization** other than a local educational agency, of demonstrated quality;

(2) the term **'eligible organization'** means any **public or private nonprofit organization with a record of providing effective services** to family literacy providers, such as the National Center for Family Literacy, Parents as Teachers, Inc., the Home Instruction Program for Preschool Youngsters, and the Home and School Institute, Inc.;

(3) the terms **'Indian tribe'** and **'tribal organization'** have the meanings given those terms in section 4 of the Indian Self-Determination and Education Assistance Act;

(4) the term **'scientifically based reading research'** has the meaning given that term in section 1208; and

(5) the term **'State'** means each of the 50 States, the District of Columbia, and the Commonwealth of Puerto Rico. (Section 1232 of NCLB Act)

20 U. S. C. § 6381b. State educational agency programs.

➔ **OVERVIEW:** Section 6381b authorizes states to use a percentage of their grant for administration and technical assistance. States can award subgrants for Even Start programs. Section (c) describes how funds may be used for family literacy services.

(a) STATE EDUCATIONAL AGENCY LEVEL ACTIVITIES - Each State educational agency that receives a grant under section 1232(d)(1) **may use not** more than a total of 6 percent of the grant funds for the costs of—

(1) administration, which amount shall not exceed half of the total;

(2) providing, through one or more subgrants or contracts, technical assistance for program improvement and replication, to eligible entities that receive subgrants under subsection (b); and

(3) carrying out sections 1240 and 1234(c).

(b) SUBGRANTS FOR LOCAL PROGRAMS -

(1) IN GENERAL - Each State educational agency shall use the grant funds received under section 1232(d)(1) and not reserved under subsection (a) to award subgrants to eligible entities to carry out Even Start programs.

(2) MINIMUM SUBGRANT AMOUNTS -

(A) IN GENERAL - Except as provided in subparagraphs (B) and (C), no State educational agency shall award a subgrant under paragraph (1) in an amount less than $75,000.

(B) SUBGRANTEES IN NINTH AND SUCCEEDING YEARS - No State educational agency shall award a subgrant under paragraph (1) in an amount less than $52,500 to an eligible entity for a fiscal year to carry out an Even Start program that is receiving assistance under this subpart or its predecessor authority for the ninth (or any subsequent) fiscal year.

(C) EXCEPTION FOR SINGLE SUBGRANT - A State educational agency may award one subgrant in each fiscal year of sufficient size, scope, and quality to be effective in an amount less than $75,000 if, after awarding subgrants under paragraph (1) for that fiscal year in accordance with subparagraphs (A) and (B), less than $75,000 is available to the State educational agency to award those subgrants. (Section 1233 of NCLB Act)

20 U. S. C. § 6381c. Uses of funds.

➡️ **OVERVIEW:** Section 6381c mandates that the funds be used to provide intense family literacy services that focus on children from birth through seven years of age.

(a) IN GENERAL - In carrying out an **Even Start** program under this subpart, a recipient of funds under this subpart shall use those funds to pay the Federal share of the cost of **providing intensive family literacy services that involve parents and children, from birth through age 7**, in a cooperative effort to **help parents become full partners in the education of their children** and to **assist children in reaching their full potential as learners.**

(b) FEDERAL SHARE LIMITATION -

(1) IN GENERAL -

(A) FEDERAL SHARE - Except as provided in paragraph (2), the Federal share under this subpart may not exceed—

(i) 90 percent of the total cost of the program in the first year that the program receives assistance under this subpart or its predecessor authority;
(ii) 80 percent in the second year;
(iii) 70 percent in the third year;
(iv) 60 percent in the fourth year;
(v) 50 percent in the fifth, sixth, seventh, and eighth such years; and
(vi) 35 percent in any subsequent year.

(B) REMAINING COST - The remaining cost of a program assisted under this subpart may be provided in cash or in kind, fairly evaluated, and may be obtained from any source, including other Federal funds under this Act.

(2) WAIVER - The State educational agency may waive, in whole or in part, the Federal share described in paragraph (1) for an eligible entity if the entity—

(A) demonstrates that it otherwise would not be able to participate in the program assisted under this subpart; and

(B) negotiates an agreement with the State educational agency with respect to the amount of the remaining cost to which the waiver will be applicable.

(3) PROHIBITION - Federal funds provided under this subpart may not be used for the indirect costs of a program assisted under this subpart, except that the Secretary may waive this paragraph if an eligible recipient of funds reserved under section 1232(a)(1)(C) demonstrates to the Secretary's satisfaction that the recipient otherwise would not be able to participate in the program assisted under this subpart.

(c) USE OF FUNDS FOR FAMILY LITERACY SERVICES -

(1) IN GENERAL - A State educational agency may use a portion of funds reserved under section 1233(a), to assist eligible entities receiving a subgrant under section 1233(b) in improving the quality of family literacy services provided under Even Start programs under this subpart, except that in no case may a State educational agency's use of funds for this purpose for a fiscal year result in a decrease from the level of activities and services provided to program participants in the preceding year.

(2) PRIORITY - In carrying out paragraph (1), a State educational agency shall give priority to programs that were of low quality, as evaluated based on the indicators of program quality developed by the State educational agency under section 1240.

(3) TECHNICAL ASSISTANCE TO HELP LOCAL PROGRAMS RAISE ADDITIONAL FUNDS - In carrying out paragraph (1), a State educational agency may use the funds referred to in that paragraph to provide technical assistance to help local programs of demonstrated effectiveness to access and leverage additional funds for the purpose of expanding services and reducing waiting lists, including requesting and applying for non-Federal resources.

(4) TECHNICAL ASSISTANCE AND TRAINING - Assistance under paragraph (1) shall be in the form of technical assistance and training, provided by a State educational agency through a grant, contract, or cooperative agreement with an entity that has experience in offering high-quality training and technical assistance to family literacy providers. (Section 1234 of NCLB Act)

20 U. S. C. § 6381d. Program elements.

➔ **OVERVIEW:** Section 6381d describes the requirements for Even Start programs. Programs must identify and recruit families most in need of services, accommodate the participants' work schedules and other responsibilities, and include high-quality, intensive instructional adult literacy programs that will empower parents to support the educational growth of their children.

Each program assisted under this subpart **shall**—

(1) include the **identification and recruitment** of families most in need of services provided under this subpart, as indicated by a low level of income, a low level of adult literacy or English language proficiency of the eligible parent or parents, and other need-related indicators;

(2) include **screening and preparation of parents, including teenage parents**, and children to enable those parents and children to participate fully in the activities and services provided under this subpart, **including testing, referral to necessary counselling,** other developmental and support services, and related services;

(3) be designed to accommodate the **participants' work schedule** and other responsibilities, including the provision of support services, when those services are unavailable from other sources, necessary for participation in the activities assisted under this subpart, such as—

(A) scheduling and locating of services to allow joint participation by parents and children;

(B) **child care** for the period that parents are involved in the program provided under this subpart; and

(C) **transportation** for the purpose of enabling parents and their children to participate in programs authorized by this subpart;

(4) **include high-quality, intensive instructional programs** that promote adult literacy and empower parents to support the educational growth of their children, developmentally appropriate early childhood educational services, and preparation of children for success in regular school programs;

(5) with respect to the **qualifications of staff** the cost of whose salaries are paid, in whole or in part, with Federal funds provided under this subpart, ensure that—

(A) **not later than December 21, 2004**—

(i) **a majority of the individuals providing academic instruction**—
(I) shall have obtained an associate's, bachelor's, or graduate **degree in a field related** to early childhood **education**, elementary school or secondary school education, or adult education; and

(II) if applicable, shall meet qualifications established by the State for early childhood education, elementary school or secondary school education, or adult education provided as part of an Even Start program or another family literacy program;

(ii) the individual responsible for administration of family literacy services under this subpart has received training in the operation of a family literacy program; and

(iii) paraprofessionals who provide support for academic instruction have a secondary school diploma or its recognized equivalent; and

(B) **all new personnel hired to provide academic instruction—**

(i) have obtained an **associate's, bachelor's, or graduate degree** in a field related to early childhood education, elementary school or secondary school education, or adult education; and

(ii) if applicable, meet qualifications established by the State for early childhood education, elementary school or secondary school education, or adult education provided as part of an Even Start program or another family literacy program;

(6) include special training of staff, including child-care staff, to develop the skills necessary to work with parents and young children in the full range of instructional services offered through this subpart;

(7) provide and monitor integrated **instructional services** to participating parents and children **through home-based programs;**

(8) **operate on a year-round basis**, including the provision of some program services, including **instructional and enrichment services, during the summer months;**

(9) be coordinated with—

(A) other programs assisted under this Act;

(B) any relevant programs under the Adult Education and Family Literacy Act, the **Individuals with Disabilities Education Act,** and title I of the Workforce Investment Act of 1998; and

(C) the Head Start program, volunteer literacy programs, and other relevant programs;

(10) use instructional programs based on **scientifically based reading research for children and adults**, to the extent that research is available;

(11) encourage participating families to attend regularly and to remain in the program a sufficient time to meet their program goals;

(12) include **reading-readiness** activities for preschool children **based on scientifically based reading research**, to the extent available, **to ensure that children enter school ready to learn to read;**

(13) if applicable, promote the continuity of family literacy to ensure that individuals retain and improve their educational outcomes;

(14) ensure that the programs will serve those families most in need of the activities and services provided by this subpart; and

(15) provide for **an independent evaluation of the program,** to be used for program improvement. (Section 1235 of NCLB Act)

20 U. S. C. § 6381e. Eligible participants.

➡ **OVERVIEW:** Eligible participants are parents and children from birth to age 7. Other family members may be eligible under specific circumstances described in Section (b).

(a) IN GENERAL - Except as provided in subsection (b), eligible participants in an Even Start program are—

(1) a parent or parents—

(A) who are eligible for participation in adult education and literacy activities under the **Adult Education and Family Literacy Act; or**

(B) who are **within the State's compulsory school attendance age** range, so long as a local educational agency provides (or ensures the availability of) the basic education component required under this subpart, or who are attending secondary school; and

(2) the child or children, from birth through age 7, of any individual described in paragraph (1).

(b) ELIGIBILITY FOR CERTAIN OTHER PARTICIPANTS -

(1) IN GENERAL - Family members of eligible participants described in subsection (a) may participate in activities and services provided under this subpart, when appropriate to serve the purpose of this subpart.

(2) SPECIAL RULE - Any family participating in a program assisted under this subpart that becomes ineligible to participate as a result of one or more members of the family becoming ineligible to participate may continue to participate in the program until all members of the family become ineligible to participate, which—

(A) in the case of a family in which ineligibility was due to the child or children of the family attaining the age of 8, shall be in 2 years or when the parent or parents become ineligible due to educational advancement, whichever occurs first; and

(B) in the case of a family in which ineligibility was due to the educational advancement of the parent or parents of the family, shall be when all children in the family attain the age of 8.

(3) CHILDREN 8 YEARS OF AGE OR OLDER - If an Even Start program assisted under this subpart collaborates with a program under part A, and funds received under the part A program contribute to paying the cost of providing programs under this subpart to children 8 years of age or older, the Even Start program may, notwithstanding subsection (a)(2), permit the participation of children 8 years of age or older if the focus of the program continues to remain on families with young children. (Section 1236 of NCLB Act)

20 U. S. C. § 6381f. Applications.

➡ **OVERVIEW:** This section describes the application process, required documentation, and plan.

(a) SUBMISSION - To be eligible to receive a subgrant under this subpart, **an eligible entity shall submit an application** to the State educational agency in such form and containing or accompanied by such information as the State educational agency shall require.

(b) REQUIRED DOCUMENTATION - Each application shall include documentation, satisfactory to the State educational agency, that the eligible entity **has the qualified personnel needed—**

(1) to develop, administer, and implement an Even Start program under this subpart; and

(2) to provide access to the special training necessary to prepare staff for the program, which may be offered by an eligible organization.

(c) PLAN -

(1) IN GENERAL - The application shall also include a plan of operation and continuous improvement for the program, that includes—

(A) a description of the program objectives, strategies to meet those objectives, and how those strategies and objectives are consistent with the program indicators established by the State;

(B) a description of the activities and services that will be provided under the program, including a description of how the program will incorporate the program elements required by section 1235;

(C) a description of the population to be served and an estimate of the number of participants to be served;

(D) as appropriate, a description of the applicant's collaborative efforts with institutions of higher education, community-based organizations, the State educational agency, private elementary schools, or other eligible organizations in carrying out the program for which assistance is sought;

(E) a statement of the methods that will be used—

(i) to ensure that the programs will serve families most in need of the activities and services provided by this subpart;
(ii) to provide services under this subpart to individuals with special needs, such as individuals with limited English proficiency and individuals with disabilities; and
(iii) to encourage participants to remain in the program for a time sufficient to meet the program's purpose;

(F) a description of how the plan is integrated with other programs under this Act or other Acts, as appropriate; and

(G) a description of how the plan provides for rigorous and objective evaluation of progress toward the program objectives described in subparagraph (A) and for continuing use of evaluation data for program improvement.

(2) DURATION OF THE PLAN - Each plan submitted under paragraph (1) shall—

(A) remain in effect for the duration of the eligible entity's participation under this subpart; and

(B) be periodically reviewed and revised by the eligible entity as necessary.

(d) CONSOLIDATED APPLICATION - The plan described in subsection (c)(1) may be submitted as part of a consolidated application under section 9305. (Section 1237 of NCLB Act)

20 U. S. C. § 6381g. Award of subgrants.

➡ **OVERVIEW:** This section describes the process by which states can award subgrants, including the role of the review panel, priorities, duration, and grant renewal.

(a) SELECTION PROCESS -

(1) IN GENERAL - The State educational agency **shall establish a review panel** in accordance with paragraph (3) that will approve applications that—

(A) are most likely to be successful in—

(i) meeting the purpose of this subpart; and
(ii) effectively implementing the program elements required under section 1235;

(B) demonstrate that the area to be served by the program has a high percentage or a large number of children and families who are in need of those services as indicated by **high levels of poverty, illiteracy, unemployment, limited English proficiency,** or other need-related indicators, such as a high percentage of children to be served by the program who reside in a school attendance area served by a local educational agency eligible for participation in programs under part A, a high number or percentage of parents who have been victims of domestic violence, or a high number or percentage of parents who are receiving assistance under a State program funded under part A of title IV of the Social Security Act (42 U.S.C. 601 et seq.);

(C) **provide services for at least a 3-year age range**, which may begin at birth;

(D) demonstrate the greatest possible cooperation and coordination between a variety of relevant service providers in all phases of the program;

(E) include cost-effective budgets, given the scope of the application;

(F) demonstrate the applicant's ability to provide the non-Federal share required by section 1234(b);

(G) are representative of urban and rural regions of the State; and

(H) show the greatest promise for providing models that may be adopted by other family literacy projects and other local educational agencies.

(2) PRIORITY FOR SUBGRANTS - The State educational agency shall give priority for subgrants under this subsection to applications that—

(A) target services primarily to families described in paragraph (1)(B); or

(B) are located in areas designated as empowerment zones or enterprise communities.

(3) REVIEW PANEL - A review panel shall consist of at least three members, including one early childhood professional, one adult education professional, and one individual with expertise in family literacy programs, and **may include other individuals,** such as one or more of the following:

(A) A representative of a parent-child education organization.

(B) A representative of a community-based literacy organization.

(C) A member of a local board of education.

(D) A representative of business and industry with a commitment to education.

(E) An individual who has been involved in the implementation of programs under this title in the State.

(b) DURATION -

(1) IN GENERAL - Subgrants under this subpart may be awarded for a period not to exceed 4 years.

(2) STARTUP PERIOD - The State educational agency may provide subgrant funds to an eligible recipient, at the recipient's request, for a 3 - to 6-month start-up period during the first year of the 4-year grant period, which may include staff recruitment and training, and the coordination of services, before requiring full implementation of the program.

(3) CONTINUING ELIGIBILITY - In awarding subgrant funds to continue a program under this subpart after the first year, the State educational agency shall review the progress of each eligible entity in meeting the objectives of the program referred to in section 1237(c)(1)(A) and shall evaluate the program based on the indicators of program quality developed by the State under section 1240.

(4) INSUFFICIENT PROGRESS - The State educational agency may refuse to award subgrant funds to an eligible entity if the agency finds that the eligible entity has not sufficiently improved the performance of the program, as evaluated based on the indicators of program quality developed by the State under section 1240, after—

(A) providing technical assistance to the eligible entity; and

(B) affording the eligible entity notice and an opportunity for a hearing.

(5) GRANT RENEWAL -

(A) An eligible entity that has previously received a subgrant under this subpart may reapply under this subpart for additional subgrants.

(B) The Federal share of any subgrant renewed under subparagraph (A) shall be limited in accordance with section 1234(b). (Section 1238 of NCLB Act)

20 U. S. C. § 6381h. Evaluation.

➔ **OVERVIEW:** This section authorizes the Secretary of Education to conduct an independent evaluation of the effectiveness of these programs.

From funds reserved under section 1232(b)(1), the Secretary shall provide for an **independent evaluation of programs** assisted under this subpart—

(1) to determine the **performance and effectiveness** of programs assisted under this subpart;

(2) to identify effective Even Start programs assisted under this subpart that can be duplicated and used in providing technical assistance to Federal, State, and local programs; and

(3) to provide State educational agencies and eligible entities receiving a subgrant under this subpart, directly or through a grant or contract with an organization with experience in the development and operation of successful family literacy services, technical assistance to ensure that local evaluations undertaken under section 1235(15) provide accurate information on the effectiveness of programs assisted under this sub-part. (Section 1329 of NCLB Act)

20 U. S. C. § 6381i. Indicators of program quality.

➔ **OVERVIEW:** The state is required to develop research and evaluation data to monitor, evaluate and improve Even Start programs. The statute includes several measures of program quality for adults and children.

Each State educational agency receiving funds under this sub-part **shall develop, based on the best available research and evaluation data**, indicators of program quality for programs assisted under this subpart. The indicators shall be used **to monitor, evaluate, and improve those programs** within the State. The indicators shall include the following:

(1) With respect to eligible participants in a program who are adults—

(A) achievement in the areas of **reading, writing, English-language acquisition**, problem solving, and numerical calculations;

(B) receipt of a **secondary school diploma** or a **general equivalency diploma (GED)**;

(C) entry into a **postsecondary school**, **job retraining** program, or **employment or career advancement**, including the **military**; and

(D) such other indicators as the State may develop.

(2) With respect to eligible participants in a program who are children—

(A) improvement in **ability to read on grade level** or reading readiness;

(B) **school attendance**;

(C) **grade retention and promotion**; and

(D) such other indicators as the State may develop. (Section 1240 of NCLB Act)

20 U. S. C. § 6381j. Research.

➡️ **OVERVIEW:** This section authorizes the Secretary of Education to carry out research into the components of successful family literacy programs, including scientifically based reading research into the most effective ways to improve the literacy skills of adults with reading problems and how to provide parents with the knowledge and skills to support their children's literacy development.

(a) IN GENERAL - The Secretary shall carry out, through grant or contract, research into the components of successful family literacy services, in order to

(1) improve the quality of existing programs assisted under this subpart or other family literacy programs carried out under this Act or the Adult Education and Family Literacy Act; and

(2) develop models for new programs to be carried out under this Act or the Adult Education and Family Literacy Act.

(b) SCIENTIFICALLY BASED RESEARCH ON FAMILY LITERACY -

(1) IN GENERAL - From amounts reserved under section 1232(b)(2), the National Institute for Literacy, in consultation with the Secretary, shall carry out research that—

(A) is **scientifically based reading research**; and

(B) determines—

(i) the most effective ways of improving the **literacy skills of adults with reading difficulties**; and

(ii) how family literacy services can best provide parents with the knowledge and skills the parents need to support their children's literacy development.

(2) USE OF EXPERT ENTITY - The National Institute for Literacy, in consultation with the Secretary, **shall carry out the research** under paragraph (1) through an entity, including a Federal agency, that has expertise in carrying out **longitudinal studies of the development of literacy skills in children** and has developed **effective interventions to help children with reading difficulties.**

(c) DISSEMINATION - The National Institute for Literacy **shall** disseminate, pursuant to section 1207, the results of the research described in subsections (a) and (b) to State educational agencies and recipients of subgrants under this subpart. (Section 1241 of NCLB Act)

20 U. S. C. § 6381k. Construction.

Nothing in this subpart shall be construed to **prohibit** a recipient of funds under this subpart from serving students participating in Even Start simultaneously with students with similar educational needs, in the same educational settings where appropriate. (Section 1242 of NCLB Act)

SUBPART 4—IMPROVING LITERACY THROUGH SCHOOL LIBRARIES

➜ **OVERVIEW:** The purpose of Subpart 4 is to increase access to well-equipped, technologically advanced school libraries. These programs provide funds to acquire books, media, Internet linkages, networks, and provide students with access to school libraries during non-school hours.

20 U. S. C. § 6383. Improving literacy through school libraries.

➜ **OVERVIEW:** Section (a) describes the purposes of this statute: to improve the literacy skills and academic achievement of students by providing them with access to well-equipped libraries and professionally certified school library media specialists. Competitive grants are available to school districts and states. Section (g) describes how funds may be used.

(a) PURPOSES - The purpose of this subpart is to **improve literacy skills and academic achievement of students** by providing students with increased access to up-to-date school library materials, a well-equipped, technologically advanced school library media center, and well-trained, **professionally certified school library media specialists.**

(b) RESERVATION - From the funds appropriated under section 1002(b)(4) for a fiscal year, the Secretary shall reserve—

(1) one-half of 1 percent to award assistance under this section to the Bureau of Indian Affairs to carry out activities consistent with the purpose of this subpart; and

(2) one-half of 1 percent to award assistance under this section to the outlying areas according to their respective needs for assistance under this subpart.

(c) GRANTS -

(1) COMPETITIVE GRANTS TO ELIGIBLE LOCAL EDUCATIONAL AGENCIES - If the amount of funds appropriated under section 1002(b)(4) for a fiscal year is less than $100,000,000, then the Secretary shall award grants, on a **competitive** basis, to eligible local educational agencies under subsection (e).

(2) FORMULA GRANTS TO STATES - If the amount of funds appropriated under section 1002(b)(4) for a fiscal year equals or exceeds $100,000,000, then the Secretary shall award grants to State educational agencies from allotments under subsection (d).

(3) DEFINITION OF ELIGIBLE LOCAL EDUCATIONAL AGENCY - In this section the term **'eligible local educational agency'** means—

(A) in the case of a local educational agency receiving assistance made available under paragraph (1), a local educational agency in which 20 percent of the students served by the local educational agency are from families with incomes below the poverty line; and

(B) in the case of a local educational agency receiving assistance from State allocations made available under paragraph (2), a local educational agency in which—
> (i) 15 percent of the students who are served by the local educational agency are from such families; or
> (ii) the percentage of students from such families who are served by the local educational agency is greater than the statewide percentage of children from such families.

(d) STATE GRANTS -

(1) ALLOTMENTS - From funds made available under subsection (c)(2) and not reserved under subsections (b) and (j) for a fiscal year, the Secretary shall allot to each State educational agency having an application approved under subsection (f)(1) an amount that bears the same relation to the funds as the amount the State educational agency received under part A for the preceding fiscal year bears to the amount all such State educational agencies received under part A for the preceding fiscal year, to increase literacy and reading skills by improving school libraries.

(2) COMPETITIVE GRANTS TO ELIGIBLE LOCAL EDUCATIONAL AGENCIES - Each State educational agency receiving an allotment under paragraph (1) for a fiscal year—

(A) may reserve not more than 3 percent of the allotted funds to provide technical assistance, **disseminate information about school library media programs that are effective and based on scientifically based research**, and pay administrative costs related to activities under this section; and

(B) shall use the allotted funds that remain after making the reservation under subparagraph (A) to award grants, for a period of 1 year, on a competitive basis, to eligible local educational agencies in the State that have an application approved under subsection (f)(2) for activities described in subsection (g).

(3) REALLOTMENT - If a State educational agency does not apply for an allotment under this section for any fiscal year, or if the State educational agency's application is not approved, the Secretary shall reallot the amount of the State educational agency's allotment to the remaining State educational agencies in accordance with paragraph (1).

(e) DIRECT COMPETITIVE GRANTS TO ELIGIBLE LOCAL EDUCATIONAL AGENCIES -

(1) IN GENERAL - From amounts made available under subsection (c)(1) and not reserved under subsections (b) and (j) for a fiscal year, the Secretary shall award grants, on a competitive basis, to eligible local educational agencies that have applications approved under subsection (f)(2) for activities described in subsection (g).

(2) DURATION - The Secretary shall award grants under this subsection for a period of 1 year.

(3) DISTRIBUTION - The Secretary shall ensure that grants under this subsection are equitably distributed among the different geographic regions of the United States, and among local educational agencies serving urban and rural areas.

(f) APPLICATIONS -

(1) STATE EDUCATIONAL AGENCY - Each State educational agency desiring assistance under this section shall submit to the Secretary an application at such time, in such manner, and containing such information as the Secretary shall require. The application shall contain a description of—

(A) how the State educational agency will assist eligible local educational agencies in meeting the requirements of this section and in using scientifically based research to implement effective school library media programs; and

(B) the standards and techniques the State educational agency will use to evaluate the quality and impact of activities carried out under this section by eligible local educational agencies to determine the need for technical assistance and whether to continue to provide additional funding to the agencies under this section.

(2) ELIGIBLE LOCAL EDUCATIONAL AGENCY - Each eligible local educational agency desiring assistance under this section shall submit to the Secretary or State educational agency, as appropriate, an application at such time, in such manner, and containing such information as the Secretary or State educational agency, respectively, shall require. The application **shall contain a description** of—

(A) a needs assessment relating to the need for school library media improvement, based on the age and condition of school library media resources, including book collections, access of school library media centers to advanced technology, and the availability of well-trained, professionally certified school library media specialists, in schools served by the eligible local educational agency;

(B) the manner in which the eligible local educational agency will use the funds made available through the grant to carry out the activities described in subsection (g);

(C) how the eligible local educational agency will extensively involve school library media specialists, teachers, administrators, and parents in the activities assisted under this section, and the manner in which the eligible local educational agency will carry out the activities described in subsection (g) using programs and materials that are grounded in scientifically based research;

(D) the manner in which the eligible local educational agency will effectively coordinate the funds and activities provided under this section with Federal, State, and local funds and activities under this subpart and other literacy, library, technology, and professional development funds and activities; and

(E) the manner in which the eligible local educational agency will collect and analyze data on the quality and impact of activities carried out under this section by schools served by the eligible local educational agency.

(g) LOCAL ACTIVITIES - Funds under this section may be used to—

(1) **acquire up-to-date school library media resources**, including books;

(2) acquire and use advanced **technology**, incorporated into the curricula of the school, to develop and enhance the information literacy, information retrieval, and critical thinking skills of students;

(3) **facilitate Internet links** and **other resourcesharing networks** among schools and school library media centers, and public and academic libraries, where possible;

(4) provide **professional development** described in section 1222(d)(2) **for school library media specialists**, and activities that foster increased collaboration between school library media specialists, teachers, and

administrators; and

(5) provide students with access to school libraries during nonschool hours, including the hours before and after school, during weekends, and during summer vacation periods.

(h) ACCOUNTABILITY AND REPORTING -

(1) LOCAL REPORTS - Each eligible local educational agency that receives funds under this section for a fiscal year shall report to the Secretary or State educational agency, as appropriate, on how the funding was used and the extent to which the availability of, the access to, and the use of, up-to-date school library media resources in the elementary schools and secondary schools served by the eligible local educational agency was increased.

(2) STATE REPORT - Each State educational agency that receives funds under this section shall compile the reports received under paragraph (1) and submit the compiled reports to the Secretary.

(i) SUPPLEMENT, NOT SUPPLANT - Funds made available under this section shall be used to supplement, and not supplant, other Federal, State, and local funds expended to carry out activities relating to library, technology, or professional development activities.

(j) NATIONAL ACTIVITIES -

(1) EVALUATIONS - From the funds appropriated under section 1002(b)(4) for each fiscal year, the Secretary shall reserve not more than 1 percent for annual, independent, national evaluations of the activities assisted under this section and their impact on improving the reading skills of students. The evaluations shall be conducted not later than 3 years after the date of enactment of the No Child Left Behind Act of 2001, (Wrightslaw Note: Enacted on January 8, 2002) and biennially thereafter.

(2) REPORT TO CONGRESS - The Secretary shall transmit the State reports received under subsection (h)(2) and the evaluations conducted under paragraph (1) to the Committee on Health, Education, Labor, and Pensions of the Senate and the Committee on Education and the Workforce of the House of Representatives. (Section 1251 of NCLB Act)

PART C—EDUCATION OF MIGRATORY CHILDREN

➜ **OVERVIEW:** The purposes of Part C, Education of Migratory Children, as described in Section 6391 are:

to provide migratory children with high-quality, comprehensive educational programs;
to reduce educational disruptions and other problems associated with repeated moves;
to ensure that schools do not penalize migratory children in curriculum, graduation requirements and state achievement standards;
to ensure that schools provide migratory children with educational services that address their special needs;
to design educational programs that help migratory children overcome cultural and language barriers, social isolation, and health problems, and
to prepare migratory children to make a successful transition to postsecondary education or employment.

Section 6392 authorizes grants. Section 6393 provides the formulas for allocations to the states and Puerto Rico. Section 6394, state applications and services, describes the application process, measurable program goals and objectives, how funds will be used, and how effectiveness will be determined. Section 6395 provides for peer review of grant applications.

Section 6396, the needs assessment and service delivery plan, specifies measurable program goals and outcomes.

Section 6397, bypass, explains that if a state is unable or unwilling to educate migratory children, the State's allocation may be given to another public or private nonprofit agency.

Section 6398 requires states to develop effective methods to electronically exchange health and educational information about migratory students. Student records shall be made available to the requesting agency at no cost. Section 6399 includes definitions of local operating agency and migratory child.

Part C, Education of Migratory Children, includes the following sections.

20 U. S. C. § 6391. Program purpose.
20 U. S. C. § 6392. Program authorized.
20 U. S. C. § 6393. State allocations.
20 U. S. C. § 6394. State applications; services.
20 U. S. C. § 6395. Secretarial approval; peer review.
20 U. S. C. § 6396. Comprehensive needs assessment and service-delivery plan; authorized activities.
20 U. S. C. § 6397. Bypass.
20 U. S. C. § 6398. Coordination of migrant education activities.
20 U. S. C. § 6399. Definitions.

20 U. S. C. § 6391. Program purpose.

It is the **purpose** of this part to assist States to—

(1) support high-quality and comprehensive educational programs for migratory children to help **reduce** the **educational disruptions** and other **problems that result from repeated moves;**

(2) ensure that migratory children who move among the States **are not penalized in** any manner by disparities among the States in curriculum, graduation requirements, and State academic content and student academic achievement standards;

(3) ensure that migratory children are provided with **appropriate educational services** (including supportive services) that address their **special needs** in a coordinated and efficient manner;

(4) ensure that migratory children receive full and appropriate opportunities to meet the same challenging State academic content and student academic achievement standards that all children are expected to meet;

(5) design programs to help migratory children overcome educational disruption, cultural and language barriers, social isolation, various health-related problems, and other factors that inhibit the ability of such children to do well in school, and to prepare such children to make a successful transition to postsecondary education or employment; and

(6) ensure that migratory children benefit from State and local systemic reforms. (Section 1301 of NCLB Act)

20 U. S. C. § 6392. Program authorized.

In order to carry out the purpose of this part, the Secretary **shall** make grants to State educational agencies, or combinations of such agencies, to establish or improve, directly or through local operating agencies, programs of education for migratory children in accordance with this part. (Section 1302 of NCLB Act)

20 U. S. C. § 6393. State allocations.

(a) STATE ALLOCATIONS -

(1) FISCAL YEAR 2002 - For fiscal year 2002, each State (other than the Commonwealth of Puerto Rico) is entitled to receive under this part an amount equal to—

(A) the sum of the estimated number of migratory children aged 3 through 21 who reside in the State full time and the full-time equivalent of the estimated number of migratory children aged 3 through 21 who reside in the State part time, as determined in accordance with subsection (e); multiplied by

(B) 40 percent of the average per-pupil expenditure in the State, except that the amount determined under this paragraph shall not be less than 32 percent, nor more than 48 percent, of the average per-pupil expenditure in the United States.

(2) SUBSEQUENT YEARS -

(A) BASE AMOUNT -

(i) IN GENERAL - Except as provided in subsection (b) and clause (ii), each State (other than the Commonwealth of Puerto Rico) is entitled to receive under this part, for fiscal year 2003 and succeeding fiscal years, an amount equal to—
   (I) the amount that such State received under this part for fiscal year 2002; plus
   (II) the amount allocated to the State under subparagraph (B).
(ii) NONPARTICIPATING STATES - In the case of a State (other than the Commonwealth of Puerto Rico) that did not receive any funds for fiscal year 2002 under this part, the State shall receive, for fiscal year 2003 and succeeding fiscal years, an amount equal to—
   (I) the amount that such State would have received under this part for fiscal year 2002 if its application under section 1304 for the year had been approved; plus
   (II) the amount allocated to the State under subparagraph (B).

(B) ALLOCATION OF ADDITIONAL AMOUNT - For fiscal year 2003 and succeeding fiscal years, the amount (if any) by which the funds appropriated to carry out this part for the year exceed such funds for fiscal year 2002 shall be allocated to a State (other than the Commonwealth of Puerto Rico) so that the State receives an amount equal to—

(i) the sum of—
   (I) the number of identified eligible migratory children, aged 3 through 21, residing in the State during the previous year; and
   (II) the number of identified eligible migratory children, aged 3 through 21, who received services under this part in summer or intersession programs provided by the State during such year; multiplied by
(ii) 40 percent of the average per-pupil expenditure in the State, except that the amount determined under this clause may not be less than 32 percent, or more than 48 percent, of the average per-pupil expenditure in the United States.

(b) ALLOCATION TO PUERTO RICO -

(1) IN GENERAL - For each fiscal year, the grant which the Commonwealth of Puerto Rico shall be eligible to receive under this part shall be the amount determined by multiplying the number of children who would be counted under subsection (a)(1)(A) if such subsection applied to the Commonwealth of Puerto Rico by the product of—

(A) the percentage which the average per-pupil expenditure in the Commonwealth of Puerto Rico is of the lowest average per-pupil expenditure of any of the 50 States; and

(B) 32 percent of the average per-pupil expenditure in the United States.

(2) MINIMUM PERCENTAGE - The percentage in paragraph (1)(A) shall not be less than—

(A) for fiscal year 2002, 77.5 percent;

(B) for fiscal year 2003, 80.0 percent;

(C) for fiscal year 2004, 82.5 percent; and

(D) for fiscal year 2005 and succeeding fiscal years, 85.0 percent.

(3) LIMITATION - If the application of paragraph (2) for any fiscal year would result in any of the 50 States or the District of Columbia receiving less under this part than it received under this part for the preceding fiscal year, then the percentage described in paragraph (1)(A) that is used for the Commonwealth of Puerto Rico for the fiscal year for which the determination is made shall be the greater of the percentage in paragraph (1)(A) for such fiscal year or the percentage used for the preceding fiscal year.

(c) RATABLE REDUCTIONS; REALLOCATIONS -

(1) IN GENERAL -

(A) If, after the Secretary reserves funds under section 1308(c), the amount appropriated to carry out this part for any fiscal year is insufficient to pay in full the amounts for which all States are eligible, the Secretary shall ratably reduce each such amount.

(B) If additional funds become available for making such payments for any fiscal year, the Secretary shall allocate such funds to States in amounts that the Secretary determines will best carry out the purpose of this part.

(2) SPECIAL RULE -

(A) The Secretary shall further reduce the amount of any grant to a State under this part for any fiscal year if the Secretary determines, based on available information on the numbers and needs of migratory children in the State and the program proposed by the State to address such needs, that such amount exceeds the amount required under section 1304.

(B) The Secretary shall reallocate such excess funds to other States whose grants under this part would otherwise be insufficient to provide an appropriate level of services to migratory children, in such amounts as the Secretary determines are appropriate.

(d) CONSORTIUM ARRANGEMENTS -

(1) IN GENERAL - In the case of a State that receives a grant of $1,000,000 or less under this section, the Secretary shall consult with the State educational agency to determine whether consortium arrangements with another State or other appropriate entity would result in delivery of services in a more effective and efficient manner.

(2) PROPOSALS - Any State, regardless of the amount of such State's allocation, may submit a consortium arrangement to the Secretary for approval.

(3) APPROVAL - The Secretary shall approve a consortium arrangement under paragraph (1) or (2) if the proposal demonstrates that the arrangement will—

(A) reduce administrative costs or program function costs for State programs; and

(B) make more funds available for direct services to add substantially to the welfare or educational attainment of children to be served under this part.

(e) DETERMINING NUMBERS OF ELIGIBLE CHILDREN - In order to determine the estimated number of migratory children residing in each State for purposes of this section, the Secretary shall—

(1) use such information as the Secretary finds most accurately reflects the actual number of migratory children;

(2) develop and implement a procedure for more accurately reflecting cost factors for different types of summer and inter-session program designs;

(3) adjust the full-time equivalent number of migratory children who reside in each State to take into account—

(A) the special needs of those children participating in special programs provided under this part that operate during the summer and intersession periods; and

(B) the additional costs of operating such programs; and

(4) conduct an analysis of the options for adjusting the formula so as to better direct services to the child whose education has been interrupted. (Section 1303 of NCLB Act)

20 U. S. C. § 6394. State applications; services.

➤ **OVERVIEW:** This statute describes the application process and requirements for measurable program goals and objectives. Section (c) states that applications must include assurances about how funds will be used and how effectiveness will be determined. Programs may provide advocacy and outreach for migratory children and their parents, professional development for teachers, and family literacy programs.

(a) APPLICATION REQUIRED - Any State desiring to receive a grant under this part for any fiscal year shall submit an application to the Secretary at such time and in such manner as the Secretary may require.

(b) PROGRAM INFORMATION - Each such application **shall include—**

(1) a description of how, in planning, implementing, and evaluating programs and projects assisted under this part, the State and its local operating agencies will ensure that the **special educational needs of migratory children, including pre-school migratory children**, are identified and addressed through—

(A) the full range of services that are available for migratory children from appropriate local, State, and Federal educational programs;

(B) joint planning among local, State, and Federal educational programs serving migrant children, including language instruction educational programs under part A or B of title III;

(C) the integration of services available under this part with services provided by those other programs; and

(D) **measurable program goals and outcomes;**

(2) a description of the steps the State is taking to provide all migratory students with the opportunity to meet the same challenging State academic content standards and challenging State student academic achievement standards that all children are expected to meet;

(3) a description of how the State will use funds received under this part to promote interstate and intrastate coordination of services for migratory children, including how, consistent with procedures the Secretary may require, the State will provide for educational continuity through the timely transfer of pertinent school records, including information on health, when children move from one school to another, whether or not

such move occurs during the regular school year;

(4) a description of the State's priorities for the use of funds received under this part, and how such priorities relate to the State's assessment of needs for services in the State;

(5) a description of how the State will determine the amount of any subgrants the State will award to local operating agencies, taking into account the numbers and needs of migratory children, the requirements of subsection (d), and the availability of funds from other Federal, State, and local programs;

(6) such budgetary and other information as the Secretary may require; and

(7) a description of how the State will encourage programs and projects assisted under this part to offer family literacy services if the program or project serves a substantial number of migratory children who have parents who do not have a high school diploma or its recognized equivalent or who have low levels of literacy.

(c) **ASSURANCES** - Each such application **shall also include assurances**, satisfactory to the Secretary, that—

(1) funds received under this part will be used only—

(A) for programs and projects, including the acquisition of equipment, in accordance with section 1306; and

(B) to coordinate such programs and projects with similar programs and projects within the State and in other States, as well as with other Federal programs that can benefit migratory children and their families;

(2) such programs and projects will be carried out in a manner consistent with the objectives of section 1114, subsections (b) and (d) of section 1115, subsections (b) and (c) of section 1120A, and part I;

(3) in the planning and operation of programs and projects at both the State and local agency operating level, there is consultation with parent advisory councils for programs of 1 school year in duration, and that all such programs and projects are carried out—

(A) in a manner that provides for the same parental involvement as is required for programs and projects under section 1118, unless extraordinary circumstances make such provision impractical; and

(B) in a format and language understandable to the parents;

(4) in planning and carrying out such programs and projects, there has been, and will be, adequate provision for addressing the unmet education needs of preschool migratory children;

(5) the effectiveness of such programs and projects will be determined, where feasible, using the same approaches and standards that will be used to assess the performance of students, schools, and local educational agencies under part A;

(6) to the extent feasible, such programs and projects will provide for—

(A) **advocacy and outreach activities for migratory children** and their families, including informing such children and families of, or helping such children and families gain access to, other education, health, nutrition, and social services;

(B) **professional development programs**, including mentoring, for teachers and other program personnel;

(C) **family literacy programs**, including such programs that use models developed under Even Start;

(D) the integration of information technology into educational and related programs; and

(E) programs to facilitate the transition of secondary school students to postsecondary education or employment; and

(7) the State will assist the Secretary in determining the number of migratory children under paragraphs (1)(A) and (2)(B)(i) of section 1303(a), through such procedures as the Secretary may require.

(d) PRIORITY FOR SERVICES - In providing services with funds received under this part, each recipient of such funds shall give priority to migratory children who are failing, or most at risk of failing, to meet the State's challenging State academic content standards and challenging State student academic achievement standards, and whose education has been interrupted during the regular school year.

(e) CONTINUATION OF SERVICES - Notwithstanding any other provision of this part—

(1) a child who ceases to be a migratory child during a school term shall be eligible for services until the end of such term;

(2) a child who is no longer a migratory child may continue to receive services for 1 additional school year, but only if comparable services are not available through other programs; and

(3) secondary school students who were eligible for services in secondary school may continue to be served through credit accrual programs until graduation. (Section 1304 of NCLB Act)

20 U. S. C. § 6395. Secretarial approval; peer review.

(a) SECRETARIAL APPROVAL - The Secretary shall approve each State application that meets the requirements of this part.

(b) PEER REVIEW - The Secretary may review any such application with the assistance and advice of State officials and other individuals with relevant expertise. (Section 1305 of NCLB Act)

20 U. S. C. § 6396. Comprehensive needs assessment and service-delivery plan; authorized activities.

➡ **OVERVIEW:** This statute describes the comprehensive needs assessment and service delivery plan. The service delivery plan must include measurable program goals and outcomes. Migratory children must have an opportunity to meet challenging state academic standards that all students are expected to meet.

(a) COMPREHENSIVE PLAN -

(1) IN GENERAL - Each State that receives assistance under this part shall ensure that the State and its local operating agencies identify and address the special educational needs of migratory children in accordance with a comprehensive State plan that—

(A) is integrated with other programs under this Act or other Acts, as appropriate;

(B) may be submitted as a part of a consolidated application under section 9302, if—

(i) the special needs of migratory children are specifically addressed in the comprehensive State plan;
(ii) the comprehensive State plan is developed in collaboration with parents of migratory children; and

(iii) the comprehensive State plan is not used to supplant State efforts regarding, or administrative funding for, this part;

(C) provides that **migratory children** will have an opportunity to meet the **same challenging State academic content standards and challenging State student academic achievement standards that all children are expected to meet;**

(D) **specifies measurable program goals and outcomes;**

(E) encompasses the full range of services that are available for migratory children from appropriate local, State, and Federal educational programs;

(F) is the product of joint planning among such local, State, and Federal programs, including programs under part A, early childhood programs, and language instruction educational programs under part A or B of title III; and

(G) provides for the integration of services available under this part with services provided by such other programs.

(2) DURATION OF THE PLAN - Each such comprehensive State plan shall—

(A) remain in effect for the duration of the State's participation under this part; and

(B) be periodically reviewed and revised by the State, as necessary, to reflect changes in the State's strategies and programs under this part.

(b) AUTHORIZED ACTIVITIES -

(1) FLEXIBILITY - In implementing the comprehensive plan described in subsection (a), each State educational agency, where applicable through its local educational agencies, shall have the flexibility to determine the activities to be provided with funds made available under this part, except that such funds first shall be used to meet the identified needs of migratory children that result from their migratory lifestyle, and to permit these children to participate effectively in school.

(2) UNADDRESSED NEEDS - Funds provided under this part shall be used to address the needs of migratory children that are not addressed by services available from other Federal or non-Federal programs, except that migratory children who are eligible to receive services under part A may receive those services through funds provided under that part, or through funds under this part that remain after the agency addresses the needs described in paragraph (1).

(3) CONSTRUCTION - Nothing in this part shall be construed to prohibit a local educational agency from serving migratory children simultaneously with students with similar educational needs in the same educational settings, where appropriate.

(4) SPECIAL RULE - Notwithstanding section 1114, a school that receives funds under this part shall continue to address the identified needs described in paragraph (1), and shall meet the special educational needs of migratory children before using funds under this part for schoolwide programs under section 1114. (Section 1306 of NCLB Act)

20 U. S. C. § 6397. Bypass.

➜ **OVERVIEW:** If a state is unable or unwilling to educate migratory children, the Department of Education may use the State's allocation to arrange for another public or private nonprofit agency to carry out these purposes in that State.

The Secretary may use all or part of any State's allocation under this part to make arrangements with **any public or private nonprofit agency** to carry out the purpose of this part in such State if the Secretary determines that—

(1) the **State is unable or unwilling** to conduct educational programs for migratory children;

(2) such arrangements would result in more efficient and economic administration of such programs; or

(3) such arrangements would add substantially to the welfare or educational attainment of such children. (Section 1307 of NCLB Act)

20 U. S. C. § 6398. Coordination of migrant education activities.

➡ **OVERVIEW:** This statute requires states to develop effective methods to electronically exchange health and educational information about migratory students. This information includes immunization and health records, academic history, credits, results from state assessments, and eligibility under the Individuals with Disabilities Education Act. Student records shall be made available to the requesting agency at no cost.

(a) IMPROVEMENT OF COORDINATION -

(1) IN GENERAL - The Secretary, in consultation with the States, may make grants to, or enter into contracts with, State educational agencies, local educational agencies, institutions of higher education, and other public and private nonprofit entities to improve the interstate and intrastate coordination among such agencies' educational programs, including the establishment or improvement of programs for credit accrual and exchange, available to migratory students.

(2) DURATION - Grants under this subsection may be awarded for not more than 5 years.

(b) STUDENT RECORDS -

(1) ASSISTANCE - The Secretary shall assist States in developing effective methods for the electronic transfer of student records and in determining the number of migratory children in each State.

(2) INFORMATION SYSTEM -

(A) IN GENERAL - The Secretary, in consultation with the States, shall ensure the **linkage of migrant student record systems for the purpose of electronically exchanging, among the States, health and educational information** regarding all migratory students. The Secretary shall ensure such linkage occurs in a cost-effective manner, utilizing systems used by the States prior to, or developed after, the date of enactment of the No Child Left Behind Act of 2001, and shall determine the minimum data elements that each State receiving funds under this part shall collect and maintain. Such elements may include—

(i) **immunization records** and other health information;
(ii) elementary and secondary **academic history** (including partial credit), credit accrual, and results from State assessments required under section 1111(b);
(iii) other academic information essential to ensuring that migratory children achieve to high standards; and
(iv) **eligibility** for services under the Individuals with Disabilities Education Act.

(B) NOTICE AND COMMENT - After consulting with the States under subparagraph (A), the Secretary shall publish a notice in the Federal Register seeking public comment on the proposed data elements that each State receiving funds under this part shall be required to collect for purposes of electronic transfer of migratory student information and the requirements that States shall meet for immediate electronic access to such information. Such publication shall occur not later than 120 days after the date of enactment of the No Child Left Behind Act of 2001.

(3) NO COST FOR CERTAIN TRANSFERS - A State educational agency or local educational agency receiving assistance under this part **shall make student records available** to another State educational agency or local educational agency that requests the records **at no cost** to the requesting agency, if the request is made in order to meet the needs of a migratory child.

(4) REPORT TO CONGRESS -

(A) IN GENERAL - Not later than April 30, 2003, the Secretary shall report to the Committee on Health, Education, Labor, and Pensions of the Senate and the Committee on Education and the Workforce of the House of Representatives the Secretary's findings and recommendations regarding the maintenance and transfer of health and educational information for migratory students by the States.

(B) REQUIRED CONTENTS - The Secretary shall include in such report—

(i) a review of the progress of States in developing and linking electronic records transfer systems;
(ii) recommendations for the development and linkage of such systems; and
(iii) recommendations for measures that may be taken to ensure the continuity of services provided for migratory students.

(c) AVAILABILITY OF FUNDS - For the purpose of carrying out this section in any fiscal year, the Secretary shall reserve not more than $10,000,000 of the amount appropriated to carry out this part for such year.

(d) INCENTIVE GRANTS - From the amounts made available to carry out this section for any fiscal year, the Secretary may reserve not more than $3,000,000 to award grants of not more than $250,000 on a competitive basis to State educational agencies that propose a consortium arrangement with another State or other appropriate entity that the Secretary determines, pursuant to criteria that the Secretary shall establish, will improve the delivery of services to migratory children whose education is interrupted.

(e) DATA COLLECTION - The Secretary shall direct the **National Center for Education Statistics** to collect data on migratory children. (Section 1308 of NCLB Act)

20 U. S. C. § 6399. Definitions.

As used in this part:

(1) LOCAL OPERATING AGENCY - The term 'local operating agency' means—

(A) a local educational agency to which a State educational agency makes a subgrant under this part;

(B) a public or **nonprofit private agency** with which a State educational agency or the Secretary makes an arrangement to carry out a project under this part; or

(C) a State educational agency, if the State educational agency operates the State's migrant education program or projects directly.

(2) MIGRATORY CHILD - The term 'migratory child' means a child who is, or whose parent or spouse is, a migratory agricultural worker, including a migratory dairy worker, or a migratory fisher, and who, **in the preceding 36 months,** in order to obtain, or accompany such parent or spouse, in order to obtain, temporary or seasonal employment in agricultural or fishing work—

(A) **has moved from one school district to another;**

(B) in a State that is comprised of a single school district, has moved from one administrative area to another within such district; or

(C) resides in a school district of more than 15,000 square miles, and migrates a distance of 20 miles or more to a temporary residence to engage in a fishing activity. (Section 1309 of NCLB Act)

PART D - PREVENTION AND INTERVENTION PROGRAMS FOR CHILDREN AND YOUTH WHO ARE NEGLECTED, DELINQUENT, OR AT-RISK

→ **OVERVIEW:** Part D focuses on the needs of children who are at-risk of academic failure. An at-risk child or youth may be in an institution or community day program for neglected or delinquent youth. The No Child Left Behind statute defines an institution as a public or private residential facility for children who are adjudicated delinquent, in need of supervision, who have been abandoned or neglected by their parents, or who are orphans.

Part D of Title I has three Subparts that begin after Section 6422:

Subpart 1 - State Agency Programs
Subpart 2 - Local Agency Programs
Subpart 3 - General Provisions.

Part D, Prevention and Intervention Programs for Children and Youth who are Neglected, Delinquent, or At-Risk, includes the following initial two sections, and three subparts.

20 U. S. C. § 6421. Purpose and program authorization.
20 U. S. C. § 6422. Payments for programs under this Part.

Subpart 1 - State Agency Programs

20 U. S. C. § 6431. Eligibility.
20 U. S. C. § 6432. Allocation of funds.
20 U. S. C. § 6433. State reallocation of funds.
20 U. S. C. § 6434. State plan and State agency applications.
20 U. S. C. § 6435. Use of funds.
20 U. S. C. § 6436. Institution-wide projects.
20 U. S. C. § 6437. Three-year programs or projects.
20 U. S. C. § 6438. Transition services.
20 U. S. C. § 6439. Evaluation; technical assistance; annual model program.

Subpart 2 - Local Agency Programs

20 U. S. C. § 6451. Purpose.
20 U. S. C. § 6452. Programs operated by local educational agencies.
20 U. S. C. § 6453. Local educational agency applications.
20 U. S. C. § 6454. Uses of funds.
20 U. S. C. § 6455. Program requirements for correctional facilities receiving funds under this section.
20 U. S. C. § 6456. Accountability.

Subpart 3 - General Provisions

20 U. S. C. § 6471. Program evaluations.
20 U. S. C. § 6472. Definitions.

20 U. S. C. § 6421. Purpose and program authorization.

(a) PURPOSE - It is the purpose of this part—

(1) **to improve educational services for children and youth in local and State institutions for neglected or delinquent children and youth** so that such children and youth have the opportunity to meet the same challenging State academic content standards and challenging State student academic achievement standards that all children in the State are expected to meet;

(2) to provide such children and youth with the services needed to make a **successful transition from institutionalization to further schooling or employment**; and

(3) **to prevent at-risk youth from dropping out of school**, and to **provide dropouts, and children and youth returning from correctional facilities or institutions** for neglected or delinquent children and youth, **with a support system to ensure their continued education.**

(b) PROGRAM AUTHORIZED - In order to carry out the purpose of this part and from amounts appropriated under section 1002(d), the Secretary shall make grants to State educational agencies to enable such agencies to award subgrants to State agencies and local educational agencies to establish or improve programs of education for neglected, delinquent, or at-risk children and youth. (Section 1401 of NCLB Act)

20 U. S. C. § 6422. Payments for programs under this part.

(a) AGENCY SUBGRANTS - Based on the allocation amount computed under section 1412, the Secretary shall allocate to each State educational agency an amount necessary to make subgrants to State agencies under subpart 1.

(b) LOCAL SUBGRANTS - Each State shall retain, for the purpose of carrying out subpart 2, funds generated throughout the State under part A of this title based on children and youth residing in local correctional facilities, or attending community day programs for delinquent children and youth. (Section 1402 of NCLB Act)

SUBPART 1 - STATE AGENCY PROGRAMS

➡ **OVERVIEW:** Subpart 1 describes state programs for at risk children, including children in institutions, children in day programs for neglected or delinquent youth, and children in adult correctional institutions. Section 6434 describes application contents and assurances by states. Section 6435 describes uses of funds. Section 6438 describes transition services.

20 U. S. C. § 6431. Eligibility.

A State agency is eligible for assistance under this subpart **if such State agency is responsible** for providing free public education for children and youth—

(1) in institutions for neglected or delinquent children and youth;

(2) attending community day programs for neglected or delinquent children and youth; or

(3) in adult correctional institutions. (Section 1411 of NCLB Act)

20 U. S. C. § 6432. Allocation of funds.

(a) SUBGRANTS TO STATE AGENCIES -

(1) IN GENERAL - Each State agency described in section 1411 (other than an agency in the Commonwealth of Puerto Rico) is eligible to receive a subgrant under this subpart, for each fiscal year, in an amount equal to the product of—

(A) the number of neglected or delinquent children and youth described in section 1411 who—

(i) are enrolled for at least 15 hours per week in education programs in adult correctional institutions; and
(ii) are enrolled for at least 20 hours per week—
    (I) in education programs in institutions for neglected or delinquent children and youth; or
    (II) in community day programs for neglected or delinquent children and youth; and

(B) 40 percent of the average per-pupil expenditure in the State, except that the amount determined under this subparagraph shall not be less than 32 percent, nor more than 48 percent, of the average per-pupil expenditure in the United States.

(2) SPECIAL RULE - The number of neglected or delinquent children and youth determined under paragraph (1) shall—

(A) be determined by the State agency by a deadline set by the Secretary, except that no State agency shall be required to determine the number of such children and youth on a specific date set by the Secretary; and

(B) be adjusted, as the Secretary determines is appropriate, to reflect the relative length of such agency's annual programs.

(b) SUBGRANTS TO STATE AGENCIES IN PUERTO RICO -

(1) IN GENERAL - For each fiscal year, the amount of the subgrant which a State agency in the Commonwealth of Puerto Rico shall be eligible to receive under this subpart shall be the amount determined by multiplying the number of children counted under subsection (a)(1)(A) for the Commonwealth of Puerto Rico by the product of—

(A) the percentage which the average per-pupil expenditure in the Commonwealth of Puerto Rico is of the lowest average per-pupil expenditure of any of the 50 States; and

(B) 32 percent of the average per-pupil expenditure in the United States.

(2) MINIMUM PERCENTAGE - The percentage in paragraph (1)(A) shall not be less than

(A) for fiscal year 2002, 77.5 percent;

(B) for fiscal year 2003, 80.0 percent;

(C) for fiscal year 2004, 82.5 percent; and

(D) for fiscal year 2005 and succeeding fiscal years, 85.0 percent.

(3) LIMITATION - If the application of paragraph (2) would result in any of the 50 States or the District of Columbia receiving less under this subpart than it received under this subpart for the preceding fiscal year, then the percentage described in paragraph (1)(A) that is used for the Commonwealth of Puerto Rico for the fiscal year for which the determination is made shall be the greater of—

(A) the percentage in paragraph (1)(A) for such fiscal year; or

(B) the percentage used for the preceding fiscal year.

(c) RATABLE REDUCTIONS IN CASE OF INSUFFICIENT APPROPRIATIONS - If the amount appropriated for any fiscal year for subgrants under subsections (a) and (b) is insufficient to pay the full amount for which all State agencies are eligible under such subsections, the Secretary shall ratably reduce each such amount. (Section 1412 of NCLB Act)

20 U. S. C. § 6433. State reallocation of funds.

If a State educational agency determines that a State agency does not need the full amount of the subgrant for which such State agency is eligible under this subpart for any fiscal year, the State educational agency may reallocate the amount that will not be needed to other eligible State agencies that need additional funds to carry out the purpose of this part, in such amounts as the State educational agency shall determine. (Section 1413 of NCLB Act)

20 U. S. C. § 6434. State plan and State agency applications.

(a) STATE PLAN -

(1) IN GENERAL - Each State educational agency that desires to receive a grant under this subpart shall submit, for approval by the Secretary, a plan—

(A) for meeting the educational needs of neglected, delinquent, and at-risk children and youth;

(B) for assisting in the transition of children and youth from correctional facilities to locally operated programs; and

(C) that is integrated with other programs under this Act or other Acts, as appropriate.

(2) CONTENTS - Each such State plan **shall—**

(A) describe the program **goals, objectives, and performance measures** established by the State that will be used to **assess the effectiveness of the program** in improving the academic, vocational, and technical skills of children in the program;

(B) provide that, to the extent feasible, such children will have the same opportunities to achieve as such children would have if such children were in the schools of local educational agencies in the State; and

(C) contain an assurance that the State educational agency will—

(i) ensure that programs assisted under this sub-part will be carried out in accordance with the State plan described in this subsection;
(ii) carry out the evaluation requirements of section 1431;
(iii) ensure that the State agencies receiving subgrants under this subpart comply with all applicable statutory and regulatory requirements; and
(iv) provide such other information as the Secretary may reasonably require.

(3) DURATION OF THE PLAN - Each such State plan shall—

(A) remain in effect for the duration of the State's participation under this part; and

(B) be periodically reviewed and revised by the State, as necessary, to reflect changes in the State's strategies and programs under this part.

(b) SECRETARIAL APPROVAL AND PEER REVIEW -

(1) SECRETARIAL APPROVAL - The Secretary shall approve each State plan that meets the requirements of this subpart.

(2) PEER REVIEW - The Secretary may review any State plan with the assistance and advice of individuals with relevant expertise.

(c) STATE AGENCY APPLICATIONS - Any State agency that desires to receive funds to carry out a program under this subpart shall submit an application to the State educational agency that—

(1) describes the procedures to be used, consistent with the State plan under section 1111, to assess the educational needs of the children to be served under this subpart;

(2) provide an assurance that in making services available to children and youth in adult correctional institutions, priority will be given to such children and youth who are likely to complete incarceration within a 2-year period;

(3) describes the program, including a budget for the first year of the program, with annual updates to be provided to the State educational agency;

(4) describes how the program will meet the goals and objectives of the State plan;

(5) describes how the State agency will consult with experts and provide the necessary training for appropriate staff, to ensure that the planning and operation of institution-wide projects under section 1416 are of high quality;

(6) describes how the State agency will carry out the evaluation requirements of section 9601 and how the results of the most recent evaluation will be used to plan and improve the program;

(7) includes data showing that the State agency has maintained the fiscal effort required of a local educational agency, in accordance with section 9521;

(8) describes how the programs will be coordinated with other appropriate State and Federal programs, such as programs under title I of Public Law 105–220, vocational and technical education programs, State and local dropout prevention programs, and special education programs;

(9) describes how the State agency will encourage correctional facilities receiving funds under this subpart to coordinate with local educational agencies or alternative education programs attended by incarcerated children and youth prior to their incarceration to ensure that student assessments and appropriate academic records are shared jointly between the correctional facility and the local educational agency or alternative education program;

(10) describes how appropriate professional development will be provided to teachers and other staff;

(11) designates an individual in each affected correctional facility or institution for neglected or delinquent children and youth to be responsible for issues relating to the **transition of children and youth** from such facility or institution to locally operated programs;

(12) describes how the State agency will endeavor to **coordinate with businesses for training and mentoring** for participating children and youth;

(13) provides an assurance that the State agency will assist in **locating alternative programs** through which

students can continue their education if the students are not returning to school after leaving the correctional facility or institution for neglected or delinquent children and youth;

(14) provides assurances that the State agency will **work with parents** to secure parents' assistance in improving the educational achievement of their children and youth, and preventing their children's and youth's further involvement in delinquent activities;

(15) provides an assurance that the State agency will work with **children and youth with disabilities in order to meet an existing individualized education** program and an assurance that the agency will notify the child's or youth's local school if the child or youth—

(A) is **identified as in need of special education services** while the child or youth is in the correctional facility or institution for neglected or delinquent children and youth; and

(B) intends to return to the local school;

(16) provides an assurance that the State agency will work with children and youth who dropped out of school before entering the correctional facility or institution for neglected or delinquent children and youth to encourage the children and youth to reenter school once the term of the incarceration is completed or provide the child or youth with the skills necessary to gain employment, continue the education of the child or youth, or achieve a secondary school diploma or its recognized equivalent if the child or youth does not intend to return to school;

(17) **provides an assurance that teachers and other qualified staff are trained to work with children and youth with disabilities and other students with special needs taking into consideration the unique needs of such students;**

(18) describes any additional services to be provided to children and youth, such as career counseling, distance learning, and assistance in securing student loans and grants; and

(19) provides an assurance that the program under this subpart will be coordinated with any programs operated under the Juvenile Justice and Delinquency Prevention Act of 1974 (42 U.S.C. 5601 et seq.) or other comparable programs, if applicable. (Section 1414 of NCLB Act)

20 U. S. C. § 6435. Use of funds.

(a) USES -

(1) IN GENERAL - A State agency shall use funds received under this subpart only for programs and projects that—

(A) are consistent with the State plan under section 1414(a); and

(B) concentrate on providing participants with the knowledge and skills needed to make a successful transition to secondary school completion, vocational or technical training, further education, or employment.

(2) PROGRAMS AND PROJECTS - Such programs and projects—

(A) may include the acquisition of equipment;

(B) shall be designed to support educational services that—

(i) except for institution-wide projects under section 1416, are provided to children and youth identified by the State agency as failing, or most at-risk of failing, to meet the State's challenging academic content standards and student academic achievement standards;

(ii) supplement and improve the quality of the educational services provided to such children and youth by the State agency; and

(iii) afford such children and youth an opportunity to meet challenging State academic achievement standards;

(C) shall be carried out in a manner consistent with section 1120A and part I (as applied to programs and projects under this part); and

(D) may include the costs of meeting the evaluation requirements of section 9601.

(b) SUPPLEMENT, NOT SUPPLANT - A program under this sub-part that **supplements** the number of hours of instruction students receive from State and local sources shall be considered to comply with **the supplement, not supplant requirement** of section 1120A (as applied to this part) without regard to the subject areas in which instruction is given during those hours. (Section 1415 of NCLB Act)

20 U. S. C. § 6436. Institution-wide projects.

A State agency that provides free public education for children and youth in an institution for neglected or delinquent children and youth (other than an adult correctional institution) or attending a community-day program for such children and youth may use funds received under this subpart to serve all children in, and upgrade the entire educational effort of, that institution or program if the State agency has developed, and the State educational agency has approved, a comprehensive plan for that institution or program that—

(1) provides for a **comprehensive assessment of the educational needs** of all children and youth in the institution or program serving juveniles;

(2) provides for a **comprehensive assessment of the educational needs of youth aged 20 and younger** in adult facilities who are expected to complete incarceration within a 2-year period;

(3) describes the steps the State agency has taken, or will take, to **provide all children and youth under age 21** with the opportunity to meet challenging State academic content standards and student academic achievement standards in order to improve the likelihood that the children and youth will complete secondary school, attain a secondary diploma or its recognized equivalent, or find employment after leaving the institution;

(4) **describes the instructional program, pupil services, and procedures that will be used to meet the needs** described in paragraph (1), including, to the extent feasible, the provision of mentors for the children and youth described in paragraph (1);

(5) specifically describes how such funds will be used;

(6) describes the **measures and procedures that will be used to assess student progress;**

(7) describes how the agency has planned, and will implement and evaluate, the institution-wide or program-wide project in consultation with personnel providing direct instructional services and support services in institutions or community-day programs for neglected or delinquent children and youth, and with personnel from the State educational agency; and

(8) includes an assurance that the State agency has provided for appropriate training for teachers and other instructional and administrative personnel to enable such teachers and personnel to carry out the project effectively. (Section 1416 of NCLB Act)

20 U. S. C. § 6437. Three-year programs or projects.

If a State agency operates a program or project under this subpart in which individual children or youth are likely to participate for more than 1 year, the State educational agency may approve the State agency's application for a subgrant under this subpart for a period of not more than 3 years. (Section 1417 of NCLB Act)

20 U. S. C. § 6438. Transition services.

(a) TRANSITION SERVICES - Each State agency shall reserve not less than 15 percent and not more than 30 percent of the amount such agency receives under this subpart for any fiscal year to support—

(1) projects that facilitate the **transition of children and youth** from State-operated institutions to schools served by local educational agencies; or

(2) the **successful reentry of youth offenders**, who are age 20 or younger and have received a secondary school diploma or its recognized equivalent, into postsecondary education, or vocational and technical training programs, through strategies designed to expose the youth to, and prepare the youth for, postsecondary education, or vocational and technical training programs, such as—

(A) **preplacement programs** that allow adjudicated or incarcerated youth to audit or attend courses on college, university, or community college campuses, or through programs provided in institutional settings;

(B) **worksite schools**, in which institutions of higher education and private or public employers partner to create programs to help students make a **successful transition to postsecondary education and employment**; and

(C) **essential support services to ensure the success of the youth**, such as

(i) personal, vocational and technical, and academic, counseling;
(ii) placement services designed to place the youth in a university, college, or junior college program;
(iii) information concerning, and assistance in obtaining, available student financial aid;
(iv) counseling services; and
(v) job placement services.

(b) CONDUCT OF PROJECTS - A project supported under this section may be conducted directly by the State agency, or through a contract or other arrangement with one or more local educational agencies, other public agencies, or private nonprofit organizations.

(c) RULE OF CONSTRUCTION - Nothing in this section shall be construed to prohibit a school that receives funds under subsection (a) from serving neglected and delinquent children and youth simultaneously with students with similar educational needs, in the same educational settings where appropriate. (Section 1418 of NCLB Act)

20 U. S. C. § 6439. Evaluation; technical assistance; annual model program.

The Secretary may reserve not more than 2.5 percent of the amount made available to carry out this subpart for a fiscal year—

(1) to develop a uniform model to evaluate the effectiveness of programs assisted under this subpart; and

(2) to provide technical assistance to and support the capacity building of State agency programs assisted under this subpart. (Section 1419 of NCLB Act)

SUBPART 2 - LOCAL AGENCY PROGRAMS

➜ **OVERVIEW:** Subpart 2 describes local school district programs for at risk children. Section 6453 is about local educational agency applications. Section 6454 is about uses of funds.

20 U. S. C. § 6451. Purpose.

The purpose of this subpart is to support the operation of **local educational agency programs** that involve collaboration with locally operated correctional facilities—

(1) to carry out high quality education programs to prepare children and youth for secondary school completion, training, employment, or further education;

(2) to provide activities to facilitate the transition of such children and youth from the correctional program to further education or employment; and

(3) to operate programs in local schools for children and youth returning from correctional facilities, and programs which may serve at-risk children and youth. (Section 1421 of NCLB Act)

20 U. S. C. § 6452. Programs operated by local educational agencies.

(a) LOCAL SUBGRANTS - With funds made available under section 1402(b), the State educational agency shall award subgrants to local educational agencies with high numbers or percentages of children and youth residing in locally operated (including county operated) correctional facilities for children and youth (including facilities involved in community day programs).

(b) SPECIAL RULE - A local educational agency that serves a school operated by a correctional facility is not required to operate a program of support for children and youth returning from such school to a school that is not operated by a correctional agency but served by such local educational agency, if more than 30 percent of the children and youth attending the school operated by the correctional facility will reside outside the boundaries served by the local educational agency after leaving such facility.

(c) NOTIFICATION - A State educational agency shall notify local educational agencies within the State of the eligibility of such agencies to receive a subgrant under this subpart.

(d) TRANSITIONAL AND ACADEMIC SERVICES - Transitional and supportive programs operated in local educational agencies under this subpart shall be designed primarily to meet the transitional and academic needs of students returning to local educational agencies or alternative education programs from correctional facilities. Services to students at-risk of dropping out of school shall not have a negative impact on meeting the transitional and academic needs of the students returning from correctional facilities. (Section 1422 of NCLB Act)

20 U. S. C. § 6453. Local educational agency applications.

Each local educational agency desiring assistance under this subpart shall submit an application to the State educational agency that contains such information as the State educational agency may require. Each such application shall include—

(1) a description of the program to be assisted;

(2) a description of formal agreements, regarding the program to be assisted, between—

(A) the local educational agency; and

(B) correctional facilities and alternative school programs serving children and youth involved with the juvenile justice system;

(3) as appropriate, a description of how participating schools will coordinate with facilities working with delinquent children and youth to ensure that such children and youth are participating in an education program comparable to one operating in the local school such youth would attend;

(4) a description of the program operated by participating schools for children and youth returning from correctional facilities and, as appropriate, the types of services that such schools will provide such children and youth and other at-risk children and youth;

(5) a description of the characteristics (including learning difficulties, substance abuse problems, and other special needs) of the children and youth who will be returning from correctional facilities and, as appropriate, other at-risk children and youth expected to be served by the program, and a description of **how the school will coordinate existing educational programs to meet the unique educational needs of such children and youth;**

(6) as appropriate, a description of **how schools will coordinate with existing social, health, and other services** to meet the needs of students returning from correctional facilities, at-risk children or youth, and other participating children or youth, including prenatal health care and nutrition services related to the health of the parent and the child or youth, parenting and child development classes, child care, targeted reentry and outreach programs, referrals to community resources, and scheduling flexibility;

(7) as appropriate, a description of any partnerships with local businesses to develop training, curriculum-based youth entrepreneurship education, and mentoring services for participating students;

(8) as appropriate, a description of **how the program will involve parents** in efforts to improve the educational achievement of their children, assist in dropout prevention activities, and prevent the involvement of their children in delinquent activities;

(9) a description of how the program under this subpart **will be coordinated with other Federal, State, and local programs,** such as programs under title I of Public Law 105–220 and vocational and technical education programs serving at-risk children and youth;

(10) a description of how the **program will be coordinated with programs operated under the Juvenile Justice and Delinquency Prevention Act of 1974** and other comparable programs, if applicable;

(11) as appropriate, a description of **how schools will work with probation officers** to assist in meeting the needs of children and youth returning from correctional facilities;

(12) a description of the **efforts participating schools will make to ensure correctional facilities working with children and youth are aware of a child's or youth's existing individualized education program;** and

(13) as appropriate, a description of the steps participating schools will take to **find alternative placements** for children and youth interested in continuing their education but **unable to participate in a regular public school program.** (Section 1423 of NCLB Act)

20 U. S. C. § 6454. Uses of funds.

Funds provided to local educational agencies under this sub-part may be used, as appropriate, for—

(1) programs that serve children and youth returning to local schools from correctional facilities, **to assist in the transition** of such children and youth **to the school environment** and **help them remain in school** in

order to complete their education;

(2) **dropout prevention programs** which serve at-risk children and youth, including pregnant and parenting teens, children and youth who have come in contact with the juvenile justice system, children and youth at least 1 year behind their expected grade level, migrant youth, immigrant youth, students with limited English proficiency, and gang members;

(3) the **coordination of health and social services** for such individuals if there is a likelihood that the provision of such services, including day care, drug and alcohol counseling, and mental health services, will improve the likelihood such individuals will complete their education;

(4) **special programs to meet the unique academic needs of participating children and youth**, including vocational and technical education, special education, career counseling, curriculum-based youth entrepreneurship education, and assistance in securing student loans or grants for postsecondary education; and

(5) programs providing mentoring and peer mediation. (Section 1424 of NCLB Act)

20 U. S. C. § 6455. Program requirements for correctional facilities receiving funds under this section.

Each correctional facility entering into an agreement with a local educational agency under section 1423(2) to provide services to children and youth under this subpart **shall**—

(1) where feasible, ensure that educational programs in the correctional facility are coordinated with the student's home school, particularly with respect to a student with an **individualized education program** under part B of the Individuals with Disabilities Education Act;

(2) if the **child or youth is identified as in need of special education services** while in the correctional facility, notify the local school of the child or youth of such need;

(3) where feasible, provide **transition assistance** to help the child or youth stay in school, including coordination of services for the family, counseling, assistance in accessing drug and alcohol abuse prevention programs, tutoring, and family counseling;

(4) provide support programs that encourage children and youth who have dropped out of school to reenter school once their term at the correctional facility has been completed, or provide such children and youth with the skills necessary to gain employment or seek a secondary school diploma or its recognized equivalent;

(5) work to ensure that the correctional facility is staffed with teachers and other qualified staff who are trained to work with children and youth with disabilities taking into consideration the unique needs of such children and youth;

(6) ensure that educational programs in the correctional facility are related to assisting students to **meet high academic achievement standards**;

(7) to the extent possible, use technology to assist in coordinating educational programs between the correctional facility and the community school;

(8) where feasible, **involve parents** in efforts to improve the educational achievement of their children and prevent the further involvement of such children in delinquent activities;

(9) coordinate funds received under this subpart with other local, State, and Federal funds available to provide services to participating children and youth, such as funds made available under title I of Public Law

105–220, and vocational and technical education funds;

(10) **coordinate programs** operated under this subpart with activities funded under the Juvenile Justice and Delinquency Prevention Act of 1974 and other comparable programs, if applicable; and

(11) if appropriate, work with local businesses to develop training, curriculum-based youth entrepreneurship education, and mentoring programs for children and youth. (Section 1425 of NCLB Act)

20 U. S. C. § 6456. Accountability.

The State educational agency may—

(1) **reduce or terminate funding** for projects under this subpart **if a local educational agency does not show progress in reducing dropout rates** for male students and for female students **over a 3-year period**; and

(2) **require correctional facilities or institutions** for neglected or delinquent children and youth to demonstrate, after receiving assistance under this subpart for 3 years, that there has been **an increase in the number of children and youth** returning to school, obtaining a secondary school diploma or its recognized equivalent, or obtaining employment after such children and youth are released. (Section 1426 of NCLB Act)

SUBPART 3 - GENERAL PROVISIONS

➜ **OVERVIEW:** Subpart 3 includes requirements about program evaluations. Section 6472 includes several definitions.

20 U. S. C. § 6471. Program evaluations.

(a) SCOPE OF EVALUATION - Each State agency or local educational agency that conducts a program under subpart 1 or 2 shall evaluate the program, disaggregating data on participation by gender, race, ethnicity, and age, not less than once every 3 years, to determine the program's impact on the ability of participants—

(1) to maintain and **improve educational achievement;**

(2) to **accrue school credits** that meet State requirements for grade promotion and secondary school graduation;

(3) to **make the transition** to a regular program or other education program operated by a local educational agency;

(4) to **complete secondary school** (or secondary school equivalency requirements) and **obtain employment** after leaving the correctional facility or institution for neglected or delinquent children and youth; and

(5) as appropriate, to **participate in postsecondary education and job training programs.**

(b) EXCEPTION - The disaggregation required under subsection (a) shall not be required in a case in which the number of students in a category is insufficient to yield statistically reliable information or the results would reveal personally identifiable information about an individual student.

(c) EVALUATION MEASURES - In conducting each evaluation under subsection (a), a State agency or local educational agency shall use multiple and appropriate measures of student progress.

(d) EVALUATION RESULTS - Each State agency and local educational agency shall—

(1) submit evaluation results to the State educational agency and the Secretary; and

(2) **use the results of evaluations under this section to plan and improve subsequent programs** for participating children and youth. (Section 1431 of NCLB Act)

20 U. S. C. § 6472. Definitions.

In this part:

(1) **ADULT CORRECTIONAL INSTITUTION** - The term **'adult correctional institution'** means a facility in which persons (including persons under 21 years of age) are confined as a result of a conviction for a criminal offense.

(2) **AT-RISK** - The term **'at-risk'**, when used with respect to a child, youth, or student, means a school aged individual who is at-risk of academic failure, has a drug or alcohol problem, is pregnant or is a parent, has come into contact with the juvenile justice system in the past, **is at least 1 year behind the expected grade level for the age of the individual,** has limited English proficiency, is a gang member, has dropped out of school in the past, or has a high absenteeism rate at school.

(3) **COMMUNITY DAY PROGRAM** - The term **'community day program'** means a regular program of instruction provided by a State agency at a community day school operated specifically for neglected or delinquent children and youth.

(4) **INSTITUTION FOR NEGLECTED OR DELINQUENT CHILDREN AND YOUTH** - The term **'institution for neglected or delinquent children and youth'** means—

(A) a public or private residential facility, other than a foster home, that is operated for the care of children who have been committed to the institution or voluntarily placed in the institution under applicable State law, due to abandonment, neglect, or death of their parents or guardians; or

(B) a public or private residential facility for the care of children who have been adjudicated to be delinquent or in need of supervision. (Section 1432 of NCLB Act)

PART E – NATIONAL ASSESSMENT OF TITLE I

➡️ **OVERVIEW:** Part E authorizes the National Assessment of Title I and includes information about state standards, state assessment systems and accountability. The essence of Part E is contained in Section 6491 - Evaluations. Section 6493 authorizes an independent review panel to advise the U. S. Department of Education about the effectiveness of the National Assessment and National Longitudinal Study.

Part E, National Assessment of Title I, includes the following four sections.

20 U. S. C. § 6491. Evaluations.
20 U. S. C. § 6492. Demonstrations of innovative practices.
20 U. S. C. § 6493. Assessment evaluation.
20 U. S. C. § 6494. Close Up fellowship program.

20 U. S. C. § 6491. Evaluations.

➡️ **OVERVIEW:** Subsection (a) authorizes the National Assessment of Title I and includes criteria for assessing programs, state definitions of adequate yearly progress, and how information about state report cards will be disseminated to the public. Subsection c describes how data and assessments will be coordinated with the National Longitudinal Study.

(a) NATIONAL ASSESSMENT OF TITLE I -

(1) IN GENERAL - The Secretary **shall conduct a national assessment** of the programs assisted under this title and the impact of this title on States, local educational agencies, schools, and students.

(2) ISSUES TO BE EXAMINED - In conducting the assessment under this subsection, the **Secretary shall examine, at a minimum,** the following:

(A) The **implementation of programs** assisted under this title and the impact of such implementation on increasing student academic achievement (particularly in schools with high concentrations of **children living in poverty**), relative to the goal of all students reaching the proficient level of achievement based on State academic assessments, challenging State academic content standards, and challenging State student academic achievement standards under section 1111.

(B) The types of programs and services that have demonstrated the **greatest likelihood of helping students reach the proficient and advanced levels** of achievement based on State student academic achievement standards and State academic content standards.

(C) The implementation of State academic standards, assessments, and accountability systems developed under this title, including—

(i) the time and cost required for the development of academic assessments for students in grades 3 through 8;
(ii) how well such State assessments meet the requirements for assessments described in this title; and
(iii) the impact of such standards, assessments, and accountability systems on educational programs and instruction at the local level.

(D) Each State's definition of **adequate yearly progress**, including—

(i) the impact of applying this definition to schools, local educational agencies, and the State;
(ii) the number of schools and local educational agencies not meeting this definition; and
(iii) the changes in the identification of schools in need of improvement as a result of such definition.

(E) How schools, local educational agencies, and States have—

(i) **publicized and disseminated the local educational agency report cards** required under section 1111(h)(2) to teachers, school staff, students, parents, and the community;
(ii) used funds made available under this title to provide preschool and family literacy services and the impact of these services on students' school readiness;
(iii) implemented the provisions of section 1118 and afforded parents meaningful opportunities to be involved in the education of their children;
(iv) used Federal, State, and local educational agency funds and resources to support schools and provide technical assistance to improve the achievement of students in low-performing schools, including the impact of the technical assistance on such achievement; and
(v) used State educational agency and local educational agency funds and resources to help schools in which 50 percent or more of the students are from families with incomes below the poverty line meet the requirement described in section 1119 of having all teachers highly qualified not later than the end of the 2005–2006 school year.

(F) The implementation of schoolwide programs and targeted assistance programs under this title and the impact of such programs on improving student academic achievement, including the extent to which schools meet the requirements of such programs.

(G) The extent to which varying models of comprehensive school reform are funded and implemented under this title, and the effect of the implementation of such models on improving achievement of disadvantaged students.

(H) The costs as compared to the benefits of the activities assisted under this title.

(I) The extent to which actions authorized under section 1116 are implemented by State educational agencies and local educational agencies to improve the academic achievement of students in low-performing schools, and the effectiveness of the implementation of such actions, including the following:

(i) The number of schools identified for school improvement and how many years the schools remain in this status.
(ii) The types of support provided by the State educational agencies and local educational agencies to schools and local educational agencies respectively identified as in need of improvement, and the impact of such support on student achievement.
(iii) The number of parents who take advantage of the public school choice provisions of this title, the costs (including transportation costs) associated with implementing these provisions, the implementation of these provisions, and the impact of these provisions (including the impact of attending another school) on student achievement.
(iv) The number of parents who choose to take advantage of the supplemental educational services option, the criteria used by the States to determine the quality of providers, the kinds of services that are available and utilized, the costs associated with implementing this option, and the impact of receiving supplemental educational services on student achievement.
(v) The implementation and impact of actions that are taken with regard to schools and local educational agencies identified for corrective action and restructuring.

(J) The extent to which State and local fiscal accounting requirements under this title affect the flexibility of schoolwide programs.

(K) The implementation and impact of the professional development activities assisted under this title and title II on instruction, student academic achievement, and teacher qualifications.

(L) The extent to which the assistance made available under this title, including funds under section 1002, is targeted to disadvantaged students, schools, and local educational agencies with the greatest need.

(M) The effectiveness of Federal administration assistance made available under this title, including monitoring and technical assistance.

(N) The academic achievement of the groups of students described in section 1111(b)(2)(C)(v)(II).

(O) Such other issues as the Secretary considers appropriate.

(3) SOURCES OF INFORMATION - In conducting the assessment under this subsection, the Secretary shall use information from a variety of sources, including the National Assessment of Educational Progress (carried out under section 411 of the National Education Statistics Act of 1994), State evaluations, and other research studies.

(4) COORDINATION - In carrying out this subsection, the Secretary shall—

(A) coordinate the national assessment under this subsection with the longitudinal study described in subsection (c); and

(B) ensure that the independent review panel described in subsection (d) participates in conducting

the national assessment under this subsection, including planning for and reviewing the assessment.

(5) DEVELOPMENTALLY APPROPRIATE MEASURES - In conducting the national assessment under this subsection, the Secretary shall use developmentally appropriate measures to assess student academic achievement.

(6) REPORTS -

(A) INTERIM REPORT - Not later **than 3 years after the date of enactment** of the No Child Left Behind Act of 2001, the Secretary **shall transmit** to the President, the Committee on Education and the Workforce of the House of Representatives, and the Committee on Health, Education, Labor, and Pensions of the Senate **an interim report** on the national assessment conducted under this subsection.

(B) FINAL REPORT - Not **later than 5 years after the date of enactment** of the No Child Left Behind Act of 2001, the Secretary **shall transmit** to the President, the Committee on Education and the Workforce of the House of Representatives, and the Committee on Health, Education, Labor, and Pensions of the Senate **a final report** on the national assessment conducted under this subsection.

(b) STUDIES AND DATA COLLECTION -

(1) IN GENERAL - In addition to other activities described in this section, the Secretary may, directly or through awarding grants to or entering into contracts with appropriate entities—

(A) assess the implementation and effectiveness of programs under this title;

(B) collect the data necessary to comply with the Government Performance and Results Act of 1993; and

(C) provide guidance and technical assistance to State educational agencies and local educational agencies in developing and maintaining management information systems through which such agencies may develop program performance indicators to improve services and performance.

(2) MINIMUM INFORMATION - In carrying out this subsection, the Secretary **shall collect, at a minimum, trend information on the effect of each program** authorized under this title, which shall complement the data collected and reported under subsections (a) and (c).

(c) NATIONAL LONGITUDINAL STUDY -

➡ **COMMENT:** The National Longitudinal Study focuses on effective educational programs for disadvantaged children. The Study includes an analysis of educational practices and programs that are effective in improving achievement and the effects of school choice options, including transfers from failing schools.

(1) IN GENERAL - The Secretary shall conduct a longitudinal study of schools receiving assistance under part A.

(2) ISSUES TO BE EXAMINED - In carrying out this subsection, the Secretary shall ensure that the study referred to in paragraph (1) provides Congress and educators with each of the following:

(A) An accurate description and analysis of the short-and long-term effect of the assistance made available under this title on academic achievement.

(B) Information that can be used to improve the effectiveness of the assistance made available under this title in enabling students to meet challenging academic achievement standards.

(C) An analysis of educational practices or model programs that are effective in improving the achievement of disadvantaged children.

(D) An analysis of the costs as compared to the benefits of the assistance made available under this title in improving the achievement of disadvantaged children.

(E) An analysis of the **effects of the availability of school choice options** under section 1116 on the academic achievement of disadvantaged students, on schools in school improvement, and on schools from which students have transferred under such options.

(F) Such other information as the Secretary considers appropriate.

(3) SCOPE - In conducting the study referred to in paragraph (1), the Secretary shall ensure that the study—

(A) **bases its analysis on a nationally representative sample of schools participating in programs under this title;**

(B) to the extent practicable, includes in its analysis students who transfer to different schools during the course of the study; and

(C) analyzes varying models or strategies for delivering school services, including—

> (i) schoolwide and targeted services; and
> (ii) comprehensive school reform models.

(d) INDEPENDENT REVIEW PANEL -

(1) **IN GENERAL** - The Secretary shall establish an independent review panel (in this subsection referred to as the '**Review Panel**') to advise the Secretary on methodological and other issues that arise in carrying out **subsections (a) and (c).**

(2) **APPOINTMENT OF MEMBERS -**

(A) **IN GENERAL** - Subject to subparagraph (B), the Secretary shall appoint members of the Review Panel from among qualified individuals who are—

> (i) **specialists in statistics, evaluation, research, and assessment;**
> (ii) **education practitioners, including teachers, principals, and local and State superintendents;**
> (iii) **parents and members of local school boards or other organizations involved with the implementation and operation of programs under this title; and**
> (iv) **other individuals with technical expertise who will contribute to the overall rigor and quality of the program evaluation.**

(B) **LIMITATIONS** - In appointing members of the Review Panel, the Secretary shall ensure that—

> (i) in order to ensure diversity, the Review Panel includes individuals appointed under subparagraph (A)(i) who represent disciplines or programs **outside the field of education**; and
> (ii) the total number of the individuals appointed under **subparagraph (A)(ii) or (A)(iv) does not exceed one-fourth** of the total number of the individuals appointed under this paragraph.

(3) FUNCTIONS - The Review Panel shall consult with and advise the Secretary—

(A) to ensure that the assessment conducted under subsection (a) and the study conducted under subsection (c)—

(i) adhere to the highest possible standards of quality with respect to research design, statistical analysis, and the dissemination of findings; and

(ii) use valid and reliable measures to document program implementation and impacts; and

(B) to ensure

(i) that the final report described in subsection (a)(6)(B) is reviewed not later than 120 days after its completion by not less than two independent experts in program evaluation (who may be from among the members of the Review Panel appointed under paragraph (2));

(ii) that such experts evaluate and comment on the degree to which the report complies with subsection (a); and

(iii) that the comments of such experts are transmitted with the report under subsection (a)(6)(B). (Section 1501 of NCLB Act)

20 U. S. C. § 6492. Demonstrations of innovative practices.

(a) IN GENERAL - From the funds appropriated for any fiscal year under section 1002(e)(1), the Secretary **may award grants** to State educational agencies, local educational agencies, other public agencies, **nonprofit organizations, public or private partnerships involving business and industry organizations**, and consortia of such entities to carry out demonstration projects that show the most promise of enabling children served under this title to meet challenging State academic content standards and challenging State student academic achievement standards.

(b) EVALUATION - The Secretary shall evaluate the demonstration projects supported under this title, **using rigorous methodological designs and techniques, including control groups and random assignment**, to the extent feasible, to produce reliable evidence of effectiveness.

(c) PARTNERSHIPS - From funds appropriated under section 1002(e)(1) for any fiscal year, the Secretary may, directly or through grants or contracts, work in partnership with State educational agencies, local educational agencies, other public agencies, and non-profit organizations to disseminate and use the highest quality research and knowledge about effective practices to improve the quality of teaching and learning in schools assisted under this title. (Section 1502 of NCLB Act)

20 U. S. C. § 6493. Assessment evaluation.

(a) IN GENERAL - The Secretary **shall conduct an independent study of assessments used for State accountability purposes** and **for making decisions about the promotion and graduation of students.** Such research shall be conducted over a period not to exceed 5 years and shall address the components described in subsection (d).

(b) CONTRACT AUTHORIZED - The Secretary is authorized to award a contract, through a peer review process, to an organization or entity capable of conducting rigorous, independent research. The Assistant Secretary of Educational Research and Improvement shall appoint peer reviewers to evaluate the applications for this contract.

(c) STUDY - The study shall—

(1) synthesize and analyze existing research that meets standards of quality and scientific rigor; and

(2) evaluate academic assessment and accountability systems in State educational agencies, local educational agencies, and schools; and

(3) make recommendations to the Department and to the Committee on Education and the Workforce of the United States House of Representatives and the Committee on Health, Education, Labor, and Pensions of the United States Senate, based on the findings of the study.

(d) COMPONENTS OF THE RESEARCH PROGRAM - The study described in subsection (a) shall examine—

(1) the effect of the assessment and accountability systems described in section (c) on students, teachers, parents, families, schools, school districts, and States, including correlations between such systems and—

(A) **student academic achievement, progress to** the State-defined level of **proficiency**, and **progress toward closing achievement gaps, based on independent measures;**

(B) changes in course offerings, teaching practices, course content, and instructional material;

(C) changes in **turnover rates among teachers, principals, and pupil-services personnel;**

(D) **changes in dropout, grade-retention, and graduation rates for students;** and

(E) such other effects as may be appropriate;

(2) the effect of the academic assessments on students with disabilities;

(3) the effect of the academic assessments on low, middle, and high socioeconomic status students, limited and nonlimited English proficient students, racial and ethnic minority students, and nonracial or nonethnic minority students;

(4) guidelines for assessing the validity, reliability, and consistency of those systems using nationally recognized professional and technical standards;

(5) the relationship between accountability systems and the inclusion or exclusion of students from the assessment system; and

(6) such other factors as the Secretary finds appropriate.

(e) REPORTING - Not later than 3 years after the contract described in subsection (b) is awarded, the organization or entity conducting the study shall submit an interim report to the Committee on Education and the Workforce of the United States House of Representatives and the Committee on Health, Education, Labor and Pensions of the United States Senate, and to the President and the States, and shall make the report widely available to the public. The organization or entity shall submit a final report to the same recipients as soon as possible after the completion of the study. Additional reports may be periodically prepared and released as necessary.

(f) RESERVATION OF FUNDS - The Secretary may reserve up to 15 percent of the funds authorized to be appropriated for this part to carry out the study, except such reservation of funds shall not exceed $1,500,000. (Section 1503 of NCLB Act)

20 U. S. C. § 6494. Close Up fellowship program.

(a) PROGRAM FOR MIDDLE SCHOOL AND SECONDARY SCHOOL STUDENTS -

(1) ESTABLISHMENT -

(A) GENERAL AUTHORITY - In accordance with this subsection, the Secretary may make grants to the Close Up Foundation of Washington, District of Columbia, a non-partisan, nonprofit foundation, for the purpose of assisting the Close Up Foundation in carrying out its programs **of increasing civic responsibility and understanding of the Federal Government** among middle school and secondary school **students**.

(B) USE OF FUNDS - Grants under this subsection shall be used only to provide financial assistance to economically disadvantaged students who participate in the programs described in subparagraph (A).

(C) NAME OF FELLOWSHIPS - Financial assistance received by students pursuant to this subsection shall be known as Close Up fellowships.

(2) APPLICATIONS -

(A) APPLICATION REQUIRED - No grant under this subsection may be made except upon an application at such time, in such manner, and accompanied by such information as the Secretary may reasonably require.

(B) CONTENTS OF APPLICATION - Each application submitted under this paragraph shall contain assurances that—

(i) Close Up fellowships provided under this subsection shall be made to economically disadvantaged middle school and secondary school students;
(ii) every effort shall be made to ensure the participation of students from rural, small town, and urban areas;
(iii) in awarding the fellowships to economically disadvantaged students, special consideration shall be given to the participation of those students with special educational needs, including students with disabilities, ethnic minority students, and students with migrant parents; and
(iv) the funds received under this subsection shall be properly disbursed.

(b) PROGRAM FOR MIDDLE SCHOOL AND SECONDARY SCHOOL TEACHERS -

(1) ESTABLISHMENT -

(A) GENERAL AUTHORITY - In accordance with this subsection, the Secretary may make grants to the Close Up Foundation of Washington, District of Columbia, a non-partisan, nonprofit foundation, for the purpose of assisting the Close Up Foundation in carrying out its programs of professional development for middle school and secondary school **teachers** and its programs to increase civic responsibility and understanding of the Federal Government among the teachers' students.

(B) USE OF FUNDS - Grants under this subsection shall be used **only to provide financial assistance to teachers** who participate in the programs described in subparagraph (A).

(C) NAME OF FELLOWSHIPS - Financial assistance received by teachers pursuant to this subsection shall be known as **Close Up fellowships**.

(2) APPLICATIONS -

(A) APPLICATION REQUIRED - No grant under this subsection may be made except upon an application at such time, in such manner, and accompanied by such information as the Secretary may reasonably require.

(B) CONTENTS OF APPLICATION - Each application submitted under this paragraph shall contain assurances that—

(i) Close Up fellowships provided under this subsection shall be made only to a teacher who has worked with at least one student from such teacher's school who participates in a program described in subsection (a)(1)(A);

(ii) no teacher shall receive more than one such fellowship in any fiscal year; and

(iii) the funds received under this subsection shall be properly disbursed.

(c) PROGRAMS FOR NEW AMERICANS -

(1) ESTABLISHMENT -

(A) GENERAL AUTHORITY - In accordance with this subsection, the Secretary may make grants to the Close Up Foundation of Washington, District of Columbia, a non-partisan, nonprofit foundation, for the purpose of assisting the Close Up Foundation in carrying out its programs of increasing civic responsibility and understanding of the Federal Government among **economically disadvantaged middle school and secondary school recent immigrant students.**

(B) DEFINITION - In this subsection, the term **'recent immigrant student'** means a student who is a member of a family that immigrated to the United States within 5 years of the student's participation in such a program.

(C) USE OF FUNDS - Grants under this subsection shall be used **only to provide financial assistance to economically disadvantaged recent immigrant students and their teachers** who participate in the programs described in subparagraph (A).

(D) NAME OF FELLOWSHIPS - Financial assistance received by students and teachers pursuant to this subsection shall be known as Close Up Fellowships for New Americans.

(2) APPLICATIONS -

(A) APPLICATION REQUIRED - No grant under this subsection may be made except upon an application at such time, in such manner, and accompanied by such information as the Secretary may reasonably require.

(B) CONTENTS OF APPLICATION - Each application submitted under this paragraph shall contain assurances that—

(i) Close Up Fellowships for New Americans shall be made to **economically disadvantaged middle school and secondary school recent immigrant students;**

(ii) every effort shall be made to ensure the participation of recent immigrant students from rural, small town, and urban areas;

(iii) in awarding the fellowships to economically disadvantaged recent immigrant students, special consideration shall be given to the participation of those students with special educational needs, including students with disabilities, students with migrant parents, and ethnic minority students;

(iv) fully describe the activities to be carried out with the proceeds of the grant made under paragraph (1); and

(v) the funds received under this subsection shall be properly disbursed.

(d) GENERAL PROVISIONS -

(1) ADMINISTRATIVE PROVISIONS -

(A) ACCOUNTABILITY - In consultation with the Secretary, the Close Up Foundation shall devise and implement procedures to measure the efficacy of the programs authorized in subsections (a), (b), and (c) in attaining objectives that include the following:

(i) Providing young people with an increased understanding of the Federal Government.
(ii) Heightening a sense of civic responsibility among young people.
(iii) Enhancing the skills of educators in teaching young people about civic responsibility, the Federal Government, and attaining citizenship competencies.

(B) GENERAL RULE - Payments under this section may be made in installments, in advance, or by way of reimbursement, with necessary adjustments on account of underpayments or overpayments.

(C) AUDIT RULE - The Comptroller General of the United States or any of the Comptroller General's duly authorized representatives shall have access for the purpose of audit and examination to any books, documents, papers, and records that are pertinent to any grant under this section.

(2) CONTINUATION OF AWARDS - Notwithstanding any other provision of this Act, any person or entity that was awarded a grant under part G of title X before the date of enactment of the No Child Left Behind Act of 2001 shall continue to receive funds in accordance with the terms of such award until the date on which the award period terminates under such terms. (Section 1504 of NCLB Act)

PART F—COMPREHENSIVE SCHOOL REFORM

➤ **OVERVIEW:** The purpose of Part F is to provide financial incentives to schools that develop comprehensive school reform strategies for basic academics and parental involvement. Section 6514 focuses on state uses of funds and priorities. Section 6516 is about local district use of funds to enable schools to implement school reforms.

Part F, Comprehensive School Reform, includes the following sections.

20 U. S. C. § 6511. Purpose.
20 U. S. C. § 6512. Program authorization.
20 U. S. C. § 6513. State applications.
20 U. S. C. § 6514. State use of funds.
20 U. S. C. § 6515. Local applications.
20 U. S. C. § 6516. Local use of funds.
20 U. S. C. § 6517. Evaluation and reports.
20 U. S. C. § 6518. Quality initiatives.

20 U. S. C. § 6511. Purpose.

The purpose of this part is to provide **financial incentives for schools to develop comprehensive school reforms, based upon scientifically based research and effective practices that include an emphasis on basic academics and parental involvement** so that all children can meet challenging State academic content and academic achievement standards. (Section 1601 of NCLB Act)

20 U. S. C. § 6512. Program authorization.

(a) PROGRAM AUTHORIZED -

(1) IN GENERAL - The Secretary is authorized to **award grants to State educational agencies**, from allotments under paragraph (2), **to enable the State educational agencies to award subgrants to local educational agencies** to carry out the purpose described in section 1601.

(2) ALLOTMENTS -

(A) RESERVATIONS - Of the amount appropriated under section 1002(f), the Secretary may reserve—

(i) not more than 1 percent for each fiscal year to provide assistance to schools supported by the Bureau of Indian Affairs and in the United States Virgin Islands, Guam, American Samoa, and the Commonwealth of the Northern Mariana Islands according to their respective needs for assistance under this part;

(ii) not more than 1 percent for each fiscal year to conduct national evaluation activities described in section 1607; and

(iii) not more than 3 percent of the amount appropriated in fiscal year 2002 to carry out this part, for quality initiatives described in section 1608.

(B) IN GENERAL - Of the amount appropriated under section 1002(f) that remains after making the reservation under subparagraph (A) for a fiscal year, the Secretary shall allot to each State for the fiscal year an amount that bears the same ratio to the remainder for that fiscal year as the amount made available under section 1124 to the State for the preceding fiscal year bears to the total amount made available under section 1124 to all States for that year.

(C) REALLOTMENT - If a State does not apply for funds under this section, the Secretary shall reallot such funds to other States that do apply in proportion to the amount allotted to such other States under subparagraph (B). (Section 1602 of NCLB Act)

20 U. S. C. § 6513. State applications.

(a) IN GENERAL - Each State educational agency that desires to receive a grant under this part shall submit an application to the Secretary at such time, in such manner, and containing such information as the Secretary may reasonably require.

(b) CONTENTS - Each such **application** shall describe—

(1) the process and selection criteria by which the State educational agency, **using expert review**, will select local educational agencies to receive subgrants under this part;

(2) how the State educational agency will ensure that funds under this part are **limited to comprehensive school reform programs** that—

(A) include each of the components described in section 1606(a);

(B) have the capacity to improve the academic achievement of all students in **core academic subjects** within participating schools; and

(C) are supported by technical assistance providers that have a successful track record, financial stability, and the capacity to deliver high quality materials, professional development for school personnel, and on-site support during the full implementation period of the reforms;

(3) **how the State educational agency will disseminate materials** and information on comprehensive school reforms that are **based on scientifically based research and effective practices**;

(4) how the State educational agency will **evaluate annually** the implementation of such reforms and **measure** the extent to which the reforms have resulted in **increased student academic achievement**; and

(5) how the State educational agency will provide technical assistance to the local educational agency or consortia of local educational agencies, and to participating schools, in evaluating, developing, and implementing comprehensive school reform. (Section 1603 of NCLB Act)

20 U. S. C. § 6514. State use of funds.

(a) IN GENERAL - Except as provided in subsection (e), a State educational agency that receives a grant under this part shall use the grant funds to award subgrants, on a **competitive basis**, to local educational agencies or consortia of local educational agencies in the State that receive funds under part A, to support comprehensive school reforms in schools that are eligible for funds under part A.

(b) SUBGRANT REQUIREMENTS - A subgrant to a local educational agency or consortium shall be—

(1) of sufficient size and scope to support the initial costs of comprehensive school reforms selected or designed by each school identified in the application of the local educational agency or consortium;

(2) in an amount not less than $50,000—

(A) for each participating school; or

(B) for each participating consortium of small schools (which for purposes of this subparagraph means a consortium of small schools serving a total of not more than 500 students); and

(3) renewable for two additional 1-year subgrant periods after the initial 1-year subgrant is made if the school is or the schools are making substantial progress in the implementation of reforms.

(c) PRIORITY - A State educational agency, in awarding subgrants under this part, shall give **priority** to local educational agencies or consortia that—

(1) plan to use the funds in schools identified as being in need of improvement or corrective action under section 1116(c); and

(2) demonstrate a commitment to assist schools with budget allocation, professional development, and other strategies necessary to ensure the comprehensive school reforms are properly implemented and are sustained in the future.

(d) GRANT CONSIDERATION - In awarding subgrants under this part, the State educational agency shall take into consideration the equitable distribution of subgrants to different geographic regions within the State, including urban and rural areas, and to schools serving elementary and secondary students.

(e) ADMINISTRATIVE COSTS - A State educational agency that receives a grant under this part **may reserve not more than 5 percent of the grant funds for administrative, evaluation, and technical assistance expenses.**

(f) SUPPLEMENT - Funds made available under this part shall be used to **supplement, and not supplant,** any other Federal, State, or local funds that would otherwise be available to carry out the activities assisted under this part.

(g) REPORTING - Each State educational agency that receives a grant under this part shall provide to the Secretary such information as the Secretary may require, including the names of local educational agencies and schools receiving assistance under this part, the amount of the assistance, a description of the comprehensive school reforms selected and used, and a copy of the State's annual evaluation of the implementation of comprehensive school reforms supported under this part and the student achievement results. (Section 1604 of NCLB Act)

20 U. S. C. § 6515. Local applications.

(a) IN GENERAL - Each local educational agency or consortium of local educational agencies desiring a subgrant under this part shall submit an application to the State educational agency at such time, in such manner, and containing such information as the State educational agency may reasonably require.

(b) CONTENTS - Each such **application shall—**

(1) identify the schools that are eligible for assistance under part A and plan to implement a comprehensive school reform program, including the projected costs of such a program;

(2) **describe the comprehensive school reforms based on scientifically based research and effective practices that such schools will implement;**

(3) describe how the local educational agency or consortium will provide technical assistance and support for the effective implementation of the comprehensive school reforms based on scientifically based research and effective practices selected by such schools; and

(4) **describe how the local educational agency or consortium will evaluate the implementation** of such comprehensive school reforms and measure the results achieved in improving student academic achievement. (Section 1605 of NCLB Act)

20 U. S. C. § 6516. Local use of funds.

(a) USES OF FUNDS - A local educational agency or consortium that receives a subgrant under this part shall provide the subgrant funds to schools that are eligible for assistance under part A and served by the agency, to enable the schools to implement a comprehensive school reform program that—

(1) employs **proven strategies and proven methods for student learning, teaching, and school management that are based on scientifically based research and effective practices and have been replicated successfully in schools;**

(2) integrates a comprehensive design for effective school functioning, including **instruction, assessment, classroom management, professional development, parental involvement, and school management**, that **aligns the school's curriculum, technology, and professional development into a comprehensive school reform plan for schoolwide change** designed to enable all students to meet challenging State content and student academic achievement standards and addresses needs identified through a school needs assessment;

(3) provides **high quality and continuous teacher and staff professional development;**

(4) **includes measurable goals for student academic achievement and benchmarks for meeting such goals;**

(5) is supported by teachers, principals, administrators, school personnel staff, and other professional staff;

(6) provides support for teachers, principals, administrators, and other school staff;

(7) provides for the **meaningful involvement of parents** and the local community in planning, implementing, and evaluating school improvement activities consistent with section 1118;

(8) uses high quality external technical support and assistance from an entity that has experience and expertise in schoolwide reform and improvement, which may include an institution of higher education;

(9) includes a plan for the **annual evaluation** of the implementation **of school reforms and the student results achieved;**

(10) identifies other resources, including Federal, State, local, and private resources, that shall be used to coordinate services that will support and sustain the comprehensive school reform effort; and

(11)

(A) has been found, through scientifically based research to significantly improve the academic achievement of students participating in such program as compared to students in schools who have not participated in such program; or

(B) has been found to have strong evidence that such program will significantly improve the academic achievement of participating children.

(b) SPECIAL RULE - A school that receives funds to develop a comprehensive school reform program shall not be limited to using nationally available approaches, but may develop the school's own comprehensive school reform program for schoolwide change as described in subsection (a). (Section 1606 of NCLB Act)

20 U. S. C. § 6517. Evaluation and reports.

(a) IN GENERAL - The Secretary shall develop a plan for a national evaluation of the programs assisted under this part.

(b) EVALUATION - The national evaluation shall—

(1) evaluate the implementation and results achieved by schools after 3 years of implementing comprehensive school reforms; and

(2) assess the effectiveness of comprehensive school reforms in schools with diverse characteristics.

(c) REPORTS - The Secretary shall submit a **report** describing the results of the evaluation under subsection (b) for the Comprehensive School Reform Program to the Committee on Education and the Workforce, and the Committee on Appropriations of the House of Representatives, and the Committee on Health, Education, Labor, and Pensions, and the Committee on Appropriations of the Senate. (Section 1607 of NCLB Act)

20 U. S. C. § 6518. Quality initiatives.

The Secretary, through grants or contracts, shall provide funds for—

(1) **a public-private effort, in which funds are matched by private organizations**, to assist States, local educational agencies, and schools, in making informed decisions regarding approving or selecting **providers** of comprehensive school reform, consistent with the requirements described in section 1606(a); and

(2) activities to foster the development of comprehensive school reform models and to provide effective capacity building for comprehensive school reform providers to expand their work in more schools, assure quality, and promote financial stability. (Section 1608 of NCLB Act)

PART G—ADVANCED PLACEMENT PROGRAMS

➜ OVERVIEW: Part G about Advanced Placement Programs notes that 600,000 students who take advanced placement courses every year do not take advanced placement exams. The purposes of Part G are:

to provide access and increase participation in advanced placement courses;
to increase access to highly trained teachers for low-income and disadvantaged students; and
to increase the number of students who receive advanced placement test scores.

Grants are available for advanced placement test fees. The number of students who take advanced placement classes and the number who take advanced placement tests will be reported by demographic and socio-economic status. Section 6537 includes definitions.

Part G, Advanced Placement Programs, includes the following sections.

20 U. S. C. § 6531. Short title.
20 U. S. C. § 6532. Purposes.
20 U. S. C. § 6533. Funding distribution rule.
20 U. S. C. § 6534. Advanced placement test fee program.
20 U. S. C. § 6535. Advanced placement incentive program grants.
20 U. S. C. § 6536. Supplement, not supplant.
20 U. S. C. § 6537. Definitions.

20 U. S. C. § 6531. Short title.

This part may be cited as the '**Access to High Standards Act**'. (Section 1701 of NCLB Act)

20 U. S. C. § 6532. Purposes.

The purposes of this part are—

(1) to support State and local efforts to **raise academic standards through advanced placement programs**, and thus further **increase the number of students who participate and succeed in advanced placement programs;**

(2) to encourage more of the 600,000 students who take advanced placement courses each year but do not take advanced placement exams each year, to **demonstrate their achievements through taking the exams;**

(3) to build on the many benefits of advanced placement programs for students, which benefits may include the acquisition of skills that are important to many employers, Scholastic Aptitude Test (SAT) scores that are 100 points above the national averages, and the achievement of better grades in secondary school and in college than the grades of students who have not participated in the programs;

(4) to increase the availability and **broaden the range of schools**, including middle schools, that have advanced placement and pre-advanced placement programs;

(5) to demonstrate that larger and more diverse groups of students can participate and succeed in advanced placement programs;

(6) to **provide greater access to advanced placement and pre-advanced placement courses** and **highly trained teachers for low-income and other disadvantaged students;**

(7) to **provide access to advanced placement courses** for secondary school students **at schools that do not offer advanced placement programs**, increase the rate at which secondary school students participate in advanced placement courses, and increase the numbers of students who receive advanced placement test scores for which college academic credit is awarded;

(8) to **increase the participation of low-income individuals in taking advanced placement tests** through the payment or partial payment of the costs of the advanced placement test fees; and

(9) to **increase the number of individuals that achieve a baccalaureate or advanced degree,** and to decrease the amount of time such individuals require to attain such degrees. (Section 1702 of NCLB Act)

20 U. S. C. § 6533. Funding distribution rule.

From amounts appropriated under section 1002(g) for a fiscal year, the Secretary shall give priority to funding activities under section 1704 and shall distribute any remaining funds under section 1705. (Section 1703 of NCLB

Act)

20 U. S. C. § 6534. Advanced placement test fee program.

(a) GRANTS AUTHORIZED - From amounts made available under section 1703 for a fiscal year, the Secretary shall grants to State educational agencies having applications approved under this section to enable the State educational agencies to reimburse low-income individuals to cover part or all of the costs of advanced placement test fees, if the low-income individuals—

(1) are enrolled in an advanced placement course; and

(2) plan to take an advanced placement test.

(b) AWARD BASIS - In determining the amount of the grant awarded to a State educational agency under this section for a fiscal year, the Secretary shall consider the number of children eligible to be counted under section 1124(c) in the State in relation to the number of such children so counted in all the States.

(c) INFORMATION DISSEMINATION - A State educational agency awarded a grant under this section shall disseminate information regarding the availability of advanced placement test fee payments under this section to eligible individuals through secondary school teachers and guidance counselors.

(d) APPLICATIONS - Each State educational agency desiring to receive a grant under this section shall submit an application to the Secretary at such time, in such manner, and accompanied by such information as the Secretary may require. At a minimum, each State educational agency application shall—

(1) describe the advanced placement test fees the State educational agency will pay on behalf of low-income individuals in the State from grant funds awarded under this section;

(2) provide an assurance that any grant funds awarded under this section shall be used only to pay for advanced placement test fees; and

(3) contain such information as the Secretary may require to demonstrate that the State educational agency will ensure that a student is eligible for payments authorized under this section, including documentation required under chapter 1 of subpart 2 of part A of title IV of the Higher Education Act of 1965.

(e) REGULATIONS - The Secretary shall prescribe such regulations as are necessary to carry out this section.

(f) REPORT -

(1) IN GENERAL - Each State educational agency awarded a grant under this section **shall**, with respect to each advanced placement subject, **annually report** to the Secretary on—

(A) the number of students in the State who are taking an advanced placement course in that subject;

(B) the number of advanced placement tests taken by students in the State who have taken an advanced placement course in that subject;

(C) the number of students in the State scoring at different levels on advanced placement tests in that subject; and

(D) demographic information regarding individuals in the State taking advanced placement courses and tests in that subject disaggregated by race, ethnicity, sex, English proficiency status, and socioeconomic status.

(2) REPORT TO CONGRESS - The Secretary shall annually compile the information received from each State educational agency under paragraph (1) and report to the appropriate committees of Congress regarding the information.

(g) BIA AS SEA - For purposes of this section the Bureau of Indian Affairs shall be treated as a State educational agency. (Section 1704 of NCLB Act)

20 U. S. C. § 6535. Advanced placement incentive program grants.

(a) GRANTS AUTHORIZED -

(1) IN GENERAL - From amounts made available under section 1703 for a fiscal year, the Secretary shall award grants, on a competitive basis, to eligible entities to enable those entities to carry out the authorized activities described in subsection (d).

(2) DURATION AND PAYMENTS -

(A) DURATION - The Secretary shall award a grant under this section for a period of not more than 3 years.

(B) PAYMENTS - The Secretary shall make grant payments under this section on an annual basis.

(3) DEFINITION OF ELIGIBLE ENTITY - In this section, the term 'eligible entity' means a State educational agency, local educational agency, or national nonprofit educational entity with expertise in advanced placement services.

(b) APPLICATION - Each eligible entity desiring a grant under this section shall submit an application to the Secretary at such time, in such manner, and accompanied by such information as the Secretary may require.

(c) PRIORITY - In awarding grants under this section, the Secretary shall give priority to an eligible entity that submits an application under subsection (b) that—

(1) demonstrates a pervasive need for access to advanced placement incentive programs;

(2) provides for the involvement of business and community organizations in the activities to be assisted;

(3) assures the availability of matching funds from State, local, or other sources to pay for the cost of activities to be assisted;

(4) demonstrates a focus on developing or expanding advanced placement programs and participation in the core academic areas of English, mathematics, and science;

(5) demonstrates an intent to carry out activities that target—

(A) local educational agencies serving schools with a high concentration of low-income students; or

(B) schools with a high concentration of low-income students; and

(6) in the case of a local educational agency, assures that the local educational agency serves schools with a high concentration of low-income students; or

(7) demonstrates an intent to carry out activities to increase the availability of, and participation in, on-line advanced placement courses.

(d) AUTHORIZED ACTIVITIES -

(1) IN GENERAL - Subject to paragraph (2), an eligible entity shall use grant funds made available under this section to expand access for low-income individuals to advanced placement incentive programs that involve—

(A) teacher training;

(B) pre-advanced placement course development;

(C) coordination and articulation between grade levels to prepare students for academic achievement in advanced placement courses;

(D) books and supplies; or

(E) activities to increase the availability of, and participation in, on-line advanced placement courses; or

(F) any other activity directly related to expanding access to and participation in advanced placement incentive programs, particularly for low-income individuals.

(2) STATE EDUCATIONAL AGENCY - In the case of an eligible entity that is a State educational agency, the entity may use grant funds made available under this section to award subgrants to local educational agencies to enable the local educational agencies to carry out the activities under paragraph (1).

(e) CONTRACTS - An eligible entity awarded a grant to provide online advanced placement courses under this part may enter into a contract with a nonprofit or for profit organization to provide the online advanced placement courses, including contracting for necessary support services.

(f) DATA COLLECTION AND REPORTING -

(1) DATA COLLECTION - Each eligible entity awarded a grant under this section **shall**, with respect to each advanced placement subject, **annually report** to the Secretary on—

(A) the number of students served by the eligible entity who are taking an advanced placement course in that subject;

(B) the number of advanced placement tests taken by students served by the eligible entity in that subject;

(C) the number of students served by the eligible entity scoring at different levels on advanced placement tests in that subject; and

(D) demographic information regarding individuals served by such agency who taking advanced placement courses and tests in that subject disaggregated by race, ethnicity, sex, English proficiency status, and socioeconomic status.

(2) REPORT - The Secretary shall annually compile the information received from each eligible entity under paragraph (1) and report to the appropriate committees of Congress regarding the information. (Section 1705 of NCLB Act)

20 U. S. C. § 6536. Supplement, not supplant.

Grant funds provided under this part shall supplement, and not supplant, other non-Federal funds that are available to assist low-income individuals to pay for the cost of advanced placement test fees or to expand access to advanced placement and pre-advanced placement courses. (Section 1706 of NCLB Act)

20 U. S. C. § 6537. Definitions.

In this part:

(1) **ADVANCED PLACEMENT TEST** - The term **'advanced placement test'** means an advanced placement test administered by the College Board or approved by the Secretary.

(2) **HIGH CONCENTRATION OF LOW-INCOME STUDENTS** - The term **'high concentration of low-income students'**, used with respect to a school, means a school that serves a student population 40 percent or more of whom are low-income individuals.

(3) **LOW-INCOME INDIVIDUAL** - The term **'low-income individual'** means an individual who is determined by a State educational agency or local educational agency to be a child, ages 5 through 17, from a low-income family, on the basis of data used by the Secretary to determine allocations under section 1124 of this Act, data on children eligible for free or reduced-price lunches under the National School Lunch Act, data on children in families receiving assistance under part A of title IV of the Social Security Act, or data on children eligible to receive medical assistance under the medicaid program under title XIX of the Social Security Act, or through an alternate method that combines or extrapolates from those data. (Section 1707 of NCLB Act)

PART H—SCHOOL DROPOUT PREVENTION

➔ **OVERVIEW:** The purposes of Part H are to prevent students from dropping out and to raise academic achievement levels.

Part H has two Subparts:

Subpart 1 - Coordinated National Strategy
Subpart 2 - School Dropout Prevention Initiative

Part H, School Dropout Prevention, includes the initial three sections followed by two subparts.

20 U. S. C. § 6551. Short title.
20 U. S. C. § 6552. Purpose.
20 U. S. C. § 6553. Authorization of appropriations.

Subpart 1—Coordinated National Strategy

20 U. S. C. § 6555. National activities.

Subpart 2—School Dropout Prevention Initiative

20 U. S. C. § 6561. Definitions. In this Subpart:
20 U. S. C. § 6561a. Program authorized.
20 U. S. C. § 6561b. Applications.
20 U. S. C. § 6561c. State reservation.
20 U. S. C. § 6561d. Strategies and capacity building
20 U. S. C. § 6561e. Selection of local educational agencies for subgrants.
20 U. S. C. § 6561f. Community based organizations.
20 U. S. C. § 6561g. Technical assistance.
20 U. S. C. § 6561h. School dropout rate calculation.
20 U. S. C. § 6561i. Reporting and accountability.

20 U. S. C. § 6551. Short title.

This part may be cited as the 'Dropout Prevention Act'. (Section 1801 of NCLB Act)

20 U. S. C. § 6552. Purpose.

The purpose of this part is to provide for **school dropout prevention and reentry** and to **raise academic achievement levels** by providing grants that—

(1) challenge all children to attain their highest academic potential; and

(2) ensure that all students have substantial and ongoing opportunities to attain their highest academic potential through schoolwide programs proven effective in school dropout prevention and reentry. (Section 1802 of NCLB Act)

20 U. S. C. § 6553. Authorization of appropriations.

For the purpose of carrying out this part, there are authorized to be appropriated $125,000,000 for fiscal year 2002 and such sums as may be necessary for each of the 5 succeeding fiscal years, of which—

(1) 10 percent shall be available to carry out subpart 1 for each fiscal year; and

(2) 90 percent shall be available to carry out subpart 2 for each fiscal year. (Section 1803 of NCLB Act)

SUBPART 1—COORDINATED NATIONAL STRATEGY

➡ **OVERVIEW:** Subpart 1 describes the Coordinated National Strategy that collects data and coordinates research into effective dropout prevention programs. Subpart 1 establishes a national recognition program to recognize and provide monetary rewards to schools that initiate comprehensive reforms.

20 U. S. C. § 6555. National activities.

(a) IN GENERAL - The Secretary is authorized—

(1) to **collect systematic data on the effectiveness of the programs** assisted under this part **in reducing school dropout rates and increasing school reentry and secondary school graduation rates;**

(2) to **establish a national clearinghouse of information on effective school dropout prevention and reentry programs** that shall disseminate to State educational agencies, local educational agencies, and schools—

(A) the results of research on school dropout prevention and reentry; and

(B) information on effective programs, best practices, and Federal resources to—

(i) reduce annual school dropout rates;
(ii) increase school reentry; and
(iii) increase secondary school graduation rates;

(3) to **provide technical assistance** to State educational agencies, local educational agencies, and schools in designing and implementing programs and securing resources **to implement effective school dropout prevention and reentry programs;**

(4) to establish and consult with an interagency working group that shall—

(A) address inter - and intra-agency program coordination issues at the Federal level with respect to school dropout prevention and reentry, and assess the targeting of existing Federal services to students who are most at risk of dropping out of school, and the cost-effectiveness of various programs and approaches used to address school dropout prevention and reentry;

(B) describe the ways in which State educational agencies and local educational agencies can implement effective school dropout prevention and reentry programs using funds from a variety of Federal programs, including the programs under this part; and

(C) examine Federal programs that may have a positive impact on secondary school graduation or school reentry;

(5) to carry out **a national recognition program** in accordance with subsection (b) that recognizes schools that have made extraordinary progress in lowering school dropout rates; and

(6) to use funds made available for this subpart to carry out the evaluation required under section 1830(c).

(b) RECOGNITION PROGRAM -

(1) ESTABLISHMENT - The Secretary shall—

(A) establish a **national recognition program**; and

(B) develop **uniform national guidelines** for the recognition program that shall be used to recognize eligible schools from nominations submitted by State educational agencies.

(2) RECOGNITION - The Secretary shall recognize, under the recognition program established under paragraph (1), eligible schools.

(3) SUPPORT - The Secretary may **make monetary awards** to an eligible school recognized under this subsection in amounts determined appropriate by the Secretary that shall be used for dissemination activities within the eligible school district or nationally.

(4) DEFINITION OF ELIGIBLE SCHOOL - In this subsection, the term **'eligible school'** means a public middle school or secondary school, including a charter school, that **has implemented comprehensive reforms** that have been **effective in lowering school dropout rates for all students**—

(A) in that secondary school or charter school; or

(B) in the case of a middle school, in the secondary school that the middle school feeds students into.

(c) CAPACITY BUILDING -

(1) IN GENERAL - The Secretary, through a **contract** with one or more **non-Federal entities**, may conduct a **capacity building and design initiative** in order to increase the types of proven strategies for school dropout prevention and reentry that **address the needs of an entire school population** rather than a subset of students.

(2) NUMBER AND DURATION.

than 5 years.

(d) SUPPORT FOR EXISTING REFORM NETWORKS -

(1) IN GENERAL - The Secretary may provide appropriate support to eligible entities to enable the eligible entities to provide training, materials, development, and staff assistance to schools assisted under this part.

(2) DEFINITION OF ELIGIBLE ENTITY - In this subsection, the term **'eligible entity'** means an entity that, prior to the date of enactment of the Dropout Prevention Act—

(A) provided training, technical assistance, and materials related to school dropout prevention or reentry to 100 or more elementary schools or secondary schools; and

(B) developed and published a specific educational program or design related to school dropout prevention or reentry for use by the schools. (Section 1811 of NCLB Act)

SUBPART 2—SCHOOL DROPOUT PREVENTION INITIATIVE

➡ **OVERVIEW:** Subpart 2, the School Dropout Prevention Initiative, provides grants to states and local school districts for effective school dropout prevention and reentry programs. These grants may be used for various purposes, including professional development, curricular materials, remedial education, reduction of pupil-teacher ratios, efforts to meet state academic achievement standards, counseling and mentoring, and comprehensive school reform models.

20 U. S. C. § 6561. Definitions. In this subpart:

(1) LOW-INCOME STUDENT - The term **'low-income student'** means a student who is determined by a local educational agency to be from a low-income family using the measures described in section 1113(c).

(2) STATE - The term **'State'** means each of the several States of the United States, the District of Columbia, the Commonwealth of Puerto Rico, the United States Virgin Islands, Guam, American Samoa, the Commonwealth of the Northern Mariana Islands, and the Bureau of Indian Affairs for purposes of serving schools funded by the Bureau. (Section 1821 of NCLB Act)

20 U. S. C. § 6561a. Program authorized.

(a) GRANTS TO STATE EDUCATIONAL AGENCIES AND LOCAL EDUCATIONAL AGENCIES -

(1) AMOUNT LESS THAN $75,000,000 -

(A) IN GENERAL - If the amount appropriated under section 1803 for a fiscal year equals or is less than $75,000,000, then the Secretary shall use such amount **to award grants, on a competitive basis**, to—

    (i) **State educational agencies** to support activities—
        (I) in schools that—
            (aa) serve students in grades 6 through 12; and
            (bb) have annual school dropout rates that are above the State average annual school dropout rate; or
        (II) in the middle schools that feed students into the schools described in subclause (I); or
    (ii) **local educational agencies** that operate—
        (I) schools that—
            (aa) serve students in grades 6 through 12; and
            (bb) have annual school dropout rates that are above the State average annual school

dropout rate; or

(II) middle schools that feed students into the schools described in subclause (I).

(B) USE OF GRANT FUNDS - Grant funds awarded under this paragraph shall be used to **fund effective, sustainable, and coordinated school dropout prevention and reentry programs** that may include the activities described in subsection (b)(2), in—

(i) schools serving students in grades 6 through 12 that have **annual school dropout rates that are above the State average** annual school dropout rate; or

(ii) the middle schools that feed students into the schools described in clause (i).

(2) AMOUNT LESS THAN $250,000,000 BUT MORE THAN $75,000,000 - If the amount appropriated under section 1803 for a fiscal year is less than $250,000,000 but more than $75,000,000, then the Secretary shall use such amount to **award grants, on a competitive basis**, to State educational agencies to enable the State educational agencies to award subgrants under subsection (b).

(3) AMOUNT EQUAL TO OR EXCEEDS $250,000,000 - If the amount appropriated under section 1803 for a fiscal year equals or exceeds $250,000,000, then the Secretary shall use such amount to award **a grant to each State educational agency** in an amount that bears the same relation to such appropriated amount as the amount the State educational agency received under part A for the preceding fiscal year bears to the amount received by all State educational agencies under such part for the preceding fiscal year, to enable the State educational agency to award subgrants under subsection (b).

(b) SUBGRANTS TO LOCAL EDUCATIONAL AGENCIES -

(1) IN GENERAL - From amounts made available to a State educational agency under paragraph (2) or (3) of subsection (a), the State educational agency shall award subgrants, **on a competitive basis, to local educational agencies** that operate public schools that serve students in grades 6 through 12 and that have **annual school dropout rates that are above the State average** annual school dropout rate, to enable those schools, or the middle schools that feed students into those schools, to implement effective, sustainable, and coordinated school dropout prevention and reentry programs that involve activities such as—

(A) **professional development**;

(B) obtaining **curricular materials**;

(C) release time for professional **staff to obtain professional development**;

(D) **planning and research**;

(E) **remedial education**;

(F) reduction in **pupil-to-teacher ratios**;

(G) efforts to **meet State student academic achievement standards**;

(H) **counseling and mentoring** for at-risk students;

(I) implementing **comprehensive school reform models**, such as creating smaller learning communities; and

(J) **school reentry activities**.

(2) **AMOUNT** - Subject to paragraph (3), a subgrant under this subpart shall be awarded—

(A) in the **first year** that a local educational agency receives a subgrant payment under this subpart, in an amount that is based on factors such as—

    (i) the size of schools operated by the local educational agency;
    (ii) costs of the model or set of prevention and reentry strategies being implemented; and
    (iii) local cost factors such as **poverty rates;**

(B) in the **second year**, in an amount that is not less than **75 percent** of the amount the local educational agency received under this subpart in the first such year;

(C) in the third year, in an amount that is not less than **50 percent** of the amount the local educational agency received under this subpart in the first such year; and

(D) in each succeeding year, in an amount that is not less than **30 percent** of the amount the local educational agency received under this subpart in the first year.

(3) DURATION - A subgrant under this subpart shall be awarded for a period of **3 years**, and may be continued for a period of 2 additional years if the State educational agency determines, based on the annual reports described in section 1830(a), that significant progress has been made in lowering the annual school dropout rate for secondary schools participating in the program assisted under this subpart. (Section 1822 of NCLB Act)

20 U. S. C. § 6561b. Applications.

(a) IN GENERAL - To receive—

(1) a grant under this subpart, a State educational agency or local educational agency shall submit an application and plan to the Secretary at such time, in such manner, and accompanied by such information as the Secretary may reasonably require; and

(2) a subgrant under this subpart, a local educational agency shall submit an application and plan to the State educational agency at such time, in such manner, and accompanied by such information as the State educational agency may reasonably require.

(b) CONTENTS -

(1) STATE EDUCATIONAL AGENCY AND LOCAL EDUCATIONAL AGENCY - Each **application and plan** submitted under subsection (a) **shall**—

    (A) **include an outline**—

        (i) of the State educational agency's or local educational agency's **strategy for reducing** the State educational agency or local educational agency's **annual school dropout rate;**
        (ii) for **targeting secondary schools, and the middle schools** that feed students into those secondary schools, that have the **highest annual school dropout rates;** and
        (iii) for **assessing the effectiveness of the efforts described in the plan;**

    (B) contain an **identification of the schools** in the State or operated by the local educational agency that have annual school dropout rates that are greater than the average annual school dropout rate for the State;

    (C) **describe the instructional strategies to be implemented,** how the strategies will serve all students, and the **effectiveness of the strategies;**

(D) describe a budget and **timeline** for implementing the strategies;

(E) contain **evidence of coordination** with existing resources;

(F) provide an assurance that funds provided under this subpart will **supplement, and not supplant**, other State and local funds available for school dropout prevention and reentry programs; and

(G) **describe how the activities to be assisted conform with research knowledge about school dropout prevention and reentry.**

(2) **LOCAL EDUCATIONAL AGENCY** - Each application and plan submitted under subsection (a) by a local educational agency shall contain, in addition to the requirements of paragraph (1)—

(A) **an assurance that the local educational agency is committed to providing ongoing operational support for such schools to address the problem of school dropouts for a period of 5 years; and**

(B) an assurance that the local educational agency will support the plan, including—

(i) provision of **release time for teacher training;**
(ii) efforts to coordinate activities for secondary schools and the middle schools that feed students into those secondary schools; and
(iii) encouraging other schools served by the local educational agency to participate in the plan. (Section 1823 of NCLB Act)

20 U. S. C. § 6561c. State reservation.

A State educational agency that receives a grant under paragraph (2) or (3) of section 1822(a) may **reserve not more than 5 percent of the grant funds for administrative costs** and State activities related to school dropout prevention and reentry activities, of which not more than 2 percent of the grant funds may be used for administrative costs. (Section 1824 of NCLB Act)

20 U. S. C. § 6561d. Strategies and capacity building

Each local educational agency receiving a grant or subgrant under this subpart and each State educational agency receiving a grant under this subpart **shall implement scientifically based, sustainable, and widely replicated strategies for school dropout prevention and reentry.** The strategies may include—

(1) **specific strategies** for targeted purposes, such as—

(A) **effective early intervention programs** designed to identify at-risk students;

(B) effective programs serving **at-risk students**, including racial and ethnic minorities and pregnant and parenting teenagers, designed to prevent such students from dropping out of school; and

(C) effective programs to identify and **encourage youth who have already dropped out of school to reenter school** and complete their secondary education; and

(2) approaches such as **breaking larger schools down into smaller learning communities** and other comprehensive reform approaches, creating alternative school programs, and developing clear linkages to career skills and employment. (Section 1825 of NCLB Act)

20 U. S. C. § 6561e. Selection of local educational agencies for subgrants.

(a) STATE EDUCATIONAL AGENCY REVIEW AND AWARD - The State educational agency shall review applications submitted under section 1823(a)(2) and award subgrants to local educational agencies with the assistance and advice of a panel of experts on school dropout prevention and reentry.

(b) ELIGIBILITY - A local educational agency is eligible to receive a subgrant under this subpart if the local educational agency operates a public school (including a public alternative school)—

(1) that is eligible to receive assistance under part A; and

(2)
  (A) that serves students 50 percent or more of whom are low-income students; or

  (B) in which a majority of the students come from feeder schools that serve students 50 percent or more of whom are low-income students. (Section 1826 of NCLB Act)

20 U. S. C. § 6561f. Community based organizations.

A local educational agency that receives a grant or subgrant under this subpart and a State educational agency that receives a grant under this subpart **may use the funds to secure necessary services from a community-based organization** or other government agency if the funds are used to provide school dropout prevention and reentry activities related to schoolwide efforts. (Section 1827 of NCLB Act)

20 U. S. C. § 6561g. Technical assistance.

Notwithstanding any other provision of law, each local educational agency that receives funds under this subpart shall use the funds to provide technical assistance to secondary schools served by the agency that have not made progress toward lowering annual school dropout rates after receiving assistance under this subpart for 2 fiscal years. (Section 1828 of NCLB Act)

20 U. S. C. § 6561h. School dropout rate calculation.

For purposes of calculating an annual school dropout rate under this subpart, a school **shall use the annual event school dropout rate** for students leaving a school in a single year determined **in accordance with the National Center for Education Statistics' Common Core of Data.** (Section 1829 of NCLB Act)

20 U. S. C. § 6561i. Reporting and accountability.

(a) LOCAL EDUCATIONAL AGENCY REPORTS -

(1) **IN GENERAL** - To receive funds under this subpart for a fiscal year **after the first fiscal year** that a local educational agency receives funds under this subpart, the local educational agency **shall provide, on an annual basis, a report** regarding the status of the implementation of activities funded under this subpart, and the **dropout data for students** at schools assisted under this subpart, **disaggregated by race and ethnicity**, to the—

  (A) Secretary, if the local educational agency receives a grant under section 1822(a)(1); or
  (B) State educational agency, if the local educational agency receives a subgrant under paragraph (2) or (3) of section 1822(a).

(2) **DROPOUT DATA** - The dropout data under paragraph (1) shall include annual school dropout rates for each fiscal year, starting with the 2 fiscal years before the local educational agency received funds under this subpart.

(b) STATE REPORT ON PROGRAM ACTIVITIES - Each State educational agency receiving funds under this subpart shall provide to the Secretary, at such time and in such format as the Secretary may require, information on the status of the implementation of activities funded under this subpart and outcome data for students in schools assisted under this subpart.

(c) ACCOUNTABILITY - The Secretary shall evaluate the effect of the activities assisted under this subpart on school dropout prevention compared, if feasible, to a control group using control procedures. The Secretary may use funds appropriated for subpart 1 to carry out this evaluation. (Section 1830 of NCLB Act)

PART I- GENERAL PROVISIONS

➜ **OVERVIEW:** Part I authorizes the Department of Education to issue No Child Left Behind regulations. Regulations issued by a federal agency are first published in the Federal Register (FR) as proposed regulations. After final regulations are enacted, these regulations are published in the Federal Register and the Code of Federal Regulations. (C.F.R.)

The No Child Left Behind regulations are published in Volume 34 of the Code of Federal Regulations.

States that receive funds under No Child Left Behind shall create State committees of practitioners that will review proposed regulations to ensure that state rules, regulations, and policies conform to the purposes of the No Child Left Behind statute. States shall eliminate or modify State and local fiscal accounting requirements so schools can consolidate funds for schoolwide programs.

Section 6575 clarifies that Title I does not authorize any Federal Government employee to control the instructional content, academic achievement standards and assessments, curriculum, or program of instruction of any State, school district or school. Title I does not require states, local school districts or schools to implement accept equal spending per pupil.

Part I, General Provisions, includes the following sections.

> 20 U. S. C. § 6571. Federal regulations.
> 20 U. S. C. § 6572. Agreements and records.
> 20 U. S. C. § 6573. State administration.
> 20 U. S. C. § 6574. Local educational agency spending audits.
> 20 U. S. C. § 6575. Prohibition against Federal mandates, direction, or control.
> 20 U. S. C. § 6576. Rule of construction on equalized spending.
> 20 U. S. C. § 6577. State report on dropout data.
> 20 U. S. C. § 6578. Regulations for sections 6311 and 6316.

20 U. S. C. § 6571. Federal regulations.

(a) IN GENERAL - The Secretary may issue such regulations as are necessary to reasonably ensure that there is compliance with this title.

(b) NEGOTIATED RULEMAKING PROCESS -

(1) IN GENERAL - Before publishing in the Federal Register proposed regulations to carry out this title, the Secretary shall obtain the advice and recommendations of representatives of Federal, State, and local administrators, parents, teachers, paraprofessionals, and members of local school boards and other organizations involved with the implementation and operation of programs under this title.

(2) MEETINGS AND ELECTRONIC EXCHANGE - Such advice and recommendations may be obtained through such mechanisms as regional meetings and electronic exchanges of information.

(3) PROPOSED REGULATIONS - After obtaining such advice and recommendations, and before publishing proposed regulations, the Secretary shall—

(A) establish a negotiated rulemaking process on, at a minimum, standards and assessments;

(B) select individuals to participate in such process from among individuals or groups that provided advice and recommendations, including representation from all geographic regions of the United States, in such numbers as will provide an equitable balance between representatives of parents and students and representatives of educators and education officials; and

(C) prepare a draft of proposed policy options that shall be provided to the individuals selected by the Secretary under subparagraph (B) not less than 15 days before the first meeting under such process.

(4) PROCESS - Such process—

(A) shall be conducted in a timely manner to ensure that final regulations are issued by the Secretary not later than 1 year after the date of enactment of the No Child Left Behind Act of 2001; and

(B) shall not be subject to the Federal Advisory Committee Act, but shall otherwise follow the provisions of the Negotiated Rulemaking Act of 1990 (5 U.S.C. 561 et seq.).

(5) EMERGENCY SITUATION - In an emergency situation in which regulations to carry out this title must be issued within a very limited time to assist State educational agencies and local educational agencies with the operation of a program under this title, the Secretary may issue proposed regulations without following such process but shall, immediately thereafter and before issuing final regulations, conduct regional meetings to review such proposed regulations.

(c) LIMITATION - Regulations to carry out this part may not require local programs to follow a particular instructional model, such as the provision of services outside the regular classroom or school program. (Section 1901 of NCLB Act)

20 U. S. C. § 6572. Agreements and records.

(a) AGREEMENTS - All published proposed regulations shall conform to agreements that result from negotiated rulemaking described in section 1901 unless the Secretary reopens the negotiated rulemaking process or provides a written explanation to the participants involved in the process explaining why the Secretary decided to depart from, and not adhere to, such agreements.

(b) RECORDS - The Secretary shall ensure that an accurate and reliable record of agreements reached during the negotiations process is maintained. (Section 1902 of NCLB Act)

20 U. S. C. § 6573. State administration.

(a) RULEMAKING -

(1) IN GENERAL - Each State that receives funds under this title shall—

(A) ensure that any State rules, regulations, and policies relating to this title conform to the purposes of this title and provide any such proposed rules, regulations, and policies to the committee of practitioners created under subsection (b) for review and comment;

(B) minimize such rules, regulations, and policies to which the State's local educational agencies and schools are subject;

(C) eliminate or modify State and local fiscal accounting requirements in order to facilitate the ability of schools to consolidate funds under schoolwide programs; and

(D) identify any such rule, regulation, or policy as a State-imposed requirement.

(2) SUPPORT AND FACILITATION - State rules, regulations, and policies under this title shall support and facilitate local educational agency and school-level systemic reform designed to enable all children to meet the challenging State student academic achievement standards.

(b) COMMITTEE OF PRACTITIONERS -

(1) IN GENERAL - Each State educational agency that receives funds under this title shall create a **State committee of practitioners** to advise the State in carrying out its responsibilities under this title.

(2) MEMBERSHIP - Each such committee shall include—

(A) **as a majority of its members, representatives from local educational agencies;**

(B) **administrators,** including the administrators of programs described in other parts of this title;

(C) **teachers,** including vocational educators;

(D) **parents;**

(E) members of local **school boards;**

(F) **representatives of private school children;** and

(G) **pupil services personnel.**

(3) DUTIES - The duties of **such committee shall include a review, before publication, of any proposed or final State rule or regulation** pursuant to this title. In an emergency situation where such rule or regulation must be issued within a very limited time to assist local educational agencies with the operation of the program under this title, the State educational agency may issue a regulation without prior consultation, but shall immediately thereafter convene the State committee of practitioners to review the emergency regulation before issuance in final form. (Section 1903 of NCLB Act)

20 U. S. C. § 6574. Local educational agency spending audits.

(a) AUDITS - The Comptroller General of the United States shall conduct audits of not less than 6 local educational agencies that receive funds under part A in each fiscal year to determine more clearly and specifically how local educational agencies are expending such funds. Such audits—

(1) shall be conducted in 6 local educational agencies that represent the size, ethnic, economic, and geographic diversity of local educational agencies; and

(2) shall examine the extent to which funds have been expended for academic instruction in the core curriculum and activities unrelated to academic instruction in the core curriculum, such as the payment of janitorial, utility, and other maintenance services, the purchase and lease of vehicles, and the payment for travel and attendance costs at conferences.

(b) REPORT - Not later than 3 months after the completion of the audits under subsection (a) each year, the Comptroller General of the United States shall submit a report on each audit to the Committee on Education and the Workforce of the House of Representatives and the Committee on Health, Education, Labor and Pensions of the Senate. (Section 1904 of NCLB Act)

20 U. S. C. § 6575. Prohibition against Federal mandates, direction, or control.

Nothing in this title **shall be construed** to authorize an officer or employee of the Federal Government to mandate, direct, or control a State, local educational agency, or school's **specific instructional content, academic achievement standards and assessments, curriculum, or program of instruction.** (Section 1905 of NCLB Act)

20 U. S. C. § 6576. Rule of construction on equalized spending.

Nothing in this title shall be construed to **mandate equalized spending per pupil** for a State, local educational agency, or school. (Section 1906 of NCLB Act)

20 U. S. C. § 6577. State report on dropout data.

Not later than 1 year after a State educational agency receives funds under this title, the agency **shall report** to the Secretary and statewide, all school district data regarding **annual school drop-out rates** in the State disaggregated by race and ethnicity according to procedures that conform with the National Center for Education Statistics' Common Core of Data. (Section 1907 of NCLB Act)

20 U. S. C. § 6578. Regulations for sections 6311 and 6316.

The Secretary shall issue regulations for sections 1111 and 1116 not later than 6 months after the date of enactment of the No Child Left Behind Act of 2001. (Section 1908 of NCLB Act)

END OF TITLE I

FOR YOUR NOTES

APPENDIX A

GLOSSARY OF ACRONYMS, ABBREVIATIONS AND TERMS

In compiling these definitions from the No Child Left Behind statute, regulations, and guidance publications from the U. S. Department of Education, the authors shortened some definitions. If you need to use a definition, be sure to get the full definition from the No Child Left Behind Act.

Depending on where a term is located in the No Child Left Behind statute, a word may have more than one definition.

ACRONYMS AND ABBREVIATIONS

ADA	Americans with Disabilities Act
AYP	Adequate Yearly Progress
CSR	Class-size Reduction
EDGAR	Education Department General Administrative Regulations
ESEA	Elementary and Secondary Education Act of 1965
ESL	English as a Second Language
FY	Fiscal Year
HEA	Higher Education Act
IDEA	Individuals with Disabilities Education Act
IHE	Institution of Higher Education
LEA	Local Educational Agency (school district)
NCLB	No Child Left Behind, the Act that amended ESEA
OMB	Office of Management and Budget
RFP	Request for Proposal
SAHE	State Agency for Higher Education
SEA	State educational agency
Secretary	Secretary of Education, U.S. Department of Education
Department	The U.S. Department of Education

GLOSSARY OF TERMS

Accountability System. Each state sets academic standards for what students should know and learn. Student achievement is measured with tests and test results are reported to the public. (20 U. S. C. § 6311)

Achievement Gap. The difference between high- and low-performing children, especially the gaps between minority and non-minority students, and between disadvantaged children and their more advantaged peers. (20 U. S. C. § 6301)

Adequate Yearly Progress (AYP). Refers to annual improvement that states, school districts and schools must make each year, as measured by academic assessments, so that all public elementary and secondary schools have the same high academic standards. (20 U. S. C. § 6311)

Alaska Native Organization. A federally recognized tribe, consortium of tribes, nonprofit Native association, or organization that has expertise in educating Alaska Natives. (20 U. S. C. § 7546)

Alternative Certification. States are encouraged states to offer alternative methods of teacher certification so talented individuals are encouraged to teach subjects they know. (20 U. S. C. § 6613)

Arts and Sciences. An institution of higher education that offer majors in content areas that correspond to academic subjects taught; an academic subject or content area that is an academic major. (20 U. S. C. § 6602)

Assessment. Another word for "test." States are required to align their academic standards and academic assessments.

Average Daily Attendance. The number of days that students attend in one school year, divided by the number of school days. (20 U. S. C. § 7801)

Average Per-pupil Expenditure. Expenditures divided by the number of children who attend school daily. (20 U. S. C. § 7801)

Beginning Teacher. A public school teacher who has taught less than three full school years. (20 U. S. C. § 7801)

Bureau. Bureau of Indian Affairs of the Department of the Interior. (25 U. S. C. § 2021)

Charter School. Independent public schools that operate under public supervision but outside traditional public school systems. Charter schools are exempt from many state and local rules, do not charge tuition, have a performance contract that specifies how the charter school will measure student performance, and complies with federal civil rights and education laws. (20 U. S. C. § 7221i)

Child. A person within the age limits for which the State provides free public education. Note: Sections of NCLB define child differently. (20 U. S. C. § 7801)

Child with a Disability. A child with mental retardation, hearing impairments (including deafness), speech or language impairments, visual impairments (including blindness), emotional disturbance, orthopedic impairments, autism, traumatic brain injury, other health impairments, or specific learning disabilities; and who needs special education and related services. (20 U. S. C. § 1401(3(A)) (See *Wrightslaw: Special Education Law*)

Classroom-Based Instructional Reading Assessment. A reading assessment that relies on teacher observations. (20 U. S. C. § 6368)

Community Based Organization. A private nonprofit organization of demonstrated effectiveness, Indian tribe, or tribally sanctioned educational authority that represents a community or segments of a community and that provides educational or related services to individuals in the community. The term includes Native Hawaiian or Native American Pacific Islander native language educational organizations. (20 U. S. C. § 7011)

Community College. An institution of higher education as defined in section 101 of the Higher Education Act of 1965 that provides not less than a 2-year program that is acceptable for full credit toward a bachelor's degree; includes institutions that receive assistance under the Tribally Controlled College or University Assistance Act of 1978. (20 U. S. C. § 7011)

Comprehension. The ability to understand and gain meaning from reading. (20 U. S. C. § 6613)

Consolidated Local Application. An application submitted by a local educational agency pursuant to section 9305. (20 U. S. C. § 7801)

Consolidated Local Plan. A plan submitted by a local educational agency (school district) pursuant to section 9305. (20 U. S. C. § 7801)

Consolidated State Application. An application submitted by a State educational agency pursuant to section 9302. (20 U. S. C. § 7801)

Consolidated State Plan. A plan submitted by a State educational agency pursuant to section 9302. (20 U. S. C. § 7801)

Core Academic Subjects. English, reading or language arts, mathematics, science, foreign languages, civics and government, economics, arts, history, and geography. (20 U. S. C. § 7801)

Corrective Action. A Title I school that failed to meet its adequate yearly progress (AYP) goals after it was identified for school improvement for two consecutive years. In general, the school failed to meet its AYP goals for four consecutive years after it was identified for school improvement. (20 U. S. C. § 6316)

County. A division of a State used by the Secretary of Commerce in compiling and reporting data regarding counties. (20 U. S. C. § 7801)

Current Expenditures. Expenditures for free public education including administration, instruction, attendance and health services, transportation, plant operation and maintenance, and expenditures for food services and student body activities; does not include expenditures for community services, capital outlay, or debt service, or expenditures from funds received under title I and part A of title V. (20 U. S. C. § 7801)

Department. The Department of Education. (20 U. S. C. § 7801)

Diagnostic Reading Assessment. A valid, reliable assessment that is based on scientifically based reading research that is used to identify a child's areas of strengths and weaknesses so the child learns to read by the end of third grade. A diagnostic reading assessment determines difficulties a child has in learning to read, the cause of these difficulties, an d possible reading intervention strategies and related special needs. (20 U. S. C. § 6368)

Director. The Director of the Office of English Language Acquisition, Language Enhancement, and Academic Achievement for Limited English Proficient Students established by the Department of Education Organization Act. (20 U. S. C. § 7011)

Disaggregated Data. The practice of sorting test results into groups of students (i.e., economically disadvantaged, racial and ethnic minority groups, disabilities, or limited English fluency) to allow parents and teachers to see how each group is performing. (20 U. S. C. § 6311)

Distance Learning. Transmission of educational or instructional programming to geographically dispersed individuals and groups via telecommunications. (20 U. S. C. § 7801)

Distinguished Schools. Schools that make the greatest gains in closing the achievement gap or exceed adequate yearly progress serve as models for other schools and provide support to other schools. (20 U. S. C. § 6317)

Early Reading First. Federal grants to school districts and public or private organizations for early language, literacy, and pre-reading for preschool children, especially children for low-income families. (20 U. S. C. § 6371)

Educational Service Agency. A regional public multi-service agency authorized by State statute to develop, manage, and provide services or programs to local educational agencies. (20 U. S. C. § 7801)

Elementary School. A nonprofit day or residential school or public elementary charter school that provides elementary education. (20 U. S. C. § 7801)

Eligible Local Educational Agency. A local educational agency with a high number or percentage of students in kindergarten through third grade who are reading below grade level. (20 U. S. C. § 6362)

Eligible Partnership. An institution of higher education that prepares teachers and principals, a school of arts and sciences; and a high-need local educational agency. (20 U. S. C. § 6631)

Eligible Professional Development Provider. A provider of reading instruction that is based on scientifically based reading research. (20 U. S. C. § 6368)

Eligible Student/Child. For the purposes of public school choice, eligible students must attend Title I schools that are in need of improvement, in corrective action, or restructuring. Note: This differs from eligibility for supplemental educational services.

Essential Components of Reading Instruction. Explicit and systematic instruction in phonemic awareness, phonics, vocabulary development, reading fluency, oral reading skills, and reading comprehension strategies. (20 U.S.C. § 6368)

Exemplary Teacher. A highly qualified teacher who taught for at least five years in a public school, private school, or institution of higher education, is regarded as exemplary by administrators and other teachers, and helps others improve instructional strategies and skills. (20 U. S. C. § 7801)

Family Education Program. A language instruction program or alternative instruction program designed to help limited English proficient adults and youth become proficient in English; provides instruction on how parents and family can facilitate the educational achievement of children. (20 U. S. C. § 7011)

Family Literacy Services. Services that are sufficiently intense to enable a family to make sustainable changes; include specific activities. (20 U. S. C. § 7801)

Flexibility. A way to fund public education; gives states and school districts authority in how they use federal funds in exchange for accountability for results. (20 U. S. C. § 7315)

Fluency. The capacity to read text accurately and quickly. (20 U. S. C. § 6613)

Free Public Education. Elementary or secondary education provided at public expense, under public supervision and direction, and without charge; does not include education beyond grade 12. (20 U. S. C. § 7491)

Gifted and Talented. Students who are capable of high achievement in intellectual, creative, artistic, or leadership areas or academic fields and who need services or activities to develop these capabilities. (20 U. S. C. § 7801)

High-Need LEA. A school district that serves at least 10,000 children from families with incomes below the poverty line or at least 20 percent of the children from families with incomes below the poverty line, with a high percentage of teachers who are not highly qualified or a high percentage of teachers who are working with emergency, provisional, or temporary certificates or licenses. (20 U. S. C. § 6602)

Highly Qualified Teacher. New teachers and teachers in Title 1 programs who are certified by the state or pass the state teacher examination, have training in the subject area they teach, and hold a license to teach. Elementary school teachers must demonstrate knowledge of teaching math and reading. Middle and high school teachers must have majors in the subjects they teach or demonstrate knowledge of that subject. Teachers who were employed when NCLB was enacted must be highly certified by 2005. Teachers who are working under license or certification waivers are not highly qualified. (20 U. S. C. § 7801)

Highly Qualified Charter School Teacher. A charter school teacher who complies with state requirements about certification or licensure. (20 U. S. C. § 7801)

Highly Qualified Paraprofessional. A paraprofessional hired after NCLB was enacted must have a high school diploma or equivalent, complete two years of study at a college or university, have an associate's degree (minimum), or take a rigorous skills test. (20 U. S. C. § 6319)

Homeless Children and Youth. Children and youth who do not have a fixed, regular, nighttime residence. Includes children who live in motels, hotels, trailer parks, or campgrounds; children who live in emergency shelters; children who are abandoned or are waiting for foster care placement; children who live in cars, parks, public spaces, abandoned buildings, substandard housing, bus or train stations; and migratory children who are homeless. (20 U. S. C. § 11434a)

Immigrant Children and Youth. Individuals between the ages of 3 and 21 who were not born in the United States and have not attended school in a state for more than three full academic years. (20 U. S. C. § 7011)

Indian. A member of an Indian tribe or band, as membership is defined by the tribe or band; a descendant of an individual described above; an Eskimo, Aleut, or other Alaska Native. (20 U. S. C. § 7491)

Indian Tribe. An Indian tribe, band, nation, or other organized group or community, including a Native village as defined in the Alaska Native Claims Settlement Act, that is eligible for the special programs and services provided to Indians because of their status as Indians. (25 U. S. C. § 2511)

Institution of Higher Education. Meaning given to term in section 101(a) of the Higher Education Act of 1965. (20 U. S. C. § 7801)

Instructional Material. Instructional content provided to a student; includes print and audio-visual materials and electronic or digital materials (Title X, Sec. 1061)

Instructional Staff. Individuals who are responsible for teaching children to read; includes principals, teachers, library media specialists, teachers of academic subjects, and other individuals who are responsible for teaching children to read. (20 U. S. C. § 6368)

Language Instruction Educational Program. An instruction course to develop English proficiency for English-language learners; meets state academic content and student academic achievement standards; may use English and the child's native language to enable the child to attain English proficiency; is designed to enable all children to be proficient in English and a second language. (20 U. S. C. § 7011)

Limited English Proficient. An individual between the ages of 3 and 21 who attends an elementary school or secondary school, who was not born in the United States or whose native language is not English, who may be a Native American, Alaska Native, or a resident of the outlying areas, or a migratory child whose native language is not English. The individual's difficulties in speaking, reading, writing, or understanding English may not permit the individual to be proficient on state assessments. (20 U. S. C. § 7801)

Local Educational Agency (LEA). A board of education or public authority that has administrative control or direction of public schools and is recognized as an administrative agency for public schools. (20 U. S. C. § 7801)

Low-Performing School. An elementary school or secondary school that is identified as in need of improvement. (20 U. S. C. § 6631)

Mentoring. The process by which a responsible individual provides a positive role model for a child, forms a supportive relationship with the child, and provides academic help and exposure to new experiences and opportunities. (20 U. S. C. § 7801)

National Assessment of Educational Progress (NAEP). Assessments in reading, mathematics, science, writing, U.S. history, geography, civics, and the arts; is the only nationally representative, continuing assessment of what American students know and can do in various subjects. (20 U.S.C. § 9010)

Native American and Native American Language. These terms have the same meaning given those terms in section 103 of the Native American Languages Act of 1990. (20 U. S. C. § 7011)

Native Hawaiian. A citizen of the United States who is a descendant of the aboriginal people who occupied the area that now comprises the State of Hawaii as evidenced by genealogical records, Kupuna (elders) or Kamaaina (long-term community residents) verification, or certified birth records. (20 U. S. C. § 7117)

Native Hawaiian Community Based Organization. An organization composed primarily of Native Hawaiians from a specific community that assists in the social, cultural, and educational development of Native Hawaiians in that community. (20 U. S. C. § 7517)

Native Hawaiian Educational Organization. A private nonprofit organization that serves Native Hawaiians, has Native Hawaiians in policy-making positions, incorporates Native Hawaiian perspective, values, language, culture, and traditions, demonstrates expertise in the education of Native Hawaiian youth, and demonstrates expertise in research and program development. (20 U. S. C. § 7517)

Native Hawaiian Language. The Native American language indigenous to the original inhabitants of the State of Hawaii. (20 U. S. C. § 7517)

Native Hawaiian; Native American Pacific Islander Native Language Educational Organization. A nonprofit organization whose board and employees are fluent speakers of the Native American languages used in the organization's educational programs, and that has at least five years successful experience in providing educational services in traditional Native American languages. (20 U. S. C. § 7011)

Native Hawaiian Organization. A private nonprofit organization that serves the interests of Native Hawaiians, has Native Hawaiians in policy-making positions, and is recognized by the Governor of Hawaii for the purpose of planning, conducting, or administering programs for the benefit of Native Hawaiians. (20 U. S. C. § 7517)

Native Language. When used to refer to an individual who has limited English proficiency, refers to the language normally used by the individual, or by the parents of a child or youth. (20 U. S. C. § 7011)

Office of Hawaiian Affairs. The Office of Hawaiian Affairs established by the Constitution of the State of Hawaii. (20 U. S. C. § 7517)

Other Staff. Pupil services personnel, librarians, career guidance and counseling personnel, education aides, and other instructional and administrative personnel. (20 U. S. C. § 7801)

Outlying Area. Includes the United States Virgin Islands, Guam, American Samoa, the Commonwealth of the Northern Mariana Islands, the freely associated states of the Republic of the Marshall Islands, the Federated States of Micronesia, and the Republic of Palau. (20 U. S. C. § 7801)

Out-of-Field Teacher. A teacher who teaches an academic subject or grade level for which the teacher is not highly qualified. (20 U. S. C. § 6602)

Paraprofessional. An individual employed in a public school who is supervised by a certified or licensed teacher; includes individuals who work in language instruction educational programs, special education, and migrant education. (20 U. S. C. § 7011)

Parent. A legal guardian or other person standing in loco parentis, a grandparent or stepparent with whom the child lives, or a person who is legally responsible for the welfare of the child. (20 U. S. C. § 7801)

Parental Involvement. Refers to participation of parents in regular, two-way, meaningful communication about learning and school activities; ensures that parents play an integral role in their child's learning, are encouraged to be actively involved in their child's education at school, are full partners in their child's education, are included in decision-making about their child's education. (20 U. S. C. § 7801)

Personal Information. Individually identifiable information; includes name, home or physical address, telephone number, or Social Security identification number. (Title X, Sec. 1061)

Phonemic Awareness. The ability to hear and identify individual sounds, or phonemes. (20 U. S. C. § 6368)

Phonics. The relationship between the letters of written language and the sounds of spoken language. (20 U. S. C. § 6368)

Poverty Line. Applies to a family of a particular size; defined the Office of Management and Budget and revised annually. (20 U. S. C. § 7801)

Principal. Includes an assistant principal. (20 U. S. C. § 6602)

Priority. The school district shall give priority to the lowest achieving children from low-income families for the purposes of public school choice. (20 U. S. C. § 6316)

Professional Development. Activities that improve teachers' knowledge of academic subjects, enable teachers to become highly qualified, give teachers and administrators' knowledge and skills so students meet high academic standards, and improve classroom management skills. Professional development is high quality, sustained, intensive, and classroom-focused, has a positive, lasting impact on classroom instruction and the teacher's performance in the classroom; does not include one-day or short-term workshops or conferences. (20 U. S. C. § 7801)

Proficient. Solid academic performance for the grade, demonstrates competence in subject matter. (20 U. S. C. § 6311)

Public School Choice. Students who attend schools identified as in need of improvement have the option to transfer to better performing public schools; districts will provide transportation to these students; priority will be given to low-income students. (20 U. S. C. § 6312)

Pupil Services Personnel. School counselors, school social workers, school psychologists, and other qualified professional personnel who provide assessment, diagnosis, counseling, educational, therapeutic, and other necessary services, including related services, as part of a comprehensive program to meet student needs. (20 U. S. C. § 7801)

Pupil Services. Services provided by pupil services personnel. (20 U. S. C. § 7801)

Reading. A complex system of deriving meaning from print that requires all of the following:
- The skills and knowledge to understand how phonemes, or speech sounds, are connected to print.
- The ability to decode unfamiliar words.
- The ability to read fluently.
- Sufficient background information and vocabulary to foster reading comprehension.
- The development of appropriate active strategies to construct meaning from print.
- The development and maintenance of a motivation to read. (20 U. S. C. § 6368)

Reading First. Grants to states and school districts to establish reading programs for students in kindergarten through grade 3 that are based on scientifically based reading research, to ensure that every student can read at grade level or above not later than the end of grade 3. (20 U. S. C. § 6361)

Restructuring. If, after one full school year of corrective action, a school fails to make adequate yearly progress, the local educational agency shall provide all students with the option to transfer to another public school, make supplemental educational services available to children who remain in the school, and carry out alternative governance arrangements for the school (i.e., replace all or most of the school staff, contract with a private management company to operate the school, turn over the school to the state). (20 U. S. C. § 6316)

School Improvement. A school that fails to make adequate yearly progress (AYP) for two consecutive years. (20 U. S. C. § 6316)

Schoolwide Program. A Title I program that upgrades the educational program of schools where at least 40 percent of children are from low-income families, or at least 40 percent of children enrolled in the school are from such families. (20 USC § 6314)

Scientifically Based Research. Refers to research that applies rigorous, systematic, and objective procedures to obtain reliable, valid knowledge about education activities and programs. Includes research that employs systematic, empirical methods that draw on observation or experiment, involves rigorous data analyses to test hypotheses and justify conclusions, relies on methods that provide reliable and valid data across evaluators and observers, and studies that are accepted by a peer-reviewed journal or approved by a panel of independent experts through rigorous, objective, and scientific review. (20 U. S. C. § 6368)

Screening Reading Assessment. An assessment that is valid, reliable, and based on scientifically based reading research; a **brief** procedure designed as a **first step** in identifying children who may be at high risk for delayed development or academic failure and **in need of further diagnosis** of their need for special services or additional reading instruction. (20 U. S. C. § 6368)

Secondary School. A nonprofit day or residential school, including a public secondary charter school, that provides secondary education, as determined by State law; does not include education beyond grade 12. (20 U. S. C. § 7801)

Secretary. The Secretary of Education. (20 U. S. C. § 7801)

State. The 50 States, the District of Columbia, the Commonwealth of Puerto Rico, and the outlying areas. (20 U. S. C. § 7801)

State Educational Agency (SEA). The agency responsible for State supervision of public elementary schools and secondary schools. (20 U. S. C. § 7801)

Supplemental Educational Services. Means tutoring and other supplemental academic enrichment services that are in addition to instruction provided during the school day and are high quality, research-based, and specifically designed to increase the academic achievement of eligible children on state academic assessments and attain proficiency in meeting the State's academic achievement standards. (20 U. S. C. § 6316)

Targeted Assistance Program. A Title I program that provides services to children who are identified as failing or most at-risk of failing to meet the state's academic achievement standards. (20 U. S. C. 6315)

Teacher Mentoring. Structured guidance and ongoing support for teachers, especially beginning teachers, to help teachers improve their teaching and develop instructional skills; may coaching, classroom observation, team teaching, and reduced teaching loads. (20 U. S. C. § 7801)

Technology. State-of- the-art technology products and services. (20 U. S. C. § 7801)

Title I. Authorizes programs to improve teaching and learning so all children have a fair, equal, and significant opportunity to obtain a high-quality education and reach, at a minimum, proficiency on challenging State academic achievement standards and state academic assessments. Title I reaches about 12.5 million students enrolled in public and private schools. ((20 U. S. C. § 6301)

Transferability. Allows states and school districts to transfer some funds they receive under Federal programs to other programs that effectively address their unique needs. (20 U. S. C. § 7305)

Unsafe School Choice Option. A student who attends a persistently dangerous public school, or has been the victim of a violent crime at school, is allowed to transfer to a safe public school. (20 U. S. C. § 7912)

Vocabulary. Words that students must know to read effectively. (20 U. S. C. § 6368)

APPENDIX B

CONTENTS OF THE NCLB CD-ROM

The *Wrightslaw NCLB CD-ROM* includes:

- Full text of No Child Left Behind (Titles I-X) with overviews, commentary and cross-references

- No Child Left Behind Act (Public Law 107-110)

- No Child Left Behind Regulations, 34 C.F.R. Part 200 (December 2, 2002)

- Proposed regulation about calculating AYP using scores of alternate assessments for children with significant cognitive impairments; change to final December 3, 2003 regulations.

- *No Child Left Behind Desktop Reference*

- *No Child Left Behind: Parent Guide*

- *No Child Left Behind Toolkits*

- Guidance publications from the U.S. Department of Education

- Fact Sheets and Brochures

PUBLICATIONS FROM U. S. DEPARTMENT OF EDUCATION

No Child Left Behind: A Desktop Reference. This comprehensive publication outlines what is new in the No Child Left Behind Act for each program supported by the Elementary and Secondary Act of 1965 and other statues; describes how the Act's four guiding principles (accountability, flexibility and local control, parental choice, and what works) work in many of these programs. (181 pages)

Parent's Guide to No Child Left Behind. This publication provides an overview of NCLB, and answers questions about accountability, testing, reading, research based instruction, teacher quality, safe schools, public school choice, supplemental educational services, and charter schools. summarizes provisions in the *No Child Left Behind Act,* answers questions about the law, explains what the law does for parents, and tells where to find additional resources. (44 pages)

No Child Left Behind: Toolkit for Teachers. This publication answers questions teachers have about No Child Left Behind; includes questions about the "highly qualified teacher" provisions, accountability, testing, reading, scientifically based research, English language learners, Reading First grants, and safe schools. (60 pages)

No Child Left Behind: Toolkit for Faith-Based and Community Organizations to Provide Extra Academic Help (Supplemental Educational Services). Answers questions about how to become a supplemental services provider; includes rules of participation, eligibility, how states identify and approve providers, delivering high-quality services, staff qualifications, and more. (27 pages)

SES In Action: A Toolkit for Parents and Community Leaders. Provides information, tips and tools that parents, community activists and others can use to help eligible families access supplemental educational services (tutoring and other academic help).

State Education Indicators with a Focus on Title I (1999-2000). This publication provides data about Title I programs in each state. The state profiles include information about demographics, statewide accountability, Title I schools, state NAEP results, and student achievement. (144 pages)

GUIDANCE PUBLICATIONS BY TITLE

Title I

The Impact of New Title I Requirements on Charter Schools. Draft guidance on how changes to Title I made by the No Child Left Behind Act affect charter schools. (16 pages)

Guidance for the Early Reading First Program. This document provides non-regulatory program guidance for the Early Reading First program. (21 pages)

LEA and School Improvement. Describes the annual review of progress, school improvement. requirements for school improvement plans, corrective action and school restructuring. (45 pages)

Paraprofessional Guidance. This publication answers questions about educational requirements for paraprofessionals, assessment, related issues, and funding. (17 pages)

Parental Involvement. Clarifies responsibilities of states and school districts in developing parental involvement plans so parents become more involved in their child's education; information about rights regarding public school choice and supplemental educational services; ways to improve parent-school communication and provide parent training programs. (61 pages)

Preschool Children. Describes requirements for high quality preschool programs including the formal teaching of reading, teacher qualifications, and professional development. (37 pages)

Public School Choice. Describes the public school choice option and provides guidance on provisions to administer and implement these requirements. (36 pages)

Guidance for the Reading First Program. This publication is the final guidance for the Reading First program. The purpose of Reading First is to ensure that all American children learn to read well by the end of third grade. (55 pages)

Report Cards, Title I, Part A. This publication answers frequently asked questions about state and school district (local educational agency) report cards. (23 pages)

Standards & Assessments. This publication is designed to help States, school districts, and schools implement standards and assessments required by the No Child Left Behind Act. (66 pages)

Supplemental Educational Services. Answers questions about academic assistance including tutoring and academic remediation; requires that these approaches be consistent with the content and instruction used by the school district and are aligned with State academic content standards. (64 pages)

Title I Services to Eligible Private School Children. Describes the required consultation between public and private school officials and the provision of equitable services to private school students. (37 pages)

Title II

Highly Qualified Teachers: Improving Teacher Quality Guidance. This document answers questions about preparing, training, and recruiting high-quality teachers and principals; requires States to develop plans with annual measurable objectives to ensure that all teachers of core academic subjects are highly qualified by the end of the 2005-2006 school year. (105 pages)

Title III

Final Non-Regulatory Guidance on the Title III State Formula Grant Program, Standards, Assessments and Accountability. Non-Regulatory Guidance on Implementation of the Title III State Formula Grant Program. (18 pages)

Title IV

21st Century Community Learning Centers. This publication helps States develop criteria to ensure that local programs are high quality and tailored to address the needs of students and their families. States and communities must identify and implement programs for which there is evidence that they are effective in helping children to succeed in school. (53 pages)

Safe and Drug-Free School and Communities Act State Grants: Guidance for State and Local Implementation of Programs. This publication provides Guidance for State and Local Implementation of Programs under Title IV, Part A, Subpart 1. (10 pages)

Title V

Charter Schools Program, Title V, Part B. This publication answers questions about charter school programs including eligibility and funding; recruitment and admissions; roles of religious and community-based organizations; administrative and fiscal responsibilities. (18 pages)

Title VI

Guidance on the Rural Education Achievement Program (REAP). The reauthorized law contains three Rural Education Achievement Program (REAP) initiatives to help rural districts that lack personnel and resources to compete for Federal grants. (39 pages)

Title VII

Education for Homeless Children and Youth Program. This publication describes the requirements of educating homeless children and recommendations for meeting these requirements.(42 pages)

Title IX

Access to High School Students and Information about Students by Military Recruiters. Congress requires school districts that receive federal funds to give military recruiters the same access to secondary school students as they provide to postsecondary institutions or to prospective employers. (4 pages)

Unsafe School Choice Option. States must implement a policy that students who attend a persistently dangerous public school, or students who are victims of a violent criminal offense while in or on the grounds of a public school ,are allowed to attend a safe public school. (17 pages)

Title X

Alternate Achievement Standards for Students with the most Significant Cognitive Disabilities. Describes requirements to include students with disabilities in state assessments; answers questions about alternate assessments, alternate achievement standards, role of IEP teams, and the 1 percent cap. (41 pages)

Note: For information about new Guidance publications issued after this book was published, please visit the No Child Left Behind section of Wrightslaw at www.wrightslaw.com/nclb/

FACT SHEETS

The *Wrightslaw NCLB CD-ROM* includes twenty printer-friendly "Fact Sheets" about No Child Left Behind topics. You can print and distribute these Fact Sheets and post them on websites.

- Facts about 21st Century Technology
- Facts about English Fluency
- Facts about Faith Based Efforts
- Facts about Getting Results
- Facts about Getting Students Help
- Facts about Good Teachers
- Facts about Local Control and Flexibility
- Facts about Making Gains Every Year
- Facts about Math Achievement
- Facts about Measuring Progress
- Facts about Reading First
- Facts about School Safety
- Facts about Science Achievement
- Facts about State Improvement Lists
- Facts about State Standards
- Facts about Supporting Charter Schools
- Raising African American Achievement
- Raising American Indian Achievement
- Raising Hispanic Achievement
- Using Data to Influence Classroom Decisions (2 page brochure)

INDEX

Note: The Index in *Wrightslaw: No Child Left Behind* is for the print version of the book and the CD-ROM.

If the subject has a page number listed adjacent to the entry, then it can be found in the print version. If it simply lists a section of the United States Code (U.S.C.) you will not find that entry in the print version, but it will be on the CD-ROM.

If the print version of this book included all of the No Child Left Behind Act, the book would be about one and a half feet thick. For this reason, we decided to include the CD-ROM. The print book includes specific chapters to help you understand and navigate No Child Left Behind and Title I of No Child Left Behind. The remaining Titles II through Title X, are located on the CD-ROM.

For example, Scientifically Based Reading Research is defined and discussed in Title I. It is in this Index with a specific page number and statute. You can locate it in the print version. However, the broader term, Scientifically Based Research, is not defined in Title I, but is discussed in elsewhere in the United States Code under Title IX, General Provisions, Definitions, at 20 U.S.C. 7801. You will find both Scientifically Based Reading Research and Scientifically Based Research in the United States Code in the CD-ROM, but you will only find Scientifically Based Reading Research in the print version.

Learn how to use the "Find" and "Search" provisions in your CD-ROM with the binocular icon, and Edit, Find and the shortcuts of "Control," letter "f" and then "Control and "g" to repeat and continue searching that entry.

Index

Wrightslaw

Special Education Complicated and Confusing!

What does the law say about -

- Evaluations and reevaluations? Test procedures? Eligibility?
- Individualized Educational Programs (IEP's) and IEP teams?
- IEP goals, objectives, benchmarks?
- Placement? Inclusion? Least restrictive environment?
- Discipline? Functional behavior assessments? Behavioral intervention plans? Interim alternative placements?
- Parent rights and responsibilities? Notice?
- Independent educational evaluations? Tuition reimbursement? Mediation? Due Process?

Get Answers to your Questions at Wrightslaw!

Advocacy Library
Articles, Columns & Tips
Advocacy Newsletter
News

Law Library
Statute & Regulations
Cases
Pleadings

Subscribe to The Special Ed Advocate, the **FREE** weekly electronic newsletter about special education law and advocacy.

To subscribe go to: http://www.wrightslaw.com/subscribe.htm

Wrightslaw Ranked #1 by Search Engines

In 2001:

- More than 750,000 people visited Wrightslaw!
- Visitors downloaded more than 2.1 million files - that's 5.3 million hits!

Wrightslaw! Open 24 Hours a Day, 365 Days a Year!
http://www.wrightslaw.com

FetaWeb.com

FetaWeb.com is the companion website to the FETA book

How the site is organized -

- Yellow Pages for Kids With Disabilities (Find Information & Support)
- Getting Started (Advocacy & Advocates, Master Plans, Project Manager)
- Advocacy 101 (Rules of Game, Obstacles to Success, Conflict, Crisis)
- Parents as Expert (The File, Learning about Disability, Tests & Measurements, IEP's)
- Special Education Laws (IDEA, Section 504 and ADA, FERPA)
- Tactics & Strategies (Assumptions, Image & Presentation, Letter Writing, Meetings)
- Free Resources "Help Section" (Directories, Appendices, Glossaries of Terms, Free Pubs and much more!)

Start your own FETA support group!

Your FETA group will help parents gain knowledge and skills to be effective advocates for their children. Instead of showing their emotions to school officials, parents can bring their problems to the group and receive guidance about how to handle specific problems.

Learn more from **FetaWeb.com**: http://www.fetaweb.com/feta.group.htm

What you will find on **FetaWeb.com** -

- Articles
- Checklists
- Sample Letters
- Charts
- Resources to supplement the book (FETA Owner's Manual)

Together the **Wrightslaw: From Emotions to Advocacy** book and **FetaWeb.com** will teach you effective advocacy skills. You will learn to recognize pitfalls and avoid mistakes that prevent parents from successfully advocating for their children.

FetaWeb.com! Open 24 Hours a Day, 365 Days a Year!
http://www.fetaweb.com